Cayman Islands

THE BRADT TRAVEL GUIDE

PUBLISHER'S FOREWORD

Hilary Bradt

The first Bradt travel guide was written in 1974 by George and Hilary Bradt on a river barge floating down a tributary of the Amazon. In the 1980s and '90s the focus shifted away from hiking to broader-based guides to new destinations – usually the first to be published on these places. In the 21st century, Bradt continues to publish these ground-breaking guides, along with others to established holiday destinations, incorporating in-depth information on culture and natural history alongside the nuts and bolts of where to stay and what to see. Bradt authors support responsible travel, with advice not only on minimum impact but also on how to give something back through local charities. Thus a true synergy is achieved between the traveller and local communities.

*   *   *

I must admit that the popular destinations of the Caribbean have formerly left me cold. I saw no reason to visit islands where local culture and the environment seemed to take second place to all-inclusive luxury resorts. Tricia Hayne's *Cayman Islands* changed all that. Through her evocative writing I now know that I could enjoy hiking and horseback riding on Grand Cayman, and immerse myself in the natural world on the less touristy sister islands. The food doesn't look bad either. It sounds like my sort of place after all!

Hilary Bradt

Hilary Bradt

19 High Street, Chalfont St Peter, Bucks SL9 9QE, England
Tel: 01753 893444; fax: 01753 892333
Email: info@bradtguides.com
Web: www.bradtguides.com

Cayman Islands

THE BRADT TRAVEL GUIDE

Second Edition

Tricia Hayne

Bradt Travel Guides Ltd, UK
The Globe Pequot Press Inc, USA

Second edition 2004
First published 2001

Bradt Travel Guides Ltd
19 High Street, Chalfont St Peter, Bucks SL9 9QE, England
Published in the USA by The Globe Pequot Press Inc, 246 Goose Lane,
PO Box 480, Guilford, Connecticut 06437-0480

British Library Cataloguing in Publication Data
A catalogue record for this book is available from the British Library

ISBN 1 84162 101 3

Photographs
Front cover Tricia Hayne
Text Mat Cottam (MC), Tricia & Bob Hayne (TH); Karen Stewart (KS),
Lawson Wood (LW)

Illustrations Carole Vincer
Maps Alan Whitaker

Typeset from the author's disc by Wakewing
Printed and bound in Spain by Grafo SA, Bilbao

Author

Tricia Hayne joined Bradt Travel Guides in 1993 and is now editorial director. She has travelled throughout North America and to many island destinations worldwide. A watersports enthusiast, she enjoys swimming, diving and sailing, as well as walking and generally exploring new places. She has had articles published in a number of national and local magazines and newspapers, including *The Daily Telegraph*, *ABTA Business Traveller*, *The Bookseller* and *The Independent on Sunday*.

FEEDBACK REQUEST
Any book about the Cayman Islands is necessarily a snapshot in time. New restaurants open, hotels change hands, dive operators come and go. The material in this guide was accurate at the time of research in spring 2004, but by the time you visit there will inevitably have been changes. Do drop me a line, whether it's to pass on details of a new venue, or to tell me about that wonderful meal – or indeed to share any negative experiences. All correspondence will be personally answered, and will help to ensure that the next edition of this guide will reflect the findings of a far wider group of people.

I look forward to hearing from you. In the meantime, have a great trip!

Bradt Travel Guides
19 High Street, Chalfont St Peter, Bucks SL9 9QE, England
Tel: +44 (0) 1753 893444; fax: +44 (0)1753 892333
Email: tricia_hayne@bradt-travelguides.com
Web: www.bradtguides.com

Contents

Acknowledgements   VIII

Introduction   IX

PART ONE   **GENERAL INFORMATION**   I

Chapter 1   **Background Information**   3
History 3, Government and politics 7, Economy 8, Geography and climate 11, Natural history and conservation 14, People 30, Education 30, Language 31, Religion 31, Culture 32

Chapter 2   **Planning and Preparation**   35
When to visit 35, Tourist information 35, Highlights 36, Cayman for specific groups 37, Tour operators 38, Red tape 41, Embassies 42, Getting there 42, Health 46, Safety 48, What to take 48, Money and banking 49, Getting around 51, Accommodation 52, Eating and drinking 55, Public holidays 57, Shopping 58, Arts and entertainment 58, Activities 60, Media and communications 61, Business 65, Other practicalities 66, Cultural dos and don'ts 67, Giving something back 67

PART TWO   **GRAND CAYMAN**   69

Chapter 3   **The Basics**   71
Arrival 71, Getting around 75, Tourist information 79, Island tours 79, Other practicalities 82

Chapter 4   **Diving and Other Activities**   85
Diving 85, Snorkelling, fishing and boat charters 102, Other watersports 108, Other sports 110, Horseriding 113, Hiking and birdwatching 114

Chapter 5   **George Town and Seven Mile Beach**   115
Where to stay 115, Where to eat 124, Bars and nightlife 133, Shopping and amenities 134, Entertainment and activities 140, Beaches 140, George Town 142

Chapter 6 **West Bay** **151**
Where to stay 151, Where to eat and drink 154,
Shopping 155, A tour by car or bike 155

Chapter 7 **East of George Town** **159**
Red Bay to Bodden Town 159, Bodden Town to East
End and North Side 164

PART THREE **THE SISTER ISLANDS** **175**
Chapter 8 **Little Cayman** **177**
History 177, Natural history 178, Getting there 179,
Getting around 179, Where to stay 180, Restaurants and
bars 184, Shopping and amenities 185, Other
practicalities 186, Activities 187, Round-the-island
tour 191

Chapter 9 **Cayman Brac** **197**
History 198, Natural history 199, Getting there 200,
Getting around 200, Where to stay 201, Restaurants and
bars 206, Shopping and amenities 208, Other
practicalities 209, Activities 210, Touring the island 217

Appendix 1 **Accommodation** **223**
Appendix 2 **Further Reading** **225**
Websites 227

Index **228**

LIST OF MAPS
Cayman Islands 12
Marine parks & other
  protected areas 28

Grand Cayman **72–3**
Grand Cayman: dive sites 98–9
Grand Cayman: other
  activities 110–11
George Town & Seven
  Mile Beach 116–17
George Town centre 144–5

West Bay 152–3
East of George Town 160–1

Little Cayman **176**
Little Cayman: west 181
Little Cayman: activities 189

Cayman Brac **196**
Cayman Brac: west 202
Cayman Brac: activities 212–13

Acknowledgements

This book would never have been written without the support of Don McDougall at the Cayman Islands Tourist Board. To him, and to the staff of McCluskey and Associates, especially Laura Shelbourne and Lisa Ferneyhough, I am very grateful. Thanks, too, to Kathy Jackson at the Department of Tourism in Cayman.

Countless people and organisations have helped in numerous ways with advice, recommendations and suggestions. More specifically, I am indebted to the following, every one of whom has made a significant contribution to this book:

In Grand Cayman: Martyn Court, Judith Burt and her mother, Margaret, for countless insights into the Cayman Islands from the inside; David Martins for his help with the cultural perspective; Rod McDowall of the Cayman Islands Tourism Association Watersports Committee for help with the text, and for organising our first dives in Cayman waters; Lesley Agostinelli at Ocean Frontiers and Nancy Easterbrook at Divetech; Gina Petrie and Tim Austin at the Department of Environment; Philip Pedley at the Cayman Islands National Archive for his advice on the history; David Carmichael of Cayman Islands Sailing Club for suggestions on the text; Mat Cottam and Wendy Moore at the National Trust; Patricia Bradley for looking over the information on birds; Geddes Hislop for showing us the secrets of the Mastic Trail; and Nicki for introducing us to the natural beauty of West Bay on horseback, and her tales of Cayman past and present. I would also like to thank Arie Barendrecht at Cobalt Coast, Tom McCallum at The Reef and Alisha Racz at Seaview Hotel for their generous hospitality.

On the sister islands: John Byrnes, both for his hefty input on climbing and for sharing his home with us; Gladys Howard, Gay Morse and all the staff at Pirates Point for showing us that Little Cayman is all about relaxation; Chevala Burke, for kindly reading through the text on Cayman Brac; Diana Scott, for her stories of life on Cayman Brac, and Genevieve Robbins for hers on Little Cayman; and Ian and Karen Stewart for help with matters photographic.

In the UK and elsewhere: John Moody of Stanley Gibbons for his contribution on philately/stamps; Jim Stevenson of the RSPB; Frank Lepore at the National Hurricane Center, Miami; Rosemary Hood for sharing her experiences and telling me about the drift seeds at Rum Point; Guy Marriott; and both Mary Chandler-Allen and Susan Watler at the government office for kindly wading through statistics.

To Hilary Bradt, whose knowledge of travel and travel writing I could never hope to emulate, thank you for the opportunity to see the other side of the coin. And finally, to my husband Bob – this is for you.

Introduction

The Cayman Islands are one of the remaining 14 outposts that comprise the British Overseas Territories. On the surface, there is an American gloss about the place, with luxury hotels and shops geared totally to the well-heeled tourist. Dig a little deeper, though, and you'll find a whole new world, where Britain meets the Caribbean, and relaxation is the key.

The approach to Seven Mile Beach from Owen Roberts Airport does not bode well. A sinking feeling dispels the Caribbean glow instilled by the airline's complementary rum punch as the scene unfolds into a sprawl of wide roads seeded with anonymous warehouses and downtown US fast-food outlets.

But first impressions are deceptive. Just a few minutes' drive from the airport and you could be sipping that rum punch, watching the sun set over the Caribbean from a pure white sandy beach. Or selecting from an almost bewildering choice of restaurants in George Town, where the atmosphere is more that of an old-fashioned market town than an international financial centre. Or dipping into an underwater world whose wonders bring divers back year after year. A little further afield, and you'll discover small sandy coves washed by a turquoise sea, or tortuous rocky shores which reward those who brave them with extraordinary coral formations and the coastline at its wildest. Better still, you will catch intriguing glimpses of an island culture founded on the sea, a proud people determined not to lose touch with their heritage.

They say that 'duppies' can only be seen by those with time to look. Perhaps the same could be said of the true Cayman Islands. So do give yourself time. Take a walk beyond your resort. Visit another island. Stop and talk to people. These islands have a story to tell, if you slow down and listen.

NOTES ABOUT ADDRESSES

Cayman addresses feature post-office box numbers rather than street names, and in many cases these bear no relationship to the physical location of an address – thus, for example, Morritt's Tortuga in East End has a George Town box number. Wherever possible, I have given the street name and/or location, as well as the box number.

Many of Cayman's restaurants, shops and services are located in small shopping malls and plazas set back from West Bay Road or in similar locations. To avoid overcluttering the maps, the name of the mall or plaza has been given, so readers should check the address when looking for a place on the map. Thus, for example, for Edoardo's in Coconut Place, find Coconut Place on the map and you have effectively pinpointed Edoardo's.

KEY TO MAP SYMBOLS

Bradt

■	Capital city
●	Main town
○	Village
	Built-up area
	National park
	Reef
	Marsh
▲	Mountain/hill *Height in metres*
✈	Airport (international)
✦	Airport (other)
✚	Airstrip
	Passenger ferry
	Cruise-liner berths
	Bridge
- - - - -	Designated walking tour
<< Rte<<	Direction of designated walking tour
....	Footpath
→	One-way street
⌂	Hotel, inn etc
✗	Restaurant
♀	Bar
ℹ	Tourist information
$	Bank
⊠	Post office
ℓ	Telephone
P	Car park
⛽	Petrol station
MW	Male/female toilets

✚	Hospital
	Bus station
⚗	Stadium (track)
	Museum
✝	Church/cathedral
✿	Garden etc
►	Golf course
●	Other attraction
	Lighthouse
	Beach
	Birdwatching/nesting sites
	Turtle-viewing/nesting sites
	Wreck site
△	Sailboat hire
◁	Windsurfer hire
	Kayak hire
	Waterskiing area
	Snorkel/scuba diving
☆	Other watersports
	Climbing
←	Off-map site/destination

Other map symbols are sometimes shown in separate key boxes with individual explanations for their meanings.

Part One

General Information

Royal palm

CAYMAN ISLANDS AT A GLANCE

Islands Grand Cayman, Little Cayman, Cayman Brac

Location In the Caribbean Sea, approximately 640km (400 miles) south of Florida, 268km (167 miles) northwest of Jamaica

Size Grand Cayman 76 square miles (197km²); Little Cayman 10 square miles (26km²); Cayman Brac 15 square miles (39km²)

Status British Dependent Territory

Population 44,144 (2003 estimate) (1999 census: Grand Cayman 37,083; Little Cayman 115; Cayman Brac 1,822)

Economy Major earners are tourism and banking

Capital George Town (1999 population 20,625)

Language English, with some regional dialects

Religion Christian

GDP US$43,703 per capita (2002)

Currency Cayman Islands dollar (CI$); CI$1 = US$0.80

Time GMT –5 (USA Eastern Standard Time). No daylight saving time.

Electricity 110 volts; 60Hz

International telephone code + 1 345

Flag Navy-blue background; Union flag top left corner; Cayman Islands coat of arms on white circular background

National anthem 'God Save the Queen'

National song 'Beloved Isle Cayman'

National emblem Green sea turtle

National flower Banana orchid

National bird Cayman parrot

National tree Silver thatch

Porcupine fish

Background Information

HISTORY
with Bob Hayne, and with particular thanks to Philip Pedley of the Cayman Islands National Archive

He hath founded it upon the seas

Cayman Islands motto (Psalm 24:2)

Looking out to sea from George Town, it takes little to imagine a renegade Spanish ship of the line hobbling into the safety of this natural harbour, its desperate crew both hungry and thirsty. In those days turtles were abundant on Seven Mile Beach, especially in May, June and July, their eggs and meat providing much-needed succour. But sailing in these waters has its dangers, and many a vessel has foundered here or on one of the many reefs that encircle these small islands.

The first recorded sighting of the Cayman Islands was not in fact of Grand Cayman, but of the Lesser Caymans, or sister islands. During Christopher Columbus' fourth and final quest in search of the New World in 1503, while en route from Panama to Hispaniola, he sailed past the two islands now known as Cayman Brac and Little Cayman. His young son, Ferdinand, described them as 'two small and low islands, full of tortoises (as was all the sea about, insomuch that they looked like little rocks), for which reason these islands were called Tortugas'. Presumably they stuck in Columbus' memory as a good place for provisions, for the turtles were collected in large numbers, effectively a living larder for the sailors.

The Turin map of 1523 showed all three islands in roughly the right position and called them Lagartos, meaning 'alligators' or 'large lizards'. The eventual name Cayman seems to have stuck around 1540, derived from a Carib word for the crocodile family, *caymanas*: the islands evidently once abounded with marine crocodiles.

Over 80 years after Columbus' sighting, when Sir Francis Drake's fleet passed within sight of the islands in 1586, they were still uninhabited. Drake anchored for two days off Grand Cayman, surrounded by crocodiles, alligators, iguanas and turtles. The lure of fresh water and turtle meat meant that the island became a regular port of call for European ships in these waters well into the 19th century.

Pirates and profiteers
Although the islands were isolated, the lack of reliable charts at the time meant that they were on one of the standard sailing routes through the Caribbean.

Ships heading east towards North America and Europe found it quicker and safer to sail west with the wind behind them, travelling as far as the western end of Cuba before turning east for Europe, with the aid of the Gulf Stream. It's not surprising, then, that the eastern tip of Grand Cayman, with an almost unbroken reef and a prevailing easterly wind, came to be labelled the 'graveyard of the Caribbean', not least as a result of the almost legendary Wreck of the Ten Sail (see page 171). Conversely, the rich pickings from shipwrecks may well have served as an attraction to privateers, who sailed under royal patronage, or renegade pirates and freebooters.

In 1670, the **Treaty of Madrid** was signed by England and Spain, in an attempt to bring peace to the region. Under the terms of the treaty, it was declared that the Cayman Islands, along with Jamaica and several others, would officially belong to England. Pirates were not to be dissuaded from their prize by a mere treaty, however, and ships in the Caribbean continued to sail in fear. It is even said that Blackbeard 'took a small turtler' off the islands, though this was a time upon which story books are based and such things are almost certainly the stuff of legends. In reality, the Cayman Islands were more frequently a staging post for merchant or naval ships than threatened by pirate invasion.

Settlers and slaves

The origin of the first settlers on Cayman is uncertain. It is possible that they were deserters from the British army in Jamaica in the mid 17th century, one surnamed Bodden. It is more likely, however, that for the most part they were small-time planters or loggers from Jamaica, who had begun to arrive in small numbers by about 1700.

THE BLACKBEARD LEGEND

Blackbeard's reign of terror in the Caribbean in fact lasted less than two years, until his demise in November 1718 at the hands of jealous pirates. Yet his colourful character and bloodthirsty exploits have become legendary, outshining the feats of more successful rivals and securing his place in the annals of history.

Born of either British or Jamaican parents (no one is quite sure), Blackbeard's real name is usually given as Edward Teach, but Tach, Tatch, Thatch or Tache have all been put forward – as indeed has Drummond! With a long, thick black beard covering most of his face, and twisted into Rastafarian-style locks, his very appearance was awesome. He wore pistols over his shoulders like bandoliers and was reputed to stick slow-burning matches under his hat to increase his look of ferocity. His mastery of his 'craft' went well beyond his appearance, of course. Once, in an idle moment in his cabin, he took out a pair of pistols, blew out the candle, crossed his hands and shot under the table at the ship's master, one Israel Hands, apparently as a random gesture to reinforce his authority in the eyes of the crew in general. Hands, lamed for life, nevertheless went on to achieve immortality as the blind Pew in Stevenson's *Treasure Island*.

Grants of land issued by the governor of Jamaica from 1734 encouraged settlers to bring their servants and slaves to the island and become planters. By 1773, there were 39 families on Grand Cayman, many of them descendants of the original Bodden, including his grandson, Isaac. Slaves at this time made up at least half of the population of 450 people, shipped out to the islands from Jamaica in increasing numbers. And when, in 1781, the slave ship *Nelly* was wrecked off the coast of Grand Cayman, several slaves were sold to the islanders in return for 'salvage and other expenses'. Other settlers were fugitives of one sort or another from Jamaica, while yet more wound up on the islands as a result of shipwreck.

When Edward Corbet visited Grand Cayman in 1802, on a fact-finding mission for the governor of Jamaica, he found a total population of 933 inhabitants, of whom 545 were slaves. Yet slavery here, with no major plantations, was not the business that it became on other Caribbean islands. Most households had fewer than ten slaves, whereas in Jamaica at the same time the norm was nearer a hundred. The relative isolation of Cayman also meant that the relationship between slaves and their owners was far more relaxed than elsewhere. Indeed, even before the release of slaves following the 1834 Abolition Act, the occasional slave owner was married to a former slave. While many of the freed slaves moved to the northern parts of Grand Cayman, others eventually emigrated to the Bay Islands off Honduras.

Trade
With the growth in population at the end of the 18th century, trade became more important to the region. Initially, merchant vessels were few, carrying cotton, turtles and timber to Jamaica, and returning with such essentials as rum, flour, candles, soap, canvas and, inevitably, slaves.

In spite of such legitimate trade, not a few islanders are reputed to have continued in 'the wrecking business', profiting from the spoils salvaged from ships that foundered on the reef.

By early in the 1800s, the stock of turtles in the seas around the islands was sufficiently depleted that they ceased to be of use to visiting ships seeking provisions, and the turtlers were forced to journey further afield to Cuba and beyond for their catch. With the need for larger vessels to undertake these longer voyages, shipbuilding became more important, taking advantage of the abundance of local timber. The majority of the craft constructed were schooners, primarily intended for the turtling industry, but later, sloops were built as well.

Social change
With changes in society – and particularly the emancipation of slaves – during the 1800s, came changes in the way that the islands were governed. In 1831, a small body of local people met at Pedro St James near Savannah, and in a historic move set about forming an elected assembly. It was not until 1863, however, that this assembly was recognised by Britain, when Cayman was officially declared a dependency of Jamaica. The three islands retained their separate administrations until 1877.

Although numerous sailing ships visited Cayman from Jamaica, Tampa or Cuba in the early 20th century, their visits were irregular and the islands

TURTLING AND THE CATBOAT

'D is for danger we fear in the night'

from 'The Turtlers' Alphabet' in
Traditional Songs from the Cayman Islands

One of the mainstays of the Cayman economy was for centuries the turtles surrounding the islands. Originally seen as a means of survival for ships in Cayman waters, the turtles experienced a rapid decline as a result of over-collection. At the beginning of the 19th century, turtlers turned their attention to the fishing grounds of Cuba, bringing their catch back to Cayman to be kept in sea pens until sold to visiting ships or transported on to Jamaica.

As the fishing grounds were further extended to the Nicaraguan cays, many Caymanian seafarers eventually settled on the mainland. In an interesting instance of reverse immigration, there are today numerous people from Central America living and working in the Cayman Islands, quite possibly some of them direct descendants from those 19th-century Caymanians who sought prosperity overseas. Trade in turtles continued until turtling was made illegal in 1970, following an international ban on turtle products in the 1960s.

At the very heart of the turtling industry from the early 1900s was the boat that took the fishermen to sea, the Caymanian catboat. In fact, the catboat was an important form of transport until the middle of the 20th century, a small boat used not just for work but for pleasure as well. A stable, single-sailed vessel, of wooden construction – usually mahogany – it was developed by seamen on Cayman Brac. It has no keel or centreboard, making it ideal for movement in shallow waters. With a crew of up to four men, it was usually 22ft (6.7m) overall. Over the years, though, catboats of different sizes have been built, such as the 14ft (4.3m) example on display upstairs in the museum in George Town.

While sometimes the boats sailed alone, at others they would be taken out to the fishing grounds on board large, ocean-going schooners or sloops. Here, eight to 12 boats and their crew of two 'rangers' would be offloaded and left to make their catch, then collected up on the schooner and returned to the island. The round trip took about eight weeks. The catch was split between the crew of the catboat and the schooner by prior agreement.

A recent revival has seen catboats being retrieved from old boathouses and restored to seaworthiness. First raced in Cayman Brac around 1905, today they take part in the occasional regatta held under the auspices of the newly founded Cayman Catboat Club.

remained somewhat cut off from the outside world, Then in May 1927 came the launch of the MV *Cimboco* (an acronym for the Cayman Islands Motor Boat Company). For the next 20 years, the motorised sailing ship became the islands' lifeline, plying once a month between Grand Cayman's East End, Cayman Brac and Jamaica, carrying the all-important post, as well as passengers, food and other goods between the three. During the 1930s, the 72ft (22m) sailing schooner, *Goldfield*, began its monthly passage between Tampa and Grand Cayman, a journey of six days that brought the first regular link with the American mainland. The arrival of one of these two ships was such an event on Grand Cayman that word would be passed round and a celebratory picnic held to welcome it into harbour.

Shipping notwithstanding, the real breakthrough in communications came with the introduction of the radio station in 1935, a joint venture between the Cayman Islands and the Cuban government. Visitors remained rare, however. Indeed, in 1939 Robert Fuller, author of *Duppies Is*, was told that he was only the twelfth American citizen to set foot on the islands.

Not surprisingly, the majority of the menfolk remained reliant on work at sea for their livelihood, particularly in the US merchant marine, and many of them spent long periods of time away from the islands. During World War II, their seamanship proved invaluable to Britain, with around a thousand Caymanian men serving in either the British Royal Navy or the merchant navy.

By the 1940s, many of the islanders, who until then had been living very much hand to mouth, found themselves with a little spare cash – a result of income earned by seamen working abroad – and the opportunity, however meagre, to invest in the government savings bank. Inevitably, this new-found wealth brought change, and with it the chance to buy such luxuries as a car. An air link between Tampa and Grand Cayman was established, with the route plied by a seaplane until 1953, when an airfield was opened on Grand Cayman. At that time, though, there were few hotels for visitors. One that did exist then was the Seaview, just to the south of George Town, and today a popular dive lodge.

When Jamaica opted for independence in 1962, the Cayman Islands elected to remain under the British Crown, with their own administrator reporting direct to Westminster. The year 1966 saw the introduction of landmark legislation to encourage banking and duty-free trade, and the boom years began. As tourism gained a hold, development began to gather speed and air traffic to Grand Cayman increased. Yet even in 1971 there were only three incoming flights a week, swelling the local population of 12,000 by a further 22,000 visitors a year.

The intervening years have seen an increasing reliance on both the tourist industry and offshore banking. Today, cruise ships and aeroplanes between them bring over two million visitors a year to a group of islands whose population is now around 44,000. While nobody would deny that the islands have gained immeasurably in financial terms, the changes wrought in the last years of the 20th century have had a social impact far greater than any of those who brought the first cars to the island could possibly have imagined.

GOVERNMENT AND POLITICS

The Cayman Islands, one of the last 14 British Overseas Territories, have experienced democratic government since 1831. The titular head of state is HM Queen Elizabeth II, represented by the governor, currently Bruce Dinwiddy, who is appointed by the British government. The governor, who has overall responsibility for defence, external affairs and internal security, including the police, oversees a democratically elected Legislative Assembly which incorporates a nine-member Cabinet. The 1972 Constitution was amended by the Crown in 1994, and again in 2003.

Until 2001, there were no political parties as such. Elections to the Legislative Assembly were fought every four years between independent candidates or loose groupings. Since then, however, two political parties have come to the fore: the United Democratic Party (UDP) and the People's Progressive Movement (PPM). Not surprisingly, the change has proved somewhat controversial.

At the last elections, held in 2000, 57 candidates stood for the 15 places on the Legislative Assembly. In November 2004, when the next elections are scheduled, these 15 elected members will vote for five from within their number to take up five ministerial positions in the Cabinet. The remaining three members of the Cabinet, the chief secretary, the financial secretary and the attorney-general, are all civil servants, appointed to the post by the governor, who also appoints a Leader of Government Business from the majority party and a Leader of the Opposition. The speaker is elected by the Legislative Assembly. The Legislative Assembly is based in George Town, opposite the law courts, while the Cabinet meets at the Government Administration Building, known locally as the Glass House, in Elgin Avenue.

The islands are divided into six districts, which on Grand Cayman are mostly synonymous with the relevant town: West Bay, George Town, Bodden Town, East End and North Side. In the sixth, which comprises the two sister islands of Cayman Brac and Little Cayman, the governor is represented by a district commissioner.

Major issues facing the government today are Cayman's role as a financial centre, and constitutional modernisation. There is a growing unease in some quarters at the lack of voice held by Cayman within the British governmental system on issues that have a direct bearing on the islands.

Legal system and the police

Cayman's legal system is based on English common law. There are two main courts: the Grand Court of the Islands (from which appeal may be made in the first instance to the Court of Appeal in Jamaica, and in the second instance to the Privy Council in London), and a lower Summary Court, as well as a Juvenile Court.

Policing is the responsibility of the Royal Cayman Islands Police, which has 314 officers on Grand Cayman, and just a handful on the sister islands. A number of British police officers are seconded to the island's force.

ECONOMY

Cayman has one of the highest standards of living in the Caribbean, with GDP per capita standing at US$43,703 in 2002. The annual growth rate had slowed to 2% by 2003, with a rate of inflation of just 0.6% at the end of 2003. There is no minimum wage, but the average hourly wage for an unskilled worker in 2001 was between US$5.60 and $9.35. Unemployment is low, at around 3.6% in October 2003; in fact, there is a deficit of skilled workers, particularly in the field of tourism, and in 2002 expatriate workers accounted for some 44% of the labour force.

SILVER THATCH ROPE

In modern terms, the silver thatch, now designated the national tree of the Cayman Islands, could be seen as something of a money tree. Not that it gave up its rewards lightly. Until the late 1940s, rope woven from its leaves formed the basis of the Cayman Islands' economy, used by the islanders to purchase everyday goods from shopkeepers, who in turn traded it for imported goods from Jamaica. Extremely durable in water, silver thatch rope was valued by seamen both in the Cayman Islands and far beyond.

Once a week, two or three 'tops cutters' would head into the dense forest of the interior to crop the leaves from the top of the tree, leaving them to dry *in situ* for a week before hauling them back for the women to start work. Each top was stripped into strings then woven into strands, which were in turn split into groups of three and stretched out. Each set of three strands was then attached to a winch, and coiled as the handle was turned to make the final length of rope. A standard length, measuring 25 fathoms (150ft/45m), was made up of around 30 leaves.

Until the early 1960s, the economy of the islands was based on fishing and farming. This can be pretty well narrowed down to fishing and rope (see above), which was almost literally a cash crop at the beginning of the 20th century. Today, however, the major sources of revenue are tourism and financial services, with only a tiny proportion of the population engaged in agriculture and fishing.

The government and private sector have an effective working relationship and industry is consulted regularly by government through several public-private committees. No direct taxes are levied.

Government revenue was estimated in 2002 to be CI$307.9 million (US$369.48 million), with expenditure at CI$302.2 million (US$362.64 million). While imports outstrip exports by about 100 to 1, the visible trade gap is more than offset by invisible earnings from tourism and financial services.

The UK accounted for exports to the islands of £7.95 million in 2003, and in return received around £73,410 worth of imports. The islands receive no direct financial aid from Britain, although the Overseas Territories Department supports a number of public-service projects including, in recent years, initiatives involving the police and nature tourism.

Tourism

From its infancy in the 1960s, tourism has developed to become a major player in Cayman's booming economy. Today, it accounts for around 70% of the islands' GNP. Indeed, the price of land facing the sea on Seven Mile Beach ranks among the highest in the world, a direct result of Cayman's popularity as a holiday resort.

While the majority of visitors come from the US, around 6.2% originate in Europe, mostly from the UK. The number of visitors grew strongly throughout the 1980s and 1990s, but in the last couple of years numbers have stabilised, with a total of 293,517 visitors in 2003. By comparison, 1970 saw just 22,891 visitors to the islands. The cruise-ship market is also significant, bringing a massive 1,818,979 passengers into George Town during 2003, an increase of over 75% in just three years. There are over 5,075 visitor bedrooms (including those in condominiums) on the islands, most of them on Grand Cayman.

Tourism-related projects have brought other rewards, too, with the erection of hotels, cruise-ship facilities at the port in George Town and high-quality residential development giving a boost to the construction industry.

Financial services

In recent years, numerous financial institutions have been attracted by the islands' tax-friendly status, making Cayman an international offshore finance centre of world renown.

The Cayman Islands Monetary Authority regulates and supervises banking, insurance and investment services. In 2000, an amendment to the Cayman Islands Monetary Law was passed enabling the authority to provide specific client information to overseas regulatory authorities, such as the UK's Financial Services Authority and the United States' Securities and Exchange Commission, to help them carry out their role.

Investment promotion is the responsibility of the Cayman Islands Investment Bureau, which was established in 2002 to encourage inward investment and to provide information and a consistent approach to potential investors.

TAX-FREE CAYMAN

The chances are that those who don't know the Cayman Islands as a holiday destination have heard of it as a Caribbean tax haven, and they'd be right. The fifth largest offshore financial centre in the world, after London, Tokyo, New York and Hong Kong, it is also the second largest captive insurance centre. By the end of 2003, there were 474 banks and trust companies registered, and 672 licences granted under insurance law. A total of 68,078 companies were registered in the Cayman Islands Registry of Companies, to which users can today gain electronic access.

Broadly, there is no direct taxation – no taxes on income, profits, capital or capital gains, property or inheritance. Companies have flocked to take advantage of the islands' current tax laws and confidentiality legislation. In addition, and in order to encourage development, there is currently a 5% reduction in stamp duty and a 50% reduction in building permit and infrastructure fees. Further incentives are in place for development initiatives on Cayman Brac and Little Cayman.

The downside of all this, of course, is that there is a significant level of indirect taxation, with prices on the islands some of the highest anywhere in the world. A 20% import duty is levied on most imported goods, licence fees are payable on bank and trust licences, and there is stamp duty on all documents. Of significant relevance for the visitor, there is also a 10% tax levied on all rented accommodation.

Agriculture and fishing

Outside of fishing charters, very few people are employed in the traditional areas of fishing, shipbuilding and farming. The size and isolation of the islands and their relative prosperity linked to tourism means that they are heavily dependent on imported foodstuffs. While large-scale agriculture is inevitably limited by a lack of water and relatively infertile soil, self-sufficiency in crops such as mangoes and green bananas is achievable, and improvements in the local production of pork and beef are having a positive effect as well.

Much of the fish consumed on the islands is caught within Cayman waters, although this is inevitably limited by marine parks regulations, and fish sold in supermarkets is rarely local. With marine life protected from commercial exploitation, very little is exported. There is no export of turtle meat or other turtle products.

GEOGRAPHY AND CLIMATE

Located in the western part of the Caribbean Sea, the Cayman Islands are situated between 19°15' and 19°45' north, and 79°44' and 81°27' west, some 167 miles (268km) northwest of Jamaica, and approximately 480 miles (768km) south of Miami in Florida. The largest of the three islands, Grand Cayman, is around 22 miles (35km) in length. The sister islands, as they are known, lie 89 miles (143km) northeast of Grand Cayman, separated from each other by a channel of less than five miles (7km): Cayman Brac is 12 miles (19.3km) long, while the smallest of the islands, Little Cayman, is just 10 miles (16km) in length. The islands cover a total combined land area of almost 100 square miles (260 km²).

The three islands are effectively the tips of the Cayman Ridge, a submarine range of mountains extending from southern Cuba. Imagine that you could see only the top floor of a 100-storey skyscraper, and you get some idea of the geology of each of these islands that effectively rise straight up from the sea bed. Forget all ideas of a mountainous environment, though. Neither Grand Cayman nor Little Cayman projects much above sea level, with the highest point on Grand Cayman just 60ft (18m). Even Cayman Brac, where the bluff runs most of the length of the island, has a high point of only 144ft (43.9m). Deep beneath the surface, between the Cayman Islands and Jamaica to the east, lies the narrow Cayman Trench, some 110 miles (176km) long and plunging to the seabed well over four miles (25,198ft/7,680m) below.

Predominantly of coral formation, the islands also feature the older, very rugged, bluff rock both on Cayman Brac and on Grand Cayman. There are essentially two types of bluff limestone. Cliffrock, the basis of the evil-looking formations found at Hell on Grand Cayman, is dark grey in colour, caused by algae which live and feed off the limestone, while the lighter grey ironshore is softer than cliffrock and breaks more easily.

The islands have no rivers, any surplus water being absorbed into the porous limestone rock. The only natural water is in saline ponds, which become brackish after rain. Vegetation consists for the most part of scrub and mangrove swamp. In fact, at least half of the land area on both Grand Cayman and Little Cayman is made up of mangrove swamps, while on Cayman Brac mangroves are to be found at the western end of the island. The combination of low rainfall,

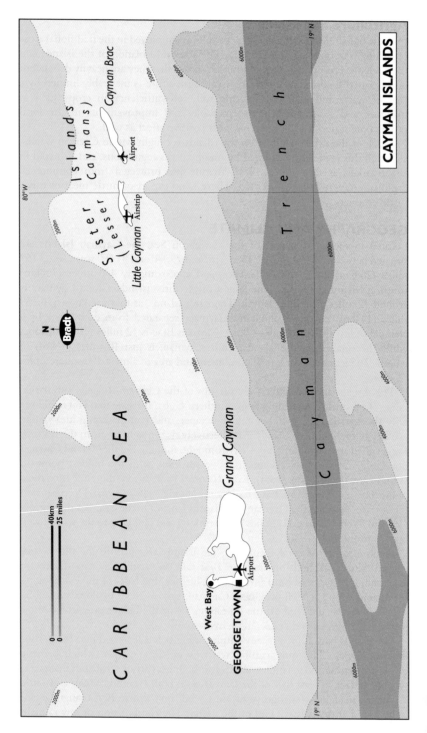

CAYMAN ISLANDS

CAYMANITE

Caymanite is a semi-precious gemstone, distinctive for its uneven bands of colour, that is specific to the Cayman Islands. Believed by geologists to have been formed millions of years ago from volcanic dust that drifted to the islands from neighbouring countries, it occurs in occasional outcrops in the bluff formation between layers of the dominant white limestone.

The colours of caymanite range from black and grey through rusty orange to light brown and cream, each the result of different metallic compounds. While the reddish colour results from a predominance of iron, it is manganese that causes the black layers, with copper, cobalt and nickel also present.

Polished caymanite jewellery can be seen in several shops on Grand Cayman, but it is illegal for visitors to take it away in its raw state.

relatively infertile soil and high labour costs means that the islands have little in the way of agriculture.

Climate

The Cayman Islands bask in a tropical climate cooled from November to March by the northeast trade winds. In the winter (December to March) there may be occasional 'nor'westers', strong winds which bring inclement weather as a result of frontal systems sweeping down from North America. May to October are warm and frequently wet, though brief showers are generally the norm; June to August can be extremely hot and humid. The average annual rainfall is around 50 inches (127mm), mostly experienced in short storms that last no more than a few hours at most. Nevertheless, flooding can occur, and it has been known for fish in the swamps to be found swimming among the trees or even down the road.

In winter, average temperatures range from 75°F to 85°F (23–29°C), with a record high of 91°F (33°C) – and a record low of just 61°F (16°C). Humidity averages around 74.5% in February and March, rising to 81% in October, although actual humidity may vary from 68% to 92%.

CLIMATE STATISTICS
Average temperature

	Jan	Feb	Mar	Apr	May	Jun	Jul	Aug	Sep	Oct	Nov	Dec
°F	78.3	78	79.3	82.4	83.8	84.5	85.3	84.5	85	83	81.6	79.3
°C	25.7	25.5	26.3	28	28.8	29.2	29.6	29.2	29.4	28.3	27.6	26.3

Average monthly rainfall

	Jan	Feb	Mar	Apr	May	Jun	Jul	Aug	Sep	Oct	Nov	Dec
in	2.2	1.2	1.9	0.4	5.4	12.4	6.5	6.1	6.8	13.2	12.2	3.4
mm	56	31	49	9	137	314	166	155	172	334	310	86

A STORM BY ANY OTHER NAME?

Hurricanes are the revolving tropical storms peculiar to the Caribbean and the Gulf of Mexico. The name 'hurricane' derives from the Caribe Indian word, *huracán*, and is, simply, the local name for the tropical cyclones that hit this region in the summer months. In the Pacific, the same weather system is known as a typhoon.

The storms form over warm seas, around 79°F/26°C, during periods of high barometric pressure. A central area of calm, known as the 'eye', is characterised by clear skies and light winds, and may grow to as much as 30 miles (48km) across. Around this, violent winds revolve at speeds in excess of 155mph (248km/h), accompanied by torrential rain (sometimes as much as 1 inch/25mm an hour) and thunder and lightning. A typical Atlantic hurricane is some 300 miles (480km) in diameter (Pacific storms may reach a staggering 1,000 miles (1,600km) across) and moves at a speed of between nine and 15mph (15–25 km/h) in the lower latitudes.

The National Hurricane Center (NHC) in Miami (www.nhc.noaa.gov/) tracks weather systems via satellite and reconnaissance aircraft. NHC issues a 72-hour forecast every six hours, at 5.00 and 11.00, both morning and evening. Hurricanes are categorised according to the Saffir-Simpson scale of one to five, with category five being the most serious. Between 1950 and 1952, hurricanes were given phonetic names, such as Able, Baker, Charlie, for ease of recognition and communication. Women's names were used exclusively between 1953 and 1979, but since then men's and women's names have been alternated. For the Atlantic, there are six alphabetical lists of 21 names, used on a rotating basis.

In the northern hemisphere, hurricanes move clockwise along a curving track from the mid Atlantic through the West Indies and into the southern USA, often leaving a trail of destruction in their wake. Worst-affected areas

Although there is a risk of hurricanes from June to November, the Cayman Islands lie further west than the typical hurricane course. The most recent significant damage was caused when Hurricane Michelle hit Grand Cayman in 2001.

NATURAL HISTORY AND CONSERVATION
Mangroves

Grand Cayman, Little Cayman and the western point of Cayman Brac were originally predominantly made up of mangrove swamps, the typical vegetation of coasts and estuaries in the tropics. The term 'mangrove' is actually a general term for fast-growing, salt-tolerant trees up to 120ft (40m) tall, with roots that are submerged at high tide. Mangroves have glands to exude excess salt, while specially modified roots provide support for the plant and act as breathing organs.

Mangroves are crucial to land stability, protecting inland areas from high winds and storm surges and helping to maintain areas of fresh water. As they grow, sediment becomes trapped between their roots, eventually creating new are low-lying coasts, which means that the Cayman Islands are highly susceptible to the havoc that can be caused by both winds and the accompanying tidal surges. The islands are theoretically at risk from June to November, when the conditions required by a hurricane are prevalent. It was close to the end of this period, in early November 1932, that Cayman was hit by the one of the worst hurricanes in living memory.

Although official records date only from 1886, information in the museum at Cayman Brac suggests that 18 hurricanes have been recorded on one or all of the islands since 1735, with no obvious pattern emerging. Indeed, in 1838 the islands were hit twice, and the years 1915–17 saw three successive hurricanes in this part of the Caribbean, whereas there have been periods of over 35 years without any direct impact. That said, on average a category 1 hurricane will pass within 60 nautical miles (or approximately 52 'land' miles) of George Town every five years.

One of the more recent hurricanes to hit the islands, Hurricane Katrina, was in 1981, when a waterspout caused by the storm uprooted a sea-grape tree and hurled it into the bar of the nearby Brac Reef Hotel! Fortunately, the ferocious Hurricane Gilbert of 1988 passed just to the southeast of Grand Cayman, making little or no impact on the island, but one of the first storms in the 21st century was rather less forgiving. In 2001, Hurricane Michelle was losing power as it approached the islands but still caused major damage, most notably to the Turtle Farm in West Bay, where many of the turtles were washed away.

Emergency hurricane procedures are in place on all three islands, with designated shelters in strategic points, including several schools. Even supermarkets produce leaflets on what to do in the event of a hurricane. Should there be a hurricane warning, tune in to Radio Cayman Two (105.3FM, or 91.9FM on the sister islands) for the latest information.

land with nutrient-rich soil that is in turn colonised by other species, such as palm trees. Additionally, fallen mangrove leaves decompose to form a complex food web that is vital for the survival of fish and other aquatic creatures. In spite of this, large tracts of mangrove swamp on the Cayman Islands are threatened with destruction by the pressure on land for development.

There are three types of mangrove found on the Cayman Islands. The red *Rhizophora mangle*, found right on the outer fringes of the swamps, has stilt or 'prop' roots, enabling it to grow in relatively deep water. The most salt-tolerant black *Avicennia germinans* grows inside, in shallower water. It has a dark-coloured bark and finger root projections, or pneumatophores, which work rather like snorkels to bring oxygen to the plants. The third, the white *Laguncularia racemosa*, with its pale trunk, prefers a drier environment.

Another plant to be found in the mangrove swamps is the gnarled buttonwood, *Concocarpus erectus*, a hardwood tree whose roots can tolerate the brackish water of this environment, while lower down the swamp fern, *Acrosticum sp*, flourishes.

Plants

The islands have numerous endemic species of plants, including many **orchids**, and all to be seen in Queen Elizabeth II Botanical Park on Grand Cayman. Most of the orchids flower in February, but the exquisite banana orchid, *Schomburgkia thomsoniana*, designated as the national flower, puts on its display in June and July. There are actually two subspecies of banana orchid. While both are tipped with a rich purple, the Grand Cayman species is predominantly white, occasionally with a yellow centre, while that found on the sister islands has a more yellowish hue. The ghost orchid *Dendrophylax fawcettii* may be found on exposed peaks of cliffrock. The yellow, purple and red colours of bromeliads, or airplants, are to be seen growing in the trees right across the islands. Among aquatic plants, there are two native species of **waterlily**, both white; one is popularly known as the water snowflake, *Nymphoides indice*, a small, daisy-like flower that proliferates in ponds on each of the islands.

Although **agriculture** plays an insignificant part in the economic success of the country today, coconuts were once an important cash crop, with all three islands dependent upon their yield throughout the 19th century. By the early 1900s, between one and two million fruits a year were exported, but by 1905 trade had peaked and, when disease struck, the industry was effectively wiped out. On a domestic level, most homes in the past would have had an area set aside for crops such as yam, plantain, sweet potato and cassava, with fruits including the soursop, avocado, tomatoes, mango and citrus fruits also grown.

Trees

Timber was once of major importance in the economy of the Cayman Islands, and many areas have been systematically stripped of trees. Most important in this trade was the **mahogany** tree, *Swietenia mahagoni*, of which few large specimens remain except on the Mastic Trail.

No matter where you are, you can't help but see the attractive **red birch**, *Bursera simaruba*, which grows readily throughout the islands but is not related to the European or North American birches. Known throughout the Caribbean as the 'tourist tree', it is easily identifiable by its peeling red bark; islanders can have a cruel sense of humour! While the broad-leaved **sea-grape** tree, *Coccoloba uvifera*, has long adorned beaches throughout the islands, the graceful **casuarinas**, *Casuarina equisetifolia*, that provide such valuable shade are not in fact native trees. Imported from Australia, these fast-growing, shallow-rooting trees actually contribute to beach erosion, as the native vegetation cannot penetrate the thick mats formed by their needle-like leaves. Along the roadside, the colourful yellow **elder** or **shamrock**, *Tecoma stans*, brightens up many a dull hedgerow around Christmas, while in the summer the vivid orange of the occasional **flame tree**, *Delonix regia*, comes into its own. And then there is that king of trees, the lofty **royal palm**, *Roystonea regia*. The favoured nesting site of the Cayman parrot, it is still to be seen in woodland areas in the interior, and is also staging a comeback in landscaped gardens in urban areas. Since the leaves of a palm fall off twice a year, you can calculate the age of the tree by counting the outer rings on its trunk and dividing the number by two.

Several trees stand out as economically valuable to Caymanians over the years. The slim **silver thatch**, *Coccothrinax proctorii*, now designated the national tree, is endemic to the islands and in times past provided the raw material both for thatching and for the locally made rope. For a seafaring nation, this rope was once a major source of revenue, even acting as a form of currency when trading with other islands (see page 9). Also of importance were the **coconut** palm, *Cocos nucifera*, with coconuts a major source of revenue until the 1930s, and the **mahogany** tree, heavily felled for timber and now quite rare – its leaves with their uneven 'shoulders' are easy to spot. The **black mangrove** was invaluable in the construction of turtle-holding pens as its tough wood is water resistant. The rough leaves of the orange-flowered **broadleaf**, *Cordia sebestena caymanensis*, were used like sandpaper to polish tortoise shells ready for export, while the waterproof latex from the **balsam**, *Clusia flava*, was used to seal the hulls of boats. Where pastures were abandoned over the years, the land was sewn with **logwood**, *Haematoxylum campechianum*, used initially for extracting indigo dye; as it took hold, however, it came to be considered a pest.

Watch out for the less friendly side of nature: Cayman has several **poisonous** native trees and shrubs. The maiden plum, *Comocladia dentata*, has dark green, serrated leaves. If touched by accident, the poisonous sap – which cannot be washed off with water – will cause blisters. You can even be affected indirectly, since rain can wash the corrosive sap on to you if you're walking beneath the tree at the wrong moment. Not dissimilar is the sap of the manchineel, *Hippomane mancinella*, although this can be rinsed off in water. Also to be avoided are the vine pear, *Selenicereus grandiflorus*, the lady hair, *Malpighia cubensis*, which has stinging hairs, the cow itch, *Mucuna pruriens,* and the leguminous vine, whose seed pods are covered in irritating hairs which blow in the wind when the pod dries and disintegrate. If you intend to wander in the forest, do ensure that you can identify these trees as all grow wild.

An excellent book, *Wild Trees in the Cayman Islands*, is available at the National Trust in George Town and in local bookshops (see *Further Reading*, page 226).

Animals
Mammals
Nine species of bat are native to the islands. Of these, the most common is the Jamaican fruit bat, *Artibeus jamaicensis*, easy to spot in the caves at Cayman Brac. Much rarer is the velvety free-tailed bat, *Molossus molossus*, and the mosquito-eating Brazilian free-tailed bat, *Tadarida brasiliensis*, a small colony of which is to be found in the Salina Reserve (not open to the public).

The agouti, an introduced rodent that was hunted in the past for its meat, and is still the object of some poaching, is occasionally seen on the Mastic Trail, and is also present in the Botanic Park.

Birds
Over 200 species of birds have been recorded in these islands, of which 17 are endemic subspecies. The only bird truly endemic to the islands, the Grand Cayman thrush, is now extinct, although recent scientific studies on the Cayman Brac parrot and a local variety of the Cuban bullfinch indicate that both should in fact be regarded as separate species.

Of course, the bird most widely associated with the Caribbean is the parrot. The **Grand Cayman parrot**, *Amazona leucocephala caymanensis*, is a gregarious and noisy bird with a wide variety of calls. The population of this parrot has stabilised since the introduction of controls on hunting, and the occasional glimpse of its distinctive red, yellow and green plumage may be caught as it flies high over the centre of the island. The endangered **Cayman Brac parrot** *Amazona leucocephala hesterna*, however, is reckoned to be the rarest parrot in the Caribbean, confined almost exclusively to old-growth forest on the bluff in Cayman Brac, where a good place to spot them is in the parrot reserve. Considerably quieter than its larger cousin, it is also far more secretive in habit. Both parrots are unique to the islands. The Cayman Brac parrot nests high up in the hollows of old Indian cedar trees, *Cedrela odorata*, while the Cayman parrot also favours both the royal palm and the black mangrove. Seed-lovers all, and fond of mangoes, they can be unpopular with farmers, but are equally attracted to almonds and the salty grapes of the sea-grape tree.

Easy to spot is the attractive little **bananaquit**, *Coeraba flaveola sharpei*, a flower-piercing bird related to the tanager. The most common bird in the Caribbean, it feeds on nectar, insects and fruits; its black and yellow colouring brightens up many a picnic or woodland walk. The **stripe-headed tanager**, *Spindalis zena*, is another native, and you may also see the yellowish **vitelline warbler**, *Dendroica vitellina vitellina*, particularly in the Botanic Park. Another native to the islands is the **northern flicker**, *Colaptes auratus gundlachi*, a species of woodpecker that also breeds in the Botanic Park, as does the West Indian woodpecker, *Melanerpes superciliaris*. The woodland **Caribbean dove**, *Leptotila jamaicensis,* known locally as the white billy dove, has red legs and is quite tame, making it popular with birdwatchers – and poachers too.

Birds of prey include the **sparrowhawk** and the ghostly **barn owl**, *Tyto alba*. Relatively common on Little Cayman, they are also to be found both on Grand Cayman and the Brac.

A small flock of the endangered **West Indian whistling-duck**, *Dendrocygna arborea*, is to be found on ponds to the north of Little Cayman (see page 194), and a second, larger group has been re-established at North Side on Grand Cayman (see page 168). On Cayman Brac, the ducks are also to be found in the wetlands to the west. Whistling-ducks are nocturnal feeders, moving from their daytime home in the mangroves to freshwater ponds in order to feed. Also known as tree ducks, they get their name from their whistling call. The only duck to breed in the islands, the whistling-duck is threatened by a combination of loss of habitat, hunting and feral predation, and is now protected under Cayman law.

A group of **cattle egrets**, *Bubulcus ibis*, interspersed with the occasional **great egret**, *Ardea alba*, is a regular sight in the wetland areas of all three islands, while the **yellow-crowned night heron**, *Nyctanassa violacea*, and the **tri-coloured heron**, *Egretta tricolour*, are also common. **Black-necked stilts**, *Himantopus mexicanus*, with their white chests, long beaks and long red legs, wade through the shallow waters searching for food. The **brown pelican**, *Pelecanus occidentalis*, is a winter visitor, occasionally to be seen cruising the coastline of Seven Mile Beach.

Of the seabirds, the large colony of **red-footed boobies**, *Sula sula*, on Little Cayman is pretty impressive, very much an ornithological success story. Both morphs (colorations) of the bird are to be seen here, the dominant brown representing some 90% of the total, with the rest white. Living in not such peaceful co-existence with the red-footed boobies is the **magnificent**

frigatebird, *Fregata magnificens*. The best time to see frigatebirds is during the mating season, from November to January, when the male flaunts his brilliant red chest in a bid to attract the female of the species. Known to locals as the 'man o' war', the frigatebird is the pirate of the skies, wheeling far overhead on watch for boobies returning from their fishing grounds. The man o' war's target is not confined to the red-foots, though, as a glance at the skies on Cayman Brac will testify. Here, high up on the bluff, lives a small colony of **brown boobies**, *Sula leucogaster*. Distinctive for its brown body and tail, with white underparts, the brown booby spends most of its waking hours out at sea, like its red-footed cousin, diving for fish. Threatened by encroaching development, Cayman Brac's resident population of brown boobies is slowly declining.

For details of birdwatching, see pages 114, 178 and 199.

Reptiles

Although crocodiles once abounded on Little Cayman (hence the name 'Cayman', from the Spanish *caymanas*), the native crocodiles, *Crocodylus rhombifer* and, to a lesser extent, *Crocodylus actutus*, are now locally extinct, although both species survive elsewhere, notably in Cuba.

There are still, however, 19 reptiles to be found in the Cayman Islands, including several sea turtles (see *Marine life*, page 25). Of the land-based reptiles, it is the **rock iguanas** with their prehistoric good looks that steal the show. Iguanas sleep in holes in the ground, emerging during the day both to feed and to soak up the heat of the sun. They eat plants and berries, with a particular fondness for wild plums. The female, shorter than the male, lays 8–20 eggs in May or June in a large burrow in the sand.

Two rock iguanas are the subject of a conservation programme under the auspices of the United Kingdom Overseas Territories Conversation Forum (UKOTCF), in conjunction with the National Trust. The territorial Grand Cayman blue iguana, *Cyclura lewisi*, is now considered to be a species in its own right and sadly tops the list of the world's most endangered lizards. A survey in 2002 found that, at most, just 10–25 of these extraordinary creatures were living in the wild. Efforts to protect the iguana are being coordinated under the National Trust's Blue Iguana Recovery Programme, which is involved in a captive-breeding initiative at the Botanic Park. In 2003, the programme's most successful year since its inception in the mid 1990s, over 80 youngsters hatched. Before being released, the iguanas are kept in captivity at the park for a couple of years to give them a better chance of survival against predation by feral cats and dogs. For further information, take a look at the programme's website, www.blueiguana.ky, or contact the National Trust.

The grey Lesser Cayman Islands iguana, *Cyclura nubila caymanensis*, a subspecies of the Cuban rock iguana, is endemic to both Little Cayman and Cayman Brac, and is frequently to be seen on Little Cayman sunning itself on the road. The common iguana, *Iguana iguana*, a green species that is not a native, is becoming widespread throughout Grand Cayman.

Geckos, too, abound, as do 'curly tails' – small creatures with their tails curled right back on themselves that are fun to watch as they scuttle along the decking in the sun. The slim, bright-blue Anolis lizards with their extendable throat patches are also in evidence.

BLUE DRAGON PROJECT

Central to the work of the National Trust's Blue Iguana Recovery Programme in raising awareness of the plight of the Cayman blue iguana is the Blue Dragon project, set up as a partnership between the National Trust for the Cayman Islands and the National Gallery.

During 2004, 16 model iguanas each measuring 8ft (2.5m) long caused quite a stir as they were brought to Grand Cayman by cargo boat. Each was given to a local artist to decorate, with some highly individual results. Some are fun and colourful, taking on the guise of a pirate or a tourist, and reflecting the exuberance of Caribbean artistic tradition. Others are more thought-provoking, and one is at first glance almost surreal, the lifebuoy around its neck symbolic of a drowning creature, with the blue of its body slowly ebbing away.

Following a display at the National Gallery, the iguanas will be released into their final homes at individual locations around Grand Cayman. From the Turtle Farm round to Rum Point, visitors will be able to see them both at attractions such as Pedro St James and the Botanic Park, and at public beaches and parks. A leaflet, the 'Blue Dragon Trail Map', is in preparation giving the background of the various artists and showing where each iguana will be permanently on view.

For further details, see www.blueiguana.ky and www.nationalgallery.org.ky.

The freshwater **pond turtle**, *Trachemys decussata*, locally known as a **hickatee**, is common in fresh or brackish ponds on Grand Cayman, where a group has set up residence in a lake in the Botanic Park, but less so on the sister islands. Hickatees grow to a length overall of 12 inches (0.3m), with the female longer than the male.

Although there are four species of **snake** on the island, none is particularly big, and none is venomous. Most, including the tiny Cayman ground boa constrictor, all of six inches (15cm) long, are rarely seen, but the aptly named racer snake, *Alsophis cantherigerus*, is often to be spotted slithering rapidly after its unsuspecting prey. And if you're in the interior, keep an eye open for the **Cuban tree frog**; its ability to 'mosaic' (change colour) through brown, green and yellow makes it quite a challenge to spot.

Insects and creepy crawlies

The one insect you are unlikely to avoid on the Cayman Islands is the **mosquito**. Once the scourge of the islands, it is now largely controlled (see box opposite). On a more benign note, there are numerous **butterflies**, including the zebra, *Heliconius charitonius*, which is almost always on the wing, and various endemic subspecies, the most dramatic of which is the Cayman swallowtail, *Heraclides andraemon tailori*. Others include the diminutive pygmy blue, *Brephidium exilis thompsoni*.

Land crabs abound in the most unlikely places. Of these, most in evidence are the large, ground-burrowing *Carsodoma*, and hermit crabs, or soldiers.

MOSQUITOES

Until relatively recently, mosquitoes were the scourge of Caymanians and their animals. In particular, the black salt-marsh mosquito, *Aedes taeniorhynchus*, was so prevalent that cattle would die from asphyxiation. Right up until the 1960s children and adults alike would take a smoke pan – a simple paint can filled with lighted coconut trash or, on Cayman Brac, rosemary and dried cow dung – if they ventured out of doors after dusk.

Smokewood, *Erythroxylum sp*, was burned on fires to help keep mosquitoes at bay. Interestingly, the 'smokewood' used by people who lived east of Bodden Town was in fact the black mangrove; it was only those who lived west of the town that burned the freshwater plant known today as the smokewood tree.

Nowadays, mosquitoes are the responsibility of the Mosquito Research and Control Unit. Established by the entomologist Dr Marco Giglioli, the unit keeps the insects under control by a combination of means. Canals or dykes have been cut through the mangrove swamps and these are flooded with sea water at strategic times to prevent mosquitoes breeding, while a second wave of control is provided by regular spraying on a rotational basis right across the islands.

Without their own natural protection, soldiers forage along the seashore for temporary homes in the form of empty shells, discarding these like secondhand clothing as they outgrow them for more appropriate cover. Capable of climbing trees, soldiers also inhabit caves and are often found on the road. If you disturb one unexpectedly, don't be surprised to hear it squeal!

Marine environment

The Cayman Islands were formed from coral, and the fringing reefs with their clear turquoise waters and myriad creatures are without doubt the greatest attraction for visitors. The seabed at this depth is alive with extraordinarily colourful and bizarre formations – great barrel sponges that grow painstakingly slowly, bright yellow tube coral and swaying sea fans provide the backdrop for a range of creatures that is almost breathtaking.

Typically, a fringing reef is an uneven platform of coral separated from the coastline by a shallow lagoon, and with a steep slope on the seaward side. In Cayman waters, though, this 'steep slope' is effectively a wall, an almost vertical drop-off straight down into the abyss. The reef forms a natural protection for the island from the waves that relentlessly roll on to its shores, and is home to over a thousand different creatures that live together in complex harmony.

Life below the surface can effectively be divided up into four zones: the reef, down to 200ft (65m), features fish and coral, and is the limit of the area in which divers can move about. Below this on the wall, between 200 and 600ft (60–182m), are sponges, while deeper still, at 600–1,000ft (182–305m) is the realm of the sharks and starfish. Below 1,000ft (305m) is classified, quite simply, as 'the deep'.

The reef

Coral reefs are home to over a quarter of all marine life, and are among the most fragile and endangered ecosystems in the world. Cayman's reefs are composed of hard coral, gorgonians and algae – there is no soft coral growing here. Most **hard coral** grows at a rate of just half an inch per year (a little over one centimetre), with the living tissue on or very near the surface. Made up of living polyps, it is incredibly fussy, requiring clear, clean water to a maximum depth of 130ft (40m), which is the limit of sunlight penetration. And if that wasn't enough, it needs sea temperatures of 21°C or above in order to thrive, which effectively limits its range to 30° north or south of the Equator. If it is disturbed, or broken, it may never recover. If sand or other sediment is stirred up around it, the polyps can suffocate. Little wonder, then, that divers should treat this living 'rock' with such caution – the coral's life, quite literally, depends on it.

The evocative names of many of the corals make them easy to identify, even for the novice. The maze-like structure of the brain coral looks just like a human brain, its swirls and coils creating endless patterns. Similarly tube corals are just that, tall narrow tube-like structures often in vivid colours, while plate coral has all the appearance of a badly stacked set of dishes after a hasty dinner party. And then there is the staghorn coral, clearly named for its resemblance to a stag's antlers. Less obvious, perhaps, is the pillar coral, one of the few corals to feed in the daytime. The distinctive 'fuzz' of its long fingers, pointing straight up by some 8ft (2.4m) or so, is actually the polyps extending to ensnare passing plankton.

The great barrel-like structures that perch atop the coral like some gargantuan drinking vessel are actually **sponges**, which obtain nutrients by filtering them out of the water. Equally slow-growing, their size does not equate with toughness: even an apparently superficial knock to the lip can result in permanent damage.

Gorgonians, although also a form of coral, look more like plants. Of these, the most in evidence is the purple common sea fan, which is to be found in shallow waters everywhere, its rather rigid structure waving back and forth with the relentless rhythm of the sea.

Far faster growing than the surrounding organisms, **algae** can gain a hold on damaged coral and if not checked can eventually swamp its host, leading to permanent damage or death. It would be easy to cast algae as the bad guy, yet there is an interdependence between these two organisms that is essential to both. Oxygen, produced by algae through photosynthesis, is essential for the coral, which in its turn produces waste on which the algae feed. It is only when the delicate balance between these two is upset that lasting damage can occur.

Other marine life

Several species of **shark** may be seen either on the reef or farther out to sea. Most common is the nurse shark, *Ginglymostoma cirratum*, which grows up to 14ft (4.3m) long and is often to be seen resting beneath an overhanging rock. Hammerheads (*Sphyrna sp*), too, are occasionally spotted offshore, while small specimens of lemon shark, *Negaprion brevirostris*, are regularly attracted by food put out by local restaurants. The reputation of these creatures goes before them, yet for the most part it is unfounded. With a similarly bad reputation, and also

BLACK CORAL

Close to the depth limits of recreational diving, you may come across the rare black coral, the raw material for much of the jewellery sold in many of Cayman's tourist shops. This fragile and slow-growing creature is on the Convention on International Trade in Endangered Species (CITES) list and takes two or three years to grow just an inch (2cm). It has been illegal to take it from Cayman waters since 1978, so the coral for jewellery is imported – in theory under licence – from Nicaragua and Honduras.

The best black coral grows at depths of 100ft (30m) or more, with delicate fronds gracing a relatively thick stem. In the wild, it actually looks light brown or even white; it is only after hours of painstaking polishing that the shiny black colour is achieved.

Although coral has been used in jewellery for thousands of years, the art of black coral sculpture was unknown in Cayman until some 20 years ago. Artists use the stem of the coral, which can be up to four inches (10cm) thick, for carving, but the technique is pretty wasteful, with a significant proportion of the coral harvested simply discarded.

an inhabitant of Cayman waters, is the **barracuda**, *Sphyraena barracuda*. Groups of youngsters are the most common, but the occasional adult is sighted as well. Divers who come across a barracuda can scare it off by swimming parallel, effectively proving that you're bigger than he is.

Another shade lover is the stunning silver **tarpon**, *Megalops atlantica*. Out in the open, though, it is spectacular, seemingly suspended motionless in the blue, as if posing to be captured on canvas by a portrait artist.

The **southern stingray**, *Dasyatis americana*, is the species to be found at Stingray City, the gentle rise and fall of their 'wings' moving them gracefully through the water. The larger **spotted eagle ray**, *Aetobatus narinari*, is more likely to be seen just off the wall.

One of several species of **grouper** that inhabit Cayman waters is the Nassau grouper, *Epinephelus striatus*, its white body patterned with irregularly spaced vertical bands in colours ranging from brown to dark green, almost at will. A lover of shade, it seeks out rocks and other outcrops on the reef where its body is well camouflaged. A slow-growing fish, it is now on the endangered list, a result of overfishing during spawning periods, and measures have been put in place to protect its spawning grounds (see page 27). All groupers start their adult lives as females, later becoming males.

Out on the reef, the kaleidoscope of colour created by so many fish is constantly changing. Several species of **parrotfish** contribute to the effect, the most common being the blue, yellow and green queen parrotfish, *Scarus vetula*. These fish, too, are hermaphrodites, starting as females but eventually ending up as males, each of a different colour. The parrotfish also has an unusual method of feeding, using its nose rather like a blunt chisel against the coral in order to extract the algae that is its food. Having helped to clean up the coral, it continues by excreting sand, thus completing the eco-friendly cycle.

Almost as colourful is the blue-and-yellow queen **angelfish**, *Holacanthus ciliaris*, although its handsome cousin, the black-and-yellow French angelfish, *Pomacanthus paru*, is far more distinctive In fact, the latter is distinctly nosy, swimming straight up to divers, its startling yellow eyes watching your every move. **Damselfish** have something of a reputation for curiosity, as well, and may even be aggressive. At least one member of this family, the little sergeant-major fish, *Abudefduf saxatilis*, with its smart black-and-white bars, is instantly recognisable. The black durgon, *Melichthys niger*, is one of several **triggerfish** to inhabit the reef, the distinctive pale-blue line that forms the meeting point between its fins and body making it easy to identify.

As **butterflyfish** and bright blue **tangs** dart in and out, shoals of blue-and-yellow-striped **French grunt** swim lazily around the reef, as do any number of the larger **jacks**. The erect dorsal fin of the reddish-orange **squirrelfish** makes it look rather like a ship in full sail. Regularly seen in shallow waters, its large dark eyes are particularly noticeable. By contrast, the expert camouflage of the **flounder** makes its presence on a sandy floor very hard to detect.

Pufferfish are curious creatures, often seen at Stingray City trying to muscle in on a free lunch. When inflated, their almost spherical bodies are unmistakable. The not dissimilar **porcupine fish** is easily distinguished from the inflated pufferfish by the spines for which it is named. It is particularly important not to touch the porcupine fish – holding it in your hands removes the mucous film which helps to protect it from many of the surrounding corals. If it's curiosity you're after, look out for the fragile-looking **trumpetfish**, *Aulostomus maculatus*, its long, thin body almost transparent, and its tail flattened.

Sea urchins in these waters are much larger than their European cousins, their long black spines decorating many a rocky cove. The subject of a conservation programme since near total extinction in the 1980s, they are only now beginning to recover, and are once again active in controlling the spread of algae. Don't tread on them of course – the spines are painful and can cause infection. Watch out, too, for the **stonefish**, well camouflaged against the rocks; its sting is poisonous.

While several shellfish may be found around the islands, it would be hard to think of any more closely associated with Cayman than the **conch**. Conch shells, immortalised in *Lord of the Flies* for the trumpet-like noise achieved if you blow through them correctly, are to be found decorating sand gardens throughout the islands, as well as on the beaches. The queen conch, *Strombus gigas*, is a large, edible sea snail which lives in shallow waters. The female lays egg masses, comprising up to half a million embryos, which take five days to hatch into veligers. The snails are mature at three years, when they weigh around 2lb (0.9g), with the shell measuring approximately eight inches (20cm) in length.

After dark, the underwater world takes on a different feel, as the world of the colourful reef fish is displaced by that of the night feeders. **Moray eels**, lurking in rocky crevices, await the arrival of the next meal to swim unsuspectingly past. The largest of the species in these waters, the green moray, *Gymnothorax funebris*, can be 6ft (1.8m) or more in length. Stories abound of morays making unprovoked attacks on humans, but contrary to popular myth they are not poisonous, though the bite may easily become infected. Interestingly, the moray can sometimes be attracted from its lair by a diver with food. The protected

spiny lobster, *Panulirus argus*, may be seen hiding under rocks or in coral nooks almost anywhere on the islands, even in the daytime, so keep your eyes open for its long antennae. At night, though, this species is on the lookout for food, and much easier to spot. **Octopus** and **squid**, too, are nocturnal, both of them capable of fast movement which enables them to outwit enemies such as the scavenging moray. And so for the most part are the **corals**, which feed during the hours of darkness.

Sea turtles

Sea turtles are pretty well synonymous with the Cayman Islands, whose sandy beaches, ideal for nesting, and the abundant supply of sea grass or – as it is known here – turtle grass (*Thallasia testudinum*) are essential to their survival. But while threats of piracy may no longer be relevant, threatened the turtles remain, suffering today more from loss of habitat than from direct hunting. All seven species of sea turtle are protected from trade under the Convention on International Trade in Endangered Species (CITES), with further protection afforded under Cayman's own marine conservation laws.

Turtles live largely in water, coming ashore only to nest. Unlike their landlubber cousins, sea turtles are unable to retract either their heads or their flippers into their shell for protection. Historically, the most common turtle around the islands was the green sea turtle, *Chelonia mydas*, so-called because its fat is a greenish colour (see box, page 26). Today, though, after centuries of commercial fishing, it is the hawksbill turtle, *Eretmochelys imbricate*, that predominates. Smaller than its cousins, it is regularly seen by divers and snorkellers. Its exquisite shell is the source of the traditional 'tortoiseshell', long coveted for ornamental purposes, but now outlawed in the Cayman Islands. Also indigenous to these waters are the loggerhead turtle, *Caretta caretta*, named for its unusually large head, and the leatherback, *Dermochelys coriacea*, although this last is pretty rare.

Wild turtles still nest on Little Cayman and Grand Cayman, but loss of habitat and nesting sites through development of the beaches on Grand Cayman has seriously affected their numbers, and the wild population remains critically threatened.

Conservation

The mangrove wetlands of the Cayman Islands give the area an importance for biodiversity much greater than their small area would suggest. Indeed, it is hoped that the islands will be the first British Overseas Territory to be covered by the protocol on specially protected areas and wildlife, following new conservation legislation that is scheduled to be passed in 2004.

Almost inevitably, pressure on land in Grand Cayman over the last 40 years has given rise to serious concern about the future of the island's mangroves. The first national park in the islands was dedicated during 2004 with the aims of conservation, recreation and education. Located on the most northerly tip of Grand Cayman, Barkers National Park is defined by its mangrove wetlands, crisscrossed by brackish channels that were originally cut to help control the island's mosquitoes, and are now home to all manner of creatures including the *Cassiopeia*, an extraordinary upside-down jellyfish that pulsates in the clear

GREEN SEA TURTLE

In the wild, the green sea turtle lays between two and seven clutches per season, each containing around 100–150 eggs, which hatch from May to November. Nesting occurs at intervals of around two to five years. Monitoring of turtles in captivity at Cayman's Turtle Farm has shown the hatchlings to grow up to 6lb (2.7kg) in their first year, and they can be expected to weigh up to 52lb (24kg) by the time they are three or four.

Turtles are cold-blooded animals, requiring warm water to survive. Even the sex of the hatchlings is determined by the temperature of the sand in which the eggs are laid: at 82°F (28°C), a balance between male and female is to be expected; cooler than that and males will dominate; hotter and there will be a predominance of females.

Turtles do not nest until they are at least 15 years old, and they may be up to 30. The female lays her eggs deep in the sand, where they take around 60 days to hatch, at which time the hatchlings make their way towards the sea, attracted by the play of moonlight on the waves. The abundance of artificial lighting in Cayman has resulted in more than one group of hatchlings heading the wrong way – and if that happens to be in the direction of a pool, then they will inevitably drown.

The Turtle Farm on Grand Cayman serves as a breeding ground for the captive green turtle (see page 156). After being bred and hatched on the farm, a number of the turtles are released into the wild, a policy that has led to a slight upturn in the previously declining sea turtle population. Although the release programme has slowed down in recent years following devastation wreaked by Hurricane Michelle in 2001, the good news is that at least two of the turtles released some 15–18 years ago have recently returned to Seven Mile Beach to nest.

waters. Along the narrow shoreline, where eagle rays and even turtles may be seen gliding through the shallows, there is an abundance of turtle grass, while sea-grape trees dominate the vegetation that lines the narrow beach.

Although the Central Mangrove Wetland Area was identified as a Ramsar site (so named after the town in Iran where, in 1971, a convention met to discuss wetlands of international importance), the status of the 8,500-acre site was never confirmed, and it remains highly vulnerable, with only 592 acres secured under the ownership of the National Trust. More positively, the 623-acre Salina Reserve, towards the east of the island, is fully owned and protected by the Trust. This wetland area is surrounded by buttonwoods and mahogany trees, bordered to the north by a rocky ridge, whose dry forest is home to white-crowned pigeons and the Cayman parrot, while in the surrounding caves lives the endangered insect-eating Brazilian free-tailed bat. In the interests of conservation, neither area is accessible to the public.

Beach erosion has become a serious issue following the high level of building along Grand Cayman's Seven Mile Beach. The width of the beach can fluctuate by as much as 200ft (65m) over the course of time, but when building is allowed too close to the shore line it can result in the virtual disappearance of the beach, as happened at the southern end in recent years. A beach erosion committee, established to monitor the situation, decided against the introduction of structures such as groins as they would forever alter the character of the beach, and the situation has since improved naturally as wind patterns have shifted. Most important of all, though, is to ensure that planning regulations prevent development too close to the shore, so that the waves can run freely up the beach, thus dissipating their energy and preventing sand from being washed away.

Of course, it is not only the environment that has suffered at the hands of man. With the increase in population has come rapid development and roadbuilding, contributing to significant loss of habitat for the island's indigenous fauna. Alongside this has been an accompanying increase in the number of domestic cats and dogs, which in turn has led to the establishment of feral populations. At stake is Cayman's native wildlife, and in particular the blue iguana, which is not adapted to defend itself against these comparatively recent predators (see page 19).

Nevertheless, there are still areas of the islands where visitors can come face to face with the wild side of Cayman. Aside from the newly designated Barkers National Park, protected highlights include the Mastic Reserve, Cayman Brac's Parrot Reserve, and Booby Pond on Little Cayman.

Marine conservation

To prevent damage from dive boats and visiting divers, marine parks have been designated throughout the islands. Yet the threat to Cayman's coral reefs is by no means limited to divers. Fishing, too, can take its toll, as can souvenir hunters and general boat traffic. And while pollution in these waters may be relatively insignificant, land reclamation is not, with the interference caused by dredging and infilling having inevitable consequences upon the surrounding ecosystems. As yet, legislation relating to issues of development, including such matters as the construction of canals, is not entirely effective, despite continued pressure from the Department of Environment.

Marine Park Zones represent the most popular diving areas, including most of West Bay, and Little Cayman's Bloody Bay Wall, with fishing almost totally banned. Boats wishing to moor outside the harbour area must use one of the 280 fixed moorings that have been placed around the three islands in order to protect the reef. These moorings, which may be used free of charge, are marked by white buoys with a blue stripe, to which are attached lengths of yellow rope. Boats up to 60ft (18m) may also anchor in sand, provided that there is no contact at any point with the coral. Conversely, 'no diving zones' have been designated at two areas of Grand Cayman's North Side.

In Replenishment Zones, such as shallow-water lagoons or sounds, line fishing is permitted, but a ban on taking conch and lobster allows these species to breed and reproduce freely. A further designation, 'grouper spawning area', protects significant areas at the eastern and western tips of each island against fishing for Nassau groupers over the next eight years, with only line fishing by Caymanian citizens permitted in the open season. Other species protected under law include angelfish, jewfish (also known as Goliath grouper) and

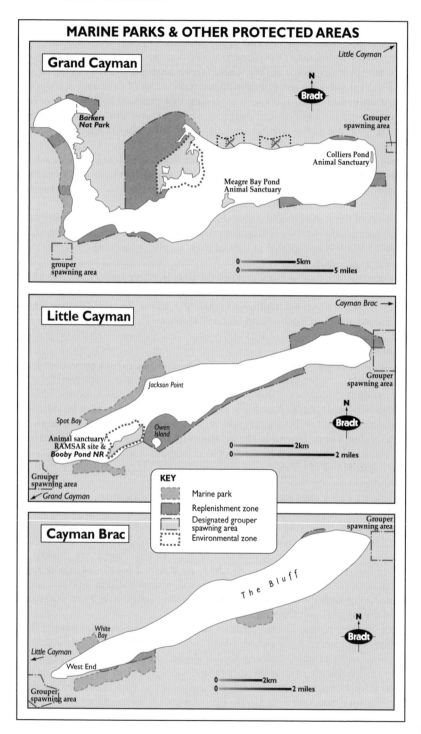

MARINE PARKS & OTHER PROTECTED AREAS

Grand Cayman

Little Cayman

N

Bradt

Barkers
Nat Park

Grouper
spawning area

Colliers Pond
Animal Sanctuary

Meagre Bay Pond
Animal Sanctuary

grouper
spawning area

0 —————5km
0 —————————5 miles

Little Cayman

Cayman Brac →

Jackson Point

Grouper
spawning area

Spot Bay

Owen
Island

N

Bradt

Animal sanctuary/
RAMSAR site &
Booby Pond NR

0 ————2km
0 ————————2 miles

Grouper
spawning area

← Grand Cayman

KEY

Marine park

Replenishment zone

Designated grouper
spawning area

Environmental zone

Cayman Brac

Grouper
spawning area

The Bluff

N

Bradt

White
Bay

Little Cayman

West End

0 ————2km
0 ————————2 miles

Grouper
spawning area

echinoderms, such as sea urchins and starfish, which may not be taken from Cayman waters at any time.

An Environmental Zone has been established to protect the mangroves that fringe the eastern side of Grand Cayman's North Sound. Here, boats are allowed at a maximum speed of 5mph (8km/h), but no in-water activity is permitted, nor any fishing or anchoring. This is particularly important as the sea grass grows in a peaty sediment that is very fragile. The protection of North Sound, however, is a thorny issue, with a considerable conflict of interest between conservationists, watersports enthusiasts and local people committed to traditional pursuits and such native dishes as conch stew.

Eight marine enforcement officers are employed by the Department of Environment to enforce the law. Infringements may be reported on VHF channel 17, or by telephoning the Department of Environment on 949 8469.

On a broader scale, further pressure on the environment comes from the greatly increased traffic from shipping. George Town hosts up to six or seven cruise ships in any one day, and the little port is struggling. Ambitious plans to build a new deep-water dock in the town will inevitably have a considerable impact on waters in this area, and further plans to build docks both in West Bay and to the eastern side of the island can only put greater pressure on the marine environment.

Conservation bodies

An institution so well known that it hardly needs any introduction, the **National Trust for the Cayman Islands** (PO Box 31116 SMB, Courts Road, Eastern Avenue, George Town; tel: 949 0121; fax: 949 7494; email: info@nationaltrust.org.ky; web: www.nationaltrust.org.ky) has a far higher profile here than its counterpart in Britain. On such small islands, the potential for upsetting the balance of nature in the interests of development is huge; the Trust works tirelessly to protect and promote the Cayman environment, both natural and cultural. It is also engaged in long-term projects to preserve the unique wildlife and flora indigenous to Cayman, central to which is the development of a system of nature reserves across the islands.

The **UK Overseas Territories Conservation Forum** (web: www.ukotcf.org) was founded in 1987 with the aim of raising awareness about the wealth of biodiversity in the UK Overseas Territories. Particularly high on the forum's current agenda is the threat to the Central Mangrove Wetlands in Grand Cayman.

The Forum is supported by a number of conservation and scientific organisations, including the Royal Society for the Protection of Birds (RSPB, The Lodge, Sandy, Beds SG19 2DL; tel: 01767 680551; fax: 01767 683211; email: wildlifeenquiries@rspb.org.uk; web: www.rspb.org.uk), and it works closely with the National Trust for the Cayman Islands.

To support the work of the Forum, you can become a Friend. Details are available from Frances Marks, Forum Co-ordinator, at 15 Insall Road, Chipping Norton, OX7 5LF, UK; tel: 01608 644425; email: fmarks@ukotcf.org.

Beneath the waves, the **Central Caribbean Marine Institute** (PO Box 31362 SMB, 238 North Church St, Grand Cayman; tel: 926 2789; fax: 949 2030; email: legacy@reefsearch.org; web: www.reefresearch.org) focuses on the study of coral reefs; its aim: 'to understand, revitalise and sustain marine biodioversity for future generations'. The institute is instrumental in the development of an ambitious project to build a marine research centre close to the unspoilt Bloody Bay Marine Park on Little Cayman (see page 194).

PEOPLE

The majority of people live on Grand Cayman, whose population in 1999 was 37,083, more than treble the number just 25 years earlier. The islands saw a 52% growth in population during the early 1980s, but this has now slowed to around 5% per year. In 2003, the total population of the islands was estimated at 44,144.

The make-up of the islands is extraordinarily diverse. Statistically, around a fifth originated from Jamaica and North America, another fifth from Europe and a similar number from Africa, with the remainder of the population of mixed race. According to one newspaper report, though, there are 'over 100 nationalities in these islands'. And that's without the large influx of expatriate workers in recent years which has led to Caymanians almost becoming a minority in their own country.

The majority of Caymanians (but less those on Cayman Brac), are employed in jobs that are for the most part unrelated to tourism. In addition to the local population, a significant number of expatriate workers live on the islands, employed in areas from tourism to construction and finance. Many of these workers originate from the UK, the US and Jamaica, with several Hondurans working on Cayman Brac.

Caymanians, long used to taking in newcomers from a variety of backgrounds and cultures, and with a seafaring history, are naturally tolerant and very welcoming. Nevertheless, the isolation of the islands over the years has meant that a few families dominate, and several names crop up time and again, in every aspect of society. Look out for Bodden, Ebanks and Scott, all of which are pretty commonplace, as are Walton and Tibbetts – the latter two particularly on the Brac – and Kirk or Kirkconnell.

Even those who have been afforded Caymanian status do not consider themselves to be truly Caymanian, which is effectively a birthright. In fact, there is a widely held view that you cannot be considered Caymanian if you haven't grown up in a world dominated by the sea, mosquitoes and conch stew!

EDUCATION

Education is compulsory for children aged 4–16, and is free for Caymanian pupils, although fees are payable for children of non-Caymanians. The curriculum is based on the British educational system, leading to CXC (Caribbean Examinations Council) exams, similar in standard to the British GCSE. After the age of 16, children may enrol at the Community College of the Cayman Islands or the International College of the Cayman Islands, or may opt to continue their studies overseas. In addition to the government schools, there are some fee-paying church schools, and others that are linked to the American educational system.

Cayman Brac has three primary schools and one high school, while since 2000 the small group of children who live on Little Cayman have been educated together in a single school room. Prior to that, children here had no choice but to attend school on Cayman Brac.

LANGUAGE

English is spoken right across the islands, though the range of accents is broad, and it's close on impossible to work out whether or not you are talking to a Caymanian. Rumours that the Cayman accent is akin to Scottish or even Welsh do not appear to be founded in truth, at least not nowadays when the influence of the United States and other Caribbean islands on the local language is immense.

RELIGION

Caymanians are for the most part very religious, and there are churches throughout the islands. In 1831, responsibility for Grand Cayman fell to the Bishop of Jamaica, who despatched the first Anglican clergyman to the island. A few years later, the Presbyterian minister William Elmslie took up residence in George Town, where he built the church that still bears his name. Today, the people of Grand Cayman are predominantly Presbyterian – as typefied by the United Church in Jamaica and the Cayman Islands (UCJCI) – but various Anglican, Catholic and other denominational churches are represented as well. There are also a number of Afro-American spiritists and Rastafarians.

On the sister islands, the Baptist church is prevalent, a legacy of the arrival of the first Baptist minister on Cayman Brac in the 1880s.

CAYMAN GRAVESITES

The simplicity of Cayman's cemeteries is for the most part accentuated by the surrounding sand that emulates the sand gardens of yesteryear. Indeed, for most ordinary people, a sand grave was the best that could be expected until relatively recently, since building materials were both scarce and expensive. Tradition had it that, following a burial, the outline of the grave was demarcated by coral stones or, if possible, conch shells, while at the head was planted a branch of 'jasmine'. Known elsewhere as the frangipani, or *Plumeria*, its highly scented white, yellow or pink blossoms bring colour and fragrance to the early spring of many an old cemetery on the islands.

While you may occasionally still come across a carefully tended sand grave in one of the more rural districts, rather more enduring are the stone house graves, complete with doors, that were the preserve of the upper classes in the 19th century. Probably the best examples of these are at the Watler cemetery at Prospect (see page 160), now owned by the National Trust, but if you look carefully you will see similar examples, some painted white, in graveyards elsewhere in the islands.

Today's graves are predominantly marked by monumental headstones and adorned with vases of artificial flowers, but keep a lookout for these charming reminders of the past – and perhaps stop for a chat with one of the people whose job it is to care for the cemeteries.

CULTURE

It's only 30 years or so since the islands' economy was based on the sea, with no electricity on the islands and very little influence from the outside world. While most men were away at sea for long periods of time, it was the women who formed the backbone of society and held the family together, with very little time or money for leisure. Games such as *waurie*, where two players compete to win each other's pieces, were the norm then, and can still be played in many homes and guesthouses, though watch out for local variations in the rules if you have played in other countries!

Although influence from the US on the local culture has been significant in recent years, it does not detract from the independence and natural tolerance of a nation whose small-town ethos makes the Cayman Islands rather different from the rest of the Caribbean. Indeed, faced with the relatively sudden influx of such strong influences from outside, many Caymanians are fighting to maintain their own cultural heritage, supported by the Cayman National Cultural Foundation and the National Trust for the Cayman Islands. The annual Cayfest (see page 58) does much to promote local culture, while Pirates Week incorporates district heritage days.

Art

Cayman art is just beginning to come to the notice of the outside world, aided by the formation of a Visual Arts Society. Native Son is a group of Caymanian

DUPPIES

'Don't never let nobody ever tell you there ain't no duppies! Duppies is!'

from *Duppies Is* by Robert Fuller

Until the second half of the 20th century, it is said that a large number of Caymanians had personal experience of duppy visitations, supernatural phenomena that could not be explained away in practical terms. Certainly numerous islanders have told of their experiences, from appearances indicating impending death to apparently freeloading duppies hitching a ride on carts or horses. Duppies seem, too, to have pointed the way to buried treasure, while others, more greedy, have been attracted to people by the occasional drop of rum or apparent promise of 'heavy cake'.

Not surprisingly, reactions to these beings have varied. While some seem to have been in tune with their ways, and accepted them as an integral part of life, others have been far from philosophical. It was not unknown for those out alone to sprinkle a trail of rum or grains of corn behind them, a sort of offering to distract potentially marauding duppies from the bottle of liquor they were carrying.

So where have the duppies gone? Robert Fuller, in his book *Duppies Is*, contends that they are still there, but that their human counterparts today no longer have the time to be in tune with the real world. Who knows?

painters and sculptors which was formed to promote their work, with exhibitions held from time to time on Grand Cayman. More far reaching, the intuitive art of 'Miss Lassie' – Gladwyn K Bush – has captured the imagination of a wider audience, and is featured in a number of books (see page 226). Examples of her work are exhibited at the art gallery in Maryland, Baltimore.

Architecture

While nobody would suggest visiting Cayman purely for its architecture, there are undoubtedly some gems of traditional buildings to be found tucked away from the eyes of most visitors. The traditional single-storey Cayman house with its corrugated iron roof and wooden porch is now the object of conservation programmes under the auspices of the National Trust, which sponsors an annual competition to reward the preservation of historic buildings.

Early houses were built of wattle and daub, based on a simple structure with wooden poles at each corner and a thatched roof. Later, wooden houses became the norm, sometimes raised off the ground both to allow air to circulate and to help keep out insects, and with a corrugated-iron roof. The kitchen, or cookhouse, was located in a separate building.

Although some of the modern buildings that have sprung up in Cayman are innovative in design, particularly the Legislative Assembly, for example, quite a few are just plain boring, and look inappropriate in the setting of a Caribbean island. It's good to see that at least one of the newer shopping complexes, Grand Harbour to the east of George Town, has addressed this issue, the resultant buildings blending into the landscape far more effectively than some of the concrete blocks down West Bay Road.

Music

Many of the folk songs that have found their way into the hearts of Caymanians over the years have been lost with the passing of an oral tradition. Some, though, have been collected by the Cayman Islands National Archive in *Traditional Songs from the Cayman Islands* (see *Further Reading*, page 225). Many of these speak of a nostalgia for the ways of Cayman, often by sailors or those who found themselves living overseas and longed to return. Others record in song the everyday world of the early 20th century, when local musicians, typically playing a fiddle, guitar and 'grater', but sometimes including shakers or a home-made drum, would come together for celebrations and other local events.

A natural progression of these traditional songs, country music gained popularity among Caymanians, influenced by the southern US radio stations which were all that were available to the islanders until the 1960s.

Today, there is no clearly defined Caymanian musical tradition accessible to visitors, although Caribbean steel bands are popular throughout the islands. Traditional calypso, with its offbeat rhythm and satirical lyrics, is complemented by *soca* – a modern variation that is faster, simpler and more dance-orientated. One international band based in the Cayman Islands is Tradewinds, who play throughout North America. Visitors to Grand Cayman may also hear about the Barefoot Man, who plays regularly at The Reef in East End (see page 173).

Sport

Not surprisingly for a Caribbean nation, cricket is popular here, as are rugby and football, but so too are more US-orientated sports such as basketball and baseball – the islands boast one of the largest baseball little leagues, with over 600 participants. Swimming is gaining in popularity among local youngsters, and is being taken very seriously: for the first time there will be a Cayman contingent of swimmers at the 2004 Athens Olympics. Athletes train and compete at the Truman Bodden Sports Complex in George Town, and in 2002 won their first medal at the Commonwealth Games in Manchester, a bronze in the men's long jump. Two track athletes will represent Cayman in Athens.

Green sea turtles

Planning and Preparation

WHEN TO VISIT

The most popular – and inevitably the most expensive – months in which to visit the Cayman Islands are from mid December to mid April, when the weather is usually dry and the temperature cooled by the northeast trade winds. Be aware, though, that the wind can occasionally veer round to the northwest, bringing spells of quite windy and cloudy weather. Caymanians reckon that April is the ideal month – calm, settled and not too hot. The rainy season officially runs from late May to late November. Rain when it comes tends to be in short bursts, usually followed by clearing skies and sunshine, and giving rise to some spectacular sunsets. That said, there are occasionally times when it rains all day, so it's as well to be prepared. June to November is the hurricane season in the Caribbean. Nevertheless, many visitors, particularly from Europe, go in the summer months, despite the greater heat at that time of year.

Divers may choose to avoid August and September when tropical storms can stir the waters, although this is by no means the norm. The variety of dive locations means that it is almost always possible to dive somewhere around the islands.

Very occasionally, you may be lucky enough to glimpse the all-too-fleeting phenomenon known as a 'green flash', a trick of the light seen at sunset just at the point when the sun dips below the horizon. Caused by a refraction of light through the Earth's atmosphere, it occurs in periods of exceptionally dry weather, and generally forecasts a clear spell during the next 24 hours.

See also *Climate*, pages 13–14.

TOURIST INFORMATION

The head office of the Cayman Islands Department of Tourism will move in September 2004 to PO Box 67 GT, George Town, Grand Cayman, BWI; tel: (+1 345) 949 0623; fax: (+ 1 345) 949 4053; web: www.caymanislands.ky. Visitors will find the office at 2nd floor, Corporate Centre, Hospital Road, George Town.

Overseas

The Cayman Islands Department of Tourism has offices in several countries, including several in the US. All share the website www.caymanislands.ky, but there are some local variations, and there's also a multilingual site, www.caymanislands.ky/europe, with information in French, Spanish, Italian, German and Portuguese, as well as English.

Canada 234 Eglinton Av E, Suite 306, Toronto, Ontario M4P 1K5; tel: 416 485 1550, toll free 1 800 263 5805; fax: 416 485 7578; web: www.caymanislands.ky/Canada
UK and Continental Europe 6 Arlington St, London SW1A 1RE; tel: 020 7491 7771; fax: 020 7409 7773; web: www.caymanislands.co.uk

US

The US toll-free number is 877 4CAYMAN; web: www.caymanislands.ky. Regional contact details are as follows:

Chicago One Lincoln Centre, 18W140 Butterfield Rd, Suite 920, Oakbrook Terrace, IL 60181; tel: 630 705 0650; fax: 630 705 1383
Houston Two Memorial City Plaza, 820 Gessner, Suite 1335, Houston, TX 77024; tel: 713 461 1317; fax: 713 461 7409
Miami Doral Centre, 8300 NW 53rd St, Suite 103, Miami, FL 33166; tel: 305 599 9033; fax: 305 599 3766
New York 3 Park Av, 39th Floor, New York, NY 10016; tel: 212 889 9009; fax: 212 889 9125

HIGHLIGHTS

With 25 years of tourism based on diving, Cayman's **underwater world** is undoubtedly a 'must see' for visitors. Whether you are a diver or snorkeller, or are happier to keep marine life behind glass, there are ample means to explore this new world. It is the walls for which Cayman **diving** is renowned, with one of the greatest attractions being Little Cayman's spectacular Bloody Bay Wall. Don't overlook the very real attractions of Cayman's numerous other dive sites, though. From shallow reefs teeming with fish to complex tunnels, swim throughs and caverns, no two dives are alike.

Among the highlights of the sea, do make time for **Stingray City**, whether as a snorkeller or a diver. Despite claims of commercialism, entering the kingdom of these magical creatures feels like something out of a fairytale.

Above the waves, all manner of **watersports** are on offer, from windsurfing and kayaking to jetskis and parasailing, and much more besides. The opportunities are here to develop an existing interest, or to try a new skill, with something for all ability levels.

Activities don't stop at the shoreline, of course: both **hikers** and **natural history** enthusiasts will find much of interest here. For the energetic, there are the hidden secrets of the Mastic Trail, an unexpectedly challenging hike that can be richly rewarding. Less demanding, but well worth a visit, is Queen Elizabeth II Botanic Park, a haven of tranquillity that offers a considerable insight into the islands' natural history and culture. And if you've ever dreamed of cantering along the beach on **horseback**, this is the place to try it.

There's also plenty to occupy the keen sports enthusiast. In particular, top-rank **golf** courses draw visitors back year on year, while many types of **fishing** are highly popular, with the annual sport-fishing tournament attracting large crowds and prize money to match.

If it's **culture** that you're after, a good start would be to visit George Town's informative National Museum, or to hire a car and follow one of the Maritime Heritage Trails that have been designated on each of the islands.

With so many activities available, it's just as well that food plays a major part in the Cayman lifestyle, and a search for **restaurants** off the beaten track would be a pretty good basis for a tour of Grand Cayman. Become a beach bum and try the Saturday barbecue at Rum Point, or spoil yourself rotten with Sunday brunch at the Westin. Take a picnic to East End and experience absolute peace less than an hour's drive from Seven Mile Beach. Or seek out that perfect waterfront setting for a romantic night out.

It's easy to think that Grand Cayman has it all, but the quieter **sister islands** of Little Cayman and Cayman Brac are much more than just add ons, as anyone who returns year after year will testify. Even if you can only squeeze in a day trip, do make time to visit one or – better still – both. And as an added bonus, the short flight from Grand Cayman affords some stunning aerial views.

CAYMAN FOR SPECIFIC GROUPS
Families
Grand Cayman is a superb place for families. Hotel rooms that routinely sleep four, a wide choice of apartments and condominiums with full kitchen facilities, plenty of friendly restaurants, long sandy beaches – what more could a family want? Many hotels will help with babysitting services, too. Some of the resorts have kids' clubs, enabling parents to indulge their own interests while their children are having a whale of a time elsewhere. For older children and teenagers, the potential for watersports is almost limitless, from snorkelling and child-orientated diving courses to jetskis and parasailing. And if all this palls, there's always bowling or the cinema.

Disabled visitors
The fact that Grand Cayman and Little Cayman are predominantly flat makes them excellent venues for those with physical disabilities, though walks in the interior are not accessible with a wheelchair. Many of the larger hotels have wheelchair access. Cayman Brac, too, is fine in the southwest where the tourist hotels are situated, but elsewhere shingle or ironshore beaches and the uneven terrain of the bluff make the island less attractive for those with special needs.

Overseas workers
The number of expatriate workers on the Cayman Islands means that by joining their ranks you will regularly come into contact with people from all over the world. The islands are popular, safe and welcoming, with a high standard of living and plenty of activities. Numerous clubs and societies are run or heavily supported by overseas workers, from charitable foundations such as the Humane Society to amateur dramatics and sports.

Those used to a broader canvas may get the urge to escape from the confines of a small island occasionally, if only to Miami for the shopping. Cayman's location in the western Caribbean makes the islands of Jamaica and Cuba a popular getaway choice, along with Central American destinations such as Panama, Honduras, Guatemala and Mexico.

If you are intending to take up residence on the islands, contact the Cayman Islands Government Information Services or the Cayman Islands Government Office in the UK (see page 66). Both can supply details of a practical nature. The

WEDDINGS FOR OVERSEAS VISITORS

The romantic prospect of a beachside wedding in the Caribbean sun appeals to many a couple planning their big day. Here, Cayman comes into its own, offering not just the idyllic setting, but also top-class hotels, a wide selection of catering possibilities and a honeymoon *in situ*.

Special marriage licences for non-resident couples may be granted in advance or on the spot by the governor of the Cayman Islands. Marriages under the special licence provisions may be performed as soon as applications have been processed – usually the same day (although licences cannot be obtained at weekends or on public holidays). During 2003, over 700 marriage licences were issued for visitors alone, some to those just stopping over on a cruise ship.

Couples will need to present proof of identity in the form of a passport or birth certificate or similar, together with either an immigration card or landing card as proof of visitor status, and any relevant divorce or death certificates. Original documents are required; photocopies are not acceptable. The minimum age for marriage in Cayman is 16, although under 18s require parental consent (or that of a legal guardian).

Licensed marriage officers are either ministers of religion or civil registrars; a full list is available on request. In addition to the marriage officer, couples will require two witnesses – if required, these can be arranged by the marriage officer. Ceremonies may be conducted between 6.00am and 8.00pm.

Licence applications forms may be obtained from the Cayman Islands Government Information Services (see page 66), or from the Deputy Chief Secretary, 3rd Floor, Government Administration Building, George Town; tel: 949 7900, ext 2222. Applicants must take or send the completed form,

official government website, www.gov.ky, is also helpful and has links to other sites, including the Chamber of Commerce and Grand Cayman's electric company, CUC. See also page 66.

TOUR OPERATORS

The rapid increase in direct booking through the internet continues apace. Nevertheless, many tour operators are in a position to negotiate favourable deals, and some can offer advice on the best places for your particular circumstances. Of those listed here, most feature only the larger resorts on Grand Cayman; a broader range is offered by the specialist dive operators. Often the smaller companies offer a personal service that makes it worthwhile seeking them out, and some will arrange tailormade trips. A comprehensive list of tour operators in Continental Europe is available on www.caymanislands.ky/europe. For cruise operators, see page 45.

UK

Caribbean Expression 104 Belsize Lane, London NW3 5BB; tel: 020 7431 2131; fax: 020 7431 4221; email: carib@expressionsholidays.co.uk; web: www.expressionsholidays.co.uk.

which should include the name of the marriage officer who will perform the ceremony, together with any relevant documentation and the fee of CI$160 (US$$200), to the deputy chief secretary.

The following is a selection of companies that specialise in Cayman Island weddings, covering everything from the licence, marriage officer and witnesses to the venue, catering and the flowers.

Bevandale Island Weddings PO Box 2122 GT; tel: 949 3435; fax: 949 7536; email: bevndale@candw.ky; web: www.bdislandweddings.com

Cayman Weddings PO Box 678 GT, George Town; tel: 949 8677/3206; fax: 949 8237; email: weddings@candw.ky; web: www.caymanweddings.com. Owned and run by Vernon and Francine Jackson, this is the most personal and individual of Cayman's wedding companies.

Celebrations PO Box 10599 APO; tel: 949 2044; fax: 949 6947; email: unique@candw.ky; web: www.celebrationsltd.com. The top-of-the-range wedding service.

Grand Old House PO Box 443 GT, tel: 949 9333; fax: 949 0635; email: grandold@candw.ky; web: www.grandoldhouse.ky. The only restaurant on Grand Cayman to have a specialist wedding co-ordinator.

Heart of Cayman PO Box 71 GT; tel: 949 8165/1343; fax: 949 0409; email: sherril@heartofcayman.com; web: www.heartofcayman.com

Trisha's Roses PO Box 2696 GT; tel: 949 2423; fax: 949 9521; email: moments@candw.ky; web: www.trishasroses.com

For further information, and a full list of both marriage officers and companies offering wedding services, write to the Cayman Islands Government Information Services for a copy of their leaflet, 'Getting Married in the Cayman Islands'.

Caribtours Kiln House, 210 New Kings Rd, London SW6 4NZ; tel: 020 7751 0660; email: escapes@caribtours.co.uk; web: www.caribtours.co.uk. Luxury resorts on Grand Cayman only.

Classic Connection Concorde House, Canal St, Chester CH1 4EJ; tel: 01244 355400; email: info@itc-uk.com; web: www.classicconnection.co.uk. Package tours for both general visitors and divers to Grand Cayman and Little Cayman.

Carrier 7–17 Church St, Wilmslow SK9 1AX; tel: 01625 547020; email: aspects@carrier.co.uk; web: www.carrier.co.uk. Grand Cayman only, and highly recommended.

Complete Caribbean St James House, 36 James St, Harrogate HG1 1RF; tel: 01423 531031; email: reservations@completecaribbean.co.uk; web: www.completecaribbean.co.uk.

Delta Vacations Leisure House, Station Rd, Kings Langley, Herts WD4 8LQ; tel: 0870 900 5001, tailormade 0870 905 4000; email: admin@deltavacations.co.uk; web: www.deltavacations.co.uk.

Harlequin Worldwide Harlequin House, 2 North Rd, South Ockendon, Essex RM15 6AZ; tel: 01708 850300; email: info@harlequinholidays.com; web: www.harlequinholidays.com. Another upmarket operator, with just Grand Cayman.

Hayes & Jarvis Groundstar House, London Rd, Crawley, W Sussex RH10 9SR; tel: 0870 366 1636; email: res@hayesandjarvis.co.uk; web: www.hayesandjarvis.co.uk. Hotel and dive packages with a range of accommodation on Grand Cayman.

Kuoni Travel Kuoni House, Deepdene Av, Dorking, Surrey RH5 4AZ; tel: 01306 747002; email: information@kuoni.co.uk; web: www.kuoni.co.uk. Tailormade and package holidays using three- to five-star hotels on Grand Cayman and Cayman Brac.

North American Travel Service Kennedy Building, 48 Victoria Rd, Leeds LS11 5AF; tel: 0113 246 1466; email: andy.abbs@nats-uk.com; web: www.northamericatravelservice.co.uk. Tailormade holidays to Grand Cayman.

Diving specialists
These specialist operators offer diving holidays on each of the three islands:

Aquatours 29A High St, Thames Ditton, Surrey KT7 0SD; tel: 020 8398 0505; email: info@aquatours.com; web: www.aquatours.com

Barefoot Traveller 204 King St, London W6 0RA; tel: 020 8741 4319; email: dive@barefoot-traveller.com; web: www.barefoot-traveller.com. Tailormade trips specialising in diving holidays.

Dive Worldwide Brayborne House, Forge Close, King's Somborne, Stockbridge, Hants SO20 6FA; tel: 01794 389372; email: info@diveworldwide.com; web: www.diveworldwide.com. Tailormade and package dive holidays.

Scuba Safaris PO Box 8, Edenbridge, Kent TN9 7ZS; tel: 01342 851196; email: info@scuba-safaris.com; web: www.scuba-safaris.com. Dive packages aboard *Cayman Aggressor IV.*

Snooba Travel PO Box 31487, London W4 2QW; tel: 0870 162 0767; email: info@snooba.com; web: www.snooba.com

US
Of the numerous tour operators in the US that cover the Cayman Islands, this is just a small selection:

Caribbean Concepts Tel: 888 918 7933 or 206 322 0617; email: dan@caribbeanconcepts.com; web: www.caribbeanconcepts.com

Cayman Express 435 Douglas Av, Suite 2205, Altamonte Springs, FL 32714; tel: 800 247 9900 and 407 682 8900; email: gotravel@caymanexpress.com; web: www.caymanexpress.com

Delta Vacations Tel: 800 221 6666; web: www.deltavacations.com; www.vacationaccess.com

Island Dreams Travel 1309 Antoine Dr, Houston, TX 77055-6942; tel: 800 346 6116 or 713 973 9300; email: info@divetrip.com; web: www.islandream.com

Island Resort Tours 300 E 40th St, New York, NY 10016; tel: 800 251 1755 or 212 476 9400; email: reservations@itr-irt.com; web: www.itrhotels.com. Feature 12 hotels on Grand Cayman.

Liberty Travel Tel: 888 271 1584; web: www.libertytravel.com

Diving specialists
Caradonna Caribbean Tours 435 Douglas Av, Suite 2205, Altamonte Springs, FL 32714; tel: 800 330 3322 and 407 774 9000; email: info@caradonna.com; web: www.caradonna.com

Sportours 2355 Honolulu Av #202, Montrose, CA 91020-1821; tel: 800 774 0295, 818 553 3333, 818 249 8877; email: reservations@sportours.com; web: www.sportours.com
World Dive Adventures 1507-C S University Dr, Plantation, FL 33324; tel: 800 433 3483 or 954 236 6611; email: info@worlddive.com; web: www.worlddive.com

Canada
Tour operators in Canada listing the Cayman Islands are Air Canada Vacations, Holiday House/Network and Total Vacations. In all cases, trips must be booked through a travel agent rather than direct.

RED TAPE
Paperwork
A valid passport is needed by all visitors, with the exception of nationals of the UK, Canada and the USA, who may provide alternative proof of nationality, such as a birth certificate with photo ID. Visitors (as against expatriate workers) are also required to have a valid return ticket showing departure from the Cayman Islands within six months of arrival, and must complete an immigration form.

Visas are not required by citizens of countries within the British Commonwealth and the former European Union, as well as a number of other nations. It is anticipated that the regulations will be amended in summer 2004 to include nationals of countries that acceded to the EU in 2004. Do note that if you are travelling via the United States, you may need a visa (and UK citizens must have a passport), so make sure that you check the current information carefully. Visas are not required by cruise-ship passengers.

Applications for visas should be made to the Passport Office in the UK (tel: 0870 521 0410; www.ukpa.gov.uk), or to the nearest British Embassy or Consulate. There are three types of visa: tourist, transit and business. Each is valid for a period of one to six months, but prices may vary according to the issuing office. Applicants should have two application forms, a valid passport, two photographs, and proof of funds available for the duration of their stay. Allow between three weeks and a month for visas to be processed. If you are planning to find a job in the islands, see *Working in the Cayman Islands*, page 66.

Entry into the Cayman Islands is normally for one month, but extensions up to six months may be obtained. Applications to extend a visa should be made to the Department of Immigration in Grand Cayman (see page 64) or Cayman Brac (tel: 948 2222), and should be accompanied by proof of funds.

Should they wish to take their animals to the islands, pet owners need a permit or valid animal passport, together with an official health certificate issued by the authorities in the country of origin.

Immigration and customs
Visitors are issued with a white immigration form on arrival. This should be kept with your passport or other travel document and given up on departure. The attractions of the Cayman Islands as a tax haven inevitably mean that the occasional person turns up in the hope of getting a job. Immigration laws are strict, and officials at the airport take a considerable amount of time going through the various formalities. As a rule, you should expect to be asked where

you are staying and, if you don't know, then you may have to provide proof of sufficient funds for the duration of your stay – usually around US$500.

Customs officers are constantly on the alert for illegal drugs. The islands lie close to major drug-trafficking routes and, although drugs are not a major problem here, they are still an issue and there is constant surveillance.

Duty-free goods
Visitors over 18 are permitted to bring in one litre of spirits, one case of beer or four litres of wine duty free, plus up to 200 cigarettes (or 25 cigars or 250 grams of tobacco). If you are staying in self-catering accommodation, it's worth buying beer and/or liquor at the duty-free shop in the US or Grand Cayman on your way in, as the cost is about a third of what you will pay in ordinary shops on the islands themselves. Note, though, that you are not allowed to get off the plane in Grand Cayman when you are on a flight that is booked through to Cayman Brac.

When returning home, visitors from the US are permitted to take goods up to a total value of US$800, while British citizens have an allowance of £145.

No visitor returning to the US, Canada or the UK may take with them products made from turtle, even at the Turtle Farm, as this contravenes the CITES agreement signed by these countries. Black coral goods (see page 23) must be accompanied by a certificate from the Department of Environment.

EMBASSIES
There are no embassies on the Cayman Islands, but there are representatives of the American and Jamaican consulates on Grand Cayman. Dates of consular visits are announced in the *Caymanian Compass*.

Consular representatives
Jamaica Tel: 949 9526; email: jamaica@candw.ky
USA Tel: 945 1511; email: consulus@candw.ky. Open Mon–Fri 8.00am–midday.

GETTING THERE
By air
The Cayman Islands have two international airports. On Grand Cayman, Owen Roberts Airport (code GCM) is situated two miles (3.5km) northeast of George Town (see page 71), while on Cayman Brac there is Gerrard Smith Airport (CYB) on the western tip of the island (see page 200). There are over a hundred direct flights a week into Grand Cayman, from the US, UK, Canada, Jamaica, Cuba and Honduras, and to Cayman Brac from Miami. Flights from London may also conveniently be routed via Miami. The national airline is Cayman Airways.

There is an airport 'departure' tax of CI$20, or US$25, payable by all visitors over the age of 12. In practice, this tax is incorporated in ticket prices, rather than collected at the airport.

From the UK
British Airways (BA) has direct flights on Boeing 767s from London Heathrow to Grand Cayman on Tuesday, Wednesday, Friday and Saturday mornings,

returning in the evening of the same days. The plane touches down for about three-quarters of an hour en route at Nassau in the Bahamas or San Juan in Puerto Rico, but passengers routed to Grand Cayman stay on board. The total flight time is approximately ten hours. Prices in economy are from around £625 return, based on travelling in May. At the same time of year, Club-class fares are from £2,600, while a first-class round-trip ticket will set you back a staggering £5,920 or so.

Via Miami

British Airways flies twice a day, seven days a week from London Heathrow to Miami, from where there are regular flights to Grand Cayman with Cayman Airways (see below). The trip to Miami takes about eight-and-a-half hours. Fares vary according to the time of year, day of travel and duration of stay, but for guidance a mid-week economy return fare based on travelling in May 2004 was £531. If tickets are booked by email or on the internet, passengers may use the self-service check in at Heathrow. There are numerous other flights between the UK and Miami, including those via Virgin (once a day) and American Airlines (at least daily).

There is no transit facility at Miami, so it's important to allow a reasonable period of time to change flights, particularly over public holiday periods; three hours would be ideal. It's a busy – some say chaotic – airport at the best of times. With the tightening of immigration procedures in the USA, the situation is unlikely to improve in the near future.

For details of connections between Miami and Cayman, see below.

From the US

Several airlines, most notably Cayman Airways and American Airlines, fly to Grand Cayman from **Miami**, between them operating some 70 flights each week, with the flight taking approximately an hour and a quarter. Other direct routes include Houston (2hr 40min), and Tampa (1hr 40min). There are also a number of charter flights from various US and Canadian airports.

The national airline, **Cayman Airways**, has friendly and helpful staff both in the US and in Grand Cayman. Once you're on board, the complementary rum or fruit punch does wonders in dispelling the hassle of hanging around airports. The airline has recently introduced a business class on international flights.There are regular flights to Grand Cayman from the US, currently as follows (though note that schedules change regularly):

Chicago	two flights a week, Wed, Sun
Fort Lauderdale	one flight daily
Houston	three flights a week, Thu, Sat, Sun
Miami	Mon, Wed, Sat, Sun (2 per day); Tue, Thu (1 per day), Sat (3 per day)
Orlando	two flights a week, Mon, Fri
Tampa	five flights a week, Mon, Thu–Sun, plus additional flights Fri, Sat

Cayman Airways also has three flights a week on Boeing 737s to Cayman Brac from Miami, via Grand Cayman. For other flights to the sister islands, see pages 81–2.

Continental Airlines has four non-stop flights a week, on Monday, Thursday, Saturday and Sunday, from **New York**'s Newark airport in Boeing 737s.

American Airlines links Grand Cayman with **New York**'s JFK airport once a week during the high season (December–April) only. Delta Airlines flies daily non-stop from **Atlanta**, Georgia, with two flights on Saturdays. Continental Airlines also operates four flights weekly from **Houston**, on Wednesday, Friday, Saturday and Sunday. US Airways fly daily from **Charlotte**, North Carolina, to Grand Cayman, and at weekends from **Philadelphia**.

On a seasonal basis, from December to April, Northwest Airlines has direct flights from **Detroit** and **Minneapolis St Paul**. **Chicago** is linked to Grand Cayman on Saturdays, December–April, by United Airlines from O'Hare airport, and by ATA from Midway airport.

From Canada
Scheduled flights from **Toronto** taking just under four hours are offered twice a week by Air Canada. Alternatively, visitors from Canada can be routed with other airlines from Montreal or Toronto via various cities in the US.

From Cuba
Cayman Airways has three flights a week from Havana to Grand Cayman, on Wednesday, Friday and Sunday. Flights with Cubana Airlines are weekly.

From Honduras
Both Cayman Airways (on Monday, Friday, Sunday) and Isleña have regular flights between Grand Cayman and **La Ceiba**, Honduras.

From Jamaica
Cayman Airways has daily flights to Grand Cayman from **Kingston**, with extra flights at weekends, and four flights a week from **Montego Bay**, on Monday, Tuesday, Wednesday and Friday. Air Jamaica also has regular connections from Kingston and Montego Bay.

From Grand Cayman to Little Cayman and Cayman Brac
Local flight connections are run by Cayman Airways Express. For details, see page 81.

Airlines
Air Canada (AC) Tel: US/Canada 888 247 2262; web: www.aircanada.ca
Air Jamaica (JM) Tel: US 800 523 5585; UK 020 8570 7999; Jamaica 1 888 FLYAIRJ; web: www.airjamaica.com
American Airlines (AA) Tel: US 800 433 7300; UK 0845 778 9789; web: www.aa.com
British Airways (BA) Tel: UK 0870 850 9850, US 800 AIRWAYS; web: www.britishairways.com
Cayman Airways (KX) Tel: US/Canada 800 422 9626; UK/Europe 020 7491 7771; Grand Cayman 345 948 2535; Cayman Brac 345 948 1221; web: www.caymanairways.com
Continental Airlines (CO) Tel: US 800 231 0856; UK 0845 607 6760; web: www.continental.com
Cubana Airlines (CUB) Tel: UK 020 7537 7909; Cuba 33 4949, 33 4950, 33 4446; web: www.cubana.cu

Delta Airlines (DL) Tel: US 800 241 4141; UK 0800 414767; web: www.delta.com
Island Air (G5) Tel: Grand Cayman 949 5252; web: www.islandaircayman.com
Isleña (WC) Tel: La Ceiba 504 443 0179; web: www.flyislena.com
Northwest Airlines (NWA) Tel: US 800 447 4747; UK 0870 507 4074; web:
www.nwa.com
United Airlines (UA) Tel: US 800 538 2929; web: www.united.com
US Airways (US) Tel: US 800 622 1015; UK 0845 600 3300; web: www.usair.com

Private aircraft

Private pilots should contact the Civil Aviation Authority of the Cayman
Islands (tel: 949 7811; web: www.caacayman.com) for information on landing
on the islands, including how to obtain an overflight permit from the Cuban
government. VOR/DME installed at Grand Cayman provides navigation
information over frequency 115.6. The ADF for Grand Cayman is 344 and for
Cayman Brac 415.

By sea

George Town is a port of registry for shipping, with a total of 729 vessels
registered in 1993, and the port is an important calling centre for cargo carriers.
Caymanian-owned ships, and those with Caymanian registration, operate
services between here and Florida, Jamaica and Costa Rica.

Cruise ships

Numerous passenger ships, sometimes as many as six a day, call in at George
Town as part of their Caribbean cruise itineraries. Most operators run their
own programmes, but visitors from cruise ships could easily organise a half
day or full day on Grand Cayman independently (see pages 79–80).
Highlights might include snorkelling at Stingray City, the Turtle Farm, the
Atlantis submarine trip and the museum in George Town. Cruise-ship
operators include the following:

Carnival Web: www.carnival-cruises.com
Celebrity Tel: US 800 722 5941; web: www.celebrity.com
Crystal Cruises Tel: US 1 866 446 6625; web: www.crystalcruises.com
Holland America Tel: US 877 SAIL HAL; web: www.hollandamerica.com
Norwegian Crown Web: www.ncl.com
Premier Cruise Line Web: www.premiercruises.com
Princess Cruises Tel: US 800 PRINCESS; web: www.princess.com
Royal Caribbean Tel: US 888 313 8883; 1 727 906 0444; web: www.royalcarib.com

Private yachts

The relative isolation of the Cayman Islands in the context of the Caribbean as
a whole means that very few yachts come into the islands. Those that do should
report to the port authority in George Town to clear customs and immigration.
For details, see *Chapter 3*, page 74. Vessels entering Cayman waters should
display the red ensign version of the Cayman flag.

The Admiralty chart of the Cayman Islands is number 462. Weather reports,
including information about the tides and a five-day forecast, are posted on the

LONG-HAUL FLIGHTS
Felicity Nicholson

There is growing evidence, albeit circumstantial, that long-haul air travel increases the risk of developing deep vein thrombosis. This condition is potentially life threatening, but it should be stressed that the danger to the average traveller is slight.

Certain risk factors specific to air travel have been identified. These include immobility, compression of the veins at the back of the knee by the edge of the seat, the decreased air pressure and slightly reduced oxygen in the cabin, and dehydration. Consuming alcohol may exacerbate the situation by increasing fluid loss and encouraging immobility.

In theory everyone is at risk, but those at highest risk are shown below:

- Passengers on journeys of longer than eight hours duration
- People over 40
- People with heart disease
- People with cancer
- People with clotting disorders
- People who have had recent surgery, especially on the legs
- Women on the pill or other oestrogen therapy
- Women who are pregnant
- People who are very tall (over 6ft/1.8m) or short (under 5ft/1.5m)

A deep vein thrombosis (DVT) is a clot of blood that forms in the leg veins. Symptoms include swelling and pain in the calf or thigh. The skin may feel hot

Department of Tourism website, www.caymanislands.ky. Alternatively, contact the National Meteorological Service, PO Box 10277 APO, George Town; tel: 949 4528.

HEALTH
Preparations

There are no immunisation requirements for visitors to the Cayman Islands, although it is suggested that visitors should be up to date on polio, diphtheria and typhoid inoculations, as they would be at home. It is worth considering routine vaccination against hepatitis A if you are a lover of seafood. This is a general precaution with seafood anywhere in the world, since shellfish are scavengers. Malaria is not a risk.

Pharmacies on the islands are comprehensively stocked, but do take sufficient prescription medicines to last your trip. Insect repellent is an essential, and plasters/Band-aids would be useful if walking in the interior forms part of your plans.

Insurance

It is important to take out travel insurance with significant health insurance coverage. If you're planning to dive, do make certain that this is covered by your policy.

to touch and becomes discoloured (light blue-red). A DVT is not dangerous in itself, but if a clot breaks down then it may travel to the lungs (pulmonary embolus). Symptoms of a pulmonary embolus (PE) include chest pain, shortness of breath and coughing up small amounts of blood.

Symptoms of a DVT rarely occur during the flight, and typically occur within three days of arrival, although symptoms of a DVT or PE have been reported up to two weeks later.

Anyone who suspects that they have these symptoms should see a doctor immediately as anticoagulation (blood-thinning) treatment can be given.

Prevention of DVT

General measures to reduce the risk of thrombosis are shown below. This advice also applies to long train or bus journeys.

- Whilst waiting to board the plane, try to walk around rather than sit.
- During the flight drink plenty of water (at least two small glasses every hour).
- Avoid excessive tea, coffee and alcohol.
- Perform leg-stretching exercises, such as pointing the toes up and down.
- Move around the cabin when practicable.

If you fit into the high-risk category (see above) ask your doctor if it is safe to travel. Additional protective measures such as graded compression stockings, aspirin or low molecular weight heparin can be given. No matter how tall you are, where possible request a seat with extra legroom.

Local facilities

Both Grand Cayman and Cayman Brac have small government hospitals, with 124 beds and 18 beds respectively. For divers, there is a decompression chamber at the hospital in George Town. There are also district clinics and a dental clinic, and a number of private medical practices. Little Cayman has only a small health clinic.

There is no free medical provision for visitors, nor any reciprocal agreement with the UK National Health Service, so it is important to take out suitable medical **insurance**, which should also cover the cost of emergency air transport should a transfer from one of the sister islands or from Grand Cayman to Miami be necessary. Health costs are similar to those in the private sector in the UK, but lower than those in the US.

In addition to the pharmacy at the hospital in George Town, and others at the two medical centres listed above, there are several **pharmacies** on Grand Cayman (see page 84) and one at the hospital on Cayman Brac (see page 209), but none on Little Cayman. Note that pharmacies may only fulfil prescriptions issued on the Cayman Islands.

Water

Water is safe to drink throughout Cayman. It is provided by desalination, either centrally or from individually run plants. Bottled water is also widely available from shops and supermarkets.

SAFETY

The islands, with their traditional emphasis on the family, are almost universally considered to be safe, friendly and welcoming, both in terms of property and of personal safety. That said, it's tempting providence to leave such things as cameras and wallets unattended on a beach or in an unlocked car. The sister islands have a laid-back attitude to security that is almost of a bygone era – on Little Cayman you're asked to leave the key in your hire car (after all, there's nowhere to take it), while on Cayman Brac the hire bikes simply don't have locks.

Women travellers need take no particular precautions, though do take care if hitchhiking, particularly at night, as you would anywhere else.

If you're out hiking, be aware that the ironshore beaches and inland rock base can be treacherous for walkers, so take particular care and wear strong shoes. And if you're heading off the beaten track, do be sure you can recognise poisonous plants such as the manchineel or the maiden plum.

The location of Cayman on the international drug-trafficking routes between North and South America makes the islands extremely vulnerable. Although constant vigilance is exercised by police and customs, drugs are still a problem, particularly ganja (marijuana) – some 80% of the prison population is in for drug-related offences. However, anti-drug laws are strict, and large fines and/or prison sentences may be imposed on anyone caught in possession of or importing any banned substance.

Marine safety

Safety on and around the sea is an important issue on islands renowned for their diving. In addition to the precautions you would always take when snorkelling or diving, watch out for currents when swimming near headlands, and for rocks just beneath the surface. Take care, too, where you put your feet – the sea urchins in these waters are huge, and venomous stonefish can be difficult to see against the camouflage of the rocks. Underwater, divers and snorkellers should avoid cutting themselves on the coral, as such wounds tend to heal slowly. If you remember that you shouldn't touch the coral, then it can't harm you!

WHAT TO TAKE

Aside from the normal clothes that you would take on holiday to a warm climate, it's worth thinking about the following:

- Snorkel, mask and fins
- Dive equipment if you have it – renting is easy but expensive
- Dive certification
- Suncream
- Sunhat
- Insect repellent
- National or international driving licence
- Camera equipment (remember that so-called 'underwater' disposable cameras cannot be used for diving)
- Binoculars

- Light sweater or cardigan for air-conditioned restaurants and that odd breezy day – or for after diving
- Light waterproof jacket for the occasional shower
- Good walking shoes if you plan to walk in the interior

MONEY AND BANKING

The unit of currency is the Cayman Islands dollar (CI$), which is subdivided into 100 cents. There are four banknotes, in denominations of 5, 10, 25 and 100 CI dollars, and four coins, respectively for 1, 5, 10 and 25 cents. US dollars are accepted throughout the islands, although change is usually given in CI dollars. The British pound is not generally in circulation.

The rate of exchange against the US dollar is fixed at CI$1 = US$1.25 (US$1 = CI$0.80). Prices may be quoted in either CI or US dollars, or indeed both, which is confusing enough for Americans and even worse for visitors from the rest of the world. As a rule of thumb, the more local establishments and most restaurants and bars seem to work in CI dollars, while the majority of hotels and dive operators quote in US dollars. The currency quoted is usually marked on menus etc, but always check if in doubt.

Travellers' cheques

US$ travellers' cheques may be used like cash in shops etc, provided that you have some form of identification (eg: passport) with you. Alternatively, you can change them for cash at the bank – a good move since the exchange rate against US$ travellers' cheques is CI$0.82.

In the event of loss or theft of travellers' cheques, contact the issuer immediately; there should be an emergency number with your cheques. Alternatively, for Thomas Cook cheques, call +44 (0)1733 318949/318950, and for those issued by American Express, call 1 800 828 0366.

Credit cards

As you would expect from a major offshore banking location, Amex, MasterCard, Visa, Discover and Diners Club credit cards are widely accepted in Cayman.

Note that payments made on credit cards are always converted to US dollars, and that conversion into a third currency is at the rate of exchange prevalent on the date of payment. So if the rate of exchange of your currency against the US dollar is falling rapidly, you would be well advised to invest in some US dollars at the beginning of your trip, rather than relying on credit cards. Cash withdrawals against Visa and MasterCard are sometimes afforded the slightly higher exchange rate for US$ travellers' cheques, ie: CI$0.82.

Credit-card emergency numbers

Amex	1 801 945 9450
Diners Club	1 303 799 1504
Discover	1 800 347 2683
MasterCard	1 800 307 7309
Visa	1 800 847 2911

Banks

Banking hours are normally 9.00am–4.00pm, Monday to Thursday, and 9.00am–4.30pm on Friday.

There are ATMs at several banks and supermarkets, except on Little Cayman. Cash withdrawals are for a minimum of CI$25.

Money-wiring services

Money wiring is available through MoneyGram or Western Union on both Grand Cayman and Cayman Brac.

Tipping

Tipping is expected in restaurants and other service-orientated establishments. The norm is 15%, which is frequently added to the bill in restaurants and elsewhere. Many hotels will add a gratuity of 10% or more to the room bill as well.

Budgeting

The cost of living on the Cayman Islands is high, and the tourist dollar doesn't go far, particularly as virtually all food and goods have to be imported. As an indication, postcards can be over US$1 each (though you'll find them if you look for US$0.30), and the going rate for a bottled beer outside of happy hours is about US$4.40.

A two-course evening meal for two people in a mid-range restaurant with a bottle of wine would be around US$95, including tax and gratuity, though eating out at lunchtime is usually significantly cheaper. In a bar, a one-course meal for two, with beer, is more likely to be around US$45. And if you really can't survive without fast food, you're looking at US$5–6.25 a head.

It would be possible to spend a small fortune if money were no object, but by being reasonably sensible two people on a mid-range budget would be fine on US$425 per day, in low season (mid April to mid December), based on the following (all prices in US dollars):

Hotel (with kitchenette & breakfast)	$245.00 (inc 10% government tax and 10% gratuity)
Lunch (self-catering)	$10.00
Dinner	$95.00 (inc 15% gratuity)
Beers or cocktails x 2	$10.00
Transport (car hire + petrol)	$45.00
Sundries (museum, ice-cream, postcards)	$20.00

This, of course, does not include activities such as diving and other watersports. Allow about US$70 per person per day for a two-tank boat dive, exclusive of equipment.

Costs for accommodation, car hire and diving can be reduced significantly if booked in advance for a period of a week or so.

Cayman on the cheap

This is something of a contradiction in terms! Those on a tight budget could be in for a shock, but it's certainly possible to keep costs down, particularly if you're prepared to slow down to the Cayman pace of life. Discover Cayman out of season, from mid April to mid December, when it's quieter and prices are lower. Two can stay for the price of one in most places, and four cost even less per person, so it's cheaper not to travel alone. Accommodation is available at the lower end of the range if you hunt around – try Seaview, or Harbour View, or perhaps one of the guesthouses – costs here are from US$70 per room. Transport using a combination of walking, local buses and maybe a hired bike for a day or two is the most realistic.

Obviously eating in is an option, but you're not going to experience much of Cayman that way. On the other hand, this offers the opportunity to try supermarket salad bars at CI$3.99 per pound (CI$8.98 per kilo), and hot buffets, too, are available for just a little more. Have a hunt round Farmer's Market (see page 136) for local produce, or try their lunchtime takeaway buffet. Prepare a picnic lunch instead of eating out, and buy drinks from one of the supermarkets too – or drink tap water; it's perfectly safe. In the evening, happy hours are a great source of budget succour: drinks on a two-for-one basis, and free buffet snacks in many bars, can set you up for the evening, while for something more substantial, try one of the roadside stalls selling jerk chicken. Alternatively, a bit of judicious research reveals gems such as all-you-can-eat barbecues, or you could head for smaller local restaurants and fill up on coconut rice and goat curry at a fraction of the price you'd pay on Seven Mile Beach. As for entertainment, bring your own mask, snorkel and fins and you'll be ready for endless hours of pleasure snorkelling on the reef at absolutely no cost.

GETTING AROUND
By air
Flights between the islands are covered on pages 81–2.

By road
Easily the best means of getting around Grand Cayman and Cayman Brac is by car. Vehicles are driven on the left, and seatbelts are compulsory. **Car hire** is available from several outlets on the islands (see pages 75, 180 and 200). You will need either an international driving permit, or your own driving licence. If you have only the latter, you will also need to purchase a visitor's driving permit. Visitor's driving permits are valid for six months or for the duration of your stay, whichever is the shorter. The minimum age to hire a car is 21, although some companies may stipulate 25. Note that the penalties for drink-driving are stiff – take a taxi.

In common with American practice, car-hire prices do not necessarily include full insurance (collision damage waiver) so do check this when comparing prices. (Note that insurance may be covered by your credit-card company, so it's worth finding out about this before paying a supplement, though do check the level of cover provided.) As a point of interest, hire cars have white number plates, in contrast to the yellow of locally owned vehicles and blue of public transport vehicles.

Bikes are easily available on all three islands, often as part of an accommodation package, and **scooters** may be hired as a practical alternative. **Hitchhiking** is relatively easy, particularly on the sister islands, but is not a good idea on Grand Cayman for women on their own at night.

Fuel is unleaded, either standard or super, or diesel. It is sold in imperial gallons, which are slightly greater than the US gallon (five imperial gallons equal six US gallons). The average price of super petrol on Grand Cayman is US$3.45 a gallon (US$0.77 per litre), but you can expect to pay a little more than this on the sister islands. Fuel stations on Grand Cayman usually keep pretty long hours, but on Little Cayman and the Brac they tend to close earlier.

Taxis are freely available in George Town and elsewhere on Grand Cayman, but less so on Cayman Brac; there are no taxis on Little Cayman. A cheap **bus** service operates throughout Grand Cayman, with a reasonably regular timetable and frequent services along Seven Mile Beach. There are no buses on either of the sister islands.

Maps
Although there are several maps available free to visitors, the accuracy of some of them is questionable if you plan to drive even slightly off the beaten track, and as for getting lost – don't! Probably the best commercial map available for the visitor is the one published by International Map Services, available at bookshops on the islands. Most useful for long-term visitors is the *Official Street Atlas of the Cayman Islands*, available from local bookshops at CI$15.

There are also detailed Ordnance Survey maps: a single sheet at a scale of 1:50,000, or four separate sheets at 1:25,000. The latter are available in the UK from Stanfords in Long Acre, London (tel: 020 7836 1321).

ACCOMMODATION
The range of accommodation in the Cayman Islands is pretty broad, from simple guesthouses to opulent hotels with everything the visitor could possibly wish for. There are no campsites, and camping is not permitted on any of the Cayman Islands. That said, you may well see Caymanians camping at Easter on Grand Cayman and, more specifically, on the tiny island of Sand Cay to the south of George Town.

Note that PO box addresses do not necessarily indicate the physical location of an establishment – where there's doubt, this has been made clear in the text.

Hotels and resorts
There is no shortage of luxury accommodation on Grand Cayman, with prices to match. There are plenty of medium-range hotels as well (many of them with self-catering facilities), but simpler establishments are thin on the ground unless you're after a dive lodge. Hotels are graded by a government board of control, with standards ranging from luxury to tourist. There is no star-rating system as such, although many of the hotels have in fact been graded by the AAA – the American Automobile Association.

Dive lodges
A number of smaller places cater specifically for the dive market, with facilities that may include on-site dive schools, rinse tanks, purpose-built swimming pools for dive training, and their own docks. Relaxed and informal, dive lodges tend to have a loyal following, with guests returning year after year to the same place.

Self-catering

There are plenty of opportunities for self-catering throughout the islands, from hotels with kitchen facilities to a bewildering selection of private condominiums and villas. Efficiencies, for the uninitiated, are effectively studio apartments, with a bedroom/living area and kitchenette. Virtually all self-catering units have a sofa bed in the living area, so that a one-bedroom suite can usually sleep four people, and a two-bedroom condominium will take six.

Many of the smaller properties are available through **Cayman Villas** (PO Box 10678 APO, Grand Cayman; tel: 945 4144, fax: 949 7471; email: reservations@caymanvillas.com; web: www.caymanvillas.com) whose office is on Owen Roberts Drive at the airport. A second possibility is **Rentals in Cayman**, PO Box 10820 APO, Grand Cayman; tel: 926 8452; fax: 945 3617; email: info@rentalsincayman.com; web: www.rentalsincayman.com. In addition, various dive outfits handle accommodation, notably **Ocean Frontiers** (PO Box 200 EE; tel: 947 7500, US toll free: 888 232 0541; fax: 947 7600; email: hq@oceanfrontiers.com; web: www.oceanfrontiers.com). Overseas, several tour operators (see pages 38–41) feature a selection of self-catering accommodation, and there's also a good range on the Department of Tourism's website, www.caymanislands.ky.

Guesthouses

Bed and breakfast and guesthouse accommodation is relatively scarce on Cayman. The few opportunities there are tend to be located inland and may be suitable for more mature visitors who are prepared to take the time to get to know their hosts.

Timeshare

There are currently six timeshare properties on Grand Cayman. Plantation Village, Grand Caymanian and the Indies Suites are on or near Seven Mile Beach, while East End boasts The Reef, Morritt's Tortuga and Grand Morritt's. Timeshare weeks can usually be exchanged through one of the two major international vacation exchange systems, RCI (www.rci.com) or II (www.intervalworld.com).

Timeshare 'invitations' and promotional offers abound for these properties, with the notable exception of The Reef, and inducements range from free diving and other watersports to savings on car hire and meals out. Be sure you know what you're taking on before you go along to one of these sessions; if you're not prepared for hard sell, don't go.

For further information, try one of the following websites:

Morritt's Tortuga Club and Resort www.morritt.com. See also page 172.
Timeshare User's Group www.tug2.net. An independent website featuring surveys of over 2,000 resorts worldwide.

Prices

Rates quoted in this guide are walk-in rates, and should be seen as a sample of the options available. Clearly it is beyond the scope of this book to detail them all. Virtually all establishments offer considerable discounts for advance booking

TRADITIONAL CAYMAN RECIPES
Rundown

Traditionally made with fish, but also with salt beef, rundown is a one-pot dish that has long been served in homes across the islands. This recipe comes from a Cayman grandmother who works at the Botanic Park. By 'coconut milk', the Caymanian is referring to blended coconut rather than the 'coconut water' that is a popular drink.

Blend the flesh from two coconuts, then strain the milk into a pan. Boil for a few minutes with onion, sweet pepper and black pepper, then add a selection of vegetables (yam, cassava, breadfruit, banana, green and red plantain, sweet potato, coco yam). Bring back to the boil. Add fish (red snapper is good). Simmer on a low heat to prevent boiling over for half an hour or so. Season with salt and pepper to taste. If you're using salt beef, adjust the timing accordingly, perhaps by cooking in a slow oven.

Crabs steamed in sea-grape or banana leaves

In Cayman, you'd be part of a family party that would go out to hunt crabs, then steam them wrapped in sea-grape or banana leaves. Since you're unlikely to go out searching for live crabs at home, this recipe assumes that you'll be using cooked crab meat.

Sauté onion, green pepper, and Scotch bonnet pepper in butter or margarine; season with pepper (not hot). Add crushed garlic and stir, then put in the crab meat and toss over a low heat for 5–10 minutes. Add a handful of fresh breadcrumbs. Pack the mixture back into the crab shells, and cook in the oven for 15 minutes. Serve with white rice, French or garlic bread and salad.

and stays of several nights, with a seemingly infinite range of possibilities available. Traditionally, rates have been split into high season, or winter (defined as mid December to mid April), and low season or summer (running from mid April to mid December), although the precise timings tend to vary from one hotel or resort to another. Increasingly, however, hotels are charging graduated rates through the year rather than distinguishing between just two separate seasons. For the most part, prices quoted in this guide reflect the lowest and highest in the year, with the exclusion of the Christmas/New Year period when rates in all but the smallest guesthouses tend towards the extortionate. Conversely, special deals abound in the low season, so it pays to shop around.

Several resort hotels and dive lodges offer all-inclusive packages for different groups, such as general holidaymakers, wedding parties, divers or fishing guests. Packages typically incorporate all meals and, in some cases, all drinks as well (particularly for divers, on the basis that few will drink heavily).

There is a 10% government accommodation tax – variously called a room tax or a tourist tax – payable on departure. Increasingly, hotels quote this as a surcharge on their rates. Gratuities, too, are usually added to the bill, from 5% to 15% depending on the establishment.

Previous page Sunset over South Sound (TH)

Above Climbing on Cayman Brac's Wave Wall presents some unusual challenges. (KS)

Above right Horseriders discover the peaceful side of Grand Cayman. (TH)

Right One of three anchors from the shipwreck *Tofa* that lie in shallow water to the south of Little Cayman (LW)

Below Kayaking at Owen Island, Little Cayman (TH)

Many resorts specify a minimum length of stay, varying from three to seven nights, particularly in high season. Cancellation charges can be hefty, so insurance is strongly advised.

EATING AND DRINKING
Food
Fresh fish and seafood are the order of the day almost everywhere on the islands. You will frequently come across dolphin on the menu – this is a fish, not to be confused with the mammal of the same name; it is sometimes listed by its Hawaiian name of 'mahi-mahi', or as 'dorado'. Other popular local fish are yellow-fin tuna and wahoo (a bit like tuna but white), also known as kingfish. On the seafood front, almost everything is available, but one thing you may not have come across is conch (pronounced 'conk'), a chewy shellfish which appears on menus in various guises, from conch stew (delicious), to conch fritters (sometimes called 'flitters'), grilled conch and even conch burgers. A staple of Caymanian cuisine, it is reputed to be a natural aphrodisiac and has a high nutritional value. Other Cayman specialities include jerk chicken (or 'jerk' anything else, for that matter – effectively a spicy barbecue) and turtle stew. In local restaurants, meals are usually served with coconut rice and beans, and fried plantain.

Fruits such as watermelon, limes, bananas and pineapples are traditionally grown inland, despite the poverty of the island's soil. Look out for the knobbly soursop, which is in fact sweet. On the vegetable front, much of Cayman's staple diet is based on crops such as breadfruit, cassava, yams and beans. Most of the fruit and vegetables eaten on the islands today are imported, but there are moves in hand to redress the balance. Local-grown fruit may look less appetising than the immaculately shaped specimens found in supermarkets, but the flavour is infinitely superior. In particular, if you're in Grand Cayman in August, head for West Bay Road and treat yourself to some of the locally grown mangoes on sale just in front of the public beach.

Widely purported to be a typical Cayman treat, rum cake is available pretty well everywhere, with plenty of outlets having free tastings (you can get quite carried away at the airport waiting for a flight!). Variations on plain rum cake include banana and chocolate flavours. Caymanians will tell you that rum cake is actually an import from elsewhere in the Caribbean. Far more traditional is the 'heavy cake' which you may be able to sample on heritage days. Rather like a cross between a suet pudding and bread and butter pudding, it is, as its name suggests, heavy. Light cake, more sponge-like in consistency, is also popular. And for a true Cayman sweet treat, see if you can get hold of coconut ice.

Eating out
Any visitor to the Cayman Islands will be spoilt for choice when it comes to eating out. The high proportion of visitors, and the affluence of the islands as a whole, make for a competitive environment and restaurateurs have risen to the challenge with a startling array of choice and extremely high standards. Seafood lovers will be in their element, but there's plenty too for meat eaters, and most restaurants have at least one vegetarian option. For youngsters, children's menus are available in many restaurants.

While standards are high, so in general are prices. In a reasonable restaurant, lunchtime meals such as salads and sandwiches fall into the US$8.50–10 range. For dinner, expect to pay a minimum of US$6 for a starter, with main courses ranging from US$16 for a pasta or simple vegetarian dish to US$35 or more for seafood and steaks. Prices in restaurants specialising in local food tend to be considerably lower. It's quite possible to find a full-blown Cayman-style meal for around US$10–15, and you probably won't have room for anything else! Look out, too, for special lunchtime deals, particularly mid week, and for Sunday brunch menus that are usually of the 'all-you-can-eat' variety. Barbecues, too, tend to offer good value for money.

For the most part, prices for restaurants listed in this guide have not been given unless there are special deals or they fall outside the norms quoted above. Most menus are priced in CI$, but always check, or that extra 25% on your US$ credit card bill may come as a bit of a shock. A 15% gratuity is usually added to the bill.

Not surprisingly, for islands that have a large proportion of visitors from the US, there are a number of brand-name fast-food outlets, from Burger King to Domino's Pizza and Pizza Hut. Or you could try fast food, Cayman style. Patties, a spicy meat pastry not dissimilar to the British Cornish pasty, are available from cafés, shops and even petrol stations for around US$1.50 each.

Street vendors are illegal throughout the islands, so there's no question of being pestered on the beach or in the street. During carnivals, though, look out for roadside stalls selling local specialities such as heavy cake or patties (see *Festivals*, page 58–9). And in the evenings, particularly at weekends, local people may set up barbecues selling jerk chicken to take away.

Drinks

Stingray beer, brewed on Grand Cayman, is available throughout the islands. There are three types: Premium, Durty and the strongest, Dark. Visitors are welcome to visit the brewery (see page 159). Also popular is Jamaican Red Stripe. Several well-known international brand names are widely available, including Heineken and Michelob.

No visit to the Caribbean is complete without at least trying the rum punch, on offer almost everywhere. So, too, are various cocktails, including the mudslide – a Cayman institution based on a rather sweet but very popular mix of vodka, Kahlua and Tia Maria on ice. For true decadence, try it frozen (liquidised with ice) or with a combination of ice-cream, chocolate sauce and whipped cream. Rather more refreshing is Cayman lemonade, a mix of gin (or vodka), peach schnapps, cranberry and sour mix, garnished with lemon. And then there's shark attack: 1oz rum, $\frac{1}{2}$oz peach schnapps, $\frac{1}{2}$oz curaçao, 2oz pineapple juice, 2oz sour mix, and a splash of grenadine.

If you care about your bank balance, keep wine for special occasions – with restaurant prices starting at US$20 a bottle for even the most ordinary wine, it's heading towards luxury status. Even in liquor stores, you're looking at US$12.50–18. However, if you're serious about your wine, then there are several restaurants on Grand Cayman that can accommodate you, notably Grand Old House, Pappagallo's, Casa Havana and the Lighthouse at Breakers, all of which hold *Wine Spectator* magazine's 2003 award of excellence.

Soft drinks such as Coca-Cola and Seven-Up are to be found pretty well everywhere, as are canned fruit juices, with a variety of flavours from mango and apricot to pineapple and orange. Most readily available, though, is fruit punch, which ranges from a rather synthetic concoction to a very tasty mix of tropical fruit juices. Iced water is served automatically in most restaurants – a very welcome import from the US. More typically, you may come across coconut water (known elsewhere as coconut milk), which is deliciously refreshing.

Under local licensing laws, all restaurants and bars must close by midnight on Saturdays and Sundays, and alcoholic drinks may not be served before 1.00pm on a Sunday. It is illegal to purchase alcohol under the age of 18 anywhere in Cayman.

PUBLIC HOLIDAYS

Banks are closed on all public holidays. All shops close on Christmas Day, and most on New Year's Day, Ash Wednesday and Good Friday, although some will open to serve cruise-ship passengers and others may open for a few hours for the convenience of customers. Every four years, Election Day, usually in November, is a public holiday. For full details, see the government website, www.gov.ky.

January

1	New Year's Day
4th Monday	National Heroes' Day

February/March
Ash Wednesday

March/April
Good Friday
Easter Monday

May

3rd Monday	Discovery Day

June

2nd/3rd Monday	Queen's Birthday. Celebrated on the Monday following the UK celebration (which is on a Saturday). There's a formal parade with marching bands, awarding of HM the Queen's Birthday honours and national honours, and a garden party open to the public in the grounds of the Governor's residence.

July

1st Monday	Constitution Day

November

Monday close to November 11	Remembrance Day. Held on the day following Remembrance Sunday.

December

25	Christmas Day
26	Boxing Day

SHOPPING

The Cayman Islands may be expensive, but George Town's status as a duty-free port makes shopping a highly attractive option for some visitors. Everything from classy boutiques to art galleries and duty-free emporia is there to attract the tourist, often in upmarket shops that would usually grace far more elegant surroundings. The majority of shops are located in George Town and along Grand Cayman's West Bay Road, where numerous small shopping plazas cater to the ever-growing demand. Shopaholics would do best to visit the sister islands after Grand Cayman; here a greater degree of normality prevails and there is little to get those shopping glands salivating.

Duty-free goods such as jewellery, china, perfume and cigars may be most in evidence, as are designer clothes, but look further and you will find opportunities to purchase the work of local artists and craftspeople. Brightly painted wooden toys, natural woven baskets and quality T-shirts make good souvenirs, as do evocative paintings in all manner of styles. Don't buy products made from turtleshell (they shouldn't be on sale anyway) and think twice about black coral. The latter is protected around Cayman, so is imported from Honduras and Nicaragua, which seems pretty iniquitous (see box, page 23). For the collector, a number of stores sell treasure coins, though few of these are from Cayman waters.

If local foods are your weakness, consider a bottle of jerk sauce to brighten up that barbecue at home. And then, of course, there's the ubiquitous, if pricey, rum cake (see *Food*, page 54). Unexpectedly, alcoholic drinks are subject to a hefty duty on the islands, so buy them tax-free at the airport.

ARTS AND ENTERTAINMENT

On Grand Cayman, several restaurants and bars have live entertainment throughout the week, offering anything from jazz to steel bands. There are also two theatres with a broad range of plays and concerts for every taste. The sister islands, however, have little to offer the night owl beyond open-air barbecues, so take a couple of good books and be prepared to relax! Gambling is prohibited everywhere.

Festivals

Various festivals held throughout the year appeal to the visitor as well as to Caymanians.

February/March

Little Cayman Mardi Gras Festival This colourful parade around Little Cayman, organised by the local branch of the National Trust, takes place around Shrove Tuesday each year.

April/May

Cayfest The national cultural festival takes over the streets of Grand Cayman and Cayman Brac for a week at Easter each year. Based around open-air cafés, craft displays, and exhibitions of photography, food and art, it incorporates activities for children, special festival days, boat launches and parties. For further information, check the Cayfest website: www.artscayman.org.

Cayman Carnival This popular one-day carnival run by the Rotary Club centres on a colourful costume street parade, to the accompaniment of live calypso and soca bands, and with local food specialities available from roadside stalls. Visitors are welcome to join in, but only costumes made on the islands may be considered by the judges.

June
International Aviation Week is celebrated in the second week of June with aerial and marine displays and a family fun day.

July
Taste of Cayman This three-day event offers the opportunity to sample various Cayman specialities, from conch fritters to rum cake, with much more in between.

October/November
Pirates Week PO Box 51 GT; tel: 949 5859/5078; fax: 949 5449; email: pirates@candw.ky; web: www.piratesweekfestival.com. This well-established annual festival, the most important in the Cayman Islands and unique in the Caribbean, takes place in the last week of October. The fun gets off to a rattling good start on the first Saturday with a blood-curdling 'pirate invasion' of George Town harbour from two old-time sailing ships, followed by a themed parade through the streets, and music and dancing until midnight. During the days that follow, over 30 events ranging from district heritage days and sports competitions to music and fireworks displays are held throughout the islands, involving local communities every bit as much as visitors.

November
Gimistory Initiated in 1999 by the Cayman National Cultural Foundation, Gimistory brings traditional storytellers to selected outdoor venues in Grand Cayman and Cayman Brac for a week-long event at the end of November. Each evening, the audience gathers free of charge to listen to stories old and new told by proponents from both Cayman and other Caribbean islands. And after the final response of 'Jack Mandora, mi nuh choose none', signifying the end of the tale, there is the traditional Caymanian dish of fried fish and fritters, washed down by 'swankie', a local lemonade. Duppy (ghost) stories on the beach are unbeatable!

The strong American influence means that **Thanksgiving** dinners also abound in Cayman.

December
Almost immediately after Thanksgiving, the islands start preparing for **Christmas**. A competition for the best Christmas lights results in some spectacular (some might say over-the-top) decorations of hotels, houses, shops and public buildings throughout the holiday period. Caymanians and visitors alike tour the streets to see the displays, many of which are open to the public in aid of local charities.

HINTS ON PHOTOGRAPHY
Nick Garbutt and John Jones

All sorts of photographic opportunities present themselves in the islands, from simple holiday snaps to that one-off encounter with a blue iguana. For the best results, give some thought to the following tips.

- As a general rule, if it doesn't look good through the viewfinder, it will never look good as a picture. Don't take photographs for the sake of taking them; be patient and wait until the image looks right.
- Photographing **people** is never easy and more often than not it requires a fair share of luck. If you want to take a portrait shot of a stranger, it is always best to ask first. Focus on the eyes of your subject since they are the most powerful ingredient of any portrait, and be prepared for the unexpected.
- There is no mystique to good **wildlife** photography. The secret is getting into the right place at the right time and then knowing what to do when you are there. Look for striking poses, aspects of behaviour and distinctive features. Try not only to take pictures of the species itself, but also to illustrate it within the context of its environment. Alternatively, focus in close on a characteristic which can be emphasised.
- Photographically, the eyes are the most important part of an animal – focus on these, make sure they are sharp and try to ensure they contain a highlight.
- Look at the surroundings – there is nothing worse than a distracting twig or highlighted leaf lurking in the background. Getting this right is often the difference between a mediocre and a memorable image.
- A powerful flashgun adds the option of punching in extra light to transform an otherwise dreary picture. Artificial light is no substitute for natural light, though, so use it judiciously.

ACTIVITIES

Without a doubt, the Cayman Islands are a haven for the outdoor enthusiast. The islands maintain their reputation for some of the best diving in the world, with the Cayman walls the greatest draw. To this have been added over the years almost every watersport imaginable, from snorkelling and jet skiing to parasailing and windsurfing. Fishing, too, is deservedly popular, with operators offering a range of fishing for all enthusiasts.

Off the water, golf is a major attraction, with three golf courses on Grand Cayman. The relatively flat terrain means that cycling is well suited to softies (though avoid cycling up on to the bluff on Cayman Brac if you fit into this mould). For the more adventurous, horse-riding is gaining in popularity, caving is easily accessible, and climbing in Cayman Brac has a steady but growing following.

Activities are not all about adventure pursuits and sport, however. The natural history enthusiast is well served by good birdwatching and hiking on all three islands, backed by the National Trust (see page 29), while photographers have plenty of scope for both land-based and underwater photography.

- Getting close to the subject correspondingly reduces the depth of field. At camera-to-subject distances of less than a metre, apertures between f16 and f32 are necessary to ensure adequate depth of field. This means using flash to provide enough light. If possible, use one or two small flashguns to illuminate the subject from the side.

Landscapes are forever changing, even on a daily basis. Good landscape photography is all about good light and capturing mood. Generally the first and last two hours of daylight are best, or when peculiar climatic conditions add drama or emphasise distinctive features. Never place the horizon in the centre – in your mind's eye divide the frame into thirds and either exaggerate the land or the sky.

Film
If you're using conventional film (as against a digital camera), select the right film for your needs. Film speed (ISO number) indicates the sensitivity of the film to light. The lower the number, the less sensitive the film, but the better quality the final image.

For general print film, ISO 100 or 200 fit the bill perfectly. If you are using transparencies for home use or for lectures, then again ISO 100 or 200 film is fine. However, if you want to get your work published, the superior quality of ISO 25 to 100 film is best.

- Try to keep your film cool. Never leave it in direct sunlight.
- Don't allow fast film (ISO 800 and above) to pass through X-ray machines.
- Under weak light conditions use a faster film (ISO 200 or 400).

For hints on underwater photography, see pages 88–9.

It is interesting to note that there are no private beaches in Cayman – land up to the high-water mark is Crown property, owned by the Queen, as are all the islands' lakes.

For details of all activities, see *Chapter 4*, and pages 187 and 210.

MEDIA AND COMMUNICATIONS
Telecommunications, as you would expect in one of the world's most important offshore banking locations, are excellent, with facilities available for every form of business link.

Telephone, fax and internet
The telephone code for the Cayman Islands from overseas is +1 345. Until recently, telephone, telex and fax were provided by Cable & Wireless (web: www.candw.ky), but the company's monopoly was broken in 2004. Both Digicel and AT&T went live in March 2004, offering mobile-phone competition and leading to significant cuts in international call rates.

For **international calls** from Cayman, dial 011, followed by the national code, then the number required without the initial 0. The national code for the

US and Canada is 1; for the UK it is 44. A US$12.50 phonecard will pay for a six-minute call to the UK, or eight minutes to the US. Calls from hotel rooms, here as anywhere else in the world, can be exorbitant – witness a US$49 charge for a five-minute call to the UK! That said, some hotels have passed on savings from deregulation so dialling direct is sometimes the cheaper option now. Check hotel rates carefully and, if they are over US$3 per minute, use your credit card or a phonecard (see below).

Local calls within Grand Cayman or between Cayman Brac and Little Cayman are very reasonable, but those between Grand Cayman and the sister islands cost significantly more.

Internet facilities are available at most of the larger hotels. In addition, there are numerous internet cafés in and around George Town (see page 83).

Credit-cards calls
Credit-card calls can be made to any destination, from any phone in the Cayman Islands, by dialling 1 800 744 7777, followed by your card number. Instructions on how to proceed are given in English. Alternatively, for calls to the USA, dial 1 800 225 5872. You can also dial 110 for Visa and Mastercard calls.

Phonecards
There are two types of phonecard available. Prepaid phonecards are available from shops and petrol stations throughout the islands in denominations of CI$5, $10, $15 and $20, or in some cases US$10 and $20, and can be used from private, public or hotel phones. They are valid for 12 months from first use. Key in the number given on the card, then follow the instructions. You will be told how much money/time is left on the card. Phonebox calls cost very slightly more than when using coins.

SmartPhone cards may be bought in denominations of CI$10 and $20 from most general shops. They can be used only in specially designated phones, which are clearly marked.

Payphones
There are over 200 payphones throughout the islands, though in practice many have been vandalised in recent years. Payphones may be used with either coins or phonecards; instructions are posted in telephone boxes. Only CI coins are accepted, in denominations of 10 and 25 cents. International calls may be made from a payphone only with a phonecard.

Mobile phones
The use of mobile phones by visitors to Cayman is now a reality, and with more companies setting up on the islands, the situation will continue to improve. Cayman now operates on the international GSM system, so most users can either roam or simply buy a pay-as-you-go SIM card from Cable &Wireless, Digicel or AT&T.

Important telephone numbers
Emergency (police, ambulance, decompression, fire)   911 or 555
Non-emergency calls to the police   949 4222

Hospital	949 8600
Electricity	949 5200 (Grand Cayman)
	948 2224 (Cayman Brac)

Telephone services

Operator	0
International operator	010
Directory enquiries	411

Post

There is no door-to-door delivery service in the Cayman Islands, so all addresses feature a PO box number. Street names and numbering have been introduced in order to assist the emergency services, but they are still relatively new, and often do not form part of the address. Letters to the Cayman Islands should be addressed as follows:

PO Box 000000 XX
Grand Cayman/Little Cayman/Cayman Brac
Cayman Islands
British West Indies

Most postboxes are painted blue and yellow. There are regular collections of mail from Monday to Friday, and on Saturday mornings, and letters normally take around five to seven working days to reach the UK or US.

Stamps for a small postcard from the Cayman Islands to the US currently cost CI$0.20, and to the UK CI$0.25; larger postcards and letters cost CI$0.30 and CI$0.40 respectively. Stamps are available at post offices and some shops and hotels. See also *Philately*, pages 64–5.

Newspapers and magazines

The *Caymanian Compass* is published daily at CI$0.50. The more expensive Friday edition (CI$0.75) features a supplement with listings of events across the islands over the weekend and through the next week. Other papers include the weekly *New Caymanian* and *Cayman Net News* (CI$0.50), which is published daily Monday to Friday. For current and archive stories, readers can also check out www.caymannetnews.com – it's updated daily, but the most recent 72 hours' news is available on a subscription-only basis.

There's no shortage of literature distributed free to tourists, supported by mountains of glossy advertising. *What's Hot* and the *Cayman Activity Guide* (www.CaymanActivityGuide.com) are free monthly magazines which are available at numerous outlets including hotels and the airport. The hardback *Key to Cayman* is a complimentary general guide to the islands, to be found in most hotel rooms. A highlight of this book is a series of recipes supplied by many of Grand Cayman's restaurants. Others include *Fun News* (from Cayman's 'far side' – the eastern end of the island), the monthly lifestyle magazine, *Inside Out*, and the annual *Destinations* and *Menu Guide* – this last useful for the inclusion of several restaurant's menus.

For the business community, the standard reference work is *The Cayman Islands Yearbook and Business Directory*, and there is also the quarterly *Cayman Executive*.

PHILATELY

John Moody of Stanley Gibbons

Visitors to the Cayman Islands are frequently surprised at the variety and colours of the country's stamps which they encounter at hotels and local post offices when they come to send postcards. In fact, the attractive designs of the stamps often match the pictures on the cards and act as miniature promotional posters for the islands' travel industry. The sale of postage stamps also contributes to the islands' economy as collectors from all over the world seek out their designs.

Although the first post office on the Cayman Islands was opened in April 1889, in the capital George Town, the islanders had to use Jamaican stamps until November 1900 when the first stamp to bear the Cayman Islands' name was issued. The stamp was a simple Victorian definitive, much beloved by collectors of early Empire stamps, although not half as interesting to visitors as the multi-coloured stamps available today. It was not until 1935, in the reign of King George V, that the islanders could display the wonders of their islands to the world through commemorative stamps. This first issue showed such images as the red-footed booby, the hawksbill turtle and conch shells, all of which can still be seen on and around Cayman shores today.

The Cayman Islands hold a strange philatelic record in so far as they are one of only two countries in the world that had postage stamps produced by the police. This happened in February 1908 when the islands ran short of 2½d stamps and local Police Inspector J H O'Sullivan took it upon himself to alter four sheets of 4d stamps by hand, to read 2½d.

Although the current stamps portray exotic scenery, plants, flowers, fish

International newspapers on sale regularly on the islands include *The Miami Herald*, the *International Herald Tribune* and the *Financial Times*.

Television and radio

Cayman's four **television** stations are all privately run. The most popular, CITN, features 24-hour transmission of Caribbean, international and local news plus various entertainment programmes. Its sister company, CTS, is targeted at visitors – you'll soon tire of *Discover Cayman*, a relentless 45-minute newsreel of tourist-oriented promotional material backed up by countless adverts. The other two channels, CATN/TV-30 and CCTV, broadcast religious programmes.

Most hotels on the islands have satellite or cable TV, making a broad range of programmes from the US available to guests.

There is a growing number of **radio** stations operating on the islands, but these are dominated by Radio Cayman. The government-owned company offers two separate stations, Radio Cayman One, on 89.9FM (93.9FM on the sister islands), and Radio Cayman Two on 105.3FM (91.9FM on the sister islands). Both feature regular news bulletins and governmental broadcasts, together with educational, religious, cultural and entertainment programmes.

Other stations include the privately run Radio Z99.9FM, which has round-the-clock music interspersed with news bulletins. There is also Vibe FM, playing and birds, they will also be vaguely familiar – at least in the eyes of British visitors – since the head of HM The Queen still appears on each stamp. As a member of the Commonwealth, the Cayman Islands has its stamps produced by the Crown Agents Stamp Bureau in Britain, on behalf of the Cayman Islands Postal Authority. Often these commemorate or celebrate British royal occasions or events from British/Cayman history. The islands also take part in what are known as omnibus editions, when each of a group of Commonwealth countries issues, in effect, the same stamps to commemorate a common theme. The celebration of HM The Queen Mother's 100th birthday in 2000 is a good example. Not all CI stamps are British orientated, however: a recent issue caused much delight amongst children with a set portraying the colourful characters from the popular US cartoon series, *Peanuts*.

Like the stamps, Cayman banknotes and coins also bear a picture of HM Queen Elizabeth II, although British visitors will be less familiar with the dollars and cents with which both money and stamps are denominated. The Cayman Island dollar replaced £sd in 1972, when Britain's money was decimalised.

It is well worthwhile popping into the Philatelic Bureau at the central post office in George Town, or at Seven Mile Beach Post Office in West Shore Centre on West Bay Road, to have a look both at current stamp issues and at earlier ones that are still held in stock. Alternatively, they can be contacted by post at the Philatelic Bureau, Seven Mile Beach Post Office, Grand Cayman, Cayman Islands, British West Indies; tel: 946 4757; fax: 949 4113; email: cistamps@candw.ky.

predominantly reggae and pop, the country-orientated Rooster (101.9FM), and Ocean FM (95.5), with hits from the 60s and later. These are balanced by Heaven FM on 97.9FM, which features predominantly Christian music.

Frequencies for the BBC World Service and Voice of America are subject to change, so check the current situation online at www.bbc.co.uk/worldservice and www.voa.gov.

BUSINESS

The tax-free status of the Cayman Islands is central to the establishment of many businesses here. In addition, there are a number of other incentives designed to encourage the establishment of local industries, of which the most significant is the possibility of concessions on import duty, linked to investment, local employment and type of market. For further details, contact the Ministry of Tourism, Environment, Development and Commerce, Government Administration Building, Grand Cayman; tel: 949 7900.

Recent initiatives have also put Cayman Brac in a good position as a business location. With the same tax advantages as Grand Cayman, it also has lower licensing and work permit fees, and a considerably quieter pace of life. Details may be obtained from the Cayman Brac Customs Department, District Administration, Cayman Brac, tel: 948 2222.

The Cayman Islands Government Information Services publish a series of booklets covering several aspects of business on the islands, including opening a business, licensing of captive insurance companies, real estate and development, and company registration, as well as details of banking and trust company operators, and a list of professional, financial, governmental and retail services. For details of these, and other information, contact the government office (see below). It is also worth approaching the **Cayman Islands Chamber of Commerce**, PO Box 1000 GT, MacDonald Square, George Town; tel: 949 8090; fax: 949 0220; email: chamber@candw.ky.

Working in the Cayman Islands

A temporary, non-renewable work permit may be obtained before arrival in the islands, entitling the holder to carry out a specific job for a maximum of six months. Do note that permits are also required by anyone on a sales trip to the islands. Applications for a work permit should be addressed to the Chief Immigration Officer, Department of Immigration, PO Box 1098 GT, Grand Cayman (tel: 949 8344; fax: 949 8486). The office is open Monday to Friday, 9.00am–4.00pm.

Under the 2003 Immigration Law, employers may take on a non-Caymanian only if they are unable to find a qualified Caymanian to fill the post. Work permits are usually limited to three years, up to a maximum of seven years. All related fees are payable in advance.

Those planning to work in the Cayman Islands need to provide the following information to their prospective employer, who will then apply for the relevant work permit:

- completed application form for work permit
- evidence of professional qualifications and experience
- 4 passport-size photographs (3 full face; 1 profile)
- police clearance certificate or similar
- medical certificate
- character references

Self-employed people need to supply the above details, together with details of the business or profession and evidence of financial status. For further information, and details of fees, contact the Chief Immigration Officer at the above address, or one of the following:

Cayman Islands Government Information Services Elgin Av, George Town, Grand Cayman; tel: 949 8092; fax: 949 5936. Normal office hours are 8.30pm–5.00pm, Mon–Fri.

Cayman Islands Government Office in the United Kingdom 6 Arlington St, London SW1A 1RE; tel: 020 7491 7772; fax: 020 7491 7944; email: info@caymangovtuk.demon.co.uk

OTHER PRACTICALITIES
Electricity

Electricity is 110 volts, 60 Hz. Flat, two-pin, US-style plugs are standard, so take an adaptor if you are visiting from the UK or elsewhere.

CULTURAL DOS AND DON'TS

The traditional pace of life in the Cayman Islands is slow and relaxed. Don't try to rush things if you're talking to Caymanians – it's not worth it, and you'll lose the opportunity to get to know what makes this country tick. Remember, too, that Cayman society is very much of the old school, with a high standard of manners born of natural courtesy and an in-bred respect for the older generation in particular. Older women are generally addressed as ma'am, or the more familiar Miss Emily, or Miss Jenny; older men as 'sir'.

For the visitor, the lifestyle in Grand Cayman is comparatively smart, and you are requested to cover swimwear when leaving your resort. Certainly in the more upmarket restaurants, men should expect to wear trousers, not shorts, when dining out in the evening. On the sister islands, swimwear and shorts are the order of the day – and evenings are generally pretty casual too. Sunbathing nude or even topless is strictly forbidden everywhere.

On the business front, the norm is to wear suits for meetings and formal occasions, with a handshake the usual greeting.

There has until recently been a ban on gay relationships, with financial penalties incurred on the rare instances that prosecutions have been made. However, in order to bring Cayman law into line with the European Convention on Human Rights, which came into effect in the UK during 2000, the British government has recently insisted that the law be revoked. The implications of this highly controversial move could well be more far reaching than the edict itself, with questions being raised about the right of Britain to impose European law on the islands, and renewed calls in some quarters for self-determination. Cayman society, meanwhile, remains deeply conservative, and in general gay relationships will not be considered acceptable.

More generally, any form of littering is subject to a hefty fine, and gambling is illegal.

GIVING SOMETHING BACK

The standard of living in the Cayman is so high compared with other Caribbean islands that it is easy to forget that even here there are groups that would benefit from the support of visitors. Of these, it is probably the environmental charities that are particularly apt for visitors. The work of the National Trust for the Cayman Islands, and particularly the Blue Iguana Recovery Programme (see page 19), is one such, while the Central Caribbean Marine Institute is involved in vital research beneath the waves. For contact details, see page 29.

Part Two

Grand Cayman

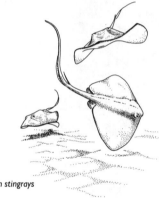

Southern stingrays

70

Take it easier...

- Increased Legroom
- Upgraded Meals
- Larger Seats
- Preferred Check-in
- Sir Turtle Lounge access

1 800 4 Cayman
www.caymanairways.com
Chicago • Houston • Tampa
Ft. Lauderdale • Miami
Montego Bay • Kingston
Cayman Brac • Little Cayman

Cayman Airways

Sir Turtle Class

available on flights to Chicago, Houston, Miami
and Ft. Lauderdale.

The Basics

Low and full of trees ... it is very dangerous
in the night, being almost surrounded by a
reef of rocks.

George Gauld,
The Island of Grand Cayman, 1773

Grand Cayman is the largest and most popular of the three Cayman islands, lying northwest of Jamaica at 19°2' north and 81° west. Fringing coral reefs hug the ragged L-shaped coast area on three sides. On the lee side, to the west, spur-and-groove coral leads out to the wall that reaches down into the abyss of the Cayman Trench. Where mangroves once covered this western shore, lines of buildings now grow, icons to the god of tourism that has brought prosperity but could so easily have swamped such a tiny island. Yet natural beauty still prevails, in the gentle sway of the trees above powdery white-sand beaches, in the rocky shores to the east, in the sunsets that bring depth to the colours of a sun-bleached landscape.

With a total land area of 76 square miles (197km²), the island is just 22 miles (35km) long, by nine miles (14.5km) wide at its widest point in the west, and narrowing to less than a mile (1.25km) near the airport. The main settlements are the capital, George Town, with a population in 1999 of 20,625, followed by West Bay (8,243) and Bodden Town (5,764).

ARRIVAL
Airport
Owen Roberts Airport is located just east of George Town, a short taxi ride from Seven Mile Beach. The small airport concourse has just one gift shop, but upstairs is a fairly substantial restaurant, the Hungry Horse (tel: 949 8056), open from 6.15am till 6.00pm, and serving everything from soft drinks and snacks and burgers to cocktails and full meals. Money can be changed at the restaurant.

Airside, there is a bar that also sells snacks of the hot dog and burger variety; it's open for all outgoing flights. Several small duty-free shops stock a selection of jewellery and souvenirs as well as the inevitable rum and rum cake. Alcohol is pretty good value at the airport shops, with a litre of spirits around US$8–12. No newspapers or books are on sale, though, so go prepared. Note that shops here will not accept credit cards for transactions of less than US$20.

GRAND CAYMAN

Getting into town

Taxis can be hired just outside the airport building: queue at the small wooden booth to be allocated the next available vehicle. Fares from the airport are set by the government, based on one to three people sharing a taxi. Sample prices (2004) are as follows:

Seven Mile Beach (southern end)	US$15.50
Seven Mile Beach (northern end)	US$23.75
East End (Morritt's Tortuga/Reef)	US$57.50
Cayman Kai	US$59.00

Additional passengers are charged at one third of these rates. If you're sharing a taxi on an ad hoc basis with another group of people, you may well be charged as two separate groups.

Alternatively, all the major car-hire companies have offices at the airport – simply turn left out of the airport building and cross the road. (See *Car hire*, page 75.) There is no bus service from the airport, and hotels are not permitted to collect guests on arrival, although most arrange for transport through a particular taxi company.

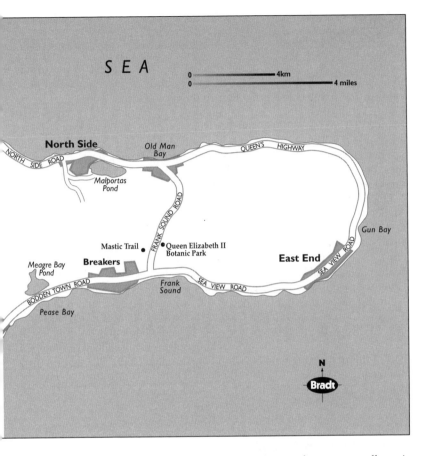

Aside from the taxi rank at Grand Cayman airport, there are usually taxis outside North Terminal at the port in George Town.

Cruise ship

Numerous cruise-ship operators include the Cayman Islands on their itineraries – several ships anchor off George Town each day. The size of Grand Cayman makes its attractions very accessible even for just a short stopover, with possibilities ranging from diving and snorkelling to sightseeing, golf and duty-free shopping.

Cruise passengers come ashore at one of the terminals in the centre of George Town, close to the museum and the shopping area. If the seas to the west of the island are rough, the ships anchor off Spotts to the south, and passengers are ferried into town from there.

During 2004, tenders were out for the construction of a new port, the Royal Water Terminal, to be located next to Fort George, almost opposite the church in George Town, to enable cruise ships to come right into the harbour instead of anchoring offshore as at present.

For a suggested walking tour of George Town, see pages 143–7.

Yacht

Very few yachts find their way to the Cayman Islands, since their relative isolation in terms of the rest of the Caribbean means that they are rarely on a natural sea route. In addition, the fringing reef makes access to the islands something of a challenge. Except in bad weather, yachts should first clear customs and immigration at the Port Authority in George Town, next to the North Terminal building The Port Authority may be contacted on channel 16 Marine VHF, or tel: 949 2055, and they'll put you on to customs. Opening hours are Mon–Fri 8.30am–4.30pm; Sat 8.30am–midday.

There are no port fees for visiting yachts during opening times, but outside these hours there is a charge of CI$56, rising to CI$72 on public holidays, so it makes sense to plan arrival times carefully.

Once formalities are complete, it is essential that you check with the Port Authority where you should anchor. Those anchoring without permission may find themselves faced with a stiff fine for inadvertently stopping in an environmental zone – easily done as the zones are not marked on the Admiralty chart. There are hundreds of permanent government moorings that can be used by the public. A full list may be obtained from either the Cayman Islands Sailing Club (see page 108) or the Department of Environment (tel: 949 8469).

Smaller yachts may head for one of the two marinas, both located in North Sound – Cayman Islands Yacht Club to the west, or Kaibo Yacht Club to the east. In theory, the marinas are accessible by craft with a draught of up to 7ft (2.1m); in practice – and without local knowledge – the likelihood of running a boat of this draught aground in North Sound is pretty high, although you may just scrape into Cayman Islands Yacht Club. There are conflicting reports of the depth of the main channel in North Sound, ranging from 9ft (2.7m) to 6ft (1.8m), but even this may be an overestimate.

For tide times around Cayman, check the daily *Caymanian Compass*.

Cayman Islands Yacht Club

Located on the west side of North Sound, in Governor's Harbour, Cayman Islands Yacht Club (PO Box 30985 SMB; tel: 945 4322; fax: 945 4432; email: ciyc@candw.ky) is the larger of the two marinas on the island. In spite of the name, there is no actual club building, with all port transactions conducted at the shop by the fuel station. The club has 138 slips, with a maximum length overall of 150ft (45.7m).

Fees are CI$8.50 per foot per month, or for short stays CI$0.95 per foot per day. Fuel, water and electricity are available, as well as toilet facilities, public telephones and a shop selling basic commodities. Opening hours are Mon–Fri 7.00am–6.00pm; Sat 7.00am–5.00pm; Sun and public holidays 7.00am–4.00pm.

Vehicular access to the marina is from West Bay Road, opposite the Anchorage Condominiums. The nearest bus stop is number 16. The flat and relatively traffic-free roads in the vicinity are often used by people out running, roller blading or just walking with their children.

Kaibo Yacht Club

Across the bay at Cayman Kai, just south of Rum Point, Kaibo Yacht Club is also something of a misnomer. There are both permanent and tie-up docks, with no fee payable if the crew is eating at the restaurant. Otherwise fees are similar to Cayman Islands Yacht Club (above). Facilities include a fuel dock and gift shop (run by Red Sail Sports). The bar, and upstairs Cecil's Restaurant, are open to all (see page 170).

Morgan's Harbour

This little harbour north of Cayman Islands Yacht Club is really not suitable for any but the smallest vessels, such as fishing boats.

GETTING AROUND
By road

The island is relatively traffic free with the exception of roads around George Town, particularly along West Bay Road, which runs parallel to Seven Mile Beach. These are best avoided Monday to Friday during the rush hours (7.15–8.45am and 4.45–6.00pm).

In spite of a very limited road network, it is surprisingly easy to get lost in the residential streets that lead off the main roads. The signposting isn't great, either, so stick to the main roads or buy a good map.

Car hire

Without doubt, the simplest means of getting around Grand Cayman is by car. Traffic is minimal outside George Town (though do avoid West Bay Road at peak hours) and parking is rarely a problem except in the centre of George Town.

Drivers must be over 21 to hire a car (some companies stipulate over 25), and in possession of either an international driving licence or a current national driving licence. If you have only the latter, you will need to purchase a visitor's driving permit from the car-hire company at a cost of around US$7.50. Those going on to one or both of the sister islands should ask for the permit to be extended to cover the whole of your stay. Vehicle insurance is run on American lines, and is fairly complex, so do check that the car you hire is comprehensively insured (including collision damage waiver, or CDW) rather than just third party.

Remember that driving in the Cayman Islands is on the left, as it is in the UK. The speed limit in Grand Cayman is 30mph (48km/h) in urban areas, and 40mph (64km/h) on most other roads, with the exception of the roads east of Bodden Town, where the limit is 50mph (80km/h) outside the villages. Should you find yourself behind a school bus, note that you must stop when children are embarking or disembarking.

Rental rates vary according to season. Winter (usually mid December to mid April) is high season, with prices some 35% greater than the rest of the year. Rates quoted below are for the most part summer rates and are exclusive of insurance and the statutory Vehicle Environmental Recovery fee (US$2.50 per day). Basic insurance starts at around US$6 per day for third party (not always available), up to approximately US$13 with CDW (sometimes with an excess or deductible), and higher for a fully insured, top-of-the-range model with no excess. Check the current rates before you sign. If you do get involved in an accident, stay at the scene until the police arrive.

Almost all companies offer a reduced rate for rentals of a week or more. You can also expect to have unlimited mileage, with free pick up and drop off, although many companies restrict the area in which this applies, so do ask in advance.

Ace Rent-a-Car Tel: 949 2280/0572, US 800 654 3131; fax: 949 0572; email: acehertz@candw.ky; web: www.acerentacarltd.com. A Hertz licensee, with locations at the airport and at the Beach Club Hotel. Over 25s only.

Andy's Rent-a-Car West Bay Rd; tel: 949 8111; fax: 949 8385; email: info@andys.ky; web: www.andys.ky. Located both at the airport (open 6.00am–10.00pm) and opposite the Marriott (open 6.00am–8.00pm). Helpful and friendly staff, and a full range of cars and jeeps at highly competitive prices. Rates from US$29 per day (US$40 in high season) for an economy two-door automatic with AC. Baby seats available.

Avis Rent-a-Car Airport office tel: 949 2468/9; fax: 949 7127; email: avisgcm@candw.ky; web: www.aviscayman.com. Open 7.00am–midnight. Also at the Hyatt Regency, Westin Casuarina, Marriott and Courtyard Marriott hotels.

Budget Rent-a-Car Tel: 949 5605; fax: 949 8223; email: budget@candw.ky. Locations at the airport and Treasure Island Resort.

Cayman Auto Rental North Church St, George Town; tel: 949 1013/6954; fax: 945 7081; email: cayauto@candw.ky; web: www.cayman.com.ky/com/auto. In the centre of George Town, close to the harbour. Chevrolets, Jeeps and Nissans. Rates from US$33 per day (US$40 in high season).

Coconut Car Rentals Tel: 949 4377/4037, US: 800 941 4562; fax: 949 7786; email: coconut@candw.ky; web: www.coconutcarrentals.com. Offices in George Town, Seven Mile Beach, Crewe Rd and the airport. Rates from US$36 per day (high season US$50).

Dollar Rent-a-Car Tel: 949 4790/0700; fax: 949 8484. Rates from US$32 (US$50 in high season). Minimum age 25.

Economy Car Rental Airport Rd; tel: 949 9550; fax: 949 1003; email: economy@candw.ky; web: www.economycarrental.com.ky. Also at The Falls, West Bay Rd, tel: 949 8992. Hyundai cars from US$37 (US$50 high season). No under 25s.

Island Paradise Rental Tel: 945 5831; fax: 945 1240. Based in George Town. Rates from US$38 all year.

Island Style Car Rental Tel/fax: 946 3233; email: islandstylevehicles@hotmail.com; web: www.islandstylecars.com. Next to Treasure Island resort.

Marshall's Rent-a-Car Tel: 949 0550/2127; fax: 949 6435; email: mar_rac@candw.ky; web: www.cayman.com.ky/com/Marshall. Based at the airport, with an office on West Bay Rd. Rates from US$35 per day (US$55 high season). Minimum age 22.

Soto's Rentals West Bay Rd; tel: 945 2424, US 800 625 6174; fax: 949 2425; email: sotos4x4@candw.ky ; web: www.sotos4x4.ky. Open-top Jeep Wranglers US$75 per day (US$85 high season); other vehicles from US$40 (US$49 high season). Also at the airport.

Sunshine Car Rentals Seven Mile Shops and the airport; tel: 949 3858; fax: 949 3636; email: sales@sunshinecarrentals.com; web: www.sunshinecarrentals.com.

Thrifty Car Rental Tel: 949 6640; US 800 367 2277; fax: 949 6354; email: thrifty@candw.ky; web: www.cayman.com.ky/com/thrifty.

Bicycles/scooters

Grand Cayman is pretty flat, and the roads relatively traffic free except for West Bay Road parallel to Seven Mile Beach and other access roads to George Town during the morning and evening rush hours. Bicycles are favoured by locals as a cheap and efficient way to get around, and many hotels have bikes available for rent to visitors. Although the island is generally considered safe, bike theft is common so do use a suitable lock.

While bikes are great for local excursions, touring the whole island on cheap hotel bikes is not an easy option. An alternative is to rent from a specialist company (where you may have the choice of mountain bikes with variable speeds) or to hire a scooter, giving a little more freedom at around US$30 a day, which includes hire of a helmet and the US$10 driver's permit. All scooter riders must wear a helmet, by law, and should have previous experience.

Bikes and scooters may be hired from the following:

Cayman Cycle Rentals Coconut Place, West Bay Rd; tel: 945 4021. Mountain bikes US$15 for 24 hours; scooters US$30 for 24 hours (comprehensive insurance an additional US$6.25).

Scooters and Wheels Aqua Mall, North Church St, George Town; tel: 949 0064; email: reidtour@candw.ky; web: www.reidtours.cayman.com. 50cc scooters at US$8 per hour, with a minimum of three hours.

Tourist Hut North Church St, George Town; tel: 946 8488. Bikes are available for US$15 per day from this central location.

In addition, both Sunshine Car Rentals and Soto's Rentals (see above) hire out bicycles at US$15 per day. In the East End, Ecoventures (see page 80) rent out mountain bikes for US$10 per half day, or US$5 per hour. They have a series of recommended trails ranging in distance from five to 20 miles (8–32km).

Taxis

There are taxi ranks at the airport, and taxis may be hired in front of the cruise-ship terminals in George Town. They are also stationed at all the major hotels on Seven Mile Beach and on Edward Street, near the post office.

Taxis at the terminals are allocated by a despatcher, who will tell you the fare payable. There is a fixed rate per person for one-way transfers to local beaches:

US$3	Beach Club Hotel; Royal Palms Beach Club
US$4	Public beach, West Bay Rd; Westin Casuarina
US$5	Cemetery Reef beach
US$6	Morgan's Harbour

To call a taxi, try one of the following, most of which offer a 24-hour service, or phone the transportation hotline on 945 5100:

AA Chauffeur Service Tel: 949 7222; cell: 926 8294; email: aatours@candw.ky; web: www.aacaymanislands.com
Ace Tel: 949 3676
All Tours Tel: 949 5702
Cayman Cab Tel: 947 1173
Charlie's Tel: 949 4748
Crown's Tel: 947 6058
Webster's Tel: 947 1718

at the airport or at the port terminals in George Town also run
᷄d – see *Island tours,* opposite.

᷄-wide bus service operates from the bus depot in George Town's
Ec᷄᷄ ᷄ Street, close to the Peace Memorial and the public library. The singular
exception to this service is the airport, which remains accessible only by taxi or
by private car.

The privately run services uses 9–29-seater minibuses, each with the route
number posted on the back of the bus in a colour appropriate to that route. All
public transport vehicles have blue number plates – helpful to prevent you
hailing a private minibus by mistake! Bus drivers may blow the horn on
approach; to stop the bus, hold out your hand. There are numbered bus stops on
Seven Mile Beach and at West Bay, where services are pretty frequent, even in
the evenings. Elsewhere, the timetable is relatively flexible – you're talking
'Cayman time' here, so don't expect total reliability.

Buses will often stop on request, and for a small additional fare will often take
you right to your destination rather than just to the nearest stop.

Fares are pretty good value, and are payable at the destination, in either US or
CI dollars; they must be posted on the buses. Round-trip tickets are double the
cost of a one-way ticket. Services start at 5.30am every day. For inquiries about
schedules and rates, phone 945 5100, which also gives details of taxis and tour
buses.

Routes

Seven Mile Beach and West Bay Route 1/yellow (Eastern Av/Turtle Farm) and Route
2/bright green (West Bay: Water Coast Rd and Spanish Bay Reef). Buses run
approximately every 15 minutes, with the last bus at 11.00pm, or midnight on Friday
and Saturday. US$2.50 one way.

Bodden Town Route 3/blue. Buses run every half-hour until around 8.00pm. Routes 4
and 5 also go through Bodden Town. US$2.50 one way.

North Side and East End Route 4/purple (East End direct); Route 5/red (North Side
via East End); Route 8/orange (North Side). There are two buses per hour on island-
wide routes, running until 9.00pm. North Side US$5; East End US$4 one way.

George Town Routes 6 and 7/dark green. Buses ply between South Church Street and
South Sound throughout the day. There is no timetable but to call a bus you can phone
from the bus station.

By sea
Ferries

The *Rum Pointer* runs across North Sound between the Hyatt Regency dock on
the east side of Seven Mile Beach and Rum Point (see box opposite). The trip,
in a large two-deck open-sided boat with a capacity of 150 people, takes around
45 minutes. Note that there are no toilets on board, and no drinks either,
though there is shade. Take a bottle of water if it's hot (note that drinks are not
sold at the shop at the Hyatt dock). Tickets are available at the dock and from
the gift shop at Rum Point itself. For the latest ferry times and reservations, tel:
947 9203.

FERRY TIMETABLE TO RUM POINT

Depart Hyatt	Depart Rum Point
9.30am	11.00am
12.00 midday	1.00pm
2.00pm*	3.00pm*
4.00pm	5.00pm (6.00pm Sunday)
6.00pm**	9.00pm**

* Departs Rum Point at 2.00pm every second Tuesday
**Except Sunday

Fares are US$10 single or US$15 round trip; children 6–11 travel half price; under 5s go free. There is a discount for Cayman residents. On Saturdays, all children travel free of charge.

TOURIST INFORMATION

The Cayman Islands **Department of Tourism** is at PO Box 67 GT, 2nd floor, Corporate Centre, Hospital Rd, George Town; tel: 949 0623; fax: 949 4053; web: www.caymanislands.ky.

The tourist office runs a privilege-card programme valid on all three islands. Holders benefit from savings of up to 25% off goods supplied by participating restaurants, car-hire companies, shops and attractions. The card is available from the tourist-information office, or at their airport information booth, tel: 949 2635.

The Heritage One passport offers savings of 25% off admission fees for four separate attractions on Grand Cayman: the National Museum, the Turtle Farm, Pedro St James and Queen Elizabeth II Botanic Park. Passports cost US$19.95 for adults or US$10.95 for children, and are available from hotels, or from the attractions themselves. There is no limit on their validity, making them particularly useful for those who visit the islands regularly. The passport cannot be bought overseas.

ISLAND TOURS

A typical day out can incorporate any number of attractions described in the following chapters, most incorporated in tours by the operators listed below. An interesting basis for a slightly different tour of the island would be to hire a car and follow the newly designated **Maritime Heritage Trail**, a series of 20 signboards around the coast that chart the impact of the sea on Cayman today. Linked to a leaflet published by the tourist board, the trail follows the mariners, shipbuilders and fishermen who have played such an influential part in shaping the island, as well as the shipwrecks that fell foul of these shores, and the fortifications that protected them. Alternatively, track the locations of the colourful **Blue Dragons** (see page 20) that have their found permanent homes from West Bay round to Rum Point.

Taxis based either at the airport or at the port terminals in George Town operate tours of the island. A 1½–2-hour tour could take in the Turtle Farm,

Hell, the Conch Shell House, the Government Administration Building, Britannia golf course, the public beach and the Governor's residence. Alternatively, create your own tour at around US$40 per hour for up to three people. For contact telephone numbers, see *Taxis* page 77. For details of areas beyond George Town, see *Chapters 6* and *7*.

Various companies run organised tours, with most spending a half day visiting the east or west of the island, or a full day encompassing the whole of Grand Cayman, as below:

Cayman Island Tours Tel: 949 7865; fax: 949 0087; email: relitran@candw.ky. A 'Cayman Highlight Tour' takes in the historic sights of George Town before heading up Seven Mile Beach to West Bay. Personalised tours are available on request.

Ecoventures PO Box 200 EE, East End; tel: 947 5200; US toll free: 866 ECO EAST; fax: 947 5201; email: info@ecoventures.ky; web: www.ecoventures.ky. Based at The Reef resort, Ecoventures offers a series of guided trips that explore the quieter, eastern side of the island, each lasting 2½–3 hours. Appealing to snorkellers, photographers, naturalists and historians, as well as the more sporty types, they range from nature treks in the East End and a (muddy) exploration of the island's bat caves through guided trips to major attractions such as the Botanic Park and Pedro St James. Other options include the maritime heritage trail, reef and beach excursions (see also page 106), mountain biking, with suggested trails (see page 77), and kayak trips.

Rates US$19–29 per adult (children under 12 US$12–19). Minimum age of 15 for bat caves' exploration. Mountain-bike hire US$10 per half day. Kayak trips US$29 single, US$49 double; kayak rentals US$10 per hour, or US$20 half day.

Explore Cayman PO Box 211 NS; tel: 947 4043; email: frank@explore-cayman.com; web: www.explore-cayman.com. Frank Roulstone's company is based on years of knowledge of the islands where he was born. Each of his three guided full-day trips starts with the ferry to Rum Point and the US$89 cost includes transport and soft drinks; lunch is extra. 'Off the beaten track' includes a two-hour hike together with a tour of the Botanic Park, while a second trip for walkers incorporates both the Botanic Park and the Mastic Trail. Rather less strenuous is a tour of Cayman's less-visited beaches, for which guests should bring their own snorkelling equipment. A donation of US$5 is given to a local nature charity for every guest.

Kirk Sea Tours North Church St, George Town; tel: 949 7278; email: info@kirkseatours.com; web: www.kirkseatours.com. Island tours are just one facet of the business here. Trips range in price from US$20 to US$59, and take in George Town and West Bay, and the East End, with an option to include the Stingray sandbar at the end.

Majestic Tours PO Box 298 GT; tel: 949 7773; fax: 949 8647; email: majtours@candw.ky; web: www.majestic-tours.com. Island-wide group tours with Mrs Annie Smith or Mrs Susy Smith are based on individual rather than predetermined itineraries.

Reality Tours PO Box 439 SAV; tel: 947 7200, mobile: 916 2517; fax: 947 7222; email: realitytours@hotmail.com. One of the more personal island-tour companies has half- and full-day tours every day, with visitors collected from West Bay around 9.00am. A full day starts at West Bay, including the Turtle Farm and Hell, followed by lunch in George Town at Champion House II (not included in the price), time for shopping, then on to Pedro St James, the East End and the Botanic Park, finishing between 4.00pm and 5.00pm. Two shorter trips take in either just the West Bay component of the same trip, finishing in George Town, or the longer East End part, finishing at around 2.30pm. On Sundays, there are two slightly different trips, with a later start, and without a stop in George Town. In addition, the company runs day trips to Little Cayman and Cayman Brac.

Prices Full day CI$69, children under 12 CI$45, excluding lunch; half day, CI$37, under 12s CI$24; East Side CI$56 per adult, CI$36 for under 12s.

Silver Thatch Excursions PO Box 344 WB; tel/fax: 945 6588, cell: 916 0678; email: silvert@hotmail.com; web: www.silverthatch.ky. Geddes Hislop and his wife Janet set up Silver Thatch to promote ecotourism on Cayman, bringing their knowledge of natural history and Caymanian culture to a wider audience. Formerly employed by the National Trust, and involved in the development of both the Botanic Park and the Mastic Trail, Geddes' enthusiasm for natural history is infectious, and his guided trips extremely rewarding. In addition to leading walks along the Mastic Trail, Geddes takes visitors to East End and the Botanic Park, with the emphasis on history or the environment. Participants are collected from Seven Mile Beach and George Town Mondays to Saturdays between 7.30 and 8.30am, returning between 12.30 and 1.30pm, while early-morning birdwatching trips run from 6.00am to 11.00am. In 2004, Geddes introduced guided kayak trips which take in both inland waters and the reef. From glass-bottomed kayaks, visitors can discover a whole new underwater world even in just a few inches of water.

Prices On request, but expect to pay around US$45 per head for the Mastic Trail. Kayak trips are US$65 (children under 12 US$40), to include transport and light snack, and last around two hours. No credit cards.

Tropicana Tours PO Box 2071 GT; tel: 949 0944; fax: 949 4507; email: info@tropicana-tours.com; web: www.tropicana-tours.com. The original tour operator on Grand Cayman, Tropicana has three separate tours running every day except Sunday, as well as handling airport transfers and more besides. At 9.00am and 3.00pm, the half-day tour C concentrates on the highlights of the western end of the island, including the Turtle Farm. Tour A extends this to a full day, encompassing the whole island, while tour B combines tour C with a visit to the National Museum followed by free time to explore George Town's shops. The company also organises snorkelling trips from CI$30 for a half day to CI$50 for a full day including lunch.

Prices (including entrance fees as appropriate): Tour C CI$25; tour A CI$75, including lunch; tour B CI$30, excluding return transportation.

Webster's PO Box 31055 SMB; tel: 945 1433; fax: 949 1422; web: www.websters.ky. In addition to airport transfers, Webster's runs three specialist tours: West Side, including the Turtle Farm, at US$41.50, East Side including Pedro St James and the Botanic Park at US$50.50, and Full Island at US$88.50. Entrance fees are included, but lunch is extra.

Trips to Little Cayman and Cayman Brac

Regular daily flights are operated by **Cayman Airways** to both of the sister islands, making a day trip perfectly feasible. There are early-morning flights to each island, with a return flight around 5.00pm. Direct flights to Cayman Brac take around 40 minutes, or an hour with a short stop in Little Cayman; flights between the two sister islands take just seven minutes. For reservations information, see page 44.

Cayman Airways (tel: 948 2535; web: www.caymanairways.com) also has three flights a week on Boeing 737s to Cayman Brac from Miami, with a short stop in Grand Cayman. The airline's subsidiary, **Cayman Airways Express** (tel: 949 2311), has four return flights a day from Grand Cayman to Little

Cayman and Cayman Brac, with additional flights on Saturday mornings and evenings to Little Cayman. Schedules vary according to the time of year. Day-return fares for non-residents from Grand Cayman to Cayman Brac or Little Cayman cost around US$110 including taxes, and between the sister islands about US$50. Prices are not fixed, however, so always check first.

Island Airways (tel: 949 5252, fax: 949 7044; web: www.islandair.ky) handles private aircraft and offers charter flights, but no longer has a scheduled service to the sister islands.

If you're not sure what to do when you get there, two of the resorts on Little Cayman offer day-trip packages. **Sam McCoy's Lodge** (tel: 948 0026, see page 182) arranges day tours of the island at US$60, which includes lunch at the lodge, or US$45 without lunch (children 4–12 US$40/33, under 3s free).

Little Cayman Beach Resort (tel: 948 1033, see page 180) has an island and snorkel tour with buffet lunch, followed by an afternoon relaxing by the pool or on the beach. Alternatively, join **Reality Tours** (see page 80) for one of their guided day trips to either of the sister islands.

For more information on the sister islands, see *Chapters 8* and *9.*

OTHER PRACTICALITIES
Banks
Cayman National Bank (tel: 949 8300; web: www.caymannational.com) has branches with cash machines throughout Grand Cayman. Visa, MasterCard etc are accepted. There is a 24-hour ATM near the port in George Town and one at Harbour Place opposite Club Paradise.

ATMs
Most banks on the island have ATMs, as do the major supermarkets. Machines can issue either US or CI dollars, so decide what you want first, but remember that there is a minimum withdrawal of CI$25. ATMs most accessible to visitors include the following:

Cayman National Bank Elgin Av and Harbour Drive in George Town; Buckingham Square and Galleria Plaza on West Bay Rd; Mirco Commerce Centre, North Sound Road; airport
First Caribbean International Bank (formerly Barclays) Main St, George Town
Foster's Food Fair Airport; The Strand
Grand Harbour Pharmacy Red Bay
Kirk Supermarket Eastern Av; North Sound Rd
Republix Supermarket West Bay
Texaco Star Mart Poinciana Dr, Savannah

Communications
Telephone, fax and internet
There are numerous public telephones throughout the island, but with vandalism becoming an increasing problem it's not always easy to find one that works. Most hotels have business centres with internet access, but many are very expensive. For an efficient, all-round service at a fraction of the price, visit:

Cable & Wireless Next to North Terminal, George Town; tel: 946 5151. US$0.25 per minute.

Communication Station Cardinall Av, George Town. Phone, fax and internet access (US$0.25 per minute; minimum five minutes), and photocopying service. Pre-paid international phonecards available at US$12.50 and US$25. Open Mon–Sat 8.30am–5.00pm.

PC Powerhouse West Shore Centre, West Bay Rd; tel: 946 1800. 20 stations, with internet use at CI$4 per hour. Also provide computer servicing and accessories. Open Mon–Sat 8.00am–10.00pm, Sun midday–6.00pm. Also at Walkers Rd (opposite the Eden Centre), open Mon–Sat 8.00am–9.00pm.

For similarly priced but rather more convivial **internet** access, there are several internet cafés to choose from, most in George Town or along Seven Mile Beach:

Azzurro Buckingham Square (opposite Ragazzi), West Bay Rd; tel: 946 7745. Internet access US$7 per hour. Open Mon–Sat 6.30am–9.00pm; Sun 6.30am–6.00pm.

Café del Sol Lawrence Bd; tel: 946 2233; email: coffee@cafedelsol.ky; web: www.cafedelsol.ky. Internet access, scanning and photocopying. CI$2.50 for half an hour; an access code valid for one month costs CI$4. Open Mon–Sat 7.00am–8.00pm; Sun 8.00am–8.00pm.

Dickens Internet Café and Coffee Shop Galleria Plaza, West Bay Rd; tel: 945 9195. US$0.12 per minute. Open Mon–Sat 8.30am–10.00pm.

PD's Galleria Plaza, West Bay Rd; tel: 949 7144. Pub-like bar with internet access available at US$0.15 per minute (no minimum charge). Open Mon–Fri 7.00am–1.00am; Sat 7.00am–midnight; Sun 11.00am–midnight.

Shooters Seven Mile Shops, West Bay Rd; tel: 946 3496. CI$6 per hour. Open Mon–Fri 10.30am–1.00pm; Sat/Sun 10.30am–midnight.

Thai Restaurant Elizabethan Sq, George Town; tel: 949 6141. US$3.50 for 15 minutes. Open Mon–Sat 7.00–10.00am, 11.00am–3.00pm, 6.00–10.00pm.

Post office
The main post office is on the corner of Edward Street in George Town, tel: 949 2474, open Mon–Fri 8.15am–5.00pm. Post-office boxes are located outside the building on Edward Street. Stamp collectors will find plenty of interest here, or at the Philatelic Bureau at Seven Mile Beach Post Office in West Shore Centre on West Bay Road (open Mon–Fri 8.30am–5.00pm).

Medical facilities
The recently renovated buildings of George Town Hospital, off Smith Road in George Town, tel: 949 8600, incorporate a full range of medical facilities, including a decompression chamber for use by divers in an emergency. In the event of specialist treatment being necessary, patients are transferred to the Baptist Hospital in Miami. Medivac facilities are available on the island. In an emergency, telephone 911 or 555.

The modern Chrissie Tomlinson Memorial Hospital on Walkers Road, George Town (tel: 949 6066) is privately owned and operated.

There are also several private medical centres, including the Professional Medical Centre in The Strand on West Bay Road (tel: 949 7077) and Cayman Medical and Surgical Centre on Eastern Avenue (tel: 949 8150).

Should you be in urgent need of a **dentist**, call one of the two private dental clinics in George Town: Cayman Dental Services, tel: 947 4447, and Cayman Medical and Surgical Centre, tel: 949 8150, or try the Dentist Clinic in The Strand, tel: 949 3367.

Pharmacies

Remember that pharmacies in Cayman may only fulfil prescriptions that have been issued on the islands, so bring sufficient quantities of any regular prescription drugs that you need to last your stay. In addition to the following, there are pharmacies at several of the supermarkets (see page 136), as well as at hospitals and health clinics.

Cayman Drug Kirk Freeport Centre, Albert Panton St, George Town; tel: 949 2957. Open Mon–Sat 8.30am–5.30pm.

Healthcare Pharmacy Grand Harbour, Red Bay; tel: 947 8900. Open Mon–Sat 8.30am–9.30pm. Their branch at Walkers Road, tel: 949 0442, is also open Sun 10.00am–5.00pm.

Strand Pharmacy The Strand, West Bay Rd; tel: 945 7759. Open Mon–Sat 7.00am–11.00pm; Sun 9.00am–6.00pm.

Religious services

With over 200 Christian churches on the islands, there is no shortage of services to attend. The majority of these are Protestant, but there is also a Catholic church, St Ignatius, in George Town's Walkers Road. Most hotels hold a list of churches with service times.

The Lord's Church in West Bay offers a free island-wide pick up to visitors for their Sunday morning service at 10.30am. To arrange to be collected, call 949 1802 at least 24 hours in advance.

Travel agency

Cayman Travel Elizabethan Sq, George Town; tel: 949 5400

Nurse shark

Diving and Other Activities

DIVING

Diving in the Cayman Islands has come a long way since Bob Soto set up in business in the 1950s with a wooden boat and tanks filled at the local gas station. Today, there are over 40 dive operators and 159 designated dive sites on Grand Cayman alone, and the islands are consistently rated among the best in the world for all-year-round diving.

Grand Cayman, like the sister islands, is effectively the tip of a submarine coral mountain surrounded by small fringing reefs which fall sharply off into the abyss, creating the walls for which the islands are famed. With visibility between 100ft and 200ft (30–60m), and the water temperature ranging from 78°F (26°C) in winter to around 84°F (29°C) in the height of summer, opportunities to explore the underwater world are almost unlimited. The lack of industry on the islands also means that the waters are relatively unpolluted and wildlife is flourishing. Inevitably, though, the relentless to and fro of cruise ships in George Town harbour is having an effect on the environment in the immediate vicinity, and of course the sheer number of divers on the reefs is bound to take its toll.

Since the fringing reefs are for the most part very shallow – some just 16ft (5m) or so – divers can combine spectacular wall dives with plenty of time along the reef, exploring in and around the rocks for the myriad creatures that inhabit this colourful world. Second and third dives offer the opportunity to navigate among the unique spur-and-groove formations – coral fingers interspersed by rivers of sand that flow towards the wall – or to weave through tunnels and runs, perhaps spotting a nurse shark lurking in the shadows or coming upon a shimmering silver tarpon suspended in the blue. Add to this a number of wrecks and it's not difficult to understand the appeal.

Many of Grand Cayman's dive sites are less than half a mile from the shore. Indeed, the proximity of the reef means that plenty of dives are accessible from the shore, while boat dives rarely require a journey of more than 20–30 minutes – and most take considerably less time. The prevailing winds are from the east, making West Bay the most sheltered area for diving at almost all times of the year.

Conservation and safety

Almost all dive operators on the islands are members of the Cayman Islands Tourism Association's Watersports Committee, which is concerned both with the safety of recreational divers and the preservation of the marine environment. The maximum depth limit permitted for recreational divers was until recently 100ft (32m). However, this has recently been revised to 130ft (40m) to allow greater flexibility for more experienced divers. Children under ten may not dive with any of the commercial organisations in the open sea. Divers should find out about the area in which they plan to dive before setting off. Briefings on dive boats are the norm, with a maximum bottom time given based on computer or dive-table calculations, as appropriate. As a rule, you should always dive with a buddy.

When diving, swimming or snorkelling from the shore, make sure that you can be seen by any boat that may be in the vicinity by clearly displaying a light or a 'diver down' flag. The 'diver down' flag may be either the blue-and-white international code 'A' flag, or the American white diagonal stripe on a red background. Lights used to indicate diving at night feature a series of three vertical lights in the sequence red, white, red, and should be visible all round.

Conservation policies, monitored by Marine Parks Officers, mean that the marine environment is strictly protected. All designated dive sites on the reef have permanent moorings to avoid anchor damage. Boats may anchor in sand away from the reef, provided that there is absolutely no contact with the coral. Moorings should never be left unattended.

Guidelines issued by the Department of Environment remind divers that it is a serious criminal offence to:

- take any marine life anywhere while scuba diving
- take corals, sponges etc from any Cayman waters
- possess a speargun without a licence from the Cayman Marine Conservation Board
- export live fish or any other marine life
- take or molest a turtle.

It's a sobering thought that poor diving practice is one of the causes of reef destruction. Before you set off, ensure that you can establish and maintain neutral buoyancy and check that trailing consoles are properly secured. Don't wear gloves – you shouldn't be touching anything underwater, so they're unnecessary, and you could inadvertently spread disease too. And watch where you put those fins. Not only can the sediment stirred up choke the surrounding life, but a quick flip against the coral or a sponge can destroy years of fragile growth.

Suggestions that you feed the fish and other aquatic life around you are fairly common, but it's not a good idea. Feeding them, even with specialist food, may give you pleasure, but it could lead to a dependence on humans that may endanger the fish and other marine life, and eventually upset the delicate balance of nature upon which the whole underwater ecosystem depends.

Equipment

Diving fees usually include the use of tanks and weights/weight belts, but that is all. European divers in particular should note that, unlike in Europe and much of the rest of the world, all other diving equipment is charged extra, even on all-inclusive dive packages. The average (but not top) rate is US$10 to rent each

Above Horse-eye jacks, *Caranx latus*, live along the edge of the outer reefs, hunting smaller fish in the current. (LW)

Below right Once hunted almost to extinction, hawksbill and green turtles are now making a come back in Cayman. (LW)

Below Spectacular yellow tube sponges at Grand Cayman's Orange Canyon (KS)

Above The giant anemone, *Condylactis gigantea*, can grow over 12in (30cm) in diameter and comes in many different colours. (LW)

Below The social featherduster worm, *Bispira brunnea*, is often found at the base of sponges. (LW)

piece of equipment for 24 hours, so if you need a buoyancy control device (BCD), regulator and wetsuit you're looking at some US$30 a day on top of your dive costs, with a dive computer a further US$10–15. Some operators limit the rental cost to US$30, but others will charge more for compasses, snorkels, fins and masks, etc. Be warned!

The warm waters around the islands mean that a full wetsuit is not necessary. A skin is useful for protection in the summer months, while in winter a thin shorty suit (approx 3mm) is usually all that is required. Most of the dive operators insist on a dive computer per person, not per pair. If you cannot fulfil this requirement, and don't want to hire a computer, you'll be restricted to diving within the limits of recreational dive tables, rather than those of a computer. The only other essential is your certification – without which you'll be back to square one.

For those with their own equipment, shore dives offer an extremely economical means of exploring many of Grand Cayman's underwater treasures. The cost of hiring a tank for a day is from US$5.

A number of shops on Grand Cayman specialise in diving equipment, and several of the dive operators also have their own shops. For details, see page 135.

Courses
Almost all the dive specialists on the island are PADI affiliated, although all will recognise other qualifications, and some are also licensed to run courses by NAUI, NASDS, SSI, HSA, IANTD, TDI and BSAC. The most popular course on the island is without doubt the resort course, or Discover Scuba, which is effectively an introduction to scuba diving. For around US$100 per person, including equipment, divers have a two-hour theory session based in a pool, followed by a boat dive to around 40ft (12m). The course may be completed in half a day, but is more usually spread out over a day with a break for lunch.

Costs for the PADI Open Water course come out at around US$400, although there are wide variations. For Open Water referral (where the classroom element has been completed in advance) expect to pay about US$250. As a rule, both these and other 'entry' courses include equipment; for more advanced courses, equipment is often payable extra. Many of the operators start courses on specified days, so do be sure to check this out in advance.

DIVE ORGANISATIONS
BSAC	British Sub Aqua Club
GUE	Global Underwater Exploration
HSA	Handicapped Scuba Association
IANTD	International Association of Nitrox and Technical Divers
NASDS	National Association Scuba Diving Schools
NAUI	National Association of Underwater Instructors
PADI	Professional Association of Dive Instructors
SSI	Scuba Schools International
TDI	Technical Diving International

TIPS FOR UNDERWATER PHOTOGRAPHY
with Karen Stewart

Many are the snorkellers and divers who have set off with a cheap throwaway camera only to find that the long-awaited results when they get home vary from bad to awful. The most important thing to remember here is that these so-called 'underwater' cameras are not intended for divers. Waterproof they may be, but you need to remain on or close to the surface. As with any other camera, you also need to compose your picture carefully, taking care to prevent movement and poor light – both of which are difficult to avoid in the water. If you are stationary, so much the better. As for light, try to keep the sun behind you and avoid reflection on the water. As the contrast right on the surface can confuse the camera (and splashing is a potential problem here too), photographs taken just below may actually be clearer.

For true underwater photography, you'll need to hire or buy a suitable camera. Several shops in Grand Cayman stock these at highly competitive prices, while rentals are available both in shops and from dive operators direct. Take a bit of time to familiarise yourself with the equipment – most shops will give you a bit of help here.

One of the most important things to remember is to get close to your subject, then look up to take your shot. Water acts like fog – the farther you are from your subject, the more blurred it will be, so get as close as you can for the lens that you are using. Many underwater cameras that you rent will

Diving for children

Several initiatives in the diving world make diving accessible even for young children. With SASY (Scuba Assisted Snorkelling for Youth), children over the age of five can try out the fun of scuba diving in open water. Equipped with a regulator and buoyancy aid, they nevertheless remain at the surface, breathing from a continuous air supply and thus with none of the risks associated with water pressure at depth. Alternatively, the Bubblemaker course is designed to introduce children from aged eight to scuba diving through various activities in the confines of a swimming pool. Costs are around US$30, and courses are run by several operators including Divetech, Ocean Frontiers, Red Sail Sports, and Bob Soto's Reef Divers.

Increasingly popular is the PADI Seals programme, similar to the SSI Rangers, where children of eight and up carry out scuba-diving 'missions' in depths of up to 12ft (3.7m), both in the pool and in open water. Badges and logbooks are all part of the fun. Half-day courses cost around US$100 per child, and are available through Divetech and Ocean Frontiers.

Diving for the less confident

SASA (Scuba Assisted Snorkelling for Adults) is the adult equivalent of SASY, above, and is ideal if you want the experience of breathing from a scuba regulator and tank without going beneath the surface.

Although the technique of 'SNUBA' diving has not proved as popular as was expected, it is nevertheless still available from some outlets on the island, be fitted with a 35mm lens. That means you need to be about three feet (1m) from the subject (underwater this is about two arm lengths). By staying at this distance you will have sharper and more colourful images. You will also want to try to make that intriguing fish, or sponge or piece of coral stand out. This can easily be accomplished by shooting upwards, effectively using the deep blue water as background. Underwater shots that are taken shooting down into the sand or coral tend to lose their three-dimensionality and everything blends together.

To really bring out the beauty of the underwater world, your camera should be outfitted with some sort of strobe. Remember that as we descend in water, we quickly lose colour and light. By the time you are at 50 feet (16m), everything appears monochromatic blue or green. If you take pictures at this depth without a strobe, your picture will also appear blue or green. Strobes bring back the vibrant colours and make your subject stand out from its background.

Before you decide to try underwater photography, make sure that you are comfortable in the water with your scuba equipment and also with your buoyancy. Adding a camera when you are not comfortable can significantly increase stress. Having good buoyancy and keeping gauges and hoses tucked away means that you can get closer to subjects without in any way injuring the reef. Watch that your feet don't kick the coral or stir up the sand as you are taking the picture, and never grab on to a live reef to steady yourself.

including Kirk Sea Tours (see page 109). It's designed for snorkellers who want to venture further but aren't ready for scuba diving and, with adaptations for children from as young as four, is an ideal option for families.

Rather than wearing heavy dive gear, participants are effectively 'moored' to an inflatable raft, and breathe from a regulator attached to a surface tank. This allows for shallow dives without wearing a BCD. After just 15–20 minutes' orientation, you can follow your guide, either towing the raft behind you, or with a long hose from the raft allowing you the freedom to explore.

Night diving

The opportunities for night diving are as varied as in the day time, but after dark there's a whole new world to explore. As darkness falls, the seas are the realm of creatures such as the octopus and squid, the lobster and the eel. Most dive operators run night dives, but many keep these to a specific day of the week, so it's worth checking well in advance. Of course, diving from the shore can be done on the night of your choice. Just remember to give advance notification of any equipment needs, including an underwater torch per diver, to the relevant organisation, and to get an orientation briefing, as most dive shops close around 5.30pm.

Nitrox, technical and speciality dives

Nitrox diving is gaining popularity for the extended bottom time it can give at shallow depths and for the greater sense of wellbeing it gives, making it particularly popular with regular divers. By adjusting the mix of air in a tank to 32/68 oxygen/nitrogen (the norm is 21/79), divers can dive to a maximum of 100ft (30m) but can stay at that depth for up to 30 minutes on a first dive. On 50/50 oxygen/nitrogen, divers are limited to 30–40 ft (9–12m) but bottom time is increased by up to 50%. Nitrox tanks (around US$12–15 per tank) and the related certification are offered by most dive schools. It takes a full day for an initial course, and up to four days for an advanced course (upwards of US$500). Nitrox can also be an entry into technical diving, for which courses are offered by Divetech, Ocean Frontiers and Sunset Divers.

Rebreather diving means effectively that you can dive without the sound of bubbles released from your regulator: the silence can be awesome. Courses in rebreather techniques take between two and six days. Other possibilities include **scooter dives**, with a DPV scooter (minimum four passengers). For more details, contact Divetech or Sunset Divers.

Free diving
The skill of diving without scuba equipment offers a whole new dimension and is great for families. For tuition in everything from proper snorkelling to advanced free-diving techniques that can lead on to opportunities in instruction or competition, contact Divetech (see page 92), who operate out of West Bay.

Underwater photography
Most of the large dive operators, and even some of the smaller ones, have their own photographic division, enabling divers to rent equipment or have instruction in underwater photography. It is possible to hire a basic 35mm underwater camera from about US$10, or a video camera for around US$75. Most outfits will also produce a video of your dive, so do ask (and check the price, too – the range is approximately US$100–150). For in-depth photography courses, see Cathy Church, page 139.

Dive operators
Among the 40 or so dive operators on Grand Cayman, costs are very similar and safety standards are exceptionally high. The things that do vary, however, are the size of the operator, from one-man bands to larger operators with a fleet of boats, the location, and the style in which the dives are run. From the super efficient to the totally laid-back, the choice is yours.

Most hotels and resorts have affiliated dive schools, but there is plenty of choice so do shop around for the one that suits you rather than your resort. The bigger operators may be efficient, but sometimes the squash on board boats with large numbers of divers can justify the analogy with cattle trucks. If it's small groups you're after, it's well worth checking out one of the more individual companies. Ask, too, about special deals. With so many dive operators, competition is fierce and almost all outfits offer discounts or extra dives for those booked for a couple of days or more.

The majority of operators listed below will have an instructor on board, and dives are usually accompanied by at least one experienced guide. That said, the short site briefing, with relevant safety instructions, means that divers may usually explore at their own pace – in pairs, of course. For dive courses, expect a ratio of one instructor to between four and six divers. The accessibility of dive sites means that the west, north and south walls are visited by pretty well all dive operators, though the east is the preserve of just three: Cayman Diving Lodge, Ocean Frontiers and Tortuga Divers. If you have a request for a particular site, do ask – with so many options, boat captains usually welcome suggestions.

Boats usually have drinking water on board for their guests, and some offer soft drinks and snacks or fruit as well. Almost all companies are also able to arrange videos of your dive on request, with costs from around US$50 for a tape of about 15–20 minutes' duration.

Costs

A typical two-tank boat dive will consist of a 30-minute dive to 100ft (30m) in the morning, followed by a 40–50-minute dive to 40ft (16m). The cost is around US$75, excluding equipment, but rates vary quite significantly. A further afternoon dive would cost an additional US$45–55. Dives to Stingray City average US$55, while snorkel trips are from around US$30.

Most of the operators listed below offer a variety of dive packages, ranging from a couple of days' diving to a full week. Alternatively you can book a dive/accommodation package with one of the resorts or dive lodges. Based on a two-tank boat dive per day, a typical dive lodge package for six days' diving would be around US$1,025 per person in low season, or US$1,500 all inclusive. Many operators will also allow unlimited shore diving for those who take out a package. It's worth noting that packages booked in advance may work out considerably cheaper than those booked once on the island. In the event of cancellation, there is unlikely to be any refund where packages have been booked on the island, while pre-booked packages are normally subject to a minimum cancellation period.

For ease of comparison, prices are given below for a two-tank boat dive, the PADI Resort course, the full Open Water course, and daily hire of BCD and regulator, with a selection of other prices given where a particular deal is on offer. These figures are walk-in prices; various discounts are available for pre-booking, package deals, and larger groups.

Abanks PO Box 31206 SMB; 96 South Church St, George Town; tel: 945 1444; fax: 945 3319; email: abanks@aol.com; web: www.abanks.com.ky
Based at Club Paradise just a few minutes' walk from the centre of George Town, Abanks has capitalised on the name of the dive company featured in *The Firm*. With diving close to the shore in the harbour marine park, and snorkelling just off the wall, this is an all-round location, popular with cruise-ship passengers. A single accompanied dive to Eden Rock and Paradise Reef, suitable for beginners, costs US$75, inclusive of all equipment.
Rates Two-tank boat dive CI$70; Resort course CI$75; Open Water CI$350. BCD/regulator CI$12; tank CI$10.

Ambassador Divers PO Box 2396 GT; tel: 949 8839, cell 916 1064; email: ambadive@candw.ky; web: www.ambassadordivers.com
Jason Washington runs a small dive operation offering a very personal service with a maximum of ten divers on board. His small, fast boat cuts down on travelling time to divesites, meaning he can sometimes go further afield than most. All PADI courses up to Divemaster.

Rates Two-tank boat dive US$65; Resort course US$100; Open Water US$375. BCD/regulator US$10 each.

Aqua Adventures PO Box 30379 SMB; tel/fax: 949 1616, 916 1616; email: aqua@candw.ky

This small, flexible company takes no more than eight divers on any trip.

Rates Two-tank boat dive US$80; Resort course US$110; Open Water US$460. BCD/regulator US$10 each.

Bob Soto's Reef Divers PO Box 1801 GT, Seven Mile Shops, West Bay Rd; tel: 949 2871, US 800 262 7686; fax: 949 8731; email: bobsotos@candw.ky; web: www.bobsotosreefdivers.com The first dive operator in the Caribbean, Bob Soto's was established in the Cayman Islands in 1957. Now owned by Reef Divers, the company has several boats, each taking a maximum of 20 people at any one time. A PADI five-star resort, it offers PADI instructor qualifications alongside many other courses. Its flagship store is on Harbour Drive in George Town, but it also has a base and shop at Treasure Island Resort. One of the more efficient operations on the island, it maintains a high reputation. Half-day snorkel excursions cost US$30 per person.

Rates Two-tank boat dive US$85; Resort course US$99; Open Water US$425. BCD/regulator US$15 each.

Cayman Diving Lodge PO Box 11 EE; tel: 947 7555, US 800 TLC DIVE; fax: 947 7560; email: divelodge@aol.com; web: www.divelodge.com

Located in the East End, the lodge is one of just three dive operations that covers this part of the island. As an all-inclusive resort, it caters for its own guests, who have unrivalled access to diving and snorkelling on site, but it also accepts the occasional non-resident diver when space permits. For details, see page 172.

Cayman Diving School PO Box 1308 GT, West Bay Rd (next to the Strand); tel: 949 4729; email: info@caymandivingschool.com; web: www.caymandivingschool.com

A PADI five-star instructor development centre (IDC), Cayman Diving School is also affiliated to IANTD, and runs two boats. Recreational, technical and professional courses, up to instructor level, are conducted in German, French, Italian and Spanish, as well as English.

Rates Two-tank boat dive US$85; Resort course US$110; Open Water US$425. BCD/regulator US$15 each.

Divers Down PO Box 1706 GT; tel/fax: 945 1611; cell: 916 3751; email: diversdown@diversdown.net; web: www.diversdown.net

With no more than eight divers per trip, the emphasis here is on the personal, with private charters also available from US$300 for one-tank dives.

Rates Two-tank boat dive US$75; Resort course US$100; Open Water US$425. BCD/regulator US$10 each.

Divetech PO Box 31435 SMB; tel: 946 5658; fax: 946 5659; email: divetech@candw.ky; web: www.divetech.com

Located at Cobalt Coast in West Bay (and with a second office next to the Turtle Farm) Divetech is one of the top dive companies on the island. The shore diving from each of their offices is considered to be among the best on Grand Cayman, with very little marine disturbance and just a three-minute swim at a depth of 25ft (7.6m) before a 60ft (18m) mini wall (tanks may be rented for US$7.50, or nitrox at US$12.50). And if you can't face the swim, they'll taxi you out for US$7.50 per diver. In addition to all the standard diving courses (the company is affiliated to and runs courses certified by PADI, SSI, IANTD, TDI and BSAC), plus scooters, rebreathers and the like, Divetech offers a range of technical and free-diving courses, from a half-day introduction to professional and competition level. For children of five and up, they operate SASY, Seals and Ranger programmes.

Rates Two-tank boat dive US$85; Resort course US$100; Open Water US$425. BCD/regulator US$10 each. Guided shore dives US$35 (night US$45); free-diving courses from US$100 for half day.

Don Foster's Dive Cayman PO Box 31486 SMB, Casuarina Point, South Church St, George Town; tel: 945 5679; fax: 945 5133; email: dfd@candw.ky; US: 800 833 4837 (accommodation packages), 972 907 9821; fax: 903 560 1654; email: dfosters@swbell.net; web: www.donfosters.com

Established in the 1980s, Don Foster's prides itself on continuity and local knowledge built up over the years. Indeed, their Texas office is manned by their own staff. With five flat-top boats, plus a comprehensive range of PADI courses up to Divemaster, theirs is one of the larger operations on Grand Cayman. Their new main office just south of George Town has a large swimming pool for the use of clients, and a shop selling masks, clothing etc. A photo centre offers underwater photo instruction and camera rentals. There is also a second office and shop at Comfort Suites (tel: 946 3483).

Rates Two-tank boat dive US$75; Resort course US$100; Open Water US$450. BCD/regulator US$10 each.

Eden Rock Dive Centre PO Box 1907 GT, South Church St, George Town; tel: 949 7243; email: edenrock@candw.ky; web: www.edenrockdive.com

This company with its small dive shop is ideally situated for shore dives of Eden Rock and Devil's Grotto, which lie just opposite to the south of Hog Sty Bay. Guided tours are available, as are underwater maps of both areas. Affiliated to PADI, NAUI, SSI and BSAC, Eden Rock runs courses for each organisation. Resort courses take place daily.

Rates Two-tank boat dive US$75; Resort course US$80; Open Water US$400.

Fisheye Dive Centre PO Box 30076 SMB, Cayman Falls Centre; tel: 945 4209. One of the dive operations for Sunshine Suites is based at the yacht club, and their boats have a capacity of 12 or 18 divers. In addition to PADI courses, Fisheye also run specialty courses including underwater naturalist and search and recovery.

Rates Two-tank boat dive US$85; Resort course US$125; Open Water US$450. BCD/regulator US$15 each.

Neptune's Divers PO Box 30520 SMB; tel: 945 3990; fax: 949 6444; email: neptunes@neptunesdivers.com; web: www.neptunesdivers.com

Neptune specialise in small groups, with a maximum of eight divers per trip, and most dives focused on the west of the island. Boats depart from the public beach opposite the Courtyard Marriott. PADI courses up to advanced, and photography service.

Rates Two-tank boat dive US$80; Resort course US$90; Open Water US$400. BCD/regulator US$15 each.

Ocean Frontiers PO Box 200 EE; tel: 947 7500; US toll free: 888 232 0541; fax: 947 7600; email: hq@oceanfrontiers.com; web: www.oceanfrontiers.com

Established early in the 1990s, this PADI five-star operator specialises in diving off the East End, one of only three dive operators to cover this area; with three boats of different sizes they can reach most sites within ten to 20 minutes. Professional but friendly and helpful, they refer to their style as 'valet diving', with a limit of 12 divers per boat and personal touches that range from setting up your equipment to illustrated dive briefings. Their 11ft-deep pool, designed specifically for dive tuition, is the deepest on the island. They are also the dive specialists for The Reef resort, and act as a full travel agent for divers islandwide. Ocean Frontiers is one of only a handful of outfits on the island to offer PADI instructor qualifications. A wide range of other courses includes nitrox, Bubblemaker and PADI Seals, as well as technical instruction under GUE. Popular with visitors is the full-day dive trip at US$129 which incorporates Stingray City and two further dives, with lunch at Kaibo Yacht Club. The company's courtesy bus collects divers from anywhere on the island free of charge. Private charters and camera rental available.

Rates Two-tank boat dive US$89; Resort course US$99; Open Water US$399 (private instruction US$599). BCD/regulator US$15 each.

Off the Wall Divers PO Box 30176 SMB; tel/fax: 945 7525, cell: 916 0303; email: fish@candw.ky; web: www.otwdivers.com

This small group operation takes between two and ten divers per trip, with courses up to advanced, and nitrox available on request.

Rates Two-tank boat dive US$75; Resort course US$95; Open Water US$400. BCD/regulator US$10 each.

Peter Milburn's Dive Cayman PO Box 596 GT; tel: 945 5770; cell: 916 0814; fax: 945 5786; email: pmilburn@candw.ky

Flat-top boats leave from the public beach on West Bay Rd, near the Courtyard Marriott.

Rates Two-tank dive US$70; Resort course US$90. BCD/regulator US$15 each

Quabo Dives PO Box 157 GT, Coconut Place, West Bay Rd; tel: 945 4769; cell: 916 4995; fax: 947 4978; email: quabo@candw.ky; web: www.caymandiving.com

Quabo is run by Arthle Evans, a Caymanian PADI instructor who has been diving here since 1972. The emphasis is on small groups, with dives to the north and west walls. Camera and video rental available.

Rates Two-tank boat dive US$75; Resort course US$100; Open Water US$400. BCD/regulator US$10 each.

Red Baron Divers PO Box 11369 APO; tel/fax: 947 0116; cell: 916 1293; email: info@redbarondivers.com; web: www.redbarondivers.com

Two fast dive boats take between five and eight people to the west, north and south sides of the island. PADI and NAUI courses although not the full Open Water certification.

Rates Two-tank dive US$75; Resort course US$95; Open Water referral US$250. BCD/regulator US$10 each.

Red Sail Sports PO Box 31473 SMB, Coconut Place, West Bay Rd; tel: 945 5965; US: 877 733 7245; fax: 945 5808; email: infocayman@redsailcayman.com; web: www.redsailcayman.com

The biggest and most organised operator on Grand Cayman, and one of the most expensive, Red Sail Sports operates throughout the western side of the island, including the north wall. The company is affiliated to five hotels on or near Seven Mile Beach – the Westin (tel: 949 8732), Marriott (tel: 949 6343), Hyatt (tel: 949 8745), Indies Suites (tel: 946 3362) and Courtyard Marriott (tel: 946 5481) and has dive shops in these as well as at Rum Point (tel: 947 9203). With several boats, each working in different locations and with space for between 12 and 24 people, Red Sail offers PADI, NAUI, NASDS, SSI and HSA courses up to Divemaster, and including Bubblemaker and SASY, under the guidance of experienced and friendly staff. Camera and video rental. Private charters available.

Rates Two-tank dive US$100; Resort course US$140; Open Water US$500. BCD/regulator US$15 each.

Seaview Dive Center PO Box 260 GT, South Church St, George Town; tel: 945 0577; email: seadive@candw.ky; web: www.seaviewdivers.com

The dive operation at Seaview is masterminded by Treasure Island Divers (see below), who have a base at the hotel. In addition to boat dives, there is excellent shore diving from the lodge itself, with an easy swim out to a shallow dive in around 45ft (15m) leading to a wall. Tanks may be rented for US$5, and weights/belt for US$3.

Seven Mile Watersports PO Box 30742 SMB, West Bay Rd; tel: 949 0332; fax: 949 0331; email: smbrsort@candw.ky; web: www.7mile.ky

The dive operation located at Seven Mile Beach Resort is affiliated to PADI and offers diving mostly to the north wall, with free pick up from Seven Mile Beach. Their 40ft (12m) dive boat operates from Cayman Islands Yacht Club. Trips are for a maximum of 15 divers, including staff.

Rates Two-tank boat dive US$75; Resort course US$100; Open Water US$400. BCD/regulator US$10 each.

Sundivers PO Box 30181 SMB; tel: 947 6606; fax: 947 6606; email: sundiver@candw.ky

A small, individually run dive company with a maximum of eight people per trip.

Rates Two-tank dive US$80; Resort course US$100; Open Water US$400. BCD/regulator US$20 each.

Sunset Divers PO Box 479 GT, South Church St, George Town; tel: 949 7111, US 800 854 4767; fax: 949 7101; email: sunsethouse@sunsethouse.com; web: www.sunsethouse.com

The dive set up at Sunset House is geared to the resort's clientele (although other divers are welcome), with a range of courses available up to Divemaster, including nitrox and rebreather programmes. Affiliated to PADI, NAUI, SSI, NASDS and IANTD, the company has a fleet of boats visiting sites to the west, north and south, while their super-fast catamaran, *Manta*, can go further afield, including to locations off East End. The reef just off the resort is excellent for shore diving, with a couple of wrecks as well, not to mention the Siren of Sunset House (see page 101).

Rates Two-tank dive US$85; Resort course US$95; Open Water US$400. BCD US$10, regulator US$15.

Tortuga Divers PO Box 496 GT, Morritt's Tortuga Club, East End; tel: 947 2097; fax: 947 9486; email: tortugad@tortugadivers.com; web: www.tortugadivers.com

This friendly outfit has been operating for 14 years, taking divers off the reef at East End and to Stingray City. Now linked to Red Sail Sports, it continues to offer PADI courses up to Divemaster.

Rates Two-tank boat dive US$100; Resort course US$140; Open Water US$500. BCD/regulator US$15 each. Discount of 20% for Golden Turtle Club members at Morritt's Tortuga Club. Prepaid packages range from three days at US$285 to six days at US$555.

Treasure Island Divers PO Box 30975 SMB; tel: 949 4456, US 800 872 7552; fax: 949 7125; email: tidivers@divers.com; web: www.tidivers.com

The dive operation based at Treasure Island condominiums on Seven Mile Beach, behind Treasure Island Resort (and not to be confused with the resort). A PADI five-star dive centre, established in the late 1980s, Treasure Island Divers has the only dock on Seven Mile Beach. Its fleet of boats leaves at 7.30am for the morning dives, which means that divers usually have first choice of the island's sites. On board, the atmosphere is relaxed, with stereo player and an upper sun deck. Nitrox diving is available.

Rates Two-tank boat dive US$85; Resort course US$100; Open Water US$395.
BCD/regulator US$12 each.

Live-aboard boats

Cayman Aggressor IV PO Box 10028 APO; tel: 949 5551, US toll free 800 348 2628; fax:
949 8729; email: cayman@aggressor.com; web: www.aggressor.com

An 18-passenger live-aboard, *Cayman Aggressor IV* covers each of the three islands during
its week-long cruise, weather permitting, with unlimited diving for passengers.
Operating out of George Town every Saturday, the 110ft (33.5m) purpose-built boat
was refitted in 2003 and is designed for luxury. Carpeted staterooms off the main salon
have en-suite facilities, AC and TV/VCR, while up above are the dive deck and sun
deck, complete with loungers, hot tub and beer on tap. Other facilities include on-board
E-6 processing, and nitrox and rebreather rentals.

Rates per person, based on double occupancy: US$1,995– 2,395

Dive sites

The sheltered western side of Grand Cayman is the most popular area for diving.
Ideal for beginners, it also boasts a wide variety of diving to challenge even the
most experienced. When the wind is coming from the west, dive operators tend
to make for the south, so it is very rare for dives to be cancelled.

The numerous tunnels to the northwest make this a fascinating place to dive,
although currents on the point can cause occasional problems for divers. The
shallow reefs to the north itself make for excellent diving. Finally, there are the
less explored waters of the East End, where few boats venture and crowds are
unknown.

There are over 200 buoyed areas around the three islands, plus infinite
possibilities for sand anchorages. It is beyond the scope of this book to give an
in-depth assessment of all the recognised dive sites around the Cayman Islands.
The following is therefore just an overview. For more details, check out the
Department of Tourism's excellent dive website – www.divecayman.ky – or
whet your appetite with their short *Undersea Guide*, available free from the tourist
office. For a selection of books on diving in Cayman waters, see *Further Reading*,
page 227.

Shore dives

It's no accident that many of Grand Cayman's dive lodges are located to the
southwest, near George Town. Grand Cayman has numerous good shore-dive
sites in this vicinity; those that follow are just a selection.

Although the harbour itself is not as clear as it once was, a result of so much
cruise-ship traffic, this is only relative to the absolute clarity of waters around the
islands generally. Rest assured, visibility in these waters is still pretty good. If diving
in the harbour, be particularly careful to take advice in advance, leave a 'diver down'
flag on the surface before you dive (see page 86) and watch out for marine traffic.

A short surface swim of some 200yds (182m) from the Lobster Pot is **Soto's
Reef**, while nearby is the wreck of the *Cali* (see page 101), easily accessible from
Kirk Sea Tours behind the Big Bamboo on North Church Street.

To the south of the harbour, well away from the disturbance caused by
shipping, **Eden Rock** and **Devil's Grotto** lie some 100ft (30m) or so offshore

from Eden Rock Dive Centre. The centre offers guided dives of the two sites, and also has underwater maps. Both sites feature a maze of tunnels and caverns, frequently visited by tarpon, at depths of 35–45ft (10.6–13.7m). Straight out from Seaview Resort is the eponymous **Seaview**, where there is an inner reef within 30ft (10m) of the shore, separated by sand from a second reef at 68ft (22m), and then a third which takes you on to the wall. And if you're looking for something a bit different, check out the sunken **mermaid**, in 40ft (12m) of water just off Sunset House (see page 101). Other possibilities for shore diving here lie out from the (presently closed) Coconut Harbour, including **Parrots Landing** and **Waldo's Reef**.

North of George Town, just beyond the Turtle Farm in West Bay, is an ideal location for shore dives, with excellent visibility and little disturbance. A three-minute swim in 25ft (8m) of water brings the diver to a 60ft (18m) mini wall, and you could well have the place to yourselves. Night diving here is popular, too. For details, contact Divetech (see page 92).

Boat dives

No matter where you are diving, Grand Cayman is unlikely to disappoint. Go with an open mind, too – even if you've set your heart on a particular dive, you're pretty well guaranteed to enjoy any alternative that may be offered. With over 50 anchored sites on the west wall alone, there's no shortage of choice, and even if the wind's blowing strongly in one area, there'll be sheltered diving somewhere else.

Stingray City

Justifiably popular among visitors, Stingray City is actually two separate locations, both in North Sound, where snorkellers and divers may experience the almost balletic grace of these extraordinary creatures as they glide among us comparatively awkward mortals. Almost all the boat trips on Grand Cayman will take you either to the sandbar, which is so shallow that you can stand, or to the nearby shallow dive spot, where divers kneel and wait just 12ft (4m) below the surface. Either way, expect a full briefing before your encounter, so you know exactly how to behave. To avoid the worst of the crowds at the sandbar, go in the afternoon.

Stingrays were originally drawn to the site by leftover bait thrown overboard by local fishermen, and they soon became accustomed to being fed. Before long, the potential for bringing divers here was realised, and the concept of Stingray City was born. The attraction of handfuls of squid is almost instantaneous, as female southern stingrays, with their wingspan of around 4ft (1.2m), appear silently from all sides. Stingrays effectively feed like underwater vacuum cleaners, sucking up their food from the sea bed. They have plates, not teeth, and although they can clamp these shut quite tight, they don't do any harm if they accidentally catch a finger – even if it does hurt momentarily. Rumour has it that the stingrays also have a penchant for certain hair conditioners, but this is probably hearsay! For what it's worth, the sting is set well back on the tail and, since the animals are attracted by food, they are not threatened; there is no record of anyone having been stung since Stingray City was established.

Of course, female stingrays are not the only animals to be attracted by squid. The smaller and far more aggressive male is likely to want to get in on the act, as

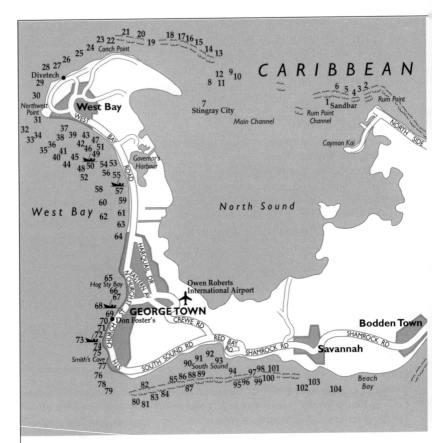

KEY TO DIVE SITES
Location of dive sites is approximate.

1 Sandbar at Stingray City
2 No-name Drop-off
3 Grand Canyon
4 Gail's Mountain
5 Chinese Wall
6 Hammerhead Hill
7 Stingray City
8 Channel's End Reef
9 Eagle Ray Pass
10 Westgate
11 Lemon Drop-off
12 Valley of the Rays
13 Josh's Canyon
14 Tarpon Alley
15 Main Street
16 Hole in the Wall
17 Cliff Hanger
18 Blue Pinnacles
19 Martin's Wall
20 Pete's Ravine
21 Bears Claw
22 Ghost Mountain
23 Sponge Point
24 Spanish Bay Reef
25 Little Tunnels
26 Schoolhouse Reef
27 Cemetery Reef

28 Hepps Pipeline
29 Turtle Farm Mini Wall
30 Hepps Wall
31 Bonnie's Arch
32 Northwest Point Drop-off
33 Orange Canyon
34 Sentinel Rock
35 Big Tunnel
36 Little Tunnel
37 Cemetery Reef
38 Slaughterhouse Reef
39 Mitch Miller Reef
40 Dragon's Hole
41 Big Dipper
42 Spanish Anchor
43 Razorback Reef
44 Little Dipper
45 Round Rock Cave
46 Aquarium
47 Angel Reef
48 Trinity Caves
49 Three Trees
50 Wreck of *Doc Polson*
51 Peter's Reef
52 Neptune's Wall
53 Jax Dax
54 Sand Chute

54 Sand Chute
55 Paradise Reef
56 Marty's Wall
57 Wreck of *Oro Verde*
58 Eagle's Nest
59 Hammerhead Hole
60 Rhapsody
61 Wildlife Reef
62 Caribbean Club Sand Chute
63 Lone Star
64 Royal Palms Ledge
65 Pageant Beach Reef
66 Soto's Reef
67 Lobster Pot Reef
68 Wreck of *Balboa*
69 Eden Rock
70 Devil's Grotto
71 Parrot's Reef
72 Seaview/Sunset Reef
73 Wreck of *David Nicholson*
74 Waldo's Reef
75 Armchair Reef
76 Eagle Ray Rock
77 Frank's Reef
78 Black Forest
79 Blackie's Hole
80 South Tarpon Alley

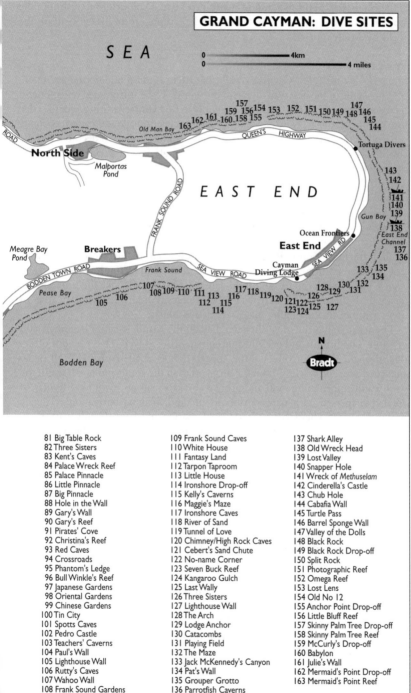

GRAND CAYMAN: DIVE SITES

81 Big Table Rock
82 Three Sisters
83 Kent's Caves
84 Palace Wreck Reef
85 Palace Pinnacle
86 Little Pinnacle
87 Big Pinnacle
88 Hole in the Wall
89 Gary's Wall
90 Gary's Reef
91 Pirates' Cove
92 Christina's Reef
93 Red Caves
94 Crossroads
95 Phantom's Ledge
96 Bull Winkle's Reef
97 Japanese Gardens
98 Oriental Gardens
99 Chinese Gardens
100 Tin City
101 Spotts Caves
102 Pedro Castle
103 Teachers' Caverns
104 Paul's Wall
105 Lighthouse Wall
106 Rutty's Caves
107 Wahoo Wall
108 Frank Sound Gardens

109 Frank Sound Caves
110 White House
111 Fantasy Land
112 Tarpon Taproom
113 Little House
114 Ironshore Drop-off
115 Kelly's Caverns
116 Maggie's Maze
117 Ironshore Caves
118 River of Sand
119 Tunnel of Love
120 Chimney/High Rock Caves
121 Cebert's Sand Chute
122 No-name Corner
123 Seven Buck Reef
124 Kangaroo Gulch
125 Last Wally
126 Three Sisters
127 Lighthouse Wall
128 The Arch
129 Lodge Anchor
130 Catacombs
131 Playing Field
132 The Maze
133 Jack McKennedy's Canyon
134 Pat's Wall
135 Grouper Grotto
136 Parrotfish Caverns

137 Shark Alley
138 Old Wreck Head
139 Lost Valley
140 Snapper Hole
141 Wreck of Methuselam
142 Cinderella's Castle
143 Chub Hole
144 Cabafia Wall
145 Turtle Pass
146 Barrel Sponge Wall
147 Valley of the Dolls
148 Black Rock
149 Black Rock Drop-off
150 Split Rock
151 Photographic Reef
152 Omega Reef
153 Lost Lens
154 Old No 12
155 Anchor Point Drop-off
156 Little Bluff Reef
157 Skinny Palm Tree Drop-off
158 Skinny Palm Tree Reef
159 McCurly's Drop-off
160 Babylon
161 Julie's Wall
162 Mermaid's Point Drop-off
163 Mermaid's Point Reef

is the occasional pufferfish, not to mention a host of colourful reef fish into the bargain. Even the menacing moray eel can be tempted from his lair beneath the rocks by a tasty morsel.

Walls and reefs

Stingray City aside, it is Cayman's walls that are its greatest underwater attraction, offering some of the best wall diving in the world. To be surrounded one moment by the sunlit world of the reef, then suddenly to find yourself staring over the edge into nothingness is truly extraordinary. Corals of every shape and pattern decorate the wall as far as the eye can see, their bright colours fading to deep blue as the abyss beckons. Here you may see the spotted eagle ray, or perhaps a hawksbill turtle, while out to sea keep an eye open for the occasional patrolling shark.

With the first dive of the day likely to be a wall dive to around 100ft (30m), the second is usually over the reef, which is for the most part shallow enough to allow periods of up to 45 minutes underwater. Here, nature's playground is in full swing. Colourful fish of all hues dart in and out of the coral; great purple sea fans wave in the currents; lobsters peer out from under rocks, often visible only by their fragile antennae. Resist any temptation to climb into those huge barrels that perch atop the coral – they've grown to that size over hundreds of years and even a slight knock can cause untold damage. Do, though, take the time to peer inside both these and the narrower tube sponges. For an extraordinary array of tiny creatures, this is a hiding place of relative safety.

The **west** wall is the most sheltered bay on the island, ideal for beginners and in windy conditions, and useful for acclimatisation as well. Don't be put off by this, though; the west offers some superb diving at all levels, with 50 or so anchored sites. With a less dramatic drop-off than the south and north walls, the west features intriguing sand and groove coral formations, with long fingers of coral interspersed with narrow ribbons of sand, making navigation relatively straightforward. There is no shortage of marine life here. Gaudy parrotfish, French and queen angelfish and smiling tangs are just a few of the numerous species that weave through the coral, with the almost transparent trumpetfish like a silent ghost and the odd algae-encrusted grouper lurking in the depths.

The names of many of the dive sites give you a flavour of what is to come. Aquarium acquired its name from the huge plastic sheets that were used during a study of the reef structure, then left behind by the scientists because it was too windy to move them. Although most of them have since been removed, one or two remain, so the occasional diver may just find out what it's like to be on the inside of a fish tank! Orange Canyon, at the northernmost tip of West Bay, is prone to strong currents, but is widely considered to be one of the west's gems, as is Texas Wall, a shallow, shelving wall with wonderful sponges and coral formations, and black durgon very much in evidence.

For most dive operators, the **north** wall involves a 20–25-minute boat ride which can occasionally be choppy. That said, the diving here is spectacular, with sharp drop offs from 40–45ft (12–13.7m) on to the wall and sites such as Eagle Ray Pass and Tarpon Alley indicating some of the highlights of the area.

The deeper reef of the **south**, at 60–70ft (18–20m), features plenty of crevices and channels to explore. Caves are very much in evidence here, with Pirate's Cove, Hole-in-the-Wall and Spotts Caves setting the scene.

Only three companies regularly run dives to the **east**: Ocean Frontiers, Tortuga Diving and Cayman Diving Lodge. Here, where the pace of life is slower and the island uncrowded, the occasional diver is something of a rarity among the marine life, and you'll be very much the stranger in their underwater world. As the walls plunge vertically from around 45ft (15.6m), the scenery is one of mazes and caverns, overhangs and chutes. In parts of the East End shark sightings are almost to be guaranteed, while very occasionally a manta ray may come into view. On a practical note, the prevailing onshore wind tends to whip up the sea a little, with waves of 3–5ft (0.9–1.5m) not uncommon.

Wrecks and other attractions

It's not surprising that Cayman waters have their fair share of wrecks, given the number of ships that plied these seas in the days of sail. In fact, the current inventory of shipwrecks stands at 111 sites off Cayman shores. Such wrecks are the property of the Crown, and protected by law, so treasure hunters should keep away, but divers and snorkellers are free to explore at their leisure.

Two that are easily visited lie to the west of George Town. The closest to shore, only 50yds (45m) out from North Church Street, is the *Cali*, a 220ft (67m) Colombian freighter that went down in the 1940s. Lying in 24ft (7m) of water, the *Cali* is now home to a wide variety of marine life, and popular with shore divers and snorkellers alike. Further out, but still in comparatively shallow water at 35ft (10.6m), is the *Balboa,* a 375ft (114m) steam-driven cargo ship which sank during the 1932 hurricane. Its proximity to the port and heavy shipping means that it is not always accessible to divers.

The *Oro Verde*, a Jamaican cargo vessel, went aground in West Bay in 1980 when its crew mutinied on discovering that the cargo of 'bananas' was in fact *ganja*. The boat, left untended, ran aground, and its cargo was washed ashore. The ship was sunk by dive operators in 1983 in 60ft (18m) of water, some 500yds (45m) off the centre of Seven Mile Beach. Now covered in coral, and home to a

THE SINKING OF A SIREN

It was on a hot morning in November 2000 that 'Amphitrite, Siren of Sunset Reef' was last seen on land. A 9ft (2.7m) bronze mermaid, the creation of Canadian sculptor Simon Morris, she was brought to Grand Cayman with a view to creating an artificial reef off Sunset House.

In a glare of publicity, the statue was unveiled to the watching crowd. Her simple lines were rapidly marred as she was trussed up in some bizarre form of bondage and hoisted by a crane into the clear waters to the southwest. From this vantage point, poised above the sea, she was slowly lowered until she seemed to be swimming, then escorted by a team from Sunset Divers to her final resting place. Here, in 50ft (15m) of warm, clear water off the southwest coast, she was set free into the underwater world, eventually to form a home for all manner of aquatic creatures. With her bronze sister attracting divers in the cold waters off British Columbia, it looks as though Amphitrite has drawn the best card.

large green moray, it is strewn across a fairly wide area and makes a popular dive both in the daytime and at night.

Although East End has been the site of many a shipwreck over the years, there is only one designated wreck dive in this area, that of the *Methuselam*. Most of the other wrecks in this area are either on the reef, so not suitable for diving, or very old and scattered, so not really classified as wreck dives. However, Ocean Frontiers runs a historical maritime snorkel trail which gives the opportunity to take a look at what is left of some of these old ships, including the *Methuselam*, the *Marybelle* and the *Geneva Kathleen*.

A relatively recent addition to the underwater world is the Siren of Sunset Reef (see box, page 101).

SNORKELLING, FISHING AND BOAT CHARTERS
Snorkelling
Even the most nervous swimmer can have a go at snorkelling: it's inexpensive, simple – and addictive! An ordinary mask and snorkel are all that is needed to open up a world that can otherwise be scarcely imagined; fins just mean you can go that much faster. If you don't have your own kit, you can always hire it for around US$10 per day from one of the many dive operators on the island. Do try the equipment on first – it's important that the mask should fit snugly and the fins shouldn't rub or you'll have blisters in next to no time.

Rules and regulations
- If you are diving or snorkelling outside a buoyed swim area or more than 200yds (180m) offshore, display a 'diver down' flag (see page 86), or a white float, light or other marker which is visible from this distance.
- Watch out for boats in the area, particularly in areas of heavy boat traffic.
- Do not touch the coral. Each time you do it affects or damages living creatures.
- Remove nothing from the water. Everything has a purpose and use; every empty shell will become a home for another creature.

Snorkelling sites
You don't have to go far to find good snorkelling on Grand Cayman. In fact, with such good visibility almost throughout the year, many of the dive sites, including several inshore wrecks, are also popular with snorkellers. And although you'll always hear of an enticing spot just that bit further on, almost every stretch of beach has its attractions.

On **Seven Mile Beach**, there may be just a narrow band of sand in front of the Marriott, but beach sand is superfluous when just offshore the shallow reef is a haven for countless colourful fish, while delicately waving antennae alert you to the presence of spiny lobsters, presumably as intrigued by us as we are by them. There's good snorkelling in front of the Westin and Indies Suites, too, while further north both Cemetery Reef (see page 141) and the public beach are good spots from which to set off. In West Bay itself, up by the Turtle Farm, the quieter waters mean that you may well have **Turtle Reef** (just offshore from Divetech) to yourself.

At the other end of the bay, in **George Town**, Eden Rock and Devil's Grotto both offer excellent snorkelling, while the wreck of the *Cali* (see page 101) is easily visible from above. To the south the rockier environment of Smith's Cove harbours its own secrets, with shoals of colourful fish and even the occasional small barracuda, though be careful not to accidentally tread on a sea urchin.

To the **north** of the island, at Rum Point, snorkelling is popular. But walk just a little way east on the beach and you'll find yourself nearer to the reef, where squirrel fish move in and out among deep purple sea fans and you may even spot a flat fish or two. And to the **east** of the island, there are any number of secluded spots, each offering almost limitless scope for anyone with a mask and snorkel and time on their hands.

If you're hankering after sites further afield, there are numerous operators who run half- and full-day snorkel trips out to Stingray City and almost anywhere on the reef. Many of these outfits also offer seafood lunch on a full-day trip as part of the deal. Half-day snorkel trips will cost upwards from US$30. In addition, Ocean Frontiers runs guided nature and historical snorkel trips from US$29.

Sandbar at Stingray City
Trips to the sandbar in North Sound, where the water is only 3ft (1m) deep in places, can be arranged through most operators on Grand Cayman for around US$30 per person. Many of the visitors here are passengers on the cruise ships that anchor off George Town, so it can get very busy when the ships are in, particularly in the mornings. That said, practicalities pale into insignificance beside the beauty of the southern stingrays that give this location its name. To share just a few moments with these magical creatures is like dancing in a dream – ignore the crowd and savour it!

Coral Gardens
Full-day snorkel trips make one of their stops at the Coral Gardens in North Sound, where sea fans beckon you to an abundance of coral formations, and multi-coloured fish dart in and out in the shallows. You may even be lucky enough to spot one of the island's turtles, either underwater or as they surface for air.

Further information
The Cayman Island Department of Tourism issues an *Undersea Guide*, which features information on 43 snorkelling sites: 18 on Grand Cayman, 12 on Cayman Brac and 13 on Little Cayman. For further information, see their website: www.divecayman.ky.

Fishing
The waters off the Cayman Islands offer a tremendous variety of fishing for both experienced anglers and complete novices. Whether your interest is in fly, bone, tarpon, reef, night or big-game fishing, there's likely to be something here that will test your skill. Fully equipped boats can be chartered for almost every type of fishing. Charters are usually for a half or full day, with prices starting from US$300 and rising to a staggering US$1,500, depending on the type of fishing and the specification of the boat. Night fishing is also available through some operators.

No licence is required for catch-and-release fishing in Cayman waters, but otherwise there are stringent regulations in place to protect various species, with fishing restricted in protected areas, and various species protected by law (see also *Marine conservation*, page 27). Those without Caymanian status may not fish without a licence from the shore, or from Cayman waters in which they can stand. It is illegal to take any lobster except the spiny lobster, for which there is a minimum size allowable. No more than five conch molluscs may be taken per person per day, or ten per boat, whichever is the fewer. Turtling is strictly controlled by licence, which may be granted only to Caymanians working in accordance with traditional practices, with further restrictions imposed regarding numbers and season. The possession or use of spearguns and Hawaiian slings by visitors is illegal; licences are granted by the Department of Environment only to Caymanians over the age of 18.

Deep-sea or **sport fishing** for blue marlin, yellowfin tuna, wahoo, dolphin and barracuda goes on throughout the year, with fish to be found relatively close to the shore, and almost always within a 20-minute boat ride. That said, certain times of the year are better than others. The best season for wahoo, for example, is said to be November to March, and fish are generally considered to be bigger during the winter and spring.

Reef fishing is best scheduled on a high incoming tide. This is light-tackle angling for fish with an average weight of 1–20lb (0.45–9kg), including snapper, grouper and jack. Conversely, **bonefishing** and **tarpon fishing** are best on a low outgoing tide, particularly in shallow waters of around 6ft (1.8m) such as Grand Cayman's North, South and Frank sounds. Bonefish averaging 3–8lb (1.4–3.6kg) are to be found on the flats of all three islands, while smaller tarpon around 4–5lb (1.8–2.3kg) may also be found in canals or dykes and brackish ponds.

Bottom fishing is popular with novices, including children, who quite often enjoy baiting their own hooks. Use natural baits wherever possible, such as squid or pilchards, available from Melody Marine in Spinnaker Square, Red Bay, tel: 947 1093, or at any of the supermarkets.

Fly fishing for bonefish, tarpon and permit is another possibility, again in the flats, with guides available, though you would be advised to bring your own tackle (a selection is available on the island at both Melody Marine and R&M Fly Shop & Charters, tel: 946 0214).

The highlight of the Cayman sport-fishing year is the annual week-long **International Fishing Tournament**, a sport-fishing jamboree that takes place at the end of April/early May. Organised by the Cayman Islands Angling Club, it's a high-value affair, with significant cash prizes. Registration is open to all comers, who compete, among other accolades, for the heaviest fish caught by a visiting angler. For details of this, or just to check out the local angling scene, contact the Cayman Islands Angling Club at PO Box 30280 SMB, Grand Cayman; email: fishing@candw.ky; web: www.fishcayman.com.

Boat operators
Many of the companies that offer boat trips cover both fishing and snorkelling. In addition to those listed below, most of the dive operators (see pages 91–6) also run snorkel trips, as do Cayman Windsurf (see page 109) and Nautilus (see page 149). Neptune's Divers also run fishing trips. Most operators running snorkel

trips include use of snorkel, mask and fins as part of the package, and most will arrange collection from your hotel.

Several companies who run snorkel and fishing trips also **charter** their boats out on a private basis, allowing you to make up your own group for fishing or snorkelling, with the freedom to choose where and when you go, and perhaps the opportunity to sail the boat as well. Many of the larger companies also act as agents for some of the individual boats listed.

For details of Cayman's submarines, or – more accurately – submersibles, see page 148.

Bayside Watersports Morgan's Harbour, West Bay; tel: 949 3200/1750; fax: 949 3700; email: bayside@candw.ky; web: www.baysidewatersports.com
Established in 1974, Bayside reckons it is the largest charter-boat booking agent on Grand Cayman, with boats ranging from 18ft (5.5m) to 60ft (18m), and is the only operator to have a truly complete fly-fishing set up. Half- and full-day trips for deep-sea, inside reef, bone, fly, flat and boat fishing.
Rates Bone, tarpon and fly fishing from US$300 per half-day (up to four anglers, or two for fly fishing). Deep-sea fishing US$500–800 half day, US$700–1,500 full day, depending on numbers. Half and full-day snorkel trips cost US$37.50/62.50 (the latter including a fish lunch on the beach).

Capt Asley's Watersports Tel: 949 3054; fax: 949 6464; email; cayfish@candw.ky
A family business based on a variety of fishing and snorkelling trips in one of their four boats, including the 41ft (12.5m) *Hit 'n' Run*.
Rates Snorkel trips US$50 per person

Capt Bryan's North Church St, George Town; tel: 949 0038, cell: 916 2093; fax: 949 2087; email: captainbryan@cayman.org
Sailing, snorkelling and fishing trips in 50ft (15m) boats. Sunset charters and private snorkel charters also available.
Rates US$35–55 per person

Capt Crosby's Watersports Coconut Place, West Bay Rd, tel: 945 4049; fax: 945 5994; email: crosby@cayman.org; web: www.cayman.org/crosby
One of the founders of Stingray City, the guitar-playing Captain Crosby takes half- and full-day snorkel trips both here and to other locations on the island on a 47ft (12m) sailing trimaran, with freshly prepared seafood lunch on offer as well. Bone and reef fishing also offered.
Rates Half-day snorkel trip US$25, full day US$40

Capt Marvin's Cayman Falls, West Bay Rd, and Waterfront Centre, George Town; tel: 945 4590/6975; fax: 945 5673; email: captmvn@candw.ky; web: www.captainmarvins.com
One of the original founders of Stingray City, Captain Marvin takes daily snorkel trips both here and to various wrecks and reefs around the coast, regaling passengers with old seafaring stories. A range of fishing charters is also available.
Rates per person: Snorkel trips half-day US$39, full day with beach lunch US$62.50. Half-day (3–4 hour) fishing charters: reef US$450–500; deep-sea US$600–800 (full day US$1,100–1,500).

Captain Ronald Ebanks Coconut Place, West Bay Rd; tel: 946 0214 (daytime), 947 3146 (after 6.00pm); email: flyfish@candw.ky; web: www.flyfishgrandcayman.com
Specialists in fly fishing and light tackle, with equipment provided. Trips leave from

Cayman Islands Yacht Club, slip A20. Captain Ebanks also has his own angling shop, R&M Fly Shop & Charters, tel: 946 0214, where anglers can buy and rent equipment.

Rates for half day: fly fishing US$340 (two people); reef fishing US$300 (up to four people)

Cayman Delight Cruises Tel: 949 6738; email: joenellp@andys.ky; web: www.caymandelightcruises.com

Half-day snorkel trips US$38 per person; children 5–10 half price; under 5s free. Book direct, or through Andy's Rent-A-Car (see page 76); packages available.

Chip Chip Charters c/o Melody Marine, Spinnaker Square, Red Bay, tel: 947 1093; fax: 949 0109; email: chipchip@candw.ky

Phil Bodden at the specialist fishing-tackle shop also arranges deep-sea fishing and snorkelling trips, which can be customised to suit.

Rates Half-day charter US$500 for up to 5 people; full day US$700. Bring your own food and drink.

Dallas Watersports Tel: 949 1538, cell: 916 2707

Deep-sea fishing in 34ft (10.4m) boat.

Rates US$450 (half day), US$600 (full day)

Ecoventures PO Box 200 EE, East End; tel: 947 5200; US toll free: 866 ECO EAST; fax: 947 5201; email: info@ecoventures.ky; web: www.ecoventures.ky

Excursions include a 2½–3-hour 'Castaway Island' trip. Visitors are taken across to an island off the East End with opportunities to snorkel and explore the surrounding reef, the site of numerous shipwrecks.

Rates US$49 per adult (children under 12 US$29), including snorkel equipment

Fantasea Tours Tel: 949 2182; fax: 949 5459; email: fantasea@candw.ky

Half-day trips from Cayman Islands Yacht Club to Stingray City and the reef in 38ft (12.5m) sailing catamaran for up to 16 people.

Rates US$31.25 per adult

Frank's Watersports Coconut Place, West Bay Rd; tel: 945 5491/949 3143; fax: 945 1992; email: cptfrank@candw.ky

Half or full-day trips with Capt Frank Ebanks in large motorboats, with complementary rum punch. Snorkelling to Stingray City, including fresh seafood lunch. Deep-sea, reef, bone and night fishing. Private charters available.

Rates Half day US$25 per person, full day US$40. Fishing charters US$300–575.

Gizmo Charters Tel: 949 1146, cell: 916 3799; fax: 949 1146

Big-game fishing aboard the *Gizmo*, with video presentations on board.

Rates Full day (7 hours) US$675; half day (4½ hours) US$500. Bottom fishing (4 hours) US$150 per person. Maximum four anglers. Snorkelling safari US$60 per person (6 hours); Stingray City US$25 per person.

Island Girl III Tel: 947 3029, cell: 916 0405; email: islgirl@candw.ky

All types of fishing and snorkelling charters in this modern 31ft (102m) fishing vessel.

Rates Half day reef US$395; half–full-day deep sea US$500–900

Jolly Roger Tel: 947 7245; email: jolroger@candw.ky; web: www.jollyrogercayman.com

The replica of a 17th-century galleon that is moored off George Town provides an interesting and Lilliputian contrast to the multi-storey cruise ships that anchor alongside. Afternoon 'pirate encounters' offer two hours of fun and frolics, with departures at 2.30pm Mon, Wed and Fri. Adults US$35, children 3–12 US$25. In the evening, there are two sunset cruises – given a choice, go for the booze (cocktail) cruise rather than dinner. Cocktail cruise US$40 (children 6–16 US$25); dinner cruise US$60 (children 6–16 US$35). Children under 6 free. All cruises depart from George Town's South Terminal.

Just Fish'n Tel: 949 8745, cell 916 0113; email: justfish@candw.ky; web: www.justfish.com.ky

Full and half-day fishing charters in 21ft (6.4m) or 38ft (11.6m) boats.

Rates Reef fishing US$400–600, deep sea 400–1,125, depending on boat.

Kellys Watersports tel: 916 0336; cell: 916 0336; fax: 949 0213; email: kellys@candw.ky; web: www.kellyswatersports.com.ky

Stingray City snorkel and dive trips with a Caymanian crew. Private charters on request.

Rates Snorkel trip US$30 per person

Kirk Sea Tours North Church St, George Town; tel: 949 7278; email: info@kirkseatours.com; web: www.kirkseatours.com

Located on the deck in front of George Town's Big Bamboo, Kirk's offers a full range of watersports, from snorkelling and diving, including SNUBA (see pages 88–9) at US$65 for 1½ hours (children US$45), to fishing.

Rates Reef/bonefishing US$300–600; fly fishing US$350–650; deep-sea fishing US$350–650; shark from US$500. Snorkel and Stingray City trips from US$15 for 1½ hours on the wreck of the *Cali* to US$49 at Stingray City with lunch at Kaibo Yacht Club.

Nina Tel: 926 5000; email: columfnd@surfbvi.com; web: www.thenina.com

Trips on this replica 500-year-old sailing vessel depart at 10.00am, 1.30pm and 5.00pm from Cayman Islands Yacht Club, and cost US$29 in the morning, or US$39 for the afternoon or evening, including soft drinks and light snacks.

Red Baron Charters PO Box 673 GT; tel/fax: 945 4744; cell: 916 4333; email: neil@sailcayman.com; web: www.sailcayman.com

Small-group (2–8 people) charters in the 39ft (11.9m) *Red Baron* or the 44ft (13.4m) *Nautigal* allow for passengers to help with the crewing – if they want to. Half- and full-day private charters with snorkelling, and sunset sailing cruises.

Rates From US$400 on *Red Baron*, US$600 on *Nautigal* (half day)

Red Sail Sports PO Box 31473 SMB, Coconut Place, West Bay Rd; tel: 946 3362; US: 877 733 7245; fax: 945 5808; email: infocayman@redsailcayman.com; web: www.redsailcayman.com

Red Sail's three luxury catamarans – the 65ft (19.8m) *Spirit of Ppalu* and *Spirit of Poseidon*, and the 62ft (18.9m) *Spirit of Cayman* – sail from the Hyatt dock for two-hour sunset cruises or 3½-hour dinner cruises, and half-day snorkel trips to Stingray City. Private charters are also available. Glass-bottomed boat cruises run Mon–Sat from Rum Point to Stingray City and the reef.

Rates Catamaran sunset sail US$35; dinner cruise US$70; snorkel trip US$80; children 3–12 half price. Glass-bottomed boat snorkel trip US$30 (snorkel equipment additional US$10 per person). Full- and half-day fishing charters for 4–8 people cost US$300–600 for reef and bottom fishing, US$500–700 for deep-sea fishing.

Soto's Cruises PO Box 30192 SMB; tel: 945 4576; fax: 945 3439; email: scruises@candw.ky; web: www.sotoscruises.com

Daily half-day trips in 40ft (12.2m) motorboat to Stingray City Sandbar, Coral Gardens and the reef.

Rates CI$19 per person

Xanax Sailing Cruises Tel: 949 1186, cell: 916 4513

Half- and full-day sailing and snorkel cruises, plus sunset dinner cruises, leave from Cayman Islands Yacht Club on a 32ft (9.8m) Erikson yacht. Private charters available on request.

Rates Snorkel trips US$37.50–62.50 per person; dinner cruise US$125 per couple

OTHER WATERSPORTS

In addition to diving and snorkelling, the range of other watersports available on the islands is vast.

The usually calm waters inside the reef make **kayaking** a real pleasure, whether you're paddling up and down Seven Mile Beach, or exploring the coves of South Sound. Kayaks are available for hire at various locations, including Kirk Sea Tours in George Town, the public beach on Seven Mile Beach, South Sound, Rum Point (see page 168), and in the East End from Ecoventures (see page 80) or Cayman Windsurf, as well as at some of the hotels. Expect to pay up to US$20 per hour for a single kayak, US$25 per hour for a double. Alternatively, you can take a guided kayak trip with Silver Thatch Excursions (see page 81), Surfside Aquasports or Ecoventures, and discover some of the secrets of Cayman's narrow inland channels and shallow lagoons.

On the safety front, remember to wear a buoyancy aid and a hat, and to take plenty of water.

Sailing dinghies, particularly Waveriders – small plastic-hulled trimarans that demand almost no previous knowledge of sailing – can be launched in minutes and are great fun, though be prepared to get wet! Waveriders are available for hire at the public beach on West Bay Road and in the East End, and will take up to three adults. Just 15 minutes' tuition and you're off.

The Cayman Islands Sailing Club at the bottom of North Sound (not far from Red Bay) offers lessons to visitors and has Lasers and Laser Picos available for hire to recreational sailors at CI$25 per hour. At weekends, the club hosts both sailing races and social events, while during April they organise the annual round-the-island regatta, a three-day event in which boats of all sizes compete to be the fastest to circumnavigate the island. For further information, contact the club on tel: 947 7913; email: sailing@candw.ky; web: www.sailing.ky.

At the other end of the spectrum are **sailing charters**, offered by several of the boat operators, some of whom will allow you to help crew the boat. See *Boat operators*, pages 105–7.

Windsurfing comes into its own off the eastern shores of the island, opposite Morritt's Tortuga and The Reef. On quiet days, in the shallow waters inside the reef, beginners can learn in calm, confined conditions with a steady wind, but when the wind is up, they would do better to head for the more sheltered waters to the west. That, however, is when experienced windsurfers and kitesurfers can really show off their skills, taking advantage of a narrow gap in the reef to surf the waves beyond. No guarantees, but if you're looking for the stronger winds then November to March is the time to be here. *The* place to go for windsurfing is Cayman Windsurf in the East End.

The sight of colourful parachutes scudding along 400ft (122m) up just off the beach is pretty tantalising. Three or four different companies offer **parasailing** along Seven Mile Beach. Participants may go up singly or in pairs, weight permitting. Just walk along the beach until you find one of the booths where parasailing is on offer, or contact an operator from the list below. Rates are around US$60 per person single, or US$100 double.

Jetbikes or **jet skis**, also known as **waverunners**, can be hired both on Seven Mile Beach and at Rum Point for around US$65 per half hour. Capable of speeds up to 15mph (24km/h), they can cause considerable damage in the wrong hands, so do read the rules before you set off. Penalties for infringement are strict, including fines or even imprisonment.

Waterskiing is available both on Seven Mile Beach and at Rum Point, through Red Sail Sports. A 15-minute session costs US$40. Waterskiing is permitted only within specifically designated watersports areas, as shown on pages 110–11. Boats must always have two crew members, in addition to the skier. Further options include **tubing**, **paddleboats** and **banana-boat** rides.

Operators

Cayman Windsurf Morritt's Tortuga, East End; tel: 947 7492; fax: 947 6763; email: cawin@candw.ky
The original windsurfing operator on Grand Cayman is now owned by Red Sail Sports. Based at the eastern end of the island, it is open to all visitors. A full windsurfing service is offered, including tuition at all levels, plus rentals – on or off site – of the latest BiC performance boards and a range of sails. For sailors – or indeed would-be sailors – there is a fleet of bright yellow Waveriders, while other rentals include Hobie Cats, ocean and glass-bottomed kayaks, and snorkel gear. Open daily 9.00am–5.00pm.
Rates per hour: Windsurfer US$35 (1-hour lesson (US$45), sailboat US$35, single kayak US$15, double kayak US$25; waverunner US$50 (1/2 hour). Snorkel equipment US$10 per day, float (raft) US$10 per day. Windsurfing tuition from US$45 for an introductory lesson; sailboat tuition US$35. Other prices on request.

Cloud Dancer Tel: 916 2944
Specialist parasailing operation on Seven Mile Beach.

D&S Charters PO Box 286 SAV; tel: 916 7566
Waterskiing and tubing off East End.

Kirk Sea Tours North Church St, George Town; tel: 949 7278; email: info@kirkseatours.com; web: www.kirkseatours.com
From the deck in front of George Town's Big Bamboo, Kirk's rent out glass-bottomed boats (US$25), and kayaks (US$15–20), and organise parasailing (US$60–100).

Parasailing Professionals Tel: 916 2953
Collections from any point along Seven Mile Beach.

Red Sail Sports Seven Mile Beach tel: 947 8745/8732; Rum Point tel: 947 9203
A broad range of watersports is offered by Red Sail, with equipment for hire, including snorkelling gear.
Rates Sailboat US$25 per hour; kayak US$20–25 per hour; paddleboat US$20 per hour. Waterskiing US$40 per 15-minute session (tuition available at US$65 for 25 minutes); tubing US$15 for ten minutes; waverunner US$65 for half an hour. Parasailing on Seven Mile Beach costs US$60 single, US$100 double. Snorkel gear US$15 per day.

Surfside Aquasports Cell: 916 2820; email: surfside@candw.ky
Surfside is the local dealer for Ocean Kayak and offers kayaking tours through the wetland areas of South Sound. The two-hour trip explores the mangrove ecosystem, its history and how it impacts the present and future of the islands, followed by a short paddle to a series of reefs, with the opportunity to snorkel. Surfside has until recently also rented out waverunners, kayaks and simple sailing trimarans at the public beach on West Bay Rd. At the time of writing, this was subject to renegotiation, but all being well it should be operational again shortly.

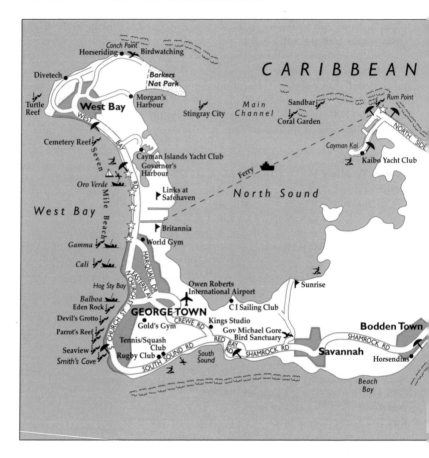

Rates per hour: Kayaks US$15 (single), US$20 (double); sailboats US$30; waverunners US$85 (US$55 per half hour)

OTHER SPORTS
Golf

Grand Cayman has two world-class golf courses, both just opposite Seven Mile Beach, and both offering a challenge to amateur and professional golfers alike. A third, the nine-hole course at the new Ritz Carlton, designed by Greg Norman, is scheduled to open in 2005. In addition, there is a family golf centre beyond George Town in the village of Savannah.

Britannia Golf Club PO Box 1588; tel: 949 1234

The only Jack Nicklaus-designed course in the Caribbean, the links-style Britannia is set back from West Bay Road behind the Hyatt, overlooking North Sound to the east. With palm trees set atop the bunkers and tropical birds for background noise, it's something of a golfer's paradise. The course is effectively two courses in one: the 9-hole championship course is 2,942yds (par 35), and within this course there are a further nine greens and tees, making it an 18-hole executive course (par 57). Play is permitted on each course on

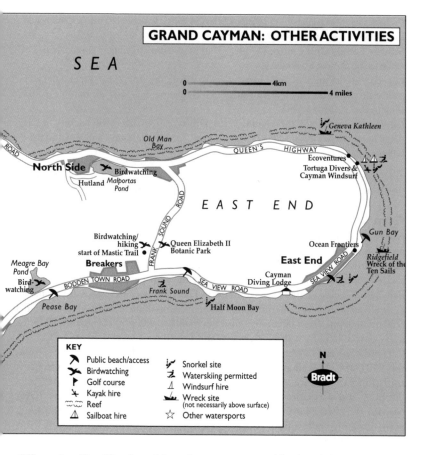

different days: Tue, Thu, Sat and Sun afternoon are reserved for the 9-hole course, and Mon, Wed, Fri and Sun morning for the 18-hole course. Allow around 2 and 3 hours respectively. Electric golf carts are compulsory, and a strict dress code is enforced, although tailored shorts are permitted. Resident professional, with lessons available on request. Tee off from 8.00am. Guests at the Hyatt may reserve tee times up to 48 hours in advance; others may make reservations up to 24 hours in advance. Golf shop open 7.30am–6.00pm. *Rates* Green fees per person, low/high season US$30–50/$40–60 for Hyatt guests, US$60–70/$85–110 for other players. Note that high season here is defined as November 1 to May 31.

The Links at Safehaven PO Box 1311GT; tel: 949 5988; fax: 949 5457; web: www.safehaven.ky

This 18-hole championship golf course off West Bay Rd on the edge of North Sound is par 71, 6,605yds. Built to USGA standards (rating 75.1), it offers a challenge to both amateur and professional golfers. Electric golf carts are compulsory, and a strict dress code is enforced. Aqua driving range. Resident professional. Tee off from 7.30am. Members may book up to 48 hours in advance; other players 24 hours in advance (four players maximum). Patio bar and restaurant. Golf shop open 7.00am–6.00pm. *Rates* Green fees per person: 9 holes US$80; 18 holes US$120 (US$75/110 in summer).

Package rates also available. Aquarange US$6 (50 balls), US$12 (110 balls). Club rental from US$15. Lessons US$36.50 per half hour.

Sunrise Family Golf Centre PO Box 10940 APO, Sunrise Landing, Savannah; tel: 947 4653; email: Sunrise1@candw.ky

Located some 15 minutes' drive east of George Town, this 9-hole, par 3 (per hole) golf course also has a full-length driving range and clubhouse. Pull carts are available. Golf shop open 7.30am–6.30pm.

Rates Green fees adults CI$17, juniors CI$8. Driving range CI$5 (small bucket), or CI$7 (large bucket). Golf lessons US$25 per half hour, US$45 per hour. Club rental adults CI$8, juniors CI$4.

There is a **mini-golf** centre next to Deckers restaurant on West Bay Road, just north of the entrance to the Hyatt Regency. Open 4.00–11.00pm daily.

Gym

Many of the top hotels have their own gyms open to residents. In addition, there are a few independent gyms open to visitors. **World Gym** on Lawrence Boulevard, tel: 949 5132, is set back from the road opposite the cinema and next to Bed restaurant. The gym is well equipped, with personal trainers on hand, daily aerobic classes and massage to boot. Daily and weekly passes are available, as well as long-term membership. Open Mon–Thu, 5.30am–10.00pm, Fri 5.30am–9.00pm, Sat 8.00am–6.00pm, Sun 8.00am–4.00pm. Prices are CI$16 for a day pass, CI$32 for a three-day pass, and CI$40 for a week.

Gold's Gym is located at Pasadora Place on Smith Road, George Town, tel: 949 7016. As well as the full range of exercise equipment, the gym has a nutrition store where you can find various vitamins and supplements, plus clothing and accessories. Rather more upbeat is the relatively new **King Studio** (tel: 946 5464) near Grand Harbour, whose facilities include a huge gym, climbing wall, squash courts and a roller-skating rink, with classes from yoga to spinning.

For details of health spas, see pages 138–9.

Rugby and football

The popular Cayman Islands Rugby Club is located at South Sound, just east of George Town, tel: 949 7960, web: www.caymanrugby.com. Matches are played most weekends, and spectators are welcome. In June, the island hosts the Cayman International Sevens tournament (www.cisevens.com).

The Football Association is based at the Truman Bodden Sports Complex on Walkers Road, George Town; for information, call 949 5775.

Squash

Visitors are welcome during the day to South Sound Squash Club (tel: 949 9469, web: www.squash.ky), which is located next to the rugby and tennis clubs in South Sound. The club has seven courts, with coaching available.

Tennis

Many hotels have their own tennis courts, and the tennis centre at the Ritz Carlton will offer professional coaching when it opens in 2005. In addition, there is the

Cayman Islands Tennis Club, located just behind the rugby club on South Sound Road, tel: 949 9464. This is a pretty active club, with resident professionals, regular tournaments, and the occasional masterclass run by pro celebrities such as Jim Courier. Visitors are welcome to play at the club during the daytime. Tennis lessons are also available through Dial-A-Tennis Pro, on 926 2776.

HORSERIDING

Unlikely though it may sound, horseriding up in West Bay is well worth fitting in, even if it's not something you'd normally consider. Cantering along a deserted beach where stingrays swim among the turtle grass has to be one of the highlights of a trip here, while walking back past mangrove swamps alive with carpet sea anemones offers an opportunity to see a side to the island that one might otherwise fear had long since fallen to the hand of the developers.

On the practical side, wear long trousers and shoes, not sandals, and bring sunscreen and a camera. Hard hats are not provided by any of the outfits below. On average, a ride lasts around an hour and a half. Experience is not necessary – these horses are pretty forgiving, and the ability of each rider, including children, is assessed in advance. Except for Coral Stone Stables, prices include collection from the vicinity of Seven Mile Beach.

Coral Stone Stables Tel: 947 2323; cell: 916 4799; fax: 947 8463; email: cstones@candw.ky; web: www.cstables.com
The newest horseriding venue on the island is based at Bodden Town. Early morning, afternoon and sunset rides through woodland in Savannah or along the beach at Bodden Town are for all levels of rider, and rates include a group photo and drink after the ride. There's also a monthly moonlit ride. Costs are from US$56.25 for an hour, with pick up a further US$10 if required.

Honeysuckle Trail Rides Tel: 947 7976, cell: 916 5420; fax: 947 1051; email: pennyhon@hotmail.com
Guided rides, including sunset tours, cost from US$60 per person for a non-private ride, walking only, to US$80 per person for a private ride, where riders may choose from walking through to galloping. Weight limit 240lb (109kg). Both English and Western tack are available. Disabled riders can be accommodated by appointment, as can large groups. Children welcome.

Nicki's Beach Rides Tel: 947 5839, cell: 916 3530
Groups of up to four people are escorted on early morning or sunset rides at Barkers, both along the beach and inland. Nicki was brought up in Grand Cayman and her enthusiasm for the island is infectious. With her raft of anecdotes about life here, and her in-depth knowledge of the local flora and fauna, this is an outing that far outlasts your hour or so in the saddle. Weight limit approximately 200lb (90kg). Morning (1 hour) US$55 per person, sunset (1½ hours) US$70.

Pampered Ponies Tel: 945 2262, cell: 916 2540; email: info@ponies.ky; web: www.ponies.ky
In addition to daily beach and trail rides, Pampered Ponies offers early morning and sunset rides, and escorted beach rides at full moon each month. A highlight here is the opportunity to ride the horses bareback in their 'swimming ride'. English as well as Western tack available. Spanish spoken. Daytime rides US$75 per person, moonlight rides US$100, swimming ride US$125 (discount specials sometimes available).

HIKING AND BIRDWATCHING

The major hiking trail on Grand Cayman is the Mastic Trail (see page 164). There are numerous other possibilities for hikers, however, particularly towards the eastern end of the island where tracts of woodland and open countryside remain undisturbed, and little-known caves are rarely visited other than by the resident bats. Don't expect marked paths, though – this is relatively uncharted and challenging terrain.

It's a good idea to take a guided walk first, if only so that you can identify Cayman's poisonous trees and take evasive action. A visit to the Botanic Park is also highly recommended – it's a lovely place to spend a morning, and the self-guided woodland trail offers another opportunity to recognise various native trees. For guided walks, including the Mastic Trail, contact Silver Thatch Excursions, Ecoventures or Explore Cayman (see pages 80–1).

Before you set off on your own, get hold of a copy of the relevant 1:25,000 Ordnance Survey map and plan your route, preferably telling someone where you're going. You'll need good shoes as the terrain can be very unforgiving. Take plenty of water and some good insect repellent, particularly in the rainy season – Cayman mosquitoes can be voracious.

The best times to see birds are in the early hours of the morning or a couple of hours before sunset. A good place to start is the Botanic Park, where all the island's landbirds have been spotted, and a good proportion of the aquatics as well. Similarly, the Mastic Trail is an excellent place for birdwatching, with some unexpected sightings at any time of the year. For aquatic birds, Meagre Bay Pond just to the east of Bodden Town is a good venue, as are Governor Michael Gore Bird Sanctuary and the bird sanctuary in West Bay by Pappagallo's restaurant. To see the West Indian whistling-duck, head for Willie Ebanks' farm in North Side. Malportas Pond at the edge of the farm is a haven for this species, Cayman's only native duck.

Keen birdwatchers are welcome to join the Cayman Islands Bird Club on one of their regular outings, usually on Saturday mornings. Contact them through the National Trust, tel: 949 0121. Alternatively, call Silver Thatch (see page 81) and get the first-hand benefit of Geddes Hislop's years of experience on a guided birdwatching trip, perhaps on the Mastic Trail.

Patricia E Bradley's *Birds of the Cayman Islands* (see *Further Reading*, page 226) not only covers around 200 species to be seen on the islands, but also gives details of the best locations for birdwatching as well. A handy checklist derived from the book is also available from bookshops and gift shops.

Zebra butterfly

George Town and
Seven Mile Beach

Mention Grand Cayman to almost anyone who
has been there, and it is usually Seven Mile
Beach that springs first to mind. This
seemingly endless stretch of white-sand beach
effectively forms the centre of Grand Cayman's
highly sophisticated tourist industry. George

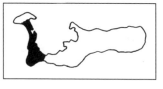

Town, by contrast, could pass for a small seaside resort town, the clapboard
houses that line the small harbour hardly being the stuff of which financial
capitals are made. Yet here, too, there is much to attract the visitor. While Seven
Mile Beach has the hotels and upmarket shops, George Town has the history
and the sense of place that, taken together, serve to make Cayman unique. A
duty-free shopping emporium par excellence, yes, but somehow George Town
seems to have taken this on board and still retained a character of its own.

WHERE TO STAY

The whole range of accommodation is available on Grand Cayman, with the
most expensive and luxurious hotels situated on Seven Mile Beach. Pressure on
building land here is huge, with beachfront land prices, at over US$50,000 per
linear foot, some of the highest in the world. The most beautiful area of Seven
Mile Beach is to the north, but hotels to the south have the added advantage of
easy proximity to George Town. Places on the southern side of George Town
tend to be smaller and more secluded, though the occasional aircraft coming in
to land may disturb your afternoon siesta. For accommodation in West Bay,
including the northern end of Seven Mile Beach, see page 151. For elsewhere on
the island, see pages 163, 167, 169 and 172. For an alphabetical list of all
accommodation, see *Appendix 1*, page 223.

All prices quoted are subject to 10% government accommodation tax and a
further 10% service charge, unless otherwise stated.

Hotels

Pretty well all hotels, villas and guesthouses have rooms with en-suite
bathrooms, and most offer a wide range of facilities for the tourist, including
some good restaurants which are for the most part described separately below.
The larger hotels are also geared to the business traveller, with well-equipped
business centres and conference suites. Note that telephone calls made from a
hotel room and use of internet services at your hotel may cost significantly more
than from payphones or external internet cafés, although this is changing. Given

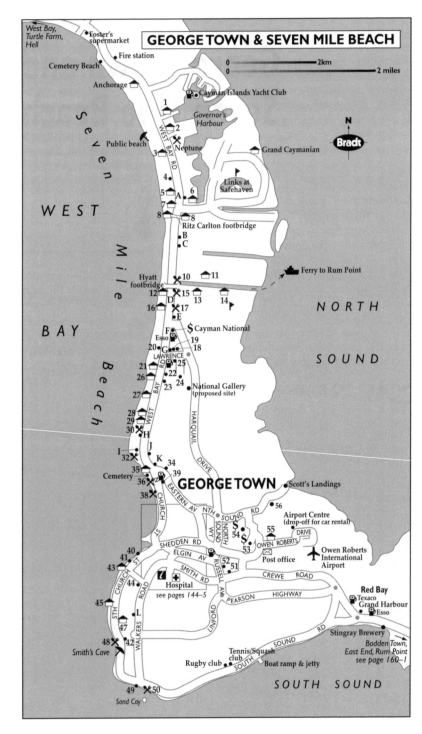

GEORGE TOWN & SEVEN MILE BEACH

0   2km
0   2 miles

West Bay,
Turtle Farm,
Hell

Foster's
supermarket

Fire station

Cemetery Beach

Anchorage

Cayman Islands Yacht Club

Public beach

Neptune

Grand Caymanian

WEST

Governor's
Harbour

Links at
Safehaven

N

Bradt

Ritz Carlton footbridge

Hyatt
footbridge

Ferry to Rum Point

NORTH

SOUND

MILE

BAY

Esso

Cayman National

LAWRENCE

National Gallery
(proposed site)

BEACH

WEST BAY ROAD

HARQUAIL DRIVE

Cemetery

GEORGE TOWN

Scott's Landings

Airport Centre
(drop-off for car rental)

EASTERN AV

NTH SOUND WY

SOUND RD

OWEN ROBERTS DRIVE

SHEDDEN RD

CHURCH ST

ELGIN AV

SMITH RD

RUSSELL AV

Post office

Owen Roberts
International
Airport

Hospital
see pages 144–5

LINFORD

PEARSON

CREWE ROAD

HIGHWAY

Red Bay

Texaco
Grand Harbour

Esso

STH CHURCH ST

WALKERS ROAD

Smith's Cove

Tennis/Squash
club

Rugby club

SOUND RD

SOUTH SOUND

Boat ramp & jetty

Stingray Brewery

Bodden Town,
East End, Rum Point
see page 160–1

Sand Cay

SOUTH SOUND

NUMERICAL KEY TO MAP OPPOSITE

Malls and squares
A Cayman Falls Centre
B Coconut Place
C The Strand
D Buckingham Square
E Regency Court
F Galleria Plaza
G West Shore Centre
H Seven Mile Shops
I Queen's Court
J Selkirk Plaza
K Merren Place
L Eden Centre

Hotels, restaurants and places of interest
1 Indies Suites
2 Courtyard Marriott/ Mangrove Grill
3 Avalon
4 Governor's Residence
5 Westin Casuarina/Casa Havana/Ferdinand's
6 Sunshine Suites
7 Villas of the Galleon
8 Ritz Carlton (under construction)

10 Ottmar's
11 Annie's Place
12 Hyatt Beach/ Hemingway's/Bamboo
13 Hyatt Regency/Garden Loggia/Britannia Grille
14 Britannia Villas
15 Decker's
16 Beach Club Hotel
17 Lone Star
18 Bed/World Gym/Matrix
19 Butterfly Farm
20 Royal Palms Beach Club/ Reef Grill
21 Marriott/Peninsula
22 Aqua Beach/Next Level
23 Coconut Joe's
24 Harquail Theatre/ Cayman National Cultural Centre
25 Cinema/Cimboco/ Marquee Plaza
26 Comfort Suites/Stingers
27 Seven Mile Beach Resort
28 Plantation Village
29 Treasure Island/Hook's Seafood Grotto/Athena

30 Big Daddy's/Mezza
32 Wharf
34 National Trust
35 Harbour View
36 Tree House
38 Lobster Pot/Bob Soto's
39 Kirk Supermarket
40 Eden Rock Dive Centre
41 Don Foster's
42 Pure Art
43 Seaview/Naked Fish
44 Adam's Guest House
45 Sunset House/Seaharvest/ Cathy Church's Photography
47 Eldemire's Guest House
48 Grand Old House
49 Dr Carey's
50 Crow's Nest
51 Farmer's Market
52 Cayman Islands National Archive
53 Foster's Supermarket
54 Tortuga Rum Cake Factory
55 Sammy's Airport Inn
56 Conch Shell House

ALPHABETICAL KEY TO MAP OPPOSITE

Malls and squares
Buckingham Square	D
Cayman Falls Centre	A
Coconut Place	B
Eden Centre	L
Galleria Plaza	F
Merren Place	K
Queen's Court	I
Regency Court	E
Selkirk Plaza	J
Seven Mile Shops	H
The Strand	C
West Shore Centre	G

Hotels, restaurants and places of interest
Adam's Guest House	44
Annie's Place	11
Aqua Beach	22
Athena	29
Avalon	3
Bamboo	12
Beach Club Hotel	16
Bed	18
Big Daddy's	30
Britannia Grille	13
Britannia Villas	14
Butterfly Farm	19
Casa Havana	5
Cayman Islands National Archive	52

Cayman National Cultural Centre	24
Cimboco	25
Cinema	25
Coconut Joe's	23
Comfort Suites	26
Conch Shell House	56
Courtyard Marriott	2
Crow's Nest	50
Decker's	15
Don Foster's	41
Dr Carey's	49
Eden Rock Dive Centre	40
Eldemire's Guest House	47
Farmer's Market	51
Ferdinand's	5
Foster's Supermarket	53
Garden Loggia	13
Governor's Residence	4
Grand Old House	48
Harbour View	35
Harquail Theatre	24
Hemingway's	12
Hook's Seafood Grotto	29
Hyatt Beach	12
Hyatt Regency	13
Indies Suites	1
Kirk Supermarket	39
Lobster Pot	38
Bob Soto's	38
Lone Star	17
Mangrove Grill	2

Marquee Plaza	25
Marriott	21
Matrix	18
Mezza	30
Naked Fish	43
National Trust	34
Next Level	22
Ottmar's	10
Peninsula	21
Plantation Village	28
Pure Art	42
Reef Grill	20
Ritz Carlton (under construction)	8
Royal Palms Beach Club	20
Sammy's Airport Inn	55
Seaview	43
Seven Mile Beach Resort	27
Stingers	26
Sunset House	45
Seaharvest	45
Cathy Church's Photography	45
Sunshine Suites	6
Tortuga Rum Cake Factory	54
Treasure Island	29
Tree House	36
Villas of the Galleon	7
Westin Casuarina	5
Wharf	32
World Gym	18

the ease with which you can pay by phonecard or credit card (see *Telephones, fax and internet*, page 61), it is simple to avoid these charges without the hassle of finding a public telephone. Note, too, that room safes may be subject to an additional daily charge of around US$2.50 – an iniquitous practice that really ought to be challenged.

Luxury

Hyatt Regency West Bay Rd; PO Box 1588 GT; tel: 949 1234, US toll free 800 55 HYATT; fax: 949 8528; web: www.hyatt.com (289 rooms, including 53 beachfront suites)

Straddling West Bay Rd just three miles north of George Town and 20 minutes from the airport, the Hyatt is really two separate hotels, linked by an integral bridge. To the east, set amid palm-lined lawns and cooling fountains, and bordering the Britannia Golf Club, all is calm and luxury, while acoss the road, right on Seven Mile Beach, the atmosphere is rather more upbeat. All rooms have one king or two double beds, AC, bath and shower, TV, minibar and safe. Restaurants include Hemingways, the Garden Loggia, the Britannia Grille and Bamboo, plus several bars and a coffee shop. Six swimming pools, whirlpools and swim-up bar; floodlit tennis courts, Jack Nicklaus-designed golf course, fitness centre and beauty spa, variety of shops. Diving and other watersports, including own marina, through Red Sail Sports. Supervised activities for children 3–12 years. Car and moped rental. Business, conference and banqueting facilities.

Rates per double room per night: low season US$220–1,350 through to high season US$415–1,750.

Marriott Beach Resort PO Box 30371, West Bay Rd; tel: 949 0088, US toll free 800 228 9290; fax: 949 0288; email: marriott@candw.ky; web: www.marriott.com (309 rooms, 4 suites)

The Marriott's beachfront location on Seven Mile Beach has in the past been somewhat undermined by erosion of the beach at this point, although a strip of sand has now returned naturally to the vicinity. The design of the hotel is one of elegance, with balconies overlooking palm-edged fountains and wrought-iron bar stools. Each room has AC, telephone, TV and minibar. Restaurants and bars include The Grille, open for breakfast 7.00–11.00am, and the Peninsula. Gift shop and boutiques; Avis car hire. For the athletic, there's a swimming pool and whirlpool, exercise room and jogging trail. Diving and watersports through Red Sail Sports.

Rates per room per night, low–high season: from standard US$199–229 to two-bedroom suite US$859–1,059

Ritz Carlton Web: www.ritzcarlton.com. When it opens in mid 2005, after considerable environmental controversy and numerous delays, the Ritz Carlton will be the first five-star hotel on the island, with a projected 366 rooms, incorporating 71 condominiums (dubbed 'The Residences'), five restaurants, a shopping arcade, a luxury spa, a tennis centre and a nine-hole golf course designed by Greg Norman. It will also be the first to be allowed to break the three-storey limit on buildings on Seven Mile Beach, an unfortunate precedent that foreshadows significant redevelopment on this already overstretched part of the island. With beachfront condos starting at US$2.1 million, the luxury doesn't come cheap.

Westin Casuarina PO Box 30620 SMB, West Bay Rd; tel: 945 3800, US toll free 800 228 3000; fax: 945 3804; email: salesing@candw.ky; web: www.westincasuarina.com (343 rooms, 4 suites)

This elegant if somewhat labyrinthine hotel is set right on Seven Mile Beach, its old-world décor masking thoroughly modern facilities. Each room has TV, minibar, ceiling fan, safe and marble bathroom, and most have French doors with balconies. Two restaurants, La Casa Havana and Ferdinand's, huge glass-fronted ballroom, and conference facilities. Two swimming pools, swim-up bar, fitness centre, Hibiscus Spa. Diving and other watersports through Red Sail Sports. Jewellery and gift shops.
Rates per room per night, low–high season, based on single/double occupancy: from island view US$226–349 up to deluxe suite US$1,390–2,050. Additional person US$25 per night.

Medium class

Comfort Suites and Resort PO Box 30238 SMB, West Bay Rd; tel: 354 945 7300, US toll free 800 517 4000; fax: 345 945 7400; email: comfort@candw.ky; web: www.caymancomfort.com (108 suites)
Conveniently located towards the southern end of Seven Mile Beach, this US chain hotel has improved in recent years. Studio and deluxe studio rooms, plus apartments, each have a kitchen, living area, TV and safe. Rooms are also available for the disabled. Gift/dive shop, fitness centre, spa, business centre, conference rooms, laundry, swimming pool; games room, scuba centre, poolside restaurant (Stingers) and bar. There's direct access to the beach from the pool via a narrow path, although shifting sands mean that the water sometimes comes quite close to the wall. Just to the right there's good snorkelling – be careful not to disturb the reef. Diving (Don Foster's), with on-site dive shop. Other watersports by arrangement.
Rates (including buffet breakfast) for two people per night, low/high season: studio US$145/205; deluxe studio US$185/215; one-bedroom suite US$175/235. Additional person US$15 per night, up to maximum of four (six in deluxe studio). Two-bedroom and master suites, sleeping six and four people respectively, from US$230/335.
Courtyard Marriott PO Box 30364 SMB, 1590 West Bay Rd; tel: 946 4433, US toll free 800 MARRIOTT; fax: 946 4434; email: hicayman@candw.ky; web: www.marriott.com (233 rooms)
Originally opened in 2000 as a Holiday Inn, the Courtyard Marriott is located on the opposite side of the road to Seven Mile Beach, close to the public beach; with its primary focus on the business market, it makes little concession to the Caribbean environment. That said, the staff are friendly and helpful, there's a good private beach immediately opposite, with a beach bar and restaurant, and facilities for the disabled are excellent. Rooms each have one king-size or two double beds, and include AC, minibar, TV and telephone. Mangrove Grill, bar, business centre, Avis car rental, gift shop, laundry. Swimming pool, fitness centre. Diving/watersports through Red Sail Sports.
Rates for one or two people per night, low/high season: island view US$145/220; ocean view US$165/240. Additional adult US$20 per night.
Indies Suites PO Box 2070 GT, Foster Drive, West Bay Rd; tel: 945 5025, US toll free 800 654 3130; fax: 945 5024; email: indiessuites@worldnet.att.net (40 suites)
Situated opposite Seven Mile Beach, the family-owned Indies Suites with its distinctive blue roof is five miles from George Town, and also offers timeshare. Each suite has one king size or two double beds, AC, kitchen, bathroom, living room with sofa bed, TV, balcony or patio. Facilities include swimming pool and Jacuzzi, with poolside bar and parties. Dive courses with Red Sail Sports. Beach access across the road.
Rates (including complimentary breakfast and sunset cruise): Low season US$180–215; high season US$299–360.

Sammy's Airport Inn PO Box 10646 APO, Owen Roberts Drive, George Town; tel: 945 2100 fax: 945 2330 (60 rooms)
Located very close to the airport, Sammy's is a modern, but rather dark old-style hotel owned by Best Western, and is best suited to business travellers on a short visit. Small, simple rooms have TV and AC, and facilities include a restaurant, bar and swimming pool. Free shuttle bus to the airport.
Rates per room: low season US$120; high season US$125 plus 20%.

Sunshine Suites PO Box 30095 SMB; 1112 West Bay Rd; tel: 949 3000, US toll free 877 786 1110; fax: 949 1200; email: mail@sunshinesuites.com; web: www.sunshinesuites.com (132 suites)
Opposite the Westin on West Bay Rd, behind Cayman Falls Plaza, this three-storey yellow-painted complex is in a peaceful location well back from the road, but within easy reach of Seven Mile Beach. Wooden outside steps lead to light, airy rooms with a personal touch. Studios, deluxe suites and one-bedroom suites all have living/dining area, kitchenette (no oven), TV and telephone. Swimming pool, picnic areas with barbecues, laundry, dive lockers. The poolside Sunshine Grill is open 7.00am–10.00pm. Diving and fishing with Fisheye, Captain Marvin's or Treasure Island Divers.
Rates per person per night, low/high season: studio US$110/195; deluxe US$170/215; one-bedroom US$195/250. Additional person US$10 per night, up to maximum of four (two in studio suites). Children under 12 stay free in parent's room. Limited maid service.

Treasure Island Resort PO Box 1817 GT, 269 West Bay Rd; tel: 949 7777; fax: 949 8672; email: admintir@candw.ky; web: www.treasureislandresort.net. US: 225 E Dania Beach Bd, Suite 210, Dania Beach, FL33004; toll free 800 203 0775 fax: 945 924 1515; fax: 945 924 1511; email: tir@vacationplaces.com (281 rooms)
At the southern end of Seven Mile Beach, just a mile from George Town, this rather functional-looking hotel is surrounded by artificial rock gardens complete with several waterfalls. All rooms have two double beds, or one king-size, with AC/ceiling fan, TV, telephone, safe, patio or balcony. Billy Bones snack bar. Hook restaurant. Two swimming pools, one with swim-up bar; tennis and beach volleyball; bicycle hire. Watersports include diving through Bob Soto, with deep-sea fishing, sailing and windsurfing by arrangement. Duty-free, dive and souvenir shops, plus beauty salon. A steel band plays in the open-plan lobby 6.30–8.00pm on Mon only.
Rates per room, per night, based on single/double occupancy, low/high season: standard US$155/220; pool view US$170/240; partial ocean view US$190/260. Additional person US$30 per night, up to maximum of four (two in studio suites). Children 17 and under stay free in parent's room.

All-inclusive resorts
Beach Club Hotel & Dive Resort PO Box 903 GT, West Bay Rd; tel: 949 8100, US toll free 800 482 DIVE; fax: 945 5167; email: cayresv@candw.ky; web: www.caymanresorthotels.com (41 rooms)
This colourful complex of Caribbean-style villas on the beach is an all-inclusive resort, under the same ownership as Spanish Bay Reef (see page 153) and popular with families. Prices include breakfast, lunch, snacks and dinner, plus unlimited bar drinks (excluding champagne), all non-motorised watersports and shore diving, dive equipment (except wetsuits), taxes and gratuities. A shuttle service runs between here and Spanish Bay. All rooms have AC, TV, bath and shower, balcony or terrace; superior and oceanfront rooms

are also available. Small swimming pool, beach bar and restaurant (the latter both open to the public); tennis court. Wide range of watersports and diving. Evening live entertainment. *Rates* per person per night, based on double occupancy, low/high season: standard US$180/375; superior US$200/420; oceanfront US$225/465 (for single occupancy, double these rates). Children under six free (maximum two per room); under 12 US$50 per night (boat dives not included). Extra person US$150 per night. Dive supplement daily two-tank dive add US$66 per day. Wedding packages available.

Dive lodges

Grand Cayman's dive lodges are located away from the bustle of Seven Mile Beach, with two just to the south of George Town where there is good shore diving. Most of the guests are here for the diving, and appreciate facilities such as dive lockers, rinse tanks and drying racks for their kit. See also Cayman Diving Lodge and Compass Point at East End, page 172.

Coconut Harbour South Church St
Once a favourite with divers, Coconut Harbour suffered severe hurricane damage a couple of years ago and in 2004 was up for sale.

Seaview Hotel and Dive Centre PO Box 260 GT; tel: 945 0558, US toll free 866 945 0558; fax: 945 0559; email: seadive@candw.ky; web: www.seaviewdivers.com (15 rooms)
Built in 1947, and probably the oldest (and least expensive) hotel on the island, the Seaview has for years been popular with the diving fraternity, who come back time and again and are welcomed by friendly and helpful staff. A cheerful yellow-and-blue building, it's a no-frills place situated on the waterfront (no beach), approximately ten minutes' walk south of George Town and a similar distance from Smith's Cove. Simple en-suite twin rooms have twin or king-size beds with AC/fan and telephone, with the recent addition of a small fridge, microwave and coffee maker, but the 'sea view' is reserved for the public rooms and terrace. Also new is the introduction of free wireless internet for guests. Outside is a bar and the Naked Fish restaurant. There's a large salt-water pool, good shore diving from the resort itself and easy access to the varied dive sites of the west coast, north wall and South Sound. Diving with Treasure Island Divers. *Rates* per night high season: single US$109; double US$119; low season US$99 up to 3 people. All-inclusive dive packages available on request.

Sunset House PO Box 479 GT, South Church St, George Town; tel: 949 711; US 888 281 3826, toll free 800 854 4767; fax: 949 7101; email: sunsethouse@sunsethouse.com; web: www.sunsethouse.com (59 rooms)
Sunset House claims to be the only resort in the Cayman Islands 'designed by divers, operated by divers, for divers'. Be that as it may, it's certainly diver orientated, with a 95% diving clientele, many of whom return year after year to this sprawling complex that feels more hotel than dive lodge. All rooms have private bathroom, AC, TV, radio alarm and telephone. Courtyard rooms have two double beds or one king or two twin beds plus shared balcony; oceanview rooms have king or two double beds, ceiling fans, private balcony; suites also have living/dining area with sofa, fridge; apartments also have kitchenette and dining room (but no fan). Swimming pool, outside bar. Seaharvest restaurant and bar. And for photographers, this is the home of Cathy Church's Photo Centre (see page 139), so advice, equipment and film developing are right on hand. *Rates* per room per night (two people, low/high season): courtyard US$130/165; ocean view US$170/210; apartment US$210/300. Two-tank dive packages per person, low/high

season, from US$421/642 for three/four nights with courtyard view, to US$1,165/1,304 for seven nights with sea view, based on two people sharing.

Guesthouses

Adam's Guest House 84 Melmac Av; tel: 949 2512; fax: 949 0919 (6 rooms)
Olga Adam has welcomed visitors to her guesthouse since 1990, offering homely accommodation with cooking facilities. Located off South Church St, it is about halfway between George Town and Smith's Cove. Each room has a private bathroom, cable TV and AC/ceiling fan. The three rooms with private entrance also have a fridge and toaster/microwave; those in the adjoining building share a kitchen with washer/dryer, dining room and living room, all with ceiling fans. Laundry, barbecue, picnic tables and telephone.
Rates per room per night: low/high season US$75/85. No personal cheques. Weekly maid service.

Annie's Place PO Box 616 GT, 282 Andrew Drive, Snug Harbour; tel: 945 5505/5693; fax: 945 4547; email: ampm@candw.ky; web: www.anniesplace.ky (2 rooms)
A few minutes' walk from Seven Mile Beach, and three miles from George Town, this comfortable home-from-home has rooms with en-suite bathroom, AC/ceiling fan, TV and safe. Guest laundry; use of telephone and fax by arrangement. A full breakfast is available in the dining room or screened courtyard.
Rates per room per night, low/high season: single US$75–85, double US$90–100

Eldemire's Guest House PO Box 482 GT, Pebbles Way, South Church St; tel: 949 5387; fax: 949 6987; email: tootie@eldemire.com; web: www.eldemire.com (13 units)
Tucked away opposite the now closed Coconut Harbour, this rather ramshackle guesthouse is just a short distance from Smith's Cove. Rooms, studios and apartment are modern and clean, though, with a private bathroom and AC/ceiling fan; the studios and apartment have kitchen facilities.
Rates per night, low/high season: double room US$86/99; studio US$99/115; apartment US$100/125 up to US$165/200, plus 10% tax. Maid service included. No credit cards or personal cheques.

Self-catering villas and apartments

The following is a small selection of the properties available on or near Seven Mile Beach. Most rates are exclusive of 10% government accommodation tax and service – which is usually around 5% for condominiums. Surcharges may apply at Christmas and New Year. Special discounts may apply for children, and dive packages are often available on request.

Anchorage Condominiums PO Box 30986 SMB, West Bay Rd; tel: 945 4088; fax: 945 5001; email: smanchor@candw.ky; web: www.theanchorage.com (15 villas)
Located at the north end of Seven Mile Beach, these two-bedroom, two-bathroom villas each have kitchen, AC, TV, telephone and balcony or screened porch overlooking the beach; some also have a third room. Daily maid service and laundry facilities. Swimming pool, tennis.
Rates per night, low/high season: garden view US$170/240; oceanfront US$265/395

Avalon Condominiums PO Box 31236 SMB, West Bay Rd; tel: 945 4171 ext 100; fax: 945 4189; email: avalon_c@candw.ky; web: www.cayman.org/Avalon/ (14 villas)
Located at the north end of Seven Mile Beach, each of these seafront three-bedroom

villas has three bathrooms, AC, kitchen, TV, telephone and screened balcony, plus private garage. Daily maid service. Swimming pool, fitness centre.

Rates per villa per night, low/high season: US$495–560/710–785. All rates subject to 6% gratuity.

Grand Caymanian Golf Resort PO Box 31495 SMB, Crystal Harbour at Safehaven; tel: 949 3100, US toll free 1 888 452 4545; fax: 949 3161; email: info@grandcaymanian.ky; web: www.grandcaymanian.ky (132 suites/villas)

Located on North Sound with direct access to the neighbouring Links at Safehaven golf course, this timeshare resort has a sandy area for beach games etc, but the coast here is ironshore so a shuttle bus ferries guests to the Hyatt's private stretch of Seven Mile Beach a couple of miles away. One-bedroom suites and two-bedroom villas have king-size beds, kitchen, bathroom, AC, private balconies and computer data ports. Daily maid service.

Rates per unit per night, low/high season: standard room US$120/185 (two people); suite US$175/255 (four people); villa US$265–330/385–550 (six people)

Harbour View PO Box 176 GT, North Church St, George Town; tel: 949 5681/4168; fax: 949 5308; email: harborvu@candw.ky; web: www.cayman.com.ky/com/harview (9 units)

One of Grand Cayman's best accommodation deals, Harbour View is an exceptionally welcoming complex located just at the start of Seven Mile Beach, and within easy walking distance of shops and restaurants. The comfortable one-bedroom apartments and studios, all en suite, have separate living area, kitchen, AC/ceiling fans, TV and telephone. There is a beach with private jetty, and a separate guest laundry.

Rates for two people per night, low/high season: studio US$75/$99, deluxe studio US$99/125, apartment US$99/$149. Additional guests US$10 per night. All rates subject to 15% gratuity.

Plantation Village PO Box 30871 SMB, West Bay Rd; tel: 949 4199, US toll free 800 822 8903; fax: 949 0646; email: pvcres@candw.ky; web: www.cayman.org/pvbr (71 apartments)

This timeshare complex, one of the first to be built on Seven Mile Beach, also has apartments for rent on a daily basis. Each apartment has two bathrooms, AC, kitchen, TV, telephone and screened patio. Laundry, maid service. Two swimming pools, tennis court, children's playground, gas barbecues, beach cabanas. Kayaks and bicycles available to guests.

Rates per night for two people, low/high season: pool view US$185–310, ocean view US$210–340; oceanfront US$265–405.

Seven Mile Beach Resort & Club PO Box 30742 SMB, West Bay Rd; tel: 949 0332; fax: 949 0331; email: smbres@candw.ky; web: www.7mile.ky (38 condominiums)

Set back off the southern end of Seven Mile Beach, close to George Town, the resort's two-bedroom condominiums each have two bathrooms, kitchen, AC, patio or private balcony and satellite TV/VCR. Swimming pool with waterfalls, tennis courts, laundry, gift and dive shop, spa. Short-term membership of World Gym included. Maid service and babysitting available.

Rates per night, up to four people, low/high season: US$250/450; children under 12 free; additional guest US$15 per night. All rates subject to 5% gratuity.

Villas of the Galleon PO Box 1797 GT, West Bay Rd; tel: 945 4311/4433; fax: 945 4705; email: vogcay@candw.ky. web: www.villasofthegalleon.com (59 apartments)

Just to the south of the Westin, these highly recommended apartments with all amenities, including AC/ceiling fans, sea view, free local phone calls and full maid service, are available for short-term rental. One- or two-bedroom units each have dining area, living room and fully equipped kitchen.

Rates per apartment per day, low/high season: one-bedroom (two people)
US$275–295/$345–385; two-bedroom (four people) US$315–350/$440–490; three-bedroom (six people) US$430–465/$620–675.

WHERE TO EAT

The standard of restaurant food throughout the island is excellent, although many locals reckon that some of the best food is to be had to the east and north of George Town (see *Chapters 6* and *7*). Sunday brunch is something of an institution, too – for a real treat, try the Westin.

For a preview of menus at some of Grand Cayman's restaurants, pick up of a copy of the free *Menu Guide*, available from hotels and tourist venues islandwide. It's an advertising vehicle, of course, so there are no independent reviews, but it's helpful nonetheless.

The geographical distinction between George Town and Seven Mile Beach is not particularly clear on the ground. For the purposes of this list, George Town is defined as the area up to and including Eastern Avenue to the north, and out towards Red Bay to the south and east.

George Town

What George Town lacks in hotels, it makes up for in restaurants. The small capital's places to eat range from top-class seafood restaurants, with views (and prices) to match, to wine bars and Italian brasseries. Cayman-style food is a speciality of some, and well worth seeking out, and even outside the main town, towards the airport for example, there are gems to be found. With the combined attentions of both the business market and visitors off the cruise ships, many venues are particularly busy at lunchtime.

Restaurants

Bacchus Fort St; tel: 949 5747. Just a short walk from the harbour, Bacchus was renovated in 2003 and has the atmosphere of a large wine bar. Frequented by ex-pats as well as tourists, it's at its most busy in the early evenings, giving way to candlelit tranquillity later. Chef/owner Keith Griffin is head of the Cayman Culinary Society and creativity is much in evidence, with tapas platters at CI$12.50 and some innovative takes on fish and seafood, as well as meat and the odd vegetarian dish. Prices are unexpectedly reasonable by Cayman standards. Open daily for lunch and dinner. Happy hour 5.00–7.00pm daily, with free tapas Fri only.

Bayside North Church St; tel: 946 2482. This delightful first-floor Indian restaurant, adorned with colourful oriental drapes and lanterns, has a regular lunchtime buffet. Open daily except Sunday lunch, 11.30–2.30pm, 5.30–10.00pm.

Big Bamboo North Church St; tel: 949 3080. The new home of the micro brewery that was formerly at Big Daddy's is in the centre of George Town, on the waterfront, and is open every day. Although strictly just a bar, it is affiliated to Harold's, a laid-back eatery on the same site, where local dishes are served Mon–Sat from breakfast onwards, and the jerk chicken is hugely popular. To complete the package, there's also Kirk's Sea Tours on the deck, with watersports, diving and snorkelling.

Brasserie Cricket Sq, off Elgin Av; tel: 945 1815. Regularly frequented at lunchtime by local business people, the colonial-style Brasserie is in a class of its own, with consistent food, welcoming service and a good ambience. A special Wed evening 'bon vivant' menu includes 12 dishes from around the world at CI$7 per course, and on Sun evenings, a three-course meal with a bottle of wine costs CI$65 per couple, plus service. Open Mon–Fri 11.30am–2.30pm, 5.30–10.00pm; Sat/Sun 5.30–10.00pm.

Breadfruit Tree Café Eastern Av; tel: 945 2124. More of a diner than a restaurant, this is a good place to come for a traditional Cayman meal after a night out. Open daily, 11.00am until the small hours.

Breezes by the Bay Cardinall Av; tel: 943 8439; web: www.breezesbythebay.com. Formerly the Landmark pub, this upstairs restaurant and bar with a wide choice of imported draught beers remains popular with expats, especially at the end of a working day during the daily 5.00–7.00pm happy hour (which on Friday extends to closing time). Live music Fri and Sat. Open Mon–Thu 8.00am–10.00pm; Fri to 11.00pm; Sat 9.00am–10.00pm; Sun 10.00am–9.00pm.

Casanova South Church St; tel: 949 7633. This small, intimate restaurant has a new location in George Town, but retains its views across West Bay. Run by 'mad Italians', it's particularly popular at lunchtimes for its excellent (and excellent-value) pasta, but evenings are busy too. Open Mon–Sat 11.30am–10.00pm.

Champion House 43 Eastern Av; tel: 949 2190. The original Champion House is independent from its larger offspring, though both are located in a large car park off Eastern Av. Traditional dishes (do try the goat curry) are served throughout the day and sometimes on until the small hours: Sun–Thu 10.00am–midnight; Fri/Sat 10.00am–3.00am. Excellent value.

Champion House II 43 Eastern Av; tel: 949 7882. Tucked away on Eastern Av, but worth a visit for its authentic Cayman dishes at reasonable prices, Champion House II also offers lunch-time buffets specialising in different world cuisines. For evening theme specials, call in advance. Open Mon–Sat 7.00am–midnight; Sun 8.00am–11.00pm. West Indian Sunday brunch 8.00am–2.00pm. Breakfast buffet Mon–Sat.

Corita's Copper Kettle Dolphin Centre, off Eastern Av; tel: 949 7078. A simple restaurant offering good-value meals in no-frills surroundings. Open from 10.00am.

Crow's Nest 104 South Sound Rd; tel: 949 9366. Situated on the right heading south from George Town on the coast road, the Crow's Nest is approximately 1½ miles beyond Grand Old House. Owned and run by Caymanians, it is set in an old Cayman house with beautiful views over to the tiny island of Sand Cay and across South Sound. Though the place has gone more upmarket in recent years, and prices are now up there with the best, the service remains relaxed and friendly; don't come in a hurry. The emphasis is on the traditional (though be prepared to be surprised): spiny Caribbean lobster stuffed and baked is a long-term favourite, and the key-lime mousse is superb; there are also several vegetarian options. Children are genuinely welcome. Open daily 11.30am–3.00pm, 5.30–10.00pm.

Grand Old House South Church St; tel: 949 9333; web: www.grandoldhouse.ky. Just a few minutes' drive south of George Town, on the waterfront, this 1908 plantation great house confers an air of timeless elegance. Lunch on the fan-cooled porch surrounded by palm trees overlooking the sea, and you won't break the bank. For a more formal affair, linger over a serious meal in the gracious surroundings of the air-conditioned dining room, or host that special party in the wine room. Cuisine is 'European and New World Caribbean'; the wine list is one of the island's best. Well patronised by the business community, the restaurant is also a popular venue for wedding parties, as attested by the 'Wedding Gallery' in the grounds. Open Mon–Fri 11.45am–2.00pm, daily 6.00–10.00pm, with pianist playing Mon–Sat evening.

Hard Rock Café 43 South Church St; tel: 945 2020; web: www.hardrock.com. Few introductions are necessary to this well-known US chain, where lively rock music accompanies huge portions of American-style food. On-site retail shop. Open daily 10.00am–10.00pm.

Lobster Pot North Church St; tel: 949 2736. A good, traditional choice, perhaps for a special occasion, the Lobster Pot is one of Grand Cayman's oldest restaurants. The first-floor dining room affords panoramic views to the west, and at 6.45pm each evening you can watch the tarpon being fed. As you'd expect from the name, the menu majors on seafood, most of which is caught by the chef himself, a keen fisherman. Set back behind the dining area is a long, dark wine bar. Open Mon–Fri 11.30am–2.30pm; daily 5.30–10.00pm.

Naked Fish South Church St; tel: 945 0558. The lively restaurant and bar adjoining the Seaview Hotel has been revamped with a menu specialising in seafood and steaks. Sit outside on a large terrace with an equally large screen showing sport, or go inside for a rather quieter meal. Open Mon–Fri 7.00am–1.00pm; Sat and Sun 7.00am–12.00pm.

Paradise Bar & Grill 96 South Church St, George Town; tel: 945 1444/3319. This lively and relaxed establishment, with its inside restaurant, bar, open deck and stretch of beach, has great views of the harbour and is popular with cruise-ship visitors. American-style food of the burger and chips variety, plus separate children's menu. Snorkels and masks available for hire. Open Mon–Fri 7.30am–10.00pm; Sat/Sun 8.30am–9.30pm. Happy hour 5.00–7.00pm daily.

Rackams Pub North Church St; tel: 945 3860. Despite the name, Rackams is also a restaurant, right in the centre of George Town on the waterfront. An upbeat, relaxed place, with an extensive cocktail menu, the service is friendly, the food varied – US orientated with a Caribbean flair – and tarpon feeding at 7.30pm from the deck is a further attraction. And with outdoor air conditioning, you can even stay outside *and* stay cool! Open daily 9.00am–10.00pm; bar 10.00am till late.

Singh's Roti Shop off Shedden Rd; tel: 946 7684. One of George Town's best-kept secrets, with a laid-back atmosphere and calypso music, is well off the beaten track. Trinidadian owned and run, it's open for lunch and dinner, with chicken roti at CI$5, and slightly more for shrimp, goat or beef. If you're not a big fan of hot food, ask for 'no pepper'!

Seaharvest South Church St, tel: 945 1383. The restaurant at Sunset House is right on the waterfront, with seafood as its speciality but with plenty of alternatives. Dine outside, or in air-conditioned comfort. Specials include an Indian night on Monday and Thursday, while on Sunday there's an 'all-you-can-eat' barbecue for just CI$15.95 plus service. Open daily 7.00am–10.00pm. Bar open Mon–Fri 9.00am–1.00am; Sat to midnight; Sun 11.00am–midnight.

Sammy's Owen Roberts Dr; tel: 945 2100. Within walking distance of the airport, the restaurant at Sammy's has a simple menu featuring seafood and West Indian dishes. Open 7.00am–10.00pm.

Smugglers Cove North Church St; tel: 945 6003; web: www.smugglers.ky. At first glance, this Caribbean café/grill is defined by dark wood décor and a cosy, old-world feel, but hidden behind is a seafront deck that's a great place to dine overlooking the water. Big on seafood, it's particularly popular at lunchtime. Open Mon–Fri 10.30am–2.30pm; daily 5.30–10.30pm.

Thai Restaurant Elizabethan Sq; tel: 949 6141; web: www.thairest.com. The setting of this new Thai restaurant may not look up to much, but the extensive menu offers authentic Thai cuisine at sensible prices, with the lunch combo at CI$8 particularly good value. Portions are 'gigantic'. Internet access on site. Open Mon–Sat 7.00–10.00am, 11.00am–3.00pm, 6.00–10.00pm.

Tree House North Church St; tel: 945 0155; web: www.almondtreehouse.com. This casual beachfront bar and grill in an idyllic tree-backed location has its own sandy beach with sun loungers, and is a good spot for snorkelling. The menu consists of grills, salads, sandwiches etc, as well as fresh seafood and tapas, and prices are very reasonable, so it's a great place for families. Live music every Tue with a buffet menu at CI$19.95. Daily happy hour; tarpon feeding at 8.30pm. Open every day, 11.00am to late.

Cafés and snack bars

While there are a few US fast-food chains to be found in George Town, including KFC near the museum and Baskin Robbins behind the post office, the town's more original venues are worth seeking out. You could also try fish fritters from Kman Time Fry Fish on the harbour, open 11.00am–4.00am.

Carib-Bean Coffee House Harbour Place; tel: 943 8463. A modern café on the first floor of this new shopping complex, overlooking the harbour and open 7.00am–4.00pm. Next door and under the same ownership is the **Grape Vine** wine bar, open Mon–Fri 11.00am–8.00pm.

Coffee & Bites Bodmer Bldg, behind the post office; tel: 945 4892

Corita's Edward St; tel: 949 2696. Old-fashioned café near the library that offers some traditional Cayman dishes and home-made 'lemon aid'. Open lunchtime only.

Craft Market Café Cardinall Av; tel: 945 7109. Simple, covered wooden café with friendly service close to the harbour and port terminals. The capital's best bargain for local fare at sensible prices, from patties to daily specials such as goat curry or jerk chicken, rice and plantain. Fruit punch or coconut water make a change from the international brands. Open daily 7.00am–4.30pm.

Daily Grind Edward St; tel: 945 1175. Located above Corita's and frequented predominantly by office workers. Freshly roasted coffee plus good selection of pastries, sandwiches etc. Open Mon–Fri 7.00am–4.00pm.

Jailhouse Café Goring Av. Simple café close to the museum with open-air seating. Snacks include local meat patties as well as hot dogs and ice-creams.

Ye Old English Bakery North Church St; tel: 945 2420; web: www.english-bakery.com. With its location at the junction with Mary St, this is a convenient place for breakfast or a snack lunch while you check out the internet. Open Mon–Sat 6.30am–4.00pm; Sun 8.00am–2.00pm.

Seven Mile Beach

In addition to the following, there will be five restaurants at the Ritz Carlton when it opens in 2005.

Aqua Beach West Bay Rd; tel: 946 6398. This laid-back newcomer opposite the Marriott dubs itself a 'power bar', similar in style to the nearby Coconut Joe's. Sit over a beer under thatched sunshades or adjourn to the deep terracotta restaurant enlivened by a large aquarium. Food with a Caribbean/Mexican slant is pretty good value. Open Tue–Fri 11.00am–1.00pm; Sat and Mon 4.00pm–1.00am; Sun midday–1.00am. Free entry to adjacent Next Level nightclub.

Asian Express Regency Court, West Bay Rd; tel: 946 0303. Small Chinese and Asian restaurant with takeaway service. Open Mon–Sat 11.00am–2.30pm; Mon–Thu 5.00–9.30pm; Fri/Sat to 10.00pm.

Athena Treasure Island Resort, West Bay Rd; tel: 945 8731. Just one of the restaurants at this resort, Athena's may sound and even look Greek, but pizzas alongside kebabs on the menu tell a different story.

Bamboo West Bay Rd; tel: 949 1234. The Hyatt's grill bar is a well-recommended sushi bar, with dark wood décor and an atmosphere more akin to downtown Tokyo or Manhattan than Cayman. Friendly service, music and cocktail menu. Open Mon–Fri 5.00pm–1.00am; Sat 5.00pm–midnight.

Bed Islander Complex, Lawrence Bd (opposite the cinema); tel: 949 7199. Popular bar and restaurant with a rather sleazy bedtime theme which belies the excellent food. Comprehensive and cosmopolitan menu with some innovative dishes reflects the background of the chefs. A good vegetarian selection includes several starters and main courses. Live music Wed, Sat. Ladies, watch out for the open-plan toilets! Open Mon–Sun 5.30pm–11.00pm; bar Mon–Fri to 1.00am; Sat/Sun to midnight.

Bella Capri West Bay Rd; tel: 945 4755. Tucked away next to The Strand, this comfortable Italian restaurant with tables on the open-air veranda was refurbished in 2004. Lunchtime 'all-you-can-eat' soup and salad bar CI$8.95 on Fridays only, 11.30am–2.30pm. Otherwise open daily 5.00–10.00pm.

Billy Bones Treasure Island Resort; tel: 945 7069. An informal poolside bar and grill.

La Bodega West Shore Centre, West Bay Rd; tel: 946 8115. Solid wooden furniture, tiled floors and simple white napiery take you to traditional Spain, but the menu is more Latin American with some Caribbean influence – and it's good. Eat in the evocatively decorated restaurant or amid the greenery on the shaded patio. Regular evening entertainment includes salsa classes on Wed and Sat from 8.00pm, and live jazz on Thu. Open Mon–Fri 11.30am–1.00am; Sat to midnight; Sun 5.00pm–midnight. Happy hour Fri.

Britannia Bar and Grille Britannia Golf Club, West Bay Rd; tel: 945 5600. Overlooking the golf course behind the Hyatt, relax in cool, screened comfort for lunch of salads, sandwiches and Mexican favourites. Open daily 11.00am–7.00pm; Sunday prime rib roast CI$28 from 5.00 to 8.00pm.

Café Mediterraneo Galleria Plaza, West Bay Rd; tel: 949 7427. This is one of those 'love it or hate it' places, with diners seemingly polarised. Sometimes excellent Italian food can be marred by decidedly erratic service. Do visit for the free salsa evenings on Thu/Fri nights from 9.00 to10.00pm, but consider going elsewhere if the boss is away. Open daily 11.00am–10.30pm; Sunday brunch 11.00am–3.00pm.

Canton Chinese Restaurant The Strand, West Bay Rd; tel: 945 3536. Open daily 11.30am–3.00pm, Sun–Thu 5.00–10.00pm; Fri/Sat to 10.30pm.

Casa Havana West Bay Rd; tel: 945 3800, ext 6017. Cayman's only AAA 4-diamond restaurant is based at the Westin Casuarina. This is a place for serious foodies, or for that very special treat, with a highly innovative menu (they call it Nuevo Latino), and a selection of tapas to make the mouth water. The opulence of the setting overlooking the Caribbean is matched by an extensive wine list, recognised by *Wine Spectator* magazine. Open daily 6.30–10.30pm.

Chicken! Chicken! West Shore Centre, West Bay Rd; tel: 945 2290. Good food based on wood-roasted chicken at affordable prices, with takeaway service available. For a change, try the crispy vegetables. Lunchtime specials CI$6.25–7.25. Open daily 11.00am–10.00pm.

Cimboco Lawrence Bd; tel: 947 2782; web: www.cimboco.com. The small, colourful restaurant tucked behind the Esso station next to the cinema lies within easy reach of Seven Mile Beach. Styled as a 'Caribbean café', it's great all-round value, with pizzas and pasta dishes as well as good jerk chicken roti. Open daily 11.00am–10.00pm to eat in or take away.

Coconut Joe's West Bay Rd; tel: 943 5637. This lively family bar/restaurant serves light meals from its relaxed location opposite the Comfort Suites. Sit outside under the spreading tree that's reputed to be a century old, or enjoy a drink on a swing seat by the bar. Open Mon–Fri 11.00am–1.00am; Sat/Sun to midnight.

Decker's West Bay Road; tel: 945 6600; web: www.deckers.ky. The double-decker London bus and pavement tables belie the smart but simple interior of this restaurant with white cloths and modern art décor. Particularly popular Fri and Sat, when local bands play, it is well patronised by staff from nearby dive schools. The international menu features eastern dishes as well as mesquite grills and steaks, and the 'all-you-can-eat' lobster special, which includes soup and salad, at CI$41.95. Open daily 5.30–10.30pm; bar open till 1.00am (midnight at weekends).

DJ's Cantina Coconut Place, West Bay Rd; tel: 945 4234. Entertainment is a major aspect of this popular bar/restaurant, with live music, including reggae, on Wednesdays, and the Tuesday DJ battles. For diners, the Mexican-style menu caters for all tastes, from chips and salsa to their speciality fajitas, with several vegetarian options. Open Mon–Fri 10.00am–3.00pm, daily 5.00–10.00pm.

Eats Café Cayman Falls Centre, West Bay Rd; tel: 945 5288/1950. The term 'café' doesn't do justice to this place opposite the Westin. The good-value American-style menu features a full breakfast at just US$6.95 (or US$10.95 for the 'hungry man' version), a varied lunch menu with salads and sandwiches, and a comprehensive dinner menu including steaks. Be prepared to queue on Sunday mornings, when the place is packed. Takeaway service available. Open daily 6.30am–11.00pm.

Edoardo's Coconut Place, West Bay Rd; tel: 945 4408; web: www.edoardos.net. A long-established favourite, this cosy restaurant with soft lighting has reasonable prices by Cayman standards – at least as far as pasta dishes are concerned, then the menu moves up through the Italian classics. 'One of the best meals I have ever eaten outside Italy,' according to one correspondent. Open daily 11.30am–2.30pm, 5.30–10.30pm.

Ferdinand's Westin Casuarina, West Bay Rd; tel: 945 3800, ext 6017. The more casual of the two restaurants at the Westin has an interesting menu with international fare that includes selected healthy-eating options. But it's Sunday brunch that really draws the crowds. A firm favourite with both Caymanians and visitors, the atmosphere is that of an English garden party on the beach – tented shade and pure white napiery against a backdrop of miles of white sand. Disregard all previous notions of 'brunch': this is something special, with dishes from around the world – Japanese sushi, old-world roast beef, Chinese, seafood, French cheeses – not to mention a full range of American breakfast food. Unstuffy waiters bring an unlimited supply of sparkling wine and orange juice, as well as soft drinks, tea and coffee. Open daily for breakfast, lunch and dinner; Sunday brunch, from 11.30am to 2.30pm, is US$42 per person.

Fidel Murphy's Queen's Court, West Bay Rd; tel: 949 5189. Not far north of George Town, Fidel Murphy's Irish pub and restaurant has a straightforward menu including Irish stew, roast chicken, and steak and Guinness pie. Specials include a Sunday carvery from 6.00pm to 9.00pm, and Monday's fish and chips with a pint of beer, both at

CI$12.95. Major sports events are shown live on big-screen TV. Happy hour Friday 5.00–8.00pm, when the place is said to be 'pumping', and there are drink specials and free buffet. Normally open Mon–Fri 10.30am–12.45am; Sat/Sun 10.30am–11.45pm, but earlier for major sports events.

Garden Loggia West Bay Rd; tel: 949 1234. Breakfast at the Hyatt Regency is reputed to be superb, with Sunday brunch at US$37.95 particularly special. A full selection of dishes is complemented by freshly squeezed orange juice, and it's waitress service to boot. Caribbean night, with entertainment from a local band, is on Tuesday, 6.30–10.30pm, reservations only. Open for breakfast 7.30–11.00am daily.

Gateway of India West Bay Rd; tel: 946 2815; fax: 946 2816. Next to the Strand, this traditional Indian restaurant has a varied menu that's pretty authentic. For the best choice, go for the lunchtime buffet during the week at CI$6.95 Mon–Wed, or CI$8.95 Thu/Fri. Open Mon–Fri 11.30am–2.30pm; daily 5.30–10.00pm.

Havana Vieja Regency Court; tel: 945 5391; email: havclub@candw.ky. The man rolling cigars in the window of this unusual venue sets the scene for a restaurant where cigars play a starring role. Not surprisingly, there's a strong Cuban emphasis on the menu, but the good news for non-smokers is that the atmosphere is smoke free. Great cocktails and substantial bar snacks as well.

Hemingways Hyatt Regency, Seven Mile Beach; tel: 945 5700. The atmosphere at midday of the Hyatt's beachfront restaurant is one of ordered calm, with its soothing décor based around indoor palm trees. Eat inside or out, making the most of gourmet sandwiches that make the average lunchtime offering seem plain boring. In the evening, the Caribbean-influenced menu is popular way beyond just hotel guests, with seafood a speciality. And on Sundays, there's an à la carte brunch from 11.00am. Parking opposite. Open daily 11.30am–2.30pm; 6.00–10.00pm.

Hook's Seafood & Sushi Bar Treasure Island Resort, West Bay Rd; tel: 945 8731. The restaurant at Treasure Island Resort tries to be all things to all people, with a cosmopolitan menu that's big on seafood with Caribbean and Chinese dishes thrown in, all at reasonable prices. If the menu's varied, that's nothing to the surroundings, with a stab at Japanese décor set against a backdrop of pirate murals. Open daily 7.00am–midnight.

Lone Star Bar & Grill West Bay Rd; tel: 945 5175. Noisy Tex-Mex restaurant and sports bar popular with the diving fraternity and good for families. Themed 'all-you-can-eat' nights. Satellite TV, with all major games (and sometimes more than one) shown in the bar. Open Mon–Fri 11.00am–1.00am; Sat/Sun to midnight. Happy hour Mon–Fri 5.00–6.30pm.

Mangrove Grill Courtyard Marriott, West Bay Rd; tel: 946 4433. The blue-and-yellow polka dot banquette seating and heavy air conditioning make this more diner than restaurant, better for quick meals than serious eating. American buffet brunch at weekends US$8.95. Open Mon–Fri 7.00–10.30am, 6.00–10.00pm; Sat/Sun 7.00am–2.00pm, 7.00–10.30pm.

Mezza West Bay Rd; tel: 949 8511. The classy restaurant above Big Daddy's liquor store is all smoked glass and mood lighting inside, or you can choose to sit outside on the terrace. The wide-ranging menu has a North American slant, and beer is still served from the micro brewery (now relocated to the Big Bamboo in George Town). Open Mon–Fri 11.30am–1.00am; Sat to midnight; Sun 11.00am–midnight.

Myrtles Queen's Court Plaza, West Bay Rd; tel: 949 7868. Unprepossessing bar and café-style venue serving local specials at good prices. Open Mon–Fri 7.00am–1.00am; Sat/Sun to midnight.

Neptune West Bay Rd; tel: 946 8709. Eat indoors amid the cool blue-and-white décor, or dine on the patio in the evening at this new restaurant near Governor's Harbour. The predominantly Italian menu also includes a good seafood curry. Open Mon–Sat 11.30–2.30pm, 5.30–10.00pm; Sun evenings only.

Ottmar's West Bay Rd (junction with Palm Heights Drive); tel: 945 5879. Established in 1972, Ottmar's serves seriously good food in graceful surroundings. Well patronised by business diners, it also has facilities for banquets and conferences. The mainly European menu specialises in the classics, alongside steaks and plenty of seafood, and the occasional Cayman dish. Open daily 6.00–11.00pm; bar open 5.00–8.00pm. Happy hour Fri.

Outback Steakhouse The Strand, West Bay Rd; tel: 945 3108. Large, Australian-themed restaurant with friendly service and 'Joey' menu for children under ten. The emphasis is on steaks and grills, with plenty of them. The range of beers is supplemented by a couple of Australian imports, with Aussie cocktails to complete the picture. Takeaway service available. Open Sun–Thu 5.30–10.00pm; Fri/Sat 5.30–11.00pm; and Sun lunch midday–3.00pm.

PD's Pub Galleria Plaza, West Bay Rd; tel: 949 7144. Don't be fooled by the exterior: behind the stark shopfront is a dark, pub-like environment (PD stands for 'pirates' den') offering good-value food and fast, friendly service. Good selection of beer, including Stingray Dark. Surprisingly comprehensive menu, from soups and salads to burgers and steaks etc, with very generous portions. Internet access available at CI$0.12 per minute (no minimum charge). Open Mon–Fri 7.00am–11.30pm; Sat/Sun to 11.00pm. Bar Mon–Fri 9.00am–1.00am; Sat 9.00am–midnight; Sun 11.00am–midnight.

Peninsula West Bay Rd; tel: 949 0088. The Marriott's exclusive restaurant overlooking the sea is open for lunch and dinner. Don't go in a hurry – the menu alone takes some reading, and making a choice from such an eclectic range could take time! Friday night is Pirates' Night Buffet, with limbo dancing and Caribbean music: adults US$34.95; children half price. Three-course Sunset Specials at US$29.95 are served Thu and Sat, 6.00–8.00pm, while on Wed and Sat there's a poolside barbecue from 11.00am to 6.00pm. Open daily 11.30am–2.30pm, 6.00–10.00pm.

Pizzeria Lago di Como Buckingham Sq, West Bay Rd; tel: 945 3484. Traditional pizza and other Italian dishes. Open daily for lunch and dinner, except Sunday lunch.

Pizzeria Vesuvio Regency Court; tel: 949 8696. Open Mon–Sat 11.30am–10.30pm; Sun and holidays 5.30–10.30pm.

Ragazzi Buckingham Sq, West Bay Rd; tel: 945 3484; web: www.ragazzi.com. Tucked away in the corner of the square, this upmarket Italian restaurant serves consistently good food, from thin pizzas to 'brilliant' lemon veal. Particularly popular at lunchtime. Takeaway service available. Open daily 11.30am–11.00pm.

Reef Grill Royal Palms Beach Club, West Bay Rd; tel: 945 6358. By no means the run-of-the-mill restaurant that the name suggests, the Reef Grill's menu has a Caribbean slant and a touch of the oriental. Strong on fish, it includes dishes such as sea bass with a Thai curry sauce. Indoor or patio dining. Open daily 6.00–11.00pm. For details of the Beach Club, see page 141.

Stingers Eating poolside at the Comfort Suites is, as you would expect, a relaxed affair, with simple meals available all day until 10.00pm. Caribbean nights on Wed and Sat feature a buffet, live music and entertainment, and Fri night each week is themed. Bar open Mon–Fri 11.00am–1.00am; Sat 11.00am–midnight; Sun midday–midnight.

Sunshine Grill West Bay Rd; tel: 949 3000. The poolside bar/restaurant at the Sunshine Suites is a colourful, casual affair, offering daily specials. Thursday night is barbecue night, at CI$15 a head, with a live band. On Monday it's the manager's party, so take advantage of free rum punch and nibbles; happy hour is 6.00–8.00pm Fridays, with half-price drinks and free finger buffet. Open 7.00am–10.00pm.

Thai Orchid Queen's Court, West Bay Rd; tel: 949 7955. Thai cuisine may not be something you would immediately associate with the Cayman Islands, but this tranquil restaurant makes a welcome change and the food, including vegetarian dishes, is reputed to be pretty good, albeit not cheap. Open Mon–Sat 11.30am–2.30pm; daily 6.00–10.00pm. Lunch buffet Tue and Thu.

Tortuga Tim's Seven Mile Shops, West Bay Rd; tel: 949 8299. A very reasonably priced Caribbean bar and grill with a selection of stir fries and some local dishes as well. Full main courses from CI$8.95. Quick, polite service. Open daily 6.30am–9.30pm for breakfast, lunch and dinner.

Verandah Tel: 943 2000. From the upstairs restaurant of the Links golf course at Safehaven (see page 111) diners look out in the early evening across the lake and lush green fairways to North Sound, a serene backdrop for a leisurely evening meal. Modern, stylish and very smart, it has food (and prices) to match – just as well that 'the food's good', according to local golfers. Open daily 5.00–10.00pm.

Wharf West Bay Rd; tel: 949 2231/7729. The stunning location of this large waterfront restaurant and bar at the beginning of Seven Mile Beach ensures its enduring popularity among locals and visitors alike, particularly for that special meal. Predominantly seafood-based menu, with daily specials and excellent service. Tarpon gather nightly in the shallows around the pier at 9.00pm to be fed by the restaurant staff. Live music Mon–Sat. Open Mon–Fri midday–2.30pm, daily 6.00–10.00pm; bar open from 3.00pm.

Yoshi Sushi Cayman Falls Centre, West Bay Rd; tel: 945 6248. The unassuming exterior here leads into an attractive Japanese restaurant dominated by colourful samurai and geisha murals. Good authentic food (and considerably cheaper than at Bamboo). Open daily 11.30am–2.30pm, 5.30–10.30pm.

Cafés, snack bars and fast food

Several US fast-food chains and ice-cream outlets, from Burger King and Pizza Hut to Subway and TCBY, have set up shop on the western side of Grand Cayman, mostly along Seven Mile Beach. But all is not lost – there are several alternatives. The area around the cinema, known as Marquee Plaza, is a good start. In addition to the following venues, jerk chicken is often available near here in the evenings.

Al La Kebab Marquee Plaza; tel: 943 4343. Close to the cinema, and opposite the Butterfly Farm, this is the place to go for that late-night kebab when you're hungry and everything else is closed. It's open in the daytime too: Mon–Fri midday–4.00am, Sat till 2.00am.

Antica Gelateria Marquee Plaza (next to the cinema); tel: 946 1400; web: www.anticagelateria.com. Forget the commercial stuff: this is the real thing – 80 different flavours of gelato, and highly recommended. Open Tue–Sun 2.30–11.00pm.

Azzurro Buckingham Square (opposite Ragazzi); tel: 946 7745. Cakes, snacks and home-made pasta are served in a relaxed atmosphere; a great place for a breakfast cappuccino. Internet access US$7 per hour. Open Mon–Sat 6.30am–9.00pm; Sun 6.30am–6.00pm.

Café del Sol Marquee Plaza (opposite Cimboco); tel: 946 2233, web: www.cafedelsol.ky. Cheerful café that also offers internet access. Open Mon–Sat 7.00am–8.00pm; Sun 8.00am–8.00pm.
Coffee Grinder Seven Mile Shops, West Bay Rd. US-style café serving sandwiches, pastries and light meals etc. Open Mon–Sat 7.00am–6.00pm; Sun 8.00am–3.00pm.
Papa John's Queen's Court, West Bay Rd; tel: 943 7272. Pizzas, pizzas and more pizzas!
Treats West Shore Centre, West Bay Rd; tel: 946 4262. Bright, cheerful and friendly, Treats serves breakfast, pastries, and fresh chocolates – and ice-creams that include bubblegum and tiramisu flavours. Open daily 7.00am–10.00pm.

Self catering?

Don't miss out on good food just because you want a night in. **Fine Dine-In** (tel: 949 3463; web: www.finedine-in.com) works with a selection of local restaurants to deliver meals to hotels, condos, or even the beach, anywhere between West Bay and Prospect (that's effectively the whole of Seven Mile Beach and a little further east than the Stingray Brewery at Red Bay). Restaurants featured include Bacchus, Bed, The Brasserie, Casanova, Champion House II, Chicken! Chicken!, Cimboco, Decker's, DJ's Cantina, Edoardo's, Gateway to India, La Bodega, Mezza, PD's Pub, Ragazzi and Thai Orchid. You'll be charged at menu prices plus a CI$5 delivery charge. Delivery is usually within 30 to 45 minutes of placing your order. For an additional fee, you can order a video at the same time – although videos may not be ordered through the website. Open Sun–Thu 5.30–10.30pm; Fri/Sat 5.30–11.00pm.

BARS AND NIGHTLIFE

The nightclub scene on Grand Cayman is evolving, but in general don't expect pumping music till dawn – many places close by 1.00am during the week, while local licensing laws insist that establishments close at midnight on Saturday and Sunday. Many of Grand Cayman's restaurants have their own bars, for which opening times are given under *Restaurants* above, and several establishments, including Bed and DJ's Cantina, feature live entertainment on different days of the week. Other bars and nightlife locations include:

The Attic Queen's Court, West Bay Rd; tel: 949 7665. This billiards lounge is situated on the second floor of Queen's Court, opposite Fidel Murphy's.
Bobo's Iguana Islander Complex, West Bay Rd; tel: 946 6900. A sports bar and lounge. Open Mon–Fri 5.00pm–1.00am; Sat 5.00pm–midnight.
Chameleon The Strand, West Bay Rd; tel: 945 0707. Large bar and dancing area above Outback Steakhouse. Themed nights with live bands – see *Caymanian Compass* for details. Open Mon–Fri 9.00pm–3.00am; Sat to midnight.
Club Oasis Tel: 949 7777. The nightclub on the third floor of Treasure Island resort is open 9.00pm–3.00am (midnight on Saturday).
Club Scene Selkirk Plaza, West Bay Rd; tel: 945 8950
Deckers West Bay Road; tel: 945 6600. Long after the last diners have left, the bar at Deckers is busy serving drinks until 1.00am (or midnight at weekends).
Jillian's Islander Complex, Lawrence Bd; tel: 949 0110. Located opposite the cinema, a billiards lounge and bar with large plasma TV screens. Free internet access. Open Mon–Fri 5.00pm–1.00am; Sat/Sun 2.00pm–midnight.

Jungle Night Club Trafalgar Place, off West Bay Rd; tel: 945 5383. Close to Neptune restaurant, this dark, jungle–themed club is popular with locals. Karaoke night Wed; disco Fri/Sat. Bar snacks. Happy hour 5.00–7.00pm. Open Mon–Fri 10.00am–1.00am; Sat 10.00am–midnight; Sun 1.00pm–midnight.

Legendz Bar Cayman Falls Centre, West Bay Rd; PO Box 30932 SMB; tel: 945 1950/5288. The bland exterior of Legendz opens into a surprisingly large, plush American bar with big plasma screens showing sport, and popular with the diving fraternity. Open Mon–Fri 11:30am–1.00am; Sat to midnight; Sun midday to midnight.

Matrix Lawrence Bd. Located above World Gym, this club with its new bar is particularly popular with ex-pats on Thursday nights, with Caymanians for the most part preferring the weekends.

Next Level West Bay Rd; tel: 946 6398; web: www.nextlevel.ky. Now relocated next to Aqua Beach, opposite the Marriott, the Next Level features regular live bands – see the *Caymanian Compass* for details. Open Mon–Fri 10.00pm–3.00am; Sat 9.00pm–midnight. Free entry for diners at Aqua Beach.

Royal Palms A great place to be in the evenings, when live music features calypso and reggae Mon–Sat in season (Wed and Sat in the summer). Bar food comes from the starters menu at the Reef Grill, so it's a cut above the norm. For details, see *Beaches* page 141.

Shooters Seven Mile Shops; tel: 946 3496. Dark, rather sleazy lounge bar with billiards table and internet café. Taped modern music. Open Mon–Fri 10.30pm–1.00am; Sat & Sun 10.30–12.00. Over 20s only after 6.00pm.

Welly's Cool Spot 110 North Sound Rd; tel: 949 2541. A local watering hole frequented mostly by Caymanians, this is definitely off the normal tourist track.

SHOPPING AND AMENITIES

Boutiques and duty-free shops abound in George Town and more are located in the malls that line West Bay Road. Many shops, particularly those catering for the tourist, are open seven days a week. For shops beyond George Town and Seven Mile Beach, see *Chapters 6* and 7.

Books, maps and games

Book Nook Galleria Plaza, West Bay Rd. Open Mon–Sat 9.00am–6.00pm.

Book Nook II Anchorage Centre, off Cardinall Av (behind Kirk Freeport), George Town; tel: 949 7392. Open Mon–Fri 9.00am–4.00pm; Sat when cruise ships are in port.

Hobbies and Books Piccadilly Centre, Elgin Av, George Town; tel: 949 0707; fax: 949 7165; email: hobbook@candw.ky. Tucked away in a modern building round the back of George Town, there's a wide variety of books and gifts here, including a good selection of books related to the Cayman Islands. Also at Grand Harbour, Red Bay. Open Mon–Sat 10.00am–8.00pm.

Books may also be bought at both of the following:

Cayman Island National Archive 37 Archive Lane, George Town; tel: 949 9809; email: cina@gov.ky. The archive houses a comprehensive series of records related to the islands, including a memory bank of non-written data. Books concerned with the islands' history are on sale. Open Mon–Fri. 8.30am–5.00pm; reading room open 9.00am–4.30pm.

National Trust Courts Rd, Eastern Av; tel: 949 0121. This attractive building is not only an excellent place to find out more about the work of the Trust, but is also a good source of books on the natural history and culture of the islands. Open Mon–Fri 9.00am–5.00pm.

Cigars

Churchill's Cigar Store Anchorage Centre, George Town; tel: 945 6141. Also at Galleria Plaza on West Bay Rd.

Havana Club West Bay Rd; tel: 945 6275. If you really want to take your time over a cigar, you can dine here at the Havana Vieja, opposite the Westin Casuarina. Outlets also at Aqua World in George Town and West Shore Centre.

Puro Rey West Bay Rd, opposite the Hyatt; tel: 945 4912/3; web: www.puroreycigars.com. Open 10.00am–10.00pm daily. Also at Seven Mile Shops.

Diving and sports supplies

Several of the dive operators on the island have their own shops selling a limited range of diving and photographic equipment, but for a wider choice you'll be better off with the retail specialists.

Divers Supply West Shore Centre, West Bay Rd; tel: 949 7621. Rentals and sales of all equipment, plus dive tuition. Open daily 8.00am–9.00pm.

Divers World Seven Mile Shops, West Bay Rd; tel: 949 8128; mobile: 916 0028; email: divworld@candw.ky. Fully comprehensive dive shop with everything a diver could possibly need, from equipment to books. Rentals available. The affiliated **Little Divers**, two doors down, has everything for younger water babes, from mini wetsuits to ocean colouring books. Open Mon–Sat 7.30am–6.00pm.

Sports Supply Galleria Plaza; tel: 949 7884. A full range of sports gear, from fishing tackle and waterskis to tennis equipment. Open Mon–Sat 9.00–8.00pm.

Scuba Sensations Tel: 949 2871. The shop next to Treasure Island Resort has a selection of dive and photographic equipment, but nothing like the range of the specialists above.

Duty free

Traditional duty-free items – jewellery, watches etc – are to be found alongside glass and china, antique coins and other similar items in the numerous duty-free shops opposite George Town harbour and lining both sides of Cardinall Avenue. The following are some of the larger duty-free centres:

24K-Mon Jewellers Buckingham Square; tel: 949 1499

Anchorage Centre corner of Cardinall Av and North Church St, George Town. Various stores sell cosmetics and perfume, crystal, jewellery and watches; leather goods; designer clothes and T-shirts; cigars.

British Outpost Duty Free Centre, Edward St; tel: 949 0742. Jewellery, watches and treasure coins. Open Mon–Fri 8.30am–5.30pm. Also at Coconut Place, West Bay Rd.

Duty Free Centre Edward St, George Town. Another umbrella outfit with shops selling jewellery, treasure coins, watches, sunglasses, designer clothes, luggage and T-shirts.

Duty Free Ltd South Church St; tel: 945 2160. Jewellery, glassware, watches and treasure coins. Also at Galleria Plaza on West Bay Rd; tel: 945 5754/4055. Open Mon–Sat 9.00am–9.15pm.

Kirk Freeport Plaza Cardinall Av, George Town; tel: 949 7477; fax: 949 8124; email: kirkfree@candw.ky. Also at The Strand, West Bay Rd.

Fishing

Fishing supplies and bait may be obtained from **Melody Marine** in Spinnaker Square, Red Bay (tel: 947 1093) or **R+M Fly Shop & Charters** (tel: 946 0214). Bait is also available from supermarkets.

Food and drink
Food
Local produce and specialities, including home-made cakes and fruits such as soursop or apple bananas in season, are available from **Farmer's Market** on Thomas Russell Avenue near the airport, open Monday to Wednesday, 7.30am to 6.00pm, and Thu–Sat to 6.30pm. There is also a daily hot-buffet takeaway, with local dishes, complete with coconut rice and beans, and fried bananas, for CI$3.99–4.99.

Grand Cayman's supermarkets are modern and efficient, with a wide variety of goods including US branded foods. Supermarkets don't sell alcoholic drinks – you'll have to go to a liquor store for these.

Fort Street Market Fort St, George Town; tel: 945 0760. Mini supermarket which also serves buffet lunch food, including soup. Pavement tables. Open Mon–Fri 7.00am–6.00pm.

Foster's Food Fair Airport Rd; tel: 949 5155. Open Mon–Sat 7.00am–11.00pm; holidays 9.00am–6.00pm. Also at The Strand, West Bay Rd, tel: 945 4748 (in-store pharmacy open Mon–Sat 9.00am–5.00pm; Sun 9.00am–midday) and Republix Plaza, West Bay, tel: 949 3214 (bus stop 18).

Hurley's Marketplace Grand Harbour, Red Bay; tel: 947 8488. Also at Walkers Rd, George Town; tel: 949 8488. ATMs at both branches. Grand Harbour open Mon–Sat 7.00am–11.00pm; holidays 7.00am–6.00pm.

Kirk Supermarket Eastern Av, George Town; tel: 949 7022. Fresh produce, salad bar, in-store pharmacy, ATM. Open Mon–Thu 7.00am–10.00pm; Fri/Sat 7.00am–11.00pm. Closed public holidays.

Simply British Galleria Plaza, West Bay Rd; tel: 945 2748; web: www.simplybritishcayman.com. Brits take note – all the comfort foods from home including McVitie's biscuits, Colman's mustard and sometimes Marmite, too. Open Mon–Sat 9.30am–5.30pm; Sun 9.00am–1.00pm.

Rum cake is a popular souvenir, with a variety of flavours available and tastings on offer in several tourist shops, or indeed straight from the factory. In addition to the following, try a branch of Blackbeard's liquor store (see below). More traditional to the Cayman Islands is coconut candy, which is sometimes available from Farmer's Market (see above).

Cayman Islands Rum Cake Centre North Church St, George Town; tel: 946 7370
Tortuga Rum Cakes Tel: 949 8866/949 2162. The company has several outlets on Grand Cayman, including two shops in the centre of George Town, and two factories – one near George Town (see page 147) and the second next to the Turtle Farm (see page 155). All offer free samples of its different varieties of rum cake.

Drink
Rum is a popular choice to take home, with flavoured rum a speciality. There are numerous liquor stores (off licences) on the island, with opening hours almost universally Mon–Sat 10.00am–7.00pm. Contrary to popular opinion, liquor stores are not duty free – a bottle of rum that costs US$33.50 on the island would cost around US$8.50 duty free at the airport. In addition to the following, some branches of Tortuga Rum (above) sell liquor.

Big Daddy's West Bay Rd; tel: 949 8511. Also at Buckingham Square and Cayman Falls Centre.

Blackbeard's 236 Crewe Rd; tel: 949 8763; web: www.blackbeardsliquors.com. One of several shops on the island featuring speciality rums, including banana and mango flavours (as well as rum cakes and a range of sauces and spices). Other outlets include The Strand, Seven Mile Shops and Grand Harbour.

Jacques Scott 384 Shedden Rd, George Town; tel: 949 7600. Also at West Shore Centre.

Red Rabbit Liquor Store Red Bay; tel: 947 1536

Tortuga Liquors Web: www.tortugarums.com. Several outlets, including South Church St, and the airport.

Wine Cellar Galleria Plaza, West Bay Rd; tel: 949 5155

Gifts, souvenirs and beachwear

There are plenty of small shops in the centre of George Town near the harbour selling everything from local arts and crafts to good-quality T-shirts and other souvenirs, while others proliferate in various shopping malls along West Bay Road. Don't forget, too, the gift shops at the museum, Butterfly Farm and other tourist attractions, which generally have something different from the run of the mill. Shops are usually open Mon–Sat, 9.00am–5.00pm unless otherwise indicated; for the most part they'll be open whenever the cruise ships are in port. The following is just a selection of these and others nearby:

Aquaworld Mall and Aquarium South Church St, George Town. This modern first-floor mall houses a number of small shops selling clothing, gifts and souvenirs – a pretty good bet for something a bit different under one roof.

Beach Boutique Seven Mile Shops; tel: 949 8128. Good range of casual clothes, sandals and beachwear. Open Mon–Sat 9.30am–6.00pm.

Casual Sports Bodmer Bldg, Shedden Rd, George Town; tel: 949 2199. T-shirts, souvenirs.

Cayman Candle Queen's Court Plaza, West Bay Rd; tel: 949 4720. The large, colourful candles sold here are made on the islands and make lovely presents. Open Mon–Fri 10.00am–9.00pm, Sat 10.00am–7.00pm.

Craft Market Cardinall Av, George Town. A small group of shops with locally produced gifts, geared primarily to the cruise market and located just across the road from the two port terminals.

Esteban Gallery North Church St, George Town; tel: 946 2787. Upmarket art and craft gallery.

Heritage Craft Goring Av, George Town; tel: 945 6041. In spite of the name, most of the huge range of items on sale here fall into the bracket of cheap souvenirs, though the occasional gem is to be found so it's worth a browse round. At least it feels real, making a change from the rather sterile duty-free shops. Open Mon–Fri 8.30am–5.30pm, Sat 10.00am–5.00pm.

Hesha West Shore Centre; tel: 949 9005. A reasonable range of gifts is available at this shop close to Seven Mile Beach. Open Mon–Sat 10.00am–6.30pm.

Hot Tropics Thompson Bldg, opposite the post office, George Town; tel: 949 7014. Large selection of T-shirts, plus a few souvenirs. Open Mon–Fri 8.00am–5.00pm; Sat 9.00am–4.30pm.

Island Art & Framing Grand Harbour, Red Bay; tel: 947 2606. Local arts and crafts and original paintings by resident artists such as Joanne Sibley, John Clarke and Gordon Hewitt. Open Mon–Fri 10.00am–6.00pm; Sat 10.00am–5.00pm.

Island Glass-Blowing North Church St, George Town; tel: 946 1483. The new glass-blowing studio in George Town opened a little further north than its predecessor in March 2004. Visitors can watch free demonstrations as all manner of rays, turtles, fish and bowls are created. Open Mon–Sat 8.00am–5.00pm.

Kennedy Gallery West Shore Centre, West Bay Rd, tel: 949 8077. An interesting selection of classy art and sculpture. Open Mon–Sat 10.00am–6.00pm.

Latitude 19 Harbour Place (opposite Eden Rock). Slightly more upmarket than most of the clothes shops in this area, with a decent range of T-shirts and other clothing. Open Mon–Sat 8.30am–5.30pm.

Occasions West Shore Centre, West Bay Rd; tel: 945 6204. A newly opened gift shop with a good selection of cards. Open Mon–Sat 9.00am–6.00pm.

Pure Art South Church St, George Town; tel: 949 9133. Located in a small cottage on the left as you head south from George Town, Pure Art has a colourful selection of individually made arts and crafts within a wide price range. Woven baskets, wooden toys and other artefacts jostle for space with original paintings (including some by owner Debbie van der Bol) and a range of prints from modern to classical. There are even local food specialities.

Shellections South Church St, George Town. Gifts and basic souvenirs are sold from a small wooden building close to the harbour.

Tropical l'Attitude Edward St, George Town; tel: 945 1233. Close to the post office, a classy gifts and clothes shop with a Caribbean theme. Open Mon–Fri 8.30am–5.30pm; Sat 8.30am–5.00pm.

Tropical Trader Galleria Plaza, West Bay Rd; tel: 949 8354. Also next to Smugglers Cove in George Town; tel: 949 6538. Arts and crafts, island music and casual clothes. Open Mon–Sat 9.00am–9.30pm.

T-Shirts of Cayman Goring Av, George Town; tel: 949 7093. In addition to a wide selection of T-shirts, browse here for sarongs, swimwear and souvenirs, to a background of calypso music.

Health and beauty

Spas have grown in popularity in recent years, and the larger hotels haven't been slow to catch on, with the latest offerings from both the Hyatt and the Westin, and a new one to come at the Ritz Carlton in 2005. Some of the following, including The Healing Touch, will visit you in your home or holiday apartment. Hair braiding is popular with visitors, whether it be single braids for around US$2 to a full head from around US$60. A full set of braids will take around 45 minutes to complete, depending on the length of hair. For details of gyms, see page 112.

Beauty Spa Tel: 945 4683/949 1234 ext 6061. The Hyatt's spa with its adjacent hair salon is also open to non-residents.

The Healing Touch Regency Court Plaza, West Bay Rd; tel: 949 2034; web: http://thehealingtouch.ky

Hibiscus Spa Tel: 945 9800, ext 6203. The Westin's luxurious spa is a haven of tranquillity with a genuine welcome. Facilities include sauna, Jacuzzi, and steam room, plus a sauna for men only, and various treatments are on offer. Options include a 'couples only' massage and hot tub at US$205. Open daily 8.00am–7.00pm.

Iris Braids and Beauty Regency Court, West Bay Rd; tel: 945 3525. Open Mon–Fri 10.00am–7.00pm; Sat from 9.00am.

Spa Esprit The Strand. Open Mon–Fri 10.00am–7.00pm; Sat 9.00am–6.00pm

Spa to Go Grand Harbour Centre; tel: 949 1525

Spa Tortuga Tel: 947 7449, ext 5944. Based at Morritt's Tortuga (see page 172).

Music and video

Blockbuster Video Outlets at Eden Centre, George Town, tel: 949 9500; West Shore Centre, West Bay Rd, tel: 949 4500, and Grand Harbour, Red Bay, tel: 947 9660. Rental of VCRs as well as videos.

Hottrax West Shore Centre, West Bay Rd; tel: 949 9047; open Mon–Sat 12.00am–10.00pm.

Also at Grand Harbour, Red Bay; tel: 947 9040. CDs and tapes for every taste. Open Mon–Sat 10.00am–10.00pm.

Pharmacy

See page 84.

Photography

There are some stunning prints of underwater life available at most gift shops on the island. For these, as well as photographic equipment at very good prices – digital cameras in particular are a real bargain – try the following:

Cathy Church's Underwater Photo Centre & Gallery Sunset House, South Church St; tel: 949 7415, US toll free 800 934 3661; web: www.cathychurch.com. Some spectacular underwater prints, some signed, makes this place worth a detour. Films available include the increasingly hard-to-find Fuji Velvia, and overnight print and slide processing is available. Underwater cameras, including a wide range of digital equipment, are on sale at duty-free prices, and rental is from US$10 per half day. Underwater photography courses go from half-day beginners' course at US$125 to private sessions costing US$45–125 per hour. Week-long package, including hotel, diving and some meals, approx US$3,000. Open daily 7.30am–6.00pm.

Cayman Camera Goring Av, George Town; tel: 949 8359; web: www.caymancamera.com. This specialist shop selling films, cameras etc has recently relocated from Harbour Drive and is well worth seeking out. Prices are said to be among the best.

Photo Centre, Bush Centre, North Church St, George Town; tel: 949 0030

Photo World Queen's Court, West Bay Rd; tel: 945 0351. Open Mon–Fri 8.30am–6.30pm; Sat 9.00am–5.30pm.

Rainbow Photo Elizabethan Sq, Shedden Rd, George Town; tel: 945 2046

Rapid Photo Merrens Place, West Bay Rd; tel: 949 7514; web: www.rapid.ky. One-hour processing for 35mm or APS films. Pick-up service available from various hotels on Seven Mile Beach. Open Mon–Fri 8.00am–6.00pm; Sat 10.00am–6.00pm.

Post and internet

See pages 82–3.

ENTERTAINMENT AND ACTIVITIES

Grand Cayman offers a wealth of activities for all interests, both on and off the water. For details of these, see *Chapter 4, Diving and Other Activities*. For information about festivals, see pages 58–9.

Music

Many restaurants and hotels feature live music on a regular basis. These include a steel band at Treasure Island Resort on Mondays, 6.30–8.00pm, and bands at the Royal Palms Beach Club (see opposite). The cost of large bands mean that most live music played today involves sequencing, with one or two players plus machines.

Theatre and cinema

The **Harquail Theatre** (tel: 949 5477; fax: 949 4519; email: cncf@candw.ky; web: www.artscayman.org), is the home of the Cayman National Cultural Foundation; it is located on the left off the Harquail Drive bypass heading north from George Town. The 330-seat, purpose-built theatre features both specially commissioned plays and musical entertainment, including classical concerts, opera, dance schools and the annual local battle of the bands. It also stages the occasional fashion show and exhibition of local art.

There is a second theatre, the **Playhouse** just off Red Bay Road in Prospect (tel: 949 1998/5585). The base of the Cayman Drama Society, which is predominantly made up of expatriate workers, the Playhouse puts on a wide variety of plays from comedies and pantomime to serious drama.

The **cinema** on Lawrence Boulevard, just off West Bay Road (tel: 949 4011), has two screens, and shows new releases twice daily in the evenings. There are also matinée showings on Saturday and Sunday. Talk of building a second cinema at Grand Harbour, near Red Bay, has yet to come to anything.

For details of what's on at all these venues, see the Friday edition of the *Caymanian Compass*, which includes a weekly entertainment guide.

Bowling is on offer at the ten-lane Stingray Bowling Centre, The Greenery, West Bay Road (next to The Strand); tel: 945 4444; fax: 949 6900; web: www.stingraybowling.com. Cost CI$4 per person, per game; CI$24 per lane for one hour; CI$3 shoe rental (children CI$2.50). There's also a snack bar, and a small amusement arcade. It's open Mon–Fri midday–1.00am; Sat–Sun midday–midnight.

Families with younger children may appreciate **Smyles** on Eastern Avenue, next to World Gym. The large activity area with ball pond is best suited to younger children, although children up to 12 are welcome, and there's a coffee area for parents. Charges for children with an adult are US$3.50 for under 2s, and US$5.50 for older ones. If you want to leave your youngsters for a while, supervised care costs US$10 for the first 1½ hours, and US$6 for each subsequent hour. Open Mon 9.00am–3.00pm; Wed/Thu 9.00am–8.00pm; Fri 9.00am–10.00pm; Sat 10.00am–10.00pm; Sun 11.00am–8.00pm.

BEACHES

Grand Cayman has no shortage of beautiful beaches, for every taste. Even within easy reach of George Town, visitors can opt for the sophistication of Seven Mile Beach or head for the more secluded coves of South Sound. Further afield, laid-back Rum Point beckons (see page 168), while choose carefully on the eastern or northern sides of the island and you could have the place to yourself.

Seven Mile Beach

Arguably the quintessential Caribbean beach, Seven Mile Beach (it's actually 4.6 miles, or 7.5km) runs the length of the western side of the island north of George Town. Hotels, villas and apartments line almost the whole of the beach, blocking any view of the sea from West Bay Road, although there are several access points to the beach, clearly marked with blue and white signs.

Just beyond the Westin, however, is one point where the builders have been kept at bay. The **public beach** (bus stop 15) is a tribute to a last vestige of commonsense, a relatively peaceful stretch of soft white sand with buoyed swimming area and natural shade provided by tall casuarina trees. Painted wooden beach shelters with barbecue grills provide ideal spots for a sand-free picnic, with toilets and telephones nearby. For children, there is a play area – and the ice-cream van pays regular visits. For more substantial fare, Rackams is to open a snack bar on the beach during 2004.

A little further north, **Cemetery Beach**, at the southern end of Boggy Sand Road (access is alongside the cemetery, opposite the fire station on West Bay Road) is another tranquil spot, with picnic benches located in the shade, and public toilets. A swim of five minutes or so brings you out to Cemetery Reef for some really good snorkelling, though the distance and relatively deep water means that this isn't for weak swimmers. Shoals of parrotfish and sergeant-major fish may be seen, and even the occasional reef shark. The fish here are well used to their graceless human companions, and may indeed swim straight up to you, which can be quite unnerving.

Facilities all along Seven Mile Beach are numerous. All the hotels along the coast have bars and restaurants open to the public, so the choice is wide. Perhaps the most reasonable is the simple beach café opposite the Courtyard Marriott, which is open for soft drinks and lunches, and has a changing area as well. Watersports, too, are easily booked: beach kiosks up near the Hyatt and Westin Casuarina hotels offer parasailing, and some of the six dive specialists that operate from here even have outlets on the beach.

For those looking for a good base, try **Royal Palms Beach Club** (West Bay Rd; tel: 945 6358; fax: 945 5360; email: rpalms@candw.ky) at the southern end of the beach, which has a beach bar, snack shop, barbecue, terrace and Reef Grill restaurant (see page 141). A lively venue, this, it has local bands playing Monday to Saturday nights in season, or Wednesday to Saturday out of season. Most watersports are available on site, and diving can be arranged through Red Sail Sports. Admission is free to residents and those staying on the island; day-trip visitors pay US$2 per person. The bar is open Mon–Sat 9.00am–midnight; Sun 1.00pm–midnight. An alternative venue for the day is **Beach Club Hotel & Dive Resort**, where visitors, including cruise-ship passengers, are welcome Mon–Sat. Here, the bar is open daily 10.00am–11.45pm, and the restaurant 6.30–9.30pm.

George Town and further south

In the centre of George Town, there's a tiny beach behind the **Tourist Hut** on North Church Street, where snorkel equipment (and even bicycles) may be hired. On the other side of George Town is **Club Paradise** (also called Paradise Bar & Grill) in South Church St, tel: 945 1444 (see page 126). With its restaurant/bar and on-the-spot diving and snorkelling, this friendly venue is a good place to spend the day, whether you want to participate in active sports or just to laze in the sun with a cool rum punch, though it does get busy when the cruise ships are in.

A little way beyond the centre of George Town lies the secluded **Smith's Cove**, a public beach that contrasts strongly with the flashier Seven Mile Beach. The small area of sand is surrounded by rocks and backed by trees under which picnic tables are set out. It is the perfect spot for snorkelling, or just to sit on the rocks and watch the sea.

Rum Point
See pages 168–70.

GEORGE TOWN
George Town, at least at first glance, is more small-town resort than offshore banking capital. Painted wooden buildings nestle among smart shopping arcades overlooking the small natural harbour, where boats tie up to ferry their passengers to and from local beaches and other attractions, or to the big cruise ships which anchor offshore on an almost daily basis. Along the waterfront, and in the area behind, the streets are lined with shops where visitors can buy anything from tacky souvenirs to top-class jewellery and watches at duty-free prices.

Although George Town itself has no real beaches, it's only a short walk to the southern end of Seven Mile Beach, or a quick bus or taxi ride to Smith's Cove or further up West Bay.

History
Once known as the Hog Sties, and overlooking what is still called Hog Sty Bay, George Town took over the role of capital from Bodden Town, some 12 miles to the east, in 1888, having been widely regarded as the capital since the 1830s. The town was probably renamed in an attempt to bestow an aura of dignity on the place.

Hog Sty Bay is a natural harbour, sheltered from the prevailing winds and the only place on the island where ships of any depth may safely anchor. In 1796, George Gauld reported that the place was:

> a small village, near which is the only place where large vessels can
> come to. The water is so clear that you can easily see where it is most
> proper to drop the anchor but without the greatest precaution you are
> in danger of having your cables cut by the rocks.

For a brief period at the end of the 19th century, the port was the centre of a phosphate-mining industry, with phosphate derived from the fossilised guano of seabirds. The formation of the Grand Cayman Phosphate Company in 1883, followed by the Carib Guano Company the next year, led to the export of tons of phosphate to the US. Within just a few years, however, large deposits of the mineral were discovered in Florida, and the industry was no longer economically viable. By the early 1890s, trading had ceased, with both companies suffering heavy losses.

Today, the harbour is a mecca for the cruise ships that bring countless passengers to the island almost daily.

What to see
A short walk around George Town

The following route takes in the major sites of George Town, starting from either South or North Terminal, close to the point at which cruise-ship passengers dock, and finishing at the nearby museum. Allow about 45 minutes for the walk, longer if you plan to stop for a drink or explore inside any of the buildings.

From North Port Terminal, turn left along Harbour Drive, with the sea to your left. Cross the road almost immediately to **Elmslie Memorial United Church**, named after the minister who brought the Presbyterian faith to the islands in the mid 19th century. The simplicity of this whitewashed church, built in the early 1920s by Captain Rayal Bodden, 'Shipwright, elder and master builder of this church', is accentuated by dark wooden pews and a stunning stained-glass window. Look up at the vaulted wooden ceiling: the rafters were designed like the upturned hull of a ship, reflecting Cayman's seafaring tradition. All are welcome to attend Sunday services, held at 9.30am, 11.00am and 7.00pm. For information, tel: 949 7923.

Just in front of the church is Cayman's **War Memorial**, a tribute to those Caymanians who lost their lives during two World Wars.

Cross back to the sea side of the road, and just past the container depot on your left you will find the old **Seamen Memorial**, a simple but chilling reminder of the almost total reliance on the sea of Caymanians through the ages.

Continue past various duty-free shops and restaurants to the rather disappointing **Fort George**, overlooking the harbour. This was never a fort in the sense of a protective building, but rather a simple enclosure surrounded by low stone walls housing just three small cannons. George Town's entire defence against late 18th-century Spanish marauders, it was later used as a look-out post in World War II, but was partially demolished in 1972. The small area that you see today, with its replica guns, is all that is left of the 'not very well constructed' fort that met Edward Corbet in 1802. A recent addition to the spot is *Tradition*, a nostalgic evocation of a fisherman and his son created by Canadian sculptor Simon Morris. Unveiled by Prince Edward in May 2003 as part of the quincentennial celebrations, it stands as a new and lasting maritime memorial to some 475 Caymanians who have lost their lives at sea.

From here, you can make a short detour north along the coast to a small new **glass-blowing studio**, where free demonstrations can be seen Mon–Sat from 8.00am. Then retrace your steps to the Fort George, and cross the road into Fort Street. Walk up here past Fort Street Market (a good place to buy a cool drink) to the modern **Legislative Assembly** (tel: 949 4236) building on your left. Visitors may attend sessions of the assembly provided that they conform with the required dress code. Alternatively, if the assembly is not in session, it may be possible to have a short guided tour by the Sergeant at Arms. Outside stands a statue of Mr Jim, a popular politician – arguably a contradiction in terms – during the 1970s and 1980s who was the brains behind the hugely successful annual Pirates Week festival.

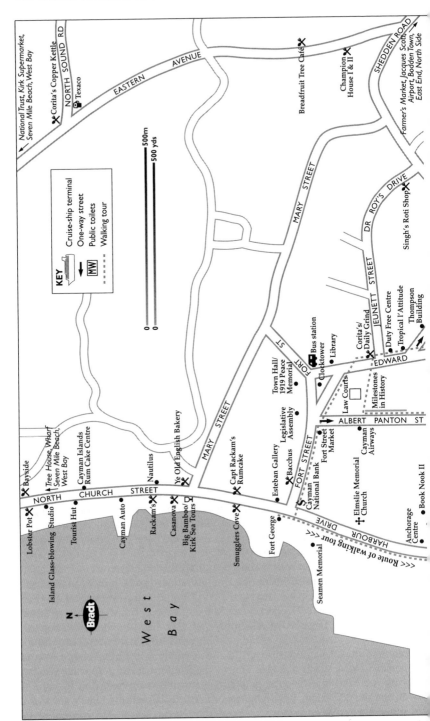

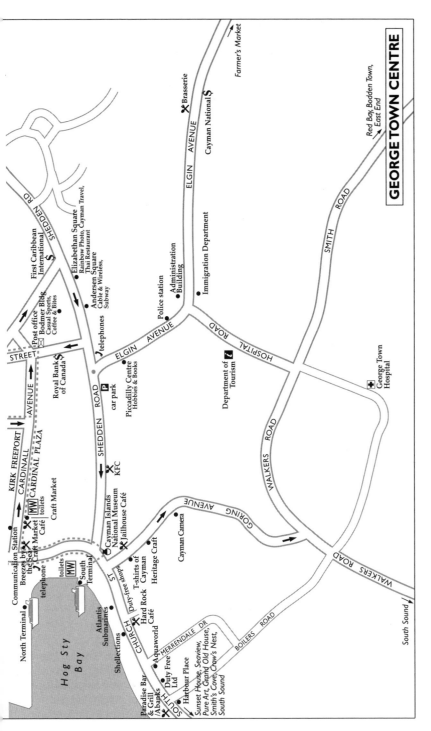

GEORGE TOWN CENTRE

The **Town Hall** next door is designated the 1919 Peace Memorial, although it was not actually built until 1923. For many years, the building was a focal point of island life, but nowadays it is used effectively as an annexe to the **Law Courts** just across the road in Edward Street. The steam-powered **clocktower** in front of the Town Hall was erected in 1937 for the princely sum of £140 (US$210) to commemorate the reign of King George V.

Diagonally opposite the Town Hall, on Edward Street, is George Town's **library** (tel: 949 5159; open Mon–Fri 10.00am–6.00pm; Sat 10.00am–1.00pm). The building dates to 1939, one of four in the town constructed by Captain Rayal Bodden, during the tenure of Allen Wolsey Cardinall. Cardinall was commissioner to the Cayman Islands from 1934 to 1941, and it is after him that George Town's Cardinall Avenue is named. Further along Edward Street, on the opposite corner, is the rounded façade of the **post office**, another of Bodden's constructions, also built in 1939. As well as central postal facilities, the office boasts a philatelic bureau (see page 83).

If you cross the square in front of the library, passing the central fountain and its attendant palm trees, you'll come to a series of polished stone walls on the other side. From the initial blocks engraved with key dates in the history of the islands, through vividly coloured depictions of Cayman culture, to poignant personal memories, these **Milestones in our History** were erected in 2003 to symbolise the passing of 500 years since the discovery of the islands by Christopher Columbus.

Follow the walls to the post office at the end, then turn west from here back towards the harbour along Cardinall Avenue, with its array of modern duty-free shops. Just before the end, on the left, is the Craft Market Café, a homely place to stop for a drink or a snack – perhaps a Cayman pattie. At the junction with Harbour Drive, turn left and cross over Shedden Avenue – the wooden buildings along here mark it out as one of George Town's older streets – to end the tour at the Old Courts building, one of Cayman's few surviving 19th-century structures and now the home of the National Museum (see below). To return to the port, turn right out of the museum and follow Harbour Drive until you are opposite the terminal.

For a more in-depth look at the town, get hold of a copy of the National Trust's **Historic Walking Tour**, which takes in the capital's historic buildings and monuments as well as several traditional homes and shops in the vicinity. The Trust's full walk takes approximately two hours, though of course you could cover just part of the route; the information in the leaflet gives considerable insight into the buildings on the route and the historical context in which they were set. For a copy of the leaflet, contact the National Trust (see page 29).

Cayman Islands National Museum
PO Box 2189, Harbour Drive; tel: 949 8368; fax: 949 0309; email: museum@candw.ky; web: www.museum.ky.
Situated opposite Hog Sty Bay in the Old Courts building, the Cayman Islands National Museum offers plenty to interest both adults and children. Don't miss the excellent 3D model, or bathymetric map, showing the Cayman Islands perched high above the sea bed of the Caribbean. A more graphic presentation of the famous walls that surround these islands would be hard to find. A laser-

disc show focusing on the underwater world is complemented by interactive displays of undersea life and Cayman natural history.

Upstairs, a moving mannequin tells stories of the sea beside the restored 14ft (4.2m) catboat, the centrepiece of displays on turtling, rope making and shipbuilding. Alongside this are numerous other cultural artefacts and paintings from the national collection, all serving to bring the history of the islands to life. The old court room has been refurbished to allow for regularly changing exhibitions of community life, including art and furniture. Heritage days, featuring all manner of traditional crafts from one of the Cayman districts, are a regular feature of the museum. Known as 'Looky ya' ('look here'), these days are usually held on the last Thursday of the month. Downstairs, there is a good gift shop and just round the corner is the Jailhouse Café.

Open Mon–Fri 9.00am–5.00pm; Sat and most public holidays 10.00am–2.00pm. Last admissions half an hour before closing. Closed first Monday of each month. Admission CI$4/US$5; concessions CI$2/US$2.50. Admission free first Saturday of each month.

Other places in or near George Town

Grand Cayman is so small that, realistically, everywhere is within easy reach of George Town. These suggestions, though, are beyond the scope of a simple walking tour. For organised tours covering the rest of the island, see pages 79–81. For details of areas beyond the town and Seven Mile Beach, have a look at *Chapters 6* and *7*.

Currently housed in the new Harbour Place, opposite Eden Rock, is the Cayman Islands' **National Gallery** (tel: 945 8111; email: nat.gal@candw.ky; web: www.nationalgallery.org.ky). Exhibits here are changed about eight times a year, showing often challenging work from both international and local artists. Entrance is free and there is a small gift shop on site. Funds permitting, there are plans to move the gallery to its final resting spot near the Harquail Theatre, off Easterly Tibbetts Drive. Open Mon–Fri 9.00am–5.00pm, Sat 11.00am–4.00pm. Admission is free.

One of the newest attractions close to George Town is the **Butterfly Farm** (tel: 946 3411; www.thebutterflyfarm.com). Set back from Lawrence Boulevard, opposite the cinema, it is home to brightly coloured tropical butterflies from around the world – although what you see when you visit will of course depend on what has recently hatched. Small display cabinets house the eggs, caterpillars and chrysalises of various tropical species, which emerge to hover over a diverse array of plants around the sand paths – a perfect opportunity for the photographer. Enjoy the spectacle, but for greater interest join one of the short guided tours that are run every 20 minutes or so. The on-site shop specialises in locally made arts and crafts. Open 8.30am–4.00pm (last tour 3.30pm). Entry US$15, children US$9.

Hidden behind George Town, opposite the CUC electricity generating station on North Sound Road, is the **Conch Shell House**. Originally built in 1935 from more than 4,000 conch shells, it later burned down but was subsequently rebuilt, and the private house that stands on the site today is rather less appealing than tour guides may suggest. Although the house is not open to the public, visitors are welcome to walk on the lawns to take photographs. Near by is the **Tortuga Rum Cake factory** (tel: 949 7701; fax: 949 6322; email: tortuga@candw.ky;

web: www.caribplace.com/foods/tortuga.htm), where visitors can get an idea of the manufacturing process as they sample the various flavours, or stop for a drink or snack. Open Mon–Fri 8.00am–5.00pm; Sat 8.00am–2.30pm.

South of George Town
Following the coast road out of George Town to the south, the streets soon give way to a quiet and exclusive residential area. On the left as you leave the town is **Pure Art** (see page 138), a colourful celebration of Cayman art, from painting and ceramics to woven baskets and wood carving. Follow the road past the Grand Old House (open Mon–Fri 11.45–2.00pm, daily 6.00–10.00pm) and continue on along the coast beyond **Smith's Cove** (the perfect place for a quick swim – see page 142). Stop, if you have time, to visit **Dr Carey's** small workshop, Bikini House, where he produces black coral jewellery and engraved glass (open Mon–Sat 8.00am–6.00pm or later). Irrespective of your views on black coral, Dr Carey is something of an institution in his own right. Take him a marble or two and you'll make his day, adding to his huge collection (36,331 in February 2004) from all over the world.

As the road veers round to the east, even the larger houses thin out to reveal a narrow coastline fringed by mangroves and casuarina trees, looking out across **South Sound.** If it's around lunch time, you could try the Crow's Nest (see page 125) for a relaxing meal in an idyllic setting.

Boat trips
Submersibles, semi-submersibles and glass-bottomed boats
You don't have to be a water baby to experience the under-sea attractions of the islands. Even if you're not a diver, you can explore the fascinating reefs and shipwrecks that surround Grand Cayman, not just from the surface but in submersibles – a form of submarine that has to return to shore regularly for its batteries to be recharged. Grand Cayman played host to the first submersible and with good reason – the reef is relatively shallow and the visibility is excellent.

For the less intrepid, semi-submersibles have a lower deck beneath the surface, enabling passengers to walk below and view the first few feet of the underwater world, as seen by a snorkeller, through large glazed windows, then return to the fresh air on the top.

Atlantis Submarines PO Box 10249 APO, Harbour Drive, George Town; tel: 949 7700, US toll free 800 887 8571; email: atlantis@candw.ky; web: www.atlantisadventures.net
The first of the world's passenger submarine operators, Atlantis was established in 1984. Passengers are ferried out to the dive site by shuttle, then transferred to the submersible for a 40-minute trip down to around 100ft (30m). For the non-diver, this is a real opportunity to see the underwater world; even divers will find the running commentary fascinating. Up to six dives a day, Mon–Sat, depart from 8.30am. Night dives are also offered Wed, Thu, Fri at 7.00pm and 8.00pm in winter, or at 7.30pm Wed, Fri in summer. Adults US$79–84 (low/high season); children half price. No children under 3ft (0.9m) tall. For the true – and well-heeled – adventurer, Atlantis boasts an altogether more serious craft capable of going to depths of up to 1,000ft (304m). The one-hour deep dive, the only one of its kind in the world, takes just two passengers per trip to

depths of 800ft (244m) for US$345–395 per person, or to 1,000ft for US$450 per person. Under the bright lights of the submarine, the true colours of coral and other marine life are clearly visible. Videos of your trip are also available. Tours depart Mon–Sat (Mon–Fri in summer) at 8.30am, 10.00am, 11.30am, 1.00pm and 2.30pm. At the other end of the scale, the semi-submersible *Seaworld Explorer* explores the harbour around George Town, including the area around two of the town's shipwrecks (departures Mon–Sat 10.00am and 2.00pm), while *Stingray Explorer* – as its name suggests – takes you out to Stingray City (departures from Morgan's Harbour Tue, Thu and Fri at 3.00pm). For information on both of these, call 949 8534. Adults US$32, children US$19.

Nautilus PO Box 10094 APO, Bush Centre, George Town; tel: 945 1355; fax: 945 3739; email: nautilus@candw.ky; web: www.nautilus.ky

Tours in the semi-submersibles *Nautilus* (named after Jules Verne's futuristic craft) and *Little R* are run from Rackam's dock (behind Rackam's Pub) in George Town. The hour-long trip with commentary offers the opportunity to see both marine life and shipwrecks, and to watch fish being fed by divers just outside the window. In the afternoons, the trip is followed by an opportunity to snorkel, either on the reef or over a nearby wreck. Mask, snorkel and fins are included, with tuition available if needed. One-hour trip: adults US$35, children US$15, under 3 free; two-hour snorkel trip: adults US$39, children US$19. Nautilus also run Aqua Boats, offering the chance to drive your own two-person inflatable on a guided tour, with three snorkelling stops. Rates US$69 per person.

Cayman Submariners/SEAmobile Submarine Tours Tel: 916 3483 (DIVE); email: info@caymansubmariners.com; web: www.caymansubmariners.com

Trips to the reef for just two passengers in this small vessel with all-round visibility make this a pretty exclusive set up, even offering the opportunity to pilot the sub – under supervision, naturally. US$139 per person.

Red Sail Sports (see page 107) offers trips in glass-bottomed boats at Rum Point.

Other boat trips

The number of companies offering boat trips is almost bewildering in its range and diversity. One that's clearly visible from George Town is the replica 17th-century galleon, the *Jolly Roger* (page 106), which offers daytime 'pirate encounters' as well as sunset, cocktail and dinner cruises. For details of this, the *Nina*, and a full range of other boat trips, including snorkelling, fishing and trips to Stingray City, see *Chapter 4*, pages 102–7.

A day trip to **Rum Point** is a must, with a regular ferry leaving from the dock alongside the Hyatt Hotel on West Bay Road several times a day. For details, see pages 78 and 168–70.

pure

Turquoise surrounding a Caribbean hideaway. Awakening to the gentle sighs of the sea on idyllic Cayman Brac. Opening shuttered windows on orchid fringed beaches on Little Cayman. Walking, cocktail in hand along the silver sands of Grand Cayman. The Cayman Islands. Three drops of pure colour.

CAYMAN ISLANDS

For more information
please call 020 7491 7771 or visit
www.caymanislands.co.uk

Above Cayman Islands National Museum, George Town (TH)

Left Shipbuilding panel from George Town's Milestones in History (TH)

Below Local boys on cannon believed to come from the Wreck of the Ten Sail (LW)

Below left Statue outside Harquail Theatre (TH)

Above Blue iguanas are frequently seen in Queen Elizabeth II Botanic Park. (TH)

Right Iguanas on Little Cayman have right of way, even by the airstrip. (TH)

Below right One of the highly original iguanas of the Blue Dragon project (TH)

Below Artist at work on an iguana for the Blue Dragon project (MC)

West Bay

Drive north past the last of the big hotels on West Bay Road, and you head back to an era when the island was rarely visited and the pace of life was slow. Painted wooden houses with airy verandas are set far back from the road in large gardens, some of them the traditional

sand gardens that are so much a part of the Cayman heritage. Once a thriving fishing community, the focal point for everyday activities from shopping and schools to the making of turtle nets, West Bay is still the second largest residential district on Grand Cayman, and popular with visitors to the Turtle Farm and Hell.

On the northern coast of West Bay you will find empty beaches and virgin mangrove forest. Here, casuarinas and sea-grape trees cast their shade over the narrow expanse of sand, and wild tamarind grows along the roadside, intertwined in season with the purple and white morning glory. Don't expect any facilities – that's the beauty of the place – although in recognition of the need to preserve this threatened environment, the eastern point of the peninsula at Barkers has recently been declared a national park.

WHERE TO STAY

Cobalt Coast Resort PO Box 159 H, 18 Sea Fan Drive; tel: 946 5656; US reservations toll free: 866 622 9626; fax: 946 5657; email: cobalt@candw.ky; web: www.cobaltcoast.com (24 rooms/suites/villas)

Refreshingly relaxed and individual, this small resort nestles in Boatswain's Bay, a secluded beachfront location on the north of West Bay, some two miles from the Turtle Farm. It is owned and efficiently run by Dutch hotelier Arie Barendrecht, whose easy-going charm is complemented by the helpfulness of his mostly Caymanian staff. Accommodation ranges from large bedrooms and suites to villas, so there are plenty of options. Each of the hotel rooms and one- or two-bedroom suites has one king or two double beds per bedroom, a living room with queen-size sofa bed, AC, TV, fridge, coffee machine, telephone and safe. In addition, the two villas have fully equipped kitchens. Duppies restaurant and bar look out over the swimming pool and Jacuzzi, and beyond to the sea – though the beach is ironshore. The hotel has its own boat dock and diving is through Divetech, who are based at the resort and have an on-site shop. The shore diving and snorkelling from here are excellent, yet the clientele remains mixed, with about a third of the guests as non-divers. It's also possible to rent kayaks at US$10 per hour, or a Laser Pico at US$30 per hour.

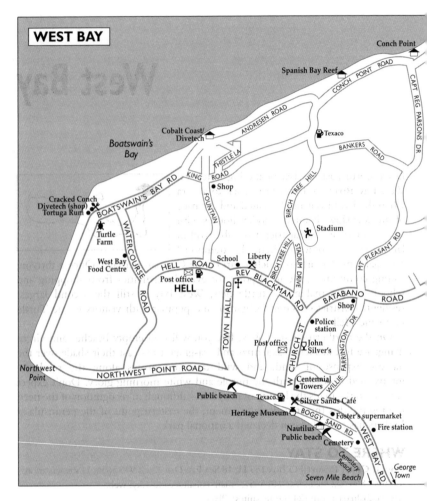

Rates per night low/high season for two people: garden view US$190/225; oceanfront US$215/250; garden suites US$235/260; one-bedroom oceanfront suite US$255/295; two-bedroom suite/villa US$410/475 (four people). Each additional person US$25. Rates subject to 20% service charge and tax. Dive packages available on request.

Jeff's Guest Homes HC2 Box 865, Winchester, WI 54557, USA; tel: US 800 484 7694 ext 5333; email: jkingstad@jeffsresorts.com; web: www.jeffsresorts.com (2 houses) Two modern individual houses in West Bay are set in attractive gardens complete with barbecue and hammocks. Each has two bedrooms, living room with sofa bed, dining room, kitchen, bathroom, AC/ceiling fans, TV/VCR and CD player, and telephone. Owner Jeff Kingstad is also a dive instructor and can arrange private lessons on request. Rates per house per week, low/high season: US$795–995/$995–1,295, plus 6% service charge.

Nautilus Apartments PO Box 634 GT, 88 Boggy Sand Rd; tel/fax: 946 0464; fax: 949 2677; email: nautiapt@candw.ky; web: www.cayman.com.ky/com/nautilus/contact.htm (4 units)

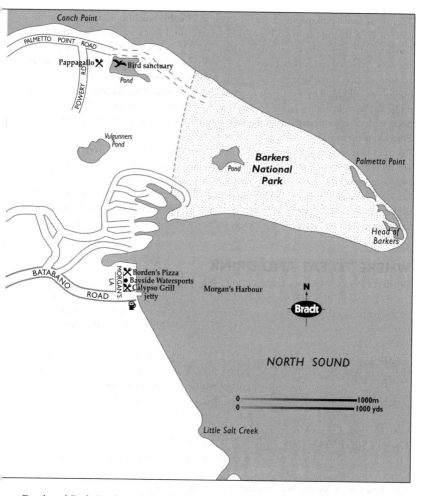

Frank and Beth Roulstone's beachside townhouses, cottage and studio in one of Grand Cayman's most historic roads offer a peaceful and personal alternative to the hotels further south. With direct access to the secluded northern end of Seven Mile Beach, each of the houses has two bedrooms, two bathrooms, kitchen and living room. The townhouses also have a balcony with sea view, AC/ceiling fans, washer/dryer and garden furniture with gas barbecue; the cottage has a screened porch and deck. The studio, ideal for two people, has ceiling fans, basin/toilet, a fridge and a cooker.

Rates per night, low/high season (inclusive of tax): townhouse (up to four people) US$220/330; cottage (up to four people) US$100/140; studio (up to two people) US$65/75. Children under 12 free. Minimum stay three days in summer, seven days in winter. No credit cards.

Spanish Bay Reef Resort PO Box 903 GT, Pikes Rd; tel: 949 3765, US toll free 1 800 482 DIVE; fax: 949 1842; email: spnshbay@candw.ky; web: www.caymanresorthotels.com (66 rooms)

This all-inclusive pink-painted resort is set on an enviable beachfront site on the north coast of West Bay, not far from Pappagallo's restaurant. Particularly popular with families and couples, the resort's rooms have AC, TV, balcony or patio with garden or sea view. Standard and superior rooms are located in the main building, while additional accommodation is available in small cottage ocean-view rooms or one-bedroom bungalows, all linked by wooden walkways. Dining is in the Spanish Main restaurant or under the stars, by Calico Jack's poolside bar. Swimming pool, private harbour and boat dock, with diving operated out of the affiliated Beach Club on Seven Mile Beach. Entertainment includes sunset party and barbecue.

Rates per person per night, based on double occupancy, vary almost from month to month. Low to high season: US$160–230 (standard) up to US$250–325 (one-bedroom bungalow). Single supplement US$100 per night. Third and fourth adults US$150 per night. Special rates for up to two children when sharing with two adults: under 6 free; 6–12 US$50 per night; 12–17 US$75 per night. Free upgrade for honeymooners. Two-tank dive package, inclusive of most equipment, additional US$50 per day.

WHERE TO EAT AND DRINK

Borden's Pizzas Morgan's Lane; tel: 949 3462. A popular place with locals, even if the smell of cooking oil is a bit overpowering. Eat in or takeaway pizzas and other fast food, including the local 'hush puppies' – deep-fried balls of flour, cornmeal and sugar. Caribbean dinner at weekends. Open Mon–Thu 5.00–11.00pm; Fri 5.00–midnight; Sat/Sun 3.00pm–midnight.

Calypso Grill Morgan's Harbour; tel: 949 3948. Tucked away right on the harbour on the east of West Bay, Calypso Grill opened in 1999 and was an instant success. It's easy to see why – the combination of waterfront setting, friendly atmosphere and good food is unbeatable. Mussels, fresh fish etc come straight from the dock, and sticky toffee pudding's a speciality. Open Tue–Sat 11.30am–2.30pm; Sun 12.30–2.30pm; daily 6.00–10.00pm. Do book at weekends.

Corita's Silver Sands Café Town Hall Rd; tel: 949 3301. Simple local café serving breakfast, lunch and dinner, as well as snacks to take out, all at very reasonable prices. Open Mon–Sat 7.30am–7.00pm.

Cracked Conch by the Sea Northwest Point Rd; tel: 945 5217; web: www.conchedout@candw.ky. This nautical-themed establishment, owned by the wife of Bob Soto (of local diving fame), is just up the road from the Turtle Farm so well frequented by tourists. Large waterfront balcony, and restaurant/bar featuring a chronology of Cayman history. Very good traditional Cayman food, including turtle and conch, as well as a range of more cosmopolitan dishes, make it an attractive choice, though many of the specials are reserved for the evening. If you're watching your weight, note that they also have an Atkins Diet menu. Takeaway service available. Sunday Caribbean buffet CI$12.95, 11.30am–3.00pm. All-evening Fri happy hour. Open daily, 11.00am till the last diners have left.

Duppies Cobalt Coast, Boatswain's Bay; tel: 946 5656. The relatively small menu at this resort restaurant is well prepared and includes a couple of vegetarian dishes at lunch and dinner and daily specials. With the stars as a backdrop, who needs designer frills? Open daily 7.00–9.00am, midday–2:30pm, 6.00–9:30pm. Live music on Saturday nights.

Liberty's 140 Rev Blackman Rd, West Bay; tel: 949 3226. The reputation of this family-owned restaurant in West Bay goes back several years. Notable for its Cayman specialities, such as conch stew, for around CI$8–12.50, it also has an 'all-you-can-eat' buffet on Wed, Fri and Sun at CI$15.95 a head. Takeaway service available. Open daily 10.30am–10.00pm.

Pappagallo Barkers, tel: 949 1119/3479; email: pappa@candw.ky; web: www.pappagallo.ky. The romantic lakeside setting of the thatched Ristorante Pappagallo on the edge of West Bay is reason enough to visit. The food here is said to be excellent, too, specialising in Italian cuisine (the pasta is mostly homemade and the gnocchi is 'unbeatable'), with a noticeably creative hand behind the scenes. Choose carefully and it won't break the bank either. The comprehensive wine list, one of the best on the island, affords plenty of choice. Open daily 6.00–10.30pm.

Bars

John Silver's This local bar tucked away off West Church Street is well off the tourist trail. Next door, at John Silver's Inn (tel: 949 4264/4242), there are basic rooms to let.

SHOPPING

There are a few local convenience stores, but just one major supermarket:

Foster's Food Fair West Bay Rd (bus stop 18). Open Mon–Sat 7.00am–11.00pm; holidays 9.00am–6.00pm. In-store pharmacy open Sun 9.00am–6.00pm.

A TOUR BY CAR OR BIKE

Heading north from George Town, at the crossroads of West Bay Road with Church Street or by bus stop 19, stop a while to take on board a little of the heritage of Grand Cayman that is rapidly disappearing. The National Trust (see page 29) has produced a walking tour of central West Bay, covering historic Cayman houses and churches, including several in nearby **Boggy Sand Road**. Tucked away behind West Bay Road, and backing on to Seven Mile Beach, this quiet lane is worth a visit to get a feel for the island as recently as the 1960s, even if you don't have time to do the whole walk. The Trust's tour takes about 2¹/₂ hours to complete, fanning out to encompass West Church Street, Pond Road, Elizabeth Street and Henning Lane, but it can sensibly be divided into three parts, each taking no longer than an hour.

On the corner of Boggy Sand Road and West Bay Road is the so-called **Heritage Museum**, tel: 949 3477, and adjacent craft shop. More a ramshackle collection of documents and artefacts accumulated by one Prentice Powell than a museum, it is really only of passing interest. That said, the examples of different types of wood – ironwood, bullet wood, black mangrove used for smoke wood, and furstic, used for boatbuilding – shed light on a number of Cayman traditions, while the building itself was originally Mr Prentice's general store. Open Mon–Thu 9.00am–4.30pm. Small admission fee.

Continuing northwest along West Bay Road, the road follows the line of the coast, bringing you eventually to the **Turtle Farm** (see box overleaf) on the left, with the Cracked Conch by the Sea (see opposite) shortly beyond, a good place to stop for lunch. The bus stop here is number 24.

Located just next to the Turtle Farm is the source of many of Grand Cayman's rum cakes, **Tortuga Rum Cake Factory**. Here you can look

TURTLE FARM

The world's only commercial green sea turtle farm was established in 1968. Now owned by the government, it welcomes visitors to observe green sea turtles, from the tiniest hatchlings to fully grown adults. The farm also has a small number of three other species of sea turtle: Kemp's ridley, loggerhead and hawksbill.

Originally set up in the natural environment of North Sound, the farm moved to its present site in 1971. Until recently, a breeding herd of 300 turtles produced some 45,000 eggs each year, but in 2001 the farm was hit by Hurricane Michelle, and many of the turtles were swept away. In subsequent years, the farm's turtle-release programme, which had been in operation since 1980, has been severely curtailed, with just ten green sea turtles released during the traditional Pirates Week ceremony in October 2003. Overall though, since the scheme was started, 28,000 hatchlings and yearlings have been released into the wild, all tagged for subsequent identification.

Although the farm is once again open to visitors and remains as popular as ever, there are ambitious plans to secure its future by rebuilding on a more sheltered site on the opposite side of the road. As part of this development, attractions at the farm will be broadened to give a wider

through the window of the bakery where some of the cakes are made and sample the various flavours before you buy. Open Mon–Fri 8.00am–5.00pm, Sat 8.00am–2.30pm. Admission free.

Follow the road on past the Turtle Farm and the Cracked Conch by the Sea, then turn right into Watercourse Road, with West Bay Food Centre on your right. Shortly after this is the turning left towards Hell.

The tiny village of **Hell**, about half a mile from the sea, acquired its name from the dark, rather evil-looking rock formations that lie behind the post office and are now much sought after by photographers. A second, unsubtantiated story has it that a one-time British governor, intent on shooting birds in the vicinity, lost his temper when he missed a target and uttered a loud 'Oh, hell!' Either way, the name stuck. Not surprisingly, cards postmarked 'Hell' are popular among tourists, and a couple of shops alongside the post office oblige with a range of postcards. The village is also said to be the setting for scenes in Defoe's *Robinson Crusoe*.

This is truly a desolate place. The blackened landscape is at its most atmospheric in the early evening, when visitors are few and the light reflects off the still, dark water. The sharp formations of karst rock seen here are similar in structure to the rock found on the Mastic Trail. Over countless years, the underlying bedrock of limestone and dolomite, originally formed under the sea, was eroded both by the action of the waves and by microscopic algae, tiny marine organisms that ate away the calcium from the rock. Whereas the rock on the Mastic Trail is white, however, the rocks here have been stained black over the years by traces of algae that still cling to them.

The post office is open Mon–Fri 8.30am–5.00pm, Sat 8.30am–midday, and family appeal: swimming with dolphins is one possibility. At present, some visitors are disappointed at the commercialism of the operation here, so it's worth stressing that it is first and foremost a working farm that is open to visitors, rather than a visitor attraction with farming on the side. There is a full-time marine biologist on the staff to look after the welfare of the turtles, some of which are second-generation turtles bred in captivity. Inevitably, work of this sort is controversial, but recently two turtles released in the 1980s have returned to Seven Mile Beach to nest, which is very encouraging. Researchers continue to monitor the situation closely. For more details of the turtles themselves, see page 26.

An on-site café selling snacks, drinks and ice-cream is surrounded by a small exhibition on the history of turtling in the islands and marine conservation. The excellent gift shop has a good selection of souvenirs and related merchandise, including books and jigsaws. For more about the history of the farm, pick up a copy of *Last Chance Lost*, which also addresses some of the conservation issues raised by the farm's programme.

PO Box 645 GT, North West Point Road, West Bay; tel: 949 3893; fax: 949 1387; email: ctfl@candw.ky; web: www.turtle.ky. Open daily, 8.30am–5.00pm. Adults US$6.00; children US$3.00.

sells special stamps. If it's closed, the shops alongside and next to the petrol station are open 7.00am–5.00pm; both sell stamps as well as postcards, so you can still post your correspondence here.

To return towards Seven Mile Beach, take the next turning right into Town Hall Road, which joins up with the northern end of West Bay Road. Alternatively, bear left on to Birch Tree Hill and make your way out towards Barkers, near Ristorante Pappagallo. The 14-acre pond and **bird sanctuary** here, overlooked by the restaurant, is a tidal lagoon that is home to tarpon. White egrets, ducks and numerous migrant birds gather here, particularly in winter. The road at this point becomes a rough track and eventually brings you to the gates of Barkers National Park (see page 25), newly dedicated in 2004 and the first part of Cayman to receive such recognition. There are plans to build a visitors' centre here with a car park, but for now the place remains relatively untouched. For an idea of the seclusion that was typical of Grand Cayman only 30 years ago, it's much nicer to leave your car or bike and explore the narrow shoreline, backed by sea-grape trees, on foot.

Turn back along the road to Captain Reginald Parsons Drive, then wend your way through to Batabano Road and east to North Sound at **Morgan's Harbour**. This quiet little backwater has a few places to moor small boats, and limited facilities including water, fuel and ice. Right by the harbour is the Calypso Grill (see page 154), a friendly place for a meal or a drink with beautiful views across North Sound. To return to Seven Mile Beach, go back along Batabano Road to the crossroads, turn left into West Church Street, and left again into West Bay Road.

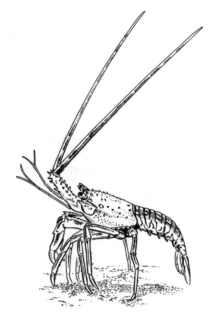

Spiny lobster

East of George Town

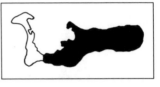

It may be thought that there's an invisible boundary dividing Grand Cayman at its narrowest point near Red Bay, as if there were some form of gateway to the more subtle charms of the eastern end of the island. The shopping mall of Grand Harbour stands like a sentinel at the crossroads, a bastion of commercialism before the greater tranquillity of the east. Marketing people like to speak of these eastern districts as 'the fourth Cayman island', and with some justification. Just a mile or so down the road and the urbanisation is replaced by small villages, peaceful coves, and a quieter, more natural side to the island that repays exploration.

While the attractions of the east are many, the highlights can also be grouped together to form a fascinating day out. If you're looking for a guided tour, or a more adventurous slant on the area, there are three tour operators who specialise in this area: Ecoventures, Explore Cayman and Silver Thatch Excursions (see pages 80–1).

RED BAY TO BODDEN TOWN

Almost three miles east of George Town, South Sound Road links up with Crewe Road, coming in from the airport area. Right on this junction is **Grand Harbour** shopping mall, and just beyond is the home of **Stingray Brewery**, which lies on Red Bay Road, tel: 947 6699. Cayman's only brewery, which is open to visitors, has three beers, available at bars throughout the islands. Durty (3%) and Dark (6%) are both available on draught only; the more popular Premium (4%) is bottled. Brewing is normally on Mondays and Thursdays, with bottling on Wednesdays. Open Mon–Sat, 9.00am–5.00pm, closed public holidays. Admission free, including beer-tasting for over 18s only. Small shop.

A little further on, set back from the road on the left, is the **Playhouse Theatre**, home to the Cayman Drama Society (see page 140). Popular with theatre-goers as well as local residents, the nearby **Durty Reid's** in Red Bay Plaza is a lively bar that also serves ice-creams and main meals, including a daily special, such as dolphin, for around CI\$10.95. It is open Mon–Fri 10.30am–1.00am, Sat–Sun 10.30am–midnight. There's a Chinese restaurant here too (tel: 947 1166), and on the small parade opposite, TCBY is a handy ice-cream stop.

Continuing east, new developments soon give way to a more verdant landscape. You could be forgiven for going through the village of **Prospect**

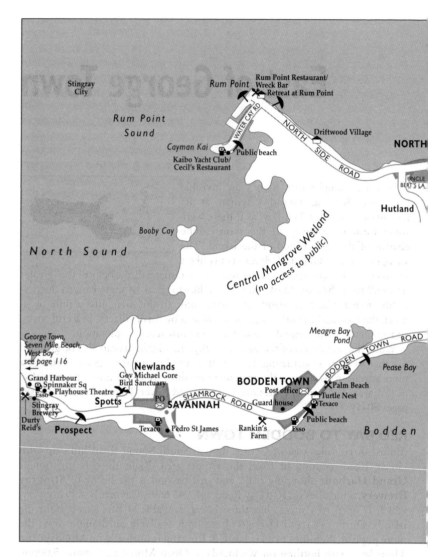

without noticing it, though it is thought to have been one of the first settlements in Grand Cayman, dating from the latter half of the 18th century. At one time there was even a fort here, now marked by a memorial. The village itself lies to the right, off the main road, but has been abandoned since 1932, the church on the coast left in ruins. Since taken over by a theological organisation, they lie on the site marked Prospect Youth Centre. Of greater interest, though, is the adjacent 19th-century Watler family cemetery, owned by the National Trust. Here, the solid stone grave markers in the shape of small houses are testament to a former, more prosperous settlement. There's a sandy beach just round the point that's a good place for snorkelling and diving, though access is very limited.

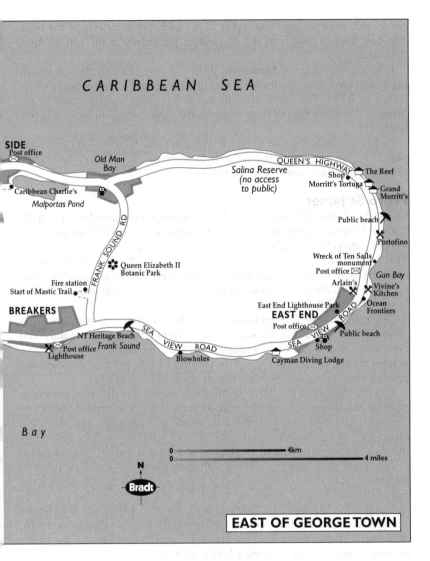

CARIBBEAN SEA

SIDE
Post office

Old Man
Bay

QUEEN'S HIGHWAY

Salina Reserve
(no access
to public)

Shop
Morritt's Tortuga

The Reef

Grand
Morritt's

Caribbean Charlie's
Malportas Pond

Public beach

Portofino

FRANK SOUND RD

Queen Elizabeth II
Botanic Park

Wreck of Ten Sails
monument
Post office

Gun Bay

Fire station
Start of Mastic Trail

Arlain's

Vivine's
Kitchen

BREAKERS

East End Lighthouse Park
EAST END

Ocean
Frontiers

Post office

SEA VIEW ROAD

NT Heritage Beach
Post office   Frank Sound
Lighthouse

SEA VIEW ROAD

Public beach

Shop

Blowholes

Cayman Diving Lodge

Bay

0   4km
0   4 miles

N

Bradt

EAST OF GEORGE TOWN

The Prospect road rejoins the main road and shortly after this you come to the village of **Spotts**, with its public beach nestled between the rocks, though currents here are strong so be careful if you plan to swim. There's a shaded picnic area under some large casuarinas trees, and ample parking. Beyond the beach is a second cemetery not dissimilar to that at Prospect, though here the 18th-century grave markers are painted white.

For the **Governor Michael Gore Bird Sanctuary**, take Spotts Newlands Road to the left, and shortly afterwards turn right; the sanctuary is about a hundred yards further on the left-hand side. More than 60 species of both water and land birds, including over a quarter of Cayman's native birds, are attracted to the small freshwater pond at the centre of this two-acre site. Walkways enable the visitor to get around, while an observation post allows undisturbed viewing of the birds. The best time to visit is in the dry season, particularly at the end of April. Admission is free.

Entering the village of **Savannah**, there is a post office on the left shortly before you come to a crossroads; on the corner is a petrol station opposite where there's an ATM. The 1940s' schoolhouse in the village was renovated by the National Trust in 1995 and is now open to the public by appointment only (tel: 949 0121).

At the crossroads, the road to the left takes you to the Sunrise Golf Centre (see page 112). Turn right into Pedro Castle Road, however, and you'll be heading towards the historic house of Pedro St James.

Pedro St James

Savannah; tel: 947 3329; fax: 947 2611; web: www.pedrostjames.ky. Open daily 8.30am–5.00pm; multimedia presentation on the hour from 10.00am to 4.00pm. Adults US$8; children 6–12 US$4, under 6 free.

This 19th-century plantation great house – categorically *not* a castle – is the oldest building in the Cayman Islands, having survived two earthquakes, three fires and over a dozen hurricanes. In fact, it was the only building on the island to survive the 1785 hurricane.

Originally built by William Eden in the 1780s, Pedro (pronounced locally as 'Peadro') St James became the seat of justice during the early 19th century, and even served time as the island's jailhouse. In 1831, the decision was taken here to form the first elected assembly of the Cayman Islands, and four years later the proclamation ending slavery in the islands was read from its steps.

Towards the end of the 19th century, the house fell into disrepair, remaining more or less abandoned over the next 60 years or so. A misguided attempt to 'restore' it as a castle led to a new lease of life as a restaurant and hotel, but successive fires eventually put paid to this venture. It was not until the early 1990s that the government purchased the property and restored it to its former elegance.

The house today features shining mahogany floors and authentic polished furniture, giving a taste of the standard of living enjoyed by the well-to-do at the end of the 18th century. Across the yard is the separate kitchen, built of wattle and daub with a thatched roof. Its traditional caboose – a large wood-fired hearth – is typical of those used for cooking throughout the islands well into the 1950s. Well-placed plaques throughout the house give a real insight into the way of life for both owners and slaves on the island at the time.

The landscaped grounds with their air of colonial grace lead down to the sea, backed by ironshore, and with unobstructed views. It's a great place for clambering on the rocks if you're careful, but do wear sensible shoes. There is also a short woodland trail.

The half-hour multi-media presentation held in the on-site theatre presents life on the islands from the time that the house was built through the birth of Cayman democracy and the abolition of slavery up to the present day. Allow at least an hour – considerably more if you're really interested – to visit the theatre and look right round the house and grounds. There's a well-stocked gift shop, where you can buy a booklet entitled *The History of Pedro St James Castle* at a swingeing US$16.50, but the chrome and plastic of the café could do with a rethink.

From the entrance to Pedro St James' car park, a track leads away from the village of Savannah. A walk of 15 minutes or so will bring you out on Pedro Bluff, some of the highest cliffs on the south coast of the island, dotted with spindly coconut palms. As you walk, you might catch a glimpse of the green parrots that inhabit the trees along the road.

Back at the crossroads, turn right and follow the road inland until you reach Bodden Town.

Bodden Town

Neatly fenced single-storeyed houses with corrugated-iron rooves and wooden verandas line the roads of this small community, whose atmosphere is more village than town, more English than American. Originally called South Side, Bodden Town was the first capital of Grand Cayman, taking its name from the 'oldest and most respectable settlers' who first made this place their home in the 18th century. Today, though, Bodden Town is a bit of a backwater, well away from the tourist frenzy of Seven Mile Beach and retaining much of its traditional charm.

Where to stay

Turtle Nest Inn PO Box 187 BT, Bodden Town Rd; tel: 947 8665; fax: 947 6379; email: turtlein@candw.ky; web: www.turtlenestinn.com (9 apartments)
Located on the beach near the post office, the hacienda-style Turtle Nest Inn is something of a revelation in Grand Cayman. Small, quiet and personal, it is owned and run by a friendly Canadian couple and offers very good value. Each of the one-bedroom apartments, and the one two-bedroom apartment, have a bathroom, living room with sofa bed, TV/VCR, telephone, AC/ceiling fans. Business facilities are available on request, as are stereos. Each week, a Caribbean night and an Indian night are held for guests, as well as a barbecue. Diving through Ocean Frontiers.
Rates per room for two people: partial sea view US$129–169, beachfront US$149–199. Additional guest US$15/20; children 3 and under free. One night free per two-week stay. Maid service included.

Where to eat

Palm Beach Bodden Town Rd; tel: 947 7044. Situated on the waterfront in Bodden Town, Palm Beach was formerly the Edge (now Over the Edge; see page 167). The reincarnation with its apricot floor and tables is certainly attractive, if a little stark, but the reputation isn't a patch on its predecessor's. The menu offers a mix of Italian and Caribbean dishes with plenty of seafood options. Open daily 11.00am–11.00pm.
Rankin's Farm Tel: 947 3283. At the other end of the spectrum, try the jerk chicken and other favourites at this farm just to the west of Bodden Town, where shaded tables set out on the grass are a pleasant place for a stop throughout the day.

Shopping

A couple of small gift shops in Bodden Town cater for the tourist market. Set back from the road towards the east of the village, the **Pirate Cave** (open 9.00am–5.00pm) has souvenirs, drinks, snacks etc. This is also the entry point to Bodden Town's so-called 'pirate' caves, for which there is a small entry charge. Further on, beyond Palm Beach restaurant, there's the aptly named **Tourist Trap** (signposted 'Wood-Works' if you're coming from the east) which sells wooden carvings and furniture; give the rather sad-looking caged rabbits and birds a miss.

What to see

Bodden Town can come as a bit of a disappointment to the visitor. Although historically significant, there is little of visual interest on the ground. **Guard House Park**, at the entrance to Bodden Town from the west, was the location of a 19th-century security post. All that is visible are some rusting cannons and a modern stone shelter that houses a few information panels about the town. A little further east, beyond a monument to Queen Victoria, the location of **Gun Square** is marked by two 18th-century cannons standing upright like sentries, a reminder of the town's need to defend itself against marauders from the sea. A leaflet covering the historic sites of Bodden Town is available from the National Trust (see page 29).

BODDEN TOWN TO EAST END AND NORTH SIDE

Just beyond Bodden Town on the left is the small Meagre Bay Pond, once frequented by hunters after teal and mallard for the pot, but now a **wildlife sanctuary** that is popular with birdwatchers. There is a bird hide here, but the pond dries out in the winter months. Park on the side of the road.

From here, the roadside vegetation becomes denser as you head for the village of **Breakers**, home to one of the island's best restaurants:

Lighthouse Breakers; tel: 947 2047. Despite the name, the 'lighthouse' was in fact built as a restaurant, and a pretty imposing one at that, with views out to sea from the screened waterside terrace backed by an air-conditioned restaurant. At lunchtime, tables are also set out on the deck over the water. Service is impeccable and the original if pricey menu focuses on Italian dishes and seafood, with daily specials; the seared scallops are unbeatable. The restaurant prides itself on a huge range of wines, with a cellar numbering some 3,000 bottles. Exclusive private room available for small parties. Open daily 11.30am–4.30pm for lunch and 5.30–9.30pm (later in high season) for dinner.

The coast road continues from here through to East End. To the left, though, is Frank Sound Road, which takes you direct to North Side and Rum Point, passing both the entrance to the Mastic Trail and Queen Elizabeth II Botanic Park.

Mastic Trail

The Mastic Trail has been used since the late 18th century to enable people to transport goods and logs from one side of the island to the other. Long disused, it was restored by the National Trust and re-opened as a public right of way in 1995. The whole area covers some 1,000 acres. To date, 399 acres of forest are owned by the Trust, which aims eventually to acquire the remaining 600 acres.

The best time to visit for birds is from October to early December, and for tree orchids, June and July. That said, it's an intriguing place at any time of the year, though note that it's subject to flooding during heavy rain.

The start of the trail is just off the Mastic Road, a turning to the left off Frank Sound Road by the fire station. Those on a guided tour will usually be collected and brought to this point. If you're in your own vehicle, park here; if the car park is full, then you are asked to return at another time as it indicates that the trail is operating at capacity level. A third option would be to get a bus to the junction of Bodden Town Road and Frank Sound Road, then walk to the beginning of the trail from there (see *Buses*, page 78, for details).

Although the trail is relatively short – around 2.5 miles (4km) in total – don't underestimate the level of difficulty. The path passes through hazardous terrain, from wetland that is in part very boggy to ancient (two-million-year-old) forest founded on treacherous and unforgiving karst rock. There is also a species of poisonous tree, the maiden plum, close to the path. Wear good strong shoes or boots (not sandals of any description), take plenty of water and stick to the path. There are no emergency facilities.

A **guide** may not be obligatory, but is strongly advisable, at least for a first trip, and infinitely more rewarding than tackling the trail alone. During our visit, we would undoubtedly have walked through the various habitats without any real understanding, and would probably have missed many of the birds and reptiles that were pointed out to us, including a nightjar and a stripe-headed tanager, as well as the Cuban tree frog, a couple of racer snakes and several land crabs. Just as interesting are the stories of island life that find their way into discussions about the surrounding flora and fauna, from the practical uses of a particular timber to the medicinal properties of an individual plant. And on a practical note, guided tours are usually one-way, with transport provided from the end of the trail to save you retracing your steps in the heat of the day.

Guided walks are run by Ecoventures, Explore Cayman and Silver Thatch Excursions (see pages 80–1). Silver Thatch is owned by Geddes Hislop, who worked for the National Trust during the restoration of the trail, and his wife, Janet. Each of his walks caters for a maximum of ten people, though in reality groups are normally smaller. Walks cost US$45 per person (children 12 and under half price), and it takes approximately two hours to cover the whole trail in one direction. Alternatively, the National Trust (see page 29) publishes a leaflet with a **self-guided walk**. It's available from the Trust for US$5, with profits going towards the purchase of land on the trail. The rugged terrain means that the trail is not suitable for young children, the elderly or the disabled.

The trail leads through an extraordinary diversity of landscape, from farmland and abandoned pasture alongside a quarry (the mahogany that once grew here has long since been felled for timber), through black mangrove swamp, across all that remains of the Mastic Bridge that once traversed the whole swamp area, and on to the bluff formation. Here, where there is no soil, trees have struggled for thousands of years to put down roots in the rocks, taking advantage of periods of rain to force their roots through holes in the rock and draw up moisture. This sharp and uneven rock is known as high rock or clift rock. Structurally it's the same as the evil-looking ground at Hell but here it is unstained by algae so is not the same distinctive black colour. It is probable that, as Grand Cayman emerged over time from the sea, this central ridge, effectively the backbone of the island, arose first, with the surrounding mangrove swamps following significantly later.

The Mastic Trail is the only place on the island to find the mastic tree, distinctive for the veins on its self-peeling bark. There are actually two different species, the yellow mastic, *Sideroxylon foetidissimum*, and the black mastic, *Terminalia eriostachya*.

Towards the end of the trail you will come to Grand Cayman's highest point.

At just 60ft (18m), 'The Mountain' may not be on a grand scale, but on this terrain it's no mean feat going uphill. From here, the trail leads out into open farmland near the island's north coast.

Those on a guided trip will be collected from this northern point of the trail. If you are on your own, however, you'll have to retrace your steps to your vehicle at the start of the trail, then you could go on to visit Queen Elizabeth II Botanic Park, a little further north on Frank Sound Road on the right-hand side. If you're planning to leave by bus, continue on foot as far as the coast road on the north of the island and catch a bus from North Side.

Queen Elizabeth II Botanic Park

PO Box 203 NS, Frank Sound Rd; tel: 947 3558; fax: 947 7873; email: guthrie@candw.ky; web: www.botanic-park.ky

Set in 65 acres in the centre of Grand Cayman, less than an hour's pleasant drive from George Town, the park was opened in 1994 by Queen Elizabeth II and specialises in Caymanian flora. One of the best times to visit is in June when the orchids are in bloom, but the design of the park and the local climate mean that there is always plenty to see.

The long avenue leading into the park is lined by logwood trees, and the smell is pervasive. Lofty royal palms guard the approach to the ticket booth.

The park is designed around a series of gardens and lakes, and has a small visitors' centre and shop. The heritage garden features a 100-year-old Cayman house, complete with separate cookhouse. Its traditional sand garden, lined by conch shells, is surrounded by local flowers, vegetables, medicinal plants and fruit trees. Here you can see such exotica as soursop and breadfruit, and learn about the traditional plants used by the islanders over the years to cure various ailments.

In the aptly named colour garden, native flowers and trees mingle with others from around the world to create ever-changing colour-themed gardens of red, blue, yellow and white. Plans are in hand for new orchid and cactus gardens, and a children's educational garden.

A woodland trail just under a mile (1.25km) long takes the visitor through Cayman's native trees, including the national silver thatch and the interestingly named duppy bush, *Phyllanthus angustifolius*, so called because it shimmers like a ghost in the moonlight. Information panels along the trail explain about some of the birds and butterflies to be seen, as well as the trees themselves, while warning signs indicate poisonous specimens.

Not surprisingly, the park is a haven for animals, birds and butterflies, with all of Cayman's landbirds to be seen and most of the aquatics as well, attracted by numerous ponds that cover some ten acres of the site. Even in winter, when much of the water in the ponds has dried up, you may see the hickatee in Kary's Pond, sculling among the delicate water snowflakes. The protected blue iguana is also present, the subject of a breeding programme at the park (see page 19). Iguanas are frequently to be spotted in the grounds, while in the iguana pen the handsome resident male seems thoroughly at ease posing for the camera.

Open daily Apr–Sep, 9.00am–6.30pm (last admission 5.30pm); Oct–Mar 9.00am–5.30pm (last admission 4.30pm). Adults US$8; children 6–12 US$4; children under 6 free. Discount of 10% for members of the National Trust for the Cayman Islands, on presentation of a valid membership card.

MEDICINAL PLANTS

The provision of modern medical facilities is taken as read nowadays, yet the use of traditional remedies is still recent enough on the islands to be remembered by many local people. Arguably the greatest cure-all, still rated highly by herbalists today, was the aloe, variously used as a laxative, a purgative and to treat worms, not to mention its application on cuts and scrapes to prevent infection. Indian mulberry was used to reduce a fever, while juniper was beneficial in easing toothache. Yellow limes served a dual purpose: not only were drops of the juice used to remove cataracts and styes, but the lime was rubbed in to a wound to cure blood poisoning.

For a good sleeping draught, the leaves of the soursop tree were boiled up as a soothing drink. Cobwebs, although hardly plants, were also part of the armoury, used to stop bleeding. And even less everyday illnesses had their cure: diabetes, for example, was kept at bay by the simple periwinkle.

All of these plants and more are to be found in the Heritage Garden at the Botanic Park.

North Side

As you complete the south–north traverse of the island, a glimpse ahead of the deep blue and turquoise sea underlines just how small Grand Cayman is. Old Man Bay is a small settlement in the sleepy district of North Side, which was once a major rope-making centre, yet was almost completely isolated from the rest of the island until Frank Sound Road was built in the early 20th century. Bear left here past a petrol station and a couple of small shops – the tiny OMB grocery and a wooden souvenir shop – and you'll come to the slightly larger village of North Side.

Where to stay and eat

Driftwood Village PO Box 143 NS; tel: 947 9791; fax: 947 9138; email: rjohnson@candw.ky (4 cottages)
The small rustic complex that is Driftwood Village straddles the road on the way to Rum Point. Basic two-bedroomed cottages sleep up to four people. The sports bar is open evenings only, with a barbecue on Fridays.
Rates on application.
North Side Surf Inn PO Box 205 NS; tel: 947 1431; fax: 947 0704; web: www.northsidesurfinn.com (10 rooms)
This small, friendly inn that occupies this spot was closed in 2004, but indications were that is was only a temporary measure.
Over the Edge Old Man Bay; tel: 947 9568. The renowned Edge restaurant has upped sticks and moved to its new location in North Side. Larger than before, and with a sturdy veranda that is a definite improvement on its decidedly rickety predecessor, it nevertheless retains much of its original charm, although standards are slightly less predictable. Come at lunchtime, when local dishes are served with salad, red potatoes and Cayman-style fried bread and you can enjoy the tranquillity of the

setting overlooking the sea. The dinner menu (and the prices) are more cosmopolitan, but we're assured that Cayman specialities may still be ordered at lunchtime prices, making this a seriously good bet. Open daily 7.30am–10.30pm for breakfast, lunch and dinner.

There's a small supermarket, Chisholm's, just west of North Side Surf Inn on the right, backing on to the sea. The beach here is rocky rather than sand, but it's quiet and not a bad place to stop for a cool drink.

On the left-hand side continuing west towards Rum Point, is a sign to **Caribbean Charlie's** (49 Uncle Bert's Lane, North Side; tel: 947 9452). Tucked away in a small lane off to the left, Caribbean Charlie's specialises in colourful wooden birdhouses and traditional *waurie* boards. Opening times are erratic, so it's best to phone first.

Shortly before Rum Point, again off to the left, is The Hut, where local farmer Willie Ebanks has a flock of West Indian whistling-ducks on **Malportas Pond**. He introduced the first pair of ducks and seven chicks in 1990; today the population of wild ducks at his farm has soared into the hundreds. The pond, which is set in largely undisturbed land, also supports herons, egrets, moorhens and coots.

Rum Point

The real-estate signs lining the approach to Rum Point are an indication of just how popular this area is becoming, although so far there is little building of any note – just a few scattered private villas. Rum Point itself, though, has developed into a popular venue for visitors, with plenty of opportunities for fun and relaxation both day and night.

The *Rum Pointer* ferry plies regularly across North Sound between the Hyatt Regency dock on the east side of Seven Mile Beach and Rum Point. For details, see pages 78–9. Tickets at Rum Point can be bought from the gift shop. By road, Rum Point is approximately 25 miles from George Town.

The beach at Rum Point is ideal for swimmers, being both sheltered and safe. Snorkelling here is pretty good, too, but walk just a few hundred yards to the east and it gets steadily better as the reef comes closer to the shoreline. With luck, you'll have the place to yourself. The underwater life at this point is wonderful, with swaying sea fans, colourful fish and much, much more.

There are changing facilities, with toilets and showers, on the beach behind the Wreck Bar.

On Saturdays, there is a barbecue, with live entertainment on the beach from Footloose between 1.00pm and 5.00pm. The rest of the week taped music enlivens the setting – or spoils it, depending on your viewpoint. If you want to bring a picnic to Rum Point, you'll need to walk along the beach away from the central area, which is privately owned. Otherwise, there's a good choice of food during the day at the Wreck Bar (see below).

The watersports operation at Rum Point is run by Red Sail Sports (tel: 947 9203). Various pieces of equipment are available for rent, from tubes, paddles and kayaks to sailboats and jetskis (waverunners), as well as snorkels, masks and fins. Waterskiing, banana boats etc are also on offer, as are trips in glass-bottomed boats (see page 107). Prices: snorkelling gear at US$15 per day. Hourly rentals: sailboats

SEEDS ON THE TIDE
with thanks to Rosemary Hood

A short stroll away from the crowds at Rum Point to the east, the eagle-eyed naturalist could find far more than just a deserted beach. Many plants cannot grow on the Cayman Islands as there are no rivers, but in 2002 Rosemary Hood found the seeds of two such plants, *Entada gigas* and *Dioclea reflexa*, lying on the beach, and presumably washed ashore from Florida, Cuba or Jamaica. While there are plenty of records of such drifts, to find *Entada gigas* so far south is considered unusual. More widely known as the sea heart, or sea bean, it will germinate in humid conditions into a rampant, vine-like plant with small, off-white flowers. The shiny black seeds, often found on beaches in northern Europe and even the Azores, are about two inches (5cm) in diameter, and have been known to remain afloat in salt water for 19 years. Sometimes called lucky beans, they have long been sold as such in fairgrounds, and are the subject of numerous superstitions, while in Scandinavian folk medicine they are used in connection with childbirth.

US$25; kayaks US$20–25; paddleboats US$20. Waterskiing US$40 per 15-minute session (tuition available at US$65 for 25 minutes); tubing US$15 for ten minutes; waverunners US$50 single, US$65 double.

Where to stay
Most of the visitors to Rum Point come over on the ferry from hotels along West Bay Road. Others take the opportunity to drive, perhaps exploring inland en route. Only a handful make the effort to stay away from the hurly burly of Seven Mile Beach, but those that do are rewarded by a gentler pace of life, some stunning snorkelling and watersports, and the chance to escape the crowds – for some of the time, anyway.

For the most part, accommodation here consists of condominiums and private villas. For details of the latter, contact Cayman Villas (see page 53). The following are also available for rent to visitors:

Retreat at Rum Point PO Box 46, North Side; tel: 947 9135; fax: 947 9058; email: retrumpt@candw.ky; web: www.theretreat.com.ky (23 rooms)
It would be hard to better the location of this seven-acre complex, on a sweeping expanse of sandy beach with panoramic views to the north, yet close to all the facilities at Rum Point. Each of the one-, two- and three-bedroom beachfront apartments has a screened-in balcony, kitchen, washer/dryer, AC/ceiling fans and TV. Facilities include tennis, swimming pool and racquetball.
Rates per night (minimum three nights), low/high season, from one-bedroom US$250/300, to oceanfront US$450/595. Maid service included.

Where to eat
Rum Point Club Restaurant Tel: 947 9412. The colourful décor of the Caribbean-style restaurant and bar at Rum Point is all fish and seahorses, clearly the work of a designer in exuberant mood. Open in the evenings, the place caters primarily for those

coming over on the 6.45pm ferry, returning to Seven Mile Beach at 9.00pm. The menu specialises in seafood – if you're spoilt for choice, try the appetizer platter at CI$10. Open Mon–Sat 5.00–8.00pm.

Wreck Bar & Grill Rum Point's beach bar is open daily 10.00am–5.00pm. On Saturdays, the popular Cayman-style barbecue (CI$9.50 for jerk chicken or pork) draws numerous visitors and locals to the beach. The rest of the week, the menu offers a wide selection of sandwiches, wraps and other dishes, with drinks including the self-indulgent mudslide.

Shopping
The **Treasure Chest** gift shop at Rum Point, run by Red Sail Sports, has a comprehensive selection of gifts and beach-orientated goods, as well as newspapers etc.

Cayman Kai
Retrace your steps to the entry to Rum Point and take the left fork to bring you to Cayman Kai, a narrow finger protruding into North Sound. Follow the road straight almost to the end, then bear right at the sign to bring you out at Kaibo Yacht Club, or bear left and you'll find yourself at the sheltered public beach, where there's plenty of shade. On the ground, the two are barely a couple of hundred yards apart, so you easily can spend the day at the beach and walk to the beach bar at the yacht club for drinks and food. A few snorkel and dive operations run their trips from here, but there is no booking office. There is, though, a small chandlery shop next to the yacht club where you can also buy cold drinks and ice-cream. Run by Red Sail Sports, it's open Mon–Fri 9.00am–6.00pm, and Sat/Sun 8.00am–7.00pm. The club is usually closed for a month or two in the autumn.

The only accommodation in this vicinity is in privately rented homes which tend towards the luxurious. For details, contact North Coast Resort Management Ltd, PO Box 1074 GT; tel: 947 9266, US 800 336 6008; fax: 947 9116; email: caykai@candw.ky; web: www.caymankai.com.

Where to eat
Cecil's Restaurant Cayman Kai; tel: 947 9975. Kaibo Yacht Club's upstairs restaurant, pronounced 'Seasil's', has a club-like atmosphere with a nautical theme and screened veranda. The menu is typical of the southern United States. Open Wed–Sun 5.00–9.00pm.

Kaibo Grill Salads, sandwiches and grills are served all day. On Tuesday evening there's a full Cayman barbecue at CI$19 per head, 6.00–10.00pm, with a live band introduced in 2004.

East End
The approach to East End from Bodden Town brings with it a gently undulating landscape with low open vegetation, quite a change from the unbroken flat terrain of the west of the island. Instead of turning left on to Frank Sound Road, continue east on Sea View Road into the district of East End.

The village of East End may have been the earliest settlement on Grand Cayman. Originally called Old Isaacs, it has been dubbed the 'graveyard of the Caribbean' as a result of the large number of ships wrecked on its shores. The

WRECK OF THE TEN SAIL

In the small hours of February 8 1794, a convoy of 58 merchant ships, most of them square-rigged sailing vessels bound for Europe, and led by HMS *Convert*, approached the reef off the district of East End from their Jamaican port of origin. The seas were rough and it was pitch dark. As the first ships struck the reef, the ensuing signal, warning the rest of the convoy of the danger, was misinterpreted, and one vessel after another foundered on the rocks. By the time that the captain of the *Convert* realised the danger, and signalled to the convoy to disperse, it was too late. Altogether, ten ships were wrecked that night, leaving their crew at the mercy of the waves, with 'the surf beating violently over the reef'.

In spite of the conditions, the villagers of East End managed to save almost all of the 400 or so people on board the ships, bringing them ashore in canoes. However, such a large contingent caused serious problems for the islanders, who were already suffering from a shortage of provisions. Captain Lawford of the *Convert* was petitioned to move the survivors, who were for the most part taken aboard the remaining ships, which then regrouped off George Town. The remainder of the men, including Lawford himself, journeyed west across the island overland. According to records in the Cayman Islands National Archive, they found themselves on 'the most execrable road imaginable... hot burning sands and sharp-pointed coral rocks that would have foiled the attempts of the most dexterous animal to pass them without injury'. To have survived the storm for a land such as this must have seemed something of a double blow.

Legend has it that George III was so grateful to the people of Cayman that he granted the islanders freedom from taxes in perpetuity. Other stories tell that, rather than freedom from taxation, Caymanians were granted freedom from conscription in times of war. Sadly, there is no evidence to support either anecdote.

most famous of these shipwrecks, now known as the 'Wreck of the Ten Sail', took place in February 1794 (see above).

Until early in the 20th century, many of the villagers 'commuted' by cat boat from here to one of the sister islands to work in the phosphate mines or the coconut trade. The village was also a trading port; indeed, until the 1940s it was the main port of entry to Grand Cayman. It was here that the *Cimboco* made its monthly visits, bringing post, passengers and cargo from Jamaica and Cayman Brac, and returning with exports of thatch rope, mahogany and turtle products.

Despite these visits, the village remained almost totally isolated until, in 1935, the road was extended from Bodden Town. Until then, journeys to George Town could only be undertaken on foot or on horseback, with goods ferried by canoe. Such were the difficulties of travel that many East Enders never went as far as the island's capital, just 25 miles away.

The quieter pace of this end of the island makes it an excellent place to come for the day and get away from the brashness of Seven Mile Beach. Countless small sandy beaches offer the perfect spot for a quiet picnic, and there are numerous little coves awaiting exploration.

Where to stay

Cayman Diving Lodge PO Box 11 EE; tel: 947 7555, US 800 TLC DIVE; fax: 947 7560; email: info@divelodge.com; web: www.divelodge.com (10 rooms)
This small, all-inclusive dive resort is idyllically located on its own on the southern shores of the island at East End, well away from any hint of mass tourism. With its family-like atmosphere, small dive groups (average 8–10) and attention to good food, it's not surprising that few guests venture far beyond the lodge, and many return year after year. Pastel-decorated rooms have AC and sea view; some are oceanfront. Meals are served in the open-air dining area above a sandy beach, fronted by a shallow lagoon that's ideal for snorkelling. *Rates* per person based on double occupancy: three-tank dive package, three–seven nights US$721–1,669; non-divers US$526–1,104. Oceanfront rooms additional US$11 per night per person. Prices include meals, government tax and airport transfers, but not alcoholic or soft (fizzy) drinks, dive equipment or certification courses. BCD/regulator US$10 each per day. Gratuities optional.

Compass Point PO Box 200 EE; tel: 947 0000; email: info@oceanfrontiers.com; web: www.oceanfrontiers.com (18 apartments)
The turquoise-painted condominiums next to Ocean Frontiers represent an expansion of the dive company's business, enabling their divers to stay right on site. Opened in summer 2004, all one- and two-bedroom apartments overlook the sea and are furnished to a high standard with AC/ceiling fans, fully equipped kitchen, whirlpool baths, cable TV, DVD and stereo, plus internet access. Outside, there are barbecue grills, and a good-sized swimming pool close to a small sandy beach. If the quality of the dive operation is anything to go by, this is definitely one to watch.
Rates low/high season: one bedroom US$145/215, two bedroom US$220/300.

Grand Morritt's With its first phase of 40 units now open, the timeshare resort adjacent to Morritt's Tortuga is almost an extension of the current site. The complex has been designed and built to be hurricane 'proof' but the result is singularly unattractive when compared with its elegant neighbour, and the height of the newer buildings doesn't help. The finished complex will have 130 units with restaurants, shops and other facilities. For information, contact Morritt's Tortuga.

Morritt's Tortuga PO Box 496 East End; tel: 947 7449/945 1571; US reservations (L&M Reservations, Florida) 800 447 0309 (177 rooms)
An upmarket timeshare in a quiet location at the eastern end of the island, Morritt's Tortuga is an attractive three-storey complex built in traditional style with wooden steps and verandas. Rooms may be rented, subject to availability, through their Florida agency, who will quote prices. Options range from one-bed studios to penthouses/townhouses suitable for families with up to eight people, and there are three rooms for disabled guests. All have AC and TV, and some have a sea view. Two restaurants – David's and Windows Bar (see below). Nightly entertainment includes comedy shows, and popular themed evenings, such as Thursday's Caribbean Night (US$18.95; children under 12 half price), are open to non-residents. Children's activities range from kids parties to one particularly innovative idea, which involves a beach walk during which children are encouraged to collect rubbish from the beach in return for free ice-cream. Swimming pool with bar, dive school (Tortuga Divers), watersports, spa, bicycles, car rental, souvenir shop, laundry.

The Reef PO Box 30865 SMB, Colliers, East End; tel: 947 3100, US 888 232 0541; fax: 947 9920; email: rentals@thereef.com.ky; web: www.thereef.com.ky (88 suites)
The sunny yellow-and-blue building of this Cayman-owned resort contrasts with the more discreet Morritt's Tortuga next door. Ongoing development will result in 166 suites, with the next phase scheduled for completion in summer 2005, and increased wheelchair access part of the plan. The resort's trump card is its location on a 1,450ft (440m) stretch of sandy beach, overlooked by every one of the light, airy and spacious suites. One- and two-bedroomed suites and studios have a TV, AC/ceiling fan and balcony; several also have the luxury of a Jacuzzi. Suites also have a living area and kitchen, while studios have a kitchenette. On site are a well-stocked dive shop and a small shop/internet café, plus Castro's Hideaway restaurant and a relaxed beach bar, while sports facilities include a beach-side swimming pool, tennis, gym, bicycles, diving with Ocean Frontiers and other watersports. Among the many other activities on offer are beach barbecues, stargazing from the dock, bike rides, and guided tours of the Botanic Park.
Rates per suite, low/high season: studio US$150/210, one-bedroom US$210/295, two-bedroom US$285/395, including twice-weekly maid service. Christmas and New Year supplement.

Where to eat and drink

Arlain's More a takeaway than a restaurant, although there are a couple of simple tables, Arlain's (almost opposite Ocean Frontiers) is open for fried chicken and similar dishes on Tue–Sun, midday–3.00pm and 7.00–11.30pm.
Castro's Hideaway The Reef; tel: 947 3100. Diners upstairs in The Reef's air-conditioned restaurant are treated to panoramic views over the sea, 8.00am–10.00pm. Speciality evenings include a Caribbean night and twice-weekly live entertainment from the Barefoot Man (on Tuesday and Thursday). For a more informal evening, sit around Castro's bar on the beach below and enjoy cocktails and a varied menu with generous portions. Open 11.00am–midnight.
David's Morritt's Tortuga; tel: 947 7449. The restaurant at Morritt's Tortuga hosts a series of themed evenings, from beach barbecues and comedy nights to Caribbean evenings and 'Steakorama'. In addition, there is a cosmopolitan à la carte menu, available at weekends. Open daily 6.00–10.00pm.
Portofino Sea View Rd; tel: 947 2700. With its seafront location, it's surprising that Portofino's has no outside eating area. The simple wooden building and blue-and-white décor contrast with the rather pricey menu, which features Italian and local dishes, including seafood curry. Cocktail menu. Open daily 11.30am–5.00pm, 5.30–10.00pm; Sunday buffet with local specialities 11.30am–3.00pm.
Vivine's Kitchen Gun Bay; tel: 947 7435. Wait in the extension to Vivine's kitchen, draped with artificial flowers, or at tables overlooking the sea, to be served enormous home-cooked meals. Absolutely no frills, but then it only costs around CI$6 a head, and you won't have room for ice-cream. Unlicensed.
Windows Bar Morritt's Tortuga; tel: 947 7449. Little more than an extension of David's (above), with a wall of windows overlooking the beach, this is open daily for breakfast and lunch, 8.00am–6.00pm.

Shops etc

There's a good general food store, **Lil Hurley's Marketplace**, in East End Village, and during 2005 Morritt's will be opening a small shopping centre with its own supermarket opposite The Reef. On the cultural side, there is the small **Wreck View Art Gallery** just outside the village, but opening hours are somewhat erratic, so you'll have to take pot luck.

What to see and do

Just beyond Frank Sound Road is the small **National Trust Heritage Beach**, with shade provided by trees, a couple of wooden cabanas, and barbecue areas, making it a good spot for a picnic. The swimming is not great, but small boats may be launched here.

A none-too-obvious sign a bit further on points towards the **blowholes**, with steps leading down to the sea. When the sea is up, the blowholes come into their own, but even on a calm day the extraordinary rock formations are worth visiting. Formed from karst limestone, the place is almost eerily barren, more lunar landscape than Caribbean beach. Don't attempt to walk on the beach without good shoes – the rocks are sharp and unforgiving.

As you drive into the village of East End, there's an excellent new public beach (see below) which makes a great place to stop, particularly for those with children who by this stage may want somewhere to let off steam. Further on, you come to the tiny **East End Lighthouse Park**, set just off the road beyond the village on the left-hand side. Owned by the National Trust, it contains the two lighthouses that have stood on this spot since 1919, with signboards explaining their historical importance. The small gravel courtyard is a miniature nature reserve, a tranquil place where birds and butterflies dart in and around the fruit trees, and wild flowers are intermingled with traditional medicinal plants.

Beyond the village of East End in Gun Bay, near the post office, are two cannons salvaged from the Wreck of the Ten Sail (see page 171). Close by, on the other side of the road, the **Wreck of the Ten Sail Park** promises more than it delivers, with portions from two different wrecks flanking a path leading to a simple memorial to those who died in this nautical disaster. As if to make the point, the wreck of yet another ship that met its end here, the *Ridgefield*, can clearly be seen lying on the reef to the east.

There are several secluded **beaches** around this area where you could be in another world to that of Seven Mile Beach. Look closely among the rocks and you may find the odd piece of caymanite – though please don't take it away. East End public beach is one step up, a tranquil, shady site overlooking a small sandy beach with its own dock. Equipped with picnic benches and wooden beach shelters, it also has recently installed toilets and public phones.

To complete the circuit, follow the road right on to Old Man Bay, past Morritt's Tortuga and The Reef. You can rent sailboats, kayaks and windsurfers at Cayman Windsurf, which is based at Morritt's, or kayaks and mountain bikes from Ecoventures at The Reef, so it's worth a stop if you'd like to explore further. Then continue to Rum Point via North Side, or return along Frank Sound Road at Old Man Bay to rejoin Bodden Town Road just east of Breakers.

Part Three

The Sister Islands

Hawksbill turtles

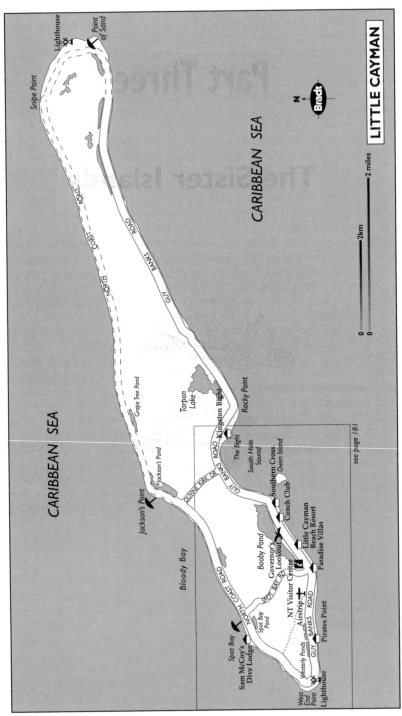

Little Cayman

Permanent home to over 20,000 red-footed boobies and just 115 humans, Little Cayman is surely the jewel in the crown of the Cayman Islands. You don't need to be an avid birdwatcher to be enthralled by the morning exodus from the booby colony, as thousands of birds head out to sea at dawn, with frigatebirds wheeling in the current overhead, anticipating their evening raid. Nor do you need to be a scuba diver to see the brightly coloured corals and sponges just below the surface of that crystal clear water, enlivened by myriads of fish of all hues. Little Cayman is a place to take time out, to relax, simply to be.

The smallest of the Cayman Islands, lying 89 miles (150km) northeast of Grand Cayman at 19°4' north, 80° west, Little Cayman is only 10 miles (16km) long and just over a mile and a half (2.7km) at its widest point. Its total land area is barely 10 square miles (26km²). Like the larger Grand Cayman, the island is more or less flat, rising to just 40ft (12m) in the centre.

Probably only 25 to 30 of the island's inhabitants – eight to ten households – are true Caymanians, the remainder being long-term residents from the US and elsewhere. There are very few children on the island; of those that do live here, the younger ones have lessons in a room next to the clinic from a teacher and a classroom assistant. Visitors account for a further 500–600 people each year.

Considered by many to be one of the three best dive areas in the world, Little Cayman is also a haven for photographers, nature lovers and those in search of real peace.

HISTORY

When Edward Corbet prepared his report on the Cayman Islands for the governor of Jamaica in 1802, Little Cayman, like Cayman Brac, was uninhabited, although fishermen regularly sailed along its shores to catch turtles and a number of isolated groups had resided here over the years. It was only in 1832, however, that the first permanent settlement began, when a small group of families came over from Grand Cayman in a deliberate move to populate the island.

Until the early 20th century, the small community on Little Cayman was augmented by labourers from Grand Cayman who commuted to the island by catboat every Sunday evening to start work in the phosphate mines at daybreak on Monday morning. As the phosphate was extracted from the mines, it was loaded on to a small-gauge train which was hauled by mules to Salt Rocks Dock on the north side of the island. Here, it would await transfer on to a ship ready for export. On Friday nights, they would make the long and frequently dangerous journey back home, with the whole process repeated week after week, month after month.

Although not hit as badly as Cayman Brac, Little Cayman suffered considerable damage during the **1932 storm**, with severe flooding and many homes destroyed. The few buildings that did survive, including the house behind the church whose second storey acted as a shelter for some of the islanders, were later pulled down. The oldest building on the island today was erected just after the storm, opposite the Village Inn in South Town (since controversially renamed Blossom Village after the British HMS *Blossom* which was engaged in surveying the island in 1831). The only structure on the island that predates the storm is the mule pen by Salt Rocks Dock, which was constructed around 1885.

The storm destroyed more than buildings of course. Prior to 1932, coconuts were a major export crop, but damage to the trees, together with a lethal yellowing blight, effectively put paid to this trade. Today, the island is dependent on tourism for its income.

It took a considerable time for the 20th century to catch up with the island. Even when the runway was finally cleared for incoming planes, it was achieved singlehandedly by one Captain Woody Bodden, using just an axe and a handmade cart. Until 1990 there was no electricity here, and it was only in 1991 that telephones were installed; prior to this VHF radios were used. It's not surprising, then, that the islanders have a strong sense of community, and some older people are extremely suspicious of the outside world. It is said that when Neil Armstrong first walked on the moon, the islanders were firm in their belief that it was a television show, rather than a live event!

Today, pretty well all the food that is consumed on the island is imported, with the singular exception of fish, some of which is caught locally, and a few plantains, limes and coconuts that are grown on the island.

NATURAL HISTORY

The flattest of the three islands, Little Cayman consists essentially of mangrove swamps, with the land along the southern coast – and much of the north as well – lined with ponds. In summer, severe storms may cause the ponds to overflow, bringing the extraordinary phenomenon of tarpon swimming down the road. Little Cayman is host to a wide variety of flora, fauna and birdlife, although curiously, there are no bees or wasps, so all pollination is done by butterflies. It also has its own bird reserve, Booby Pond (see page 192), which is the only wetland area on the islands to be designated as a Ramsar site.

No matter where you go on the island, you're likely to come across one of Little Cayman's most intriguing inhabitants, the grey Lesser Cayman Islands iguana, which to all appearances is in charge here. These anachronistic creatures are frequently to be seen sunning themselves on porches or making the most of the quiet roads across the island in the heat of the day, perhaps secure in the knowledge that they have right of way over vehicles. One particularly cheeky specimen has been known to lie by the airstrip waiting for incoming planes – and presumably a tasty morsel!

Over 100 species of coral grace the reefs that fringe the island, with more than 500 species of fish to be found in Little Cayman's unblemished waters. Sea turtles, rarely seen on the surface elsewhere, are easily spotted from boats here, as well as beneath the waves, while the abundance of all manner of marine creatures seems just that much greater in these relatively tranquil seas. Interestingly, the shallow reef is the result of countless storms over the years. One of the local fisherman, Castro, remembers that a couple of generations ago there was some 65ft (20m) of water inside the reef, but a gradual build up of sand during the intervening years has left the shallows that you see today. At least some of the islanders believe that nature should be given a helping hand with digging it out again.

GETTING THERE

Cayman Airways Express have regular flights from Grand Cayman to Little Cayman, taking 35 minutes (or an hour if it stops in Cayman Brac), and Cayman Brac, taking just seven minutes, making Little Cayman very accessible. Planes are either 19-seater de Havilland DHC 6-300 Twin Otters, or 8-seater Piper Navahos. Charter flights are operated by Island Airways. For details, see page 81.

The first hint of the mood of the island comes at the approach to the grass airstrip at the westernmost point of the island. As the plane touches down, it turns across the road and parks in front of the 'airport' – a small group of wooden buildings housing the local fire station, post office and Island Airways office; the Cayman Airways office is just by Paradise Villas. In both cases, baggage is weighed outside – the offices are too small for the scales. If you're travelling on one of the smaller planes, don't be surprised if your luggage is not on the same plane as you – this is not uncommon. It will usually arrive on the next one (but as that may be the following morning, it would be sensible to hang on to your toothbrush and swimming things). Sometimes, passengers are asked to take just one bag on their flight, with the other to follow, or to send a piece of luggage in advance of their departure.

There are controversial plans in hand to move the airport nearer to the middle of the island, towards the north side. It is understood, though, that the proposed new tarmac airstrip will be no longer than the existing grass strip, so with luck the move will have little impact on traffic, noise or environmental pollution.

GETTING AROUND

You have four choices if you wish to remain independent – walk, cycle or hire a jeep or scooter. Most of the hotels and guesthouses have **bicycles** for loan or hire and, with so little traffic, cycling on the paved roads is a real pleasure. If you're just visiting for a day, you can rent bikes from Little Cayman Beach Resort for US$5 per day. Do be careful though; the last mile or so before Point or Sand is unpaved and very bumpy, as is the road beyond Sam McCoy's Dive Lodge on the northern side. Add to this drifting sand, and a bike at these points can prove treacherous, particularly one with no gears and back-pedal brakes.

Scooters and **mountain bikes** may be hired from the Island Airways office by the airstrip, tel: 926 2921. Note that you need a driving permit (CI$7) to hire a scooter.

The rule on bikes on the islands is to lock them when unattended. Although theft is not a problem, bikes have been known to 'walk' when visitors leave them outside a restaurant then take the wrong one after a drink or two. Hire bikes are not really an option after dark – they don't have lights and only a short stretch of road east of the airport is lit. If you want to go out in the evening, most of the restaurants will collect you if you ring them in advance.

Jeeps are available for hire from McLaughlin Enterprises, PO Box 46 L; tel: 948 1000; mobile: 916 3755; fax: 948 1001; email: littlcay@candw.ky. Their office/shop is on the small shopping parade within walking distance of the airstrip; they have a courtesy phone at the airstrip which rings directly through for visitors to be picked up on arrival. Note that the jeeps are not four-wheel drive, so may not be driven on soft sand. This is a deliberate policy to prevent driving on the beach and thus the potential destruction of turtle nests. Since theft is not an issue, you'll be asked to leave the keys in the vehicle at all times.

The office is open Mon–Sat 8.30am–midday, 2.30–6.00pm; Sun 8.30–11.00am. Rates are US$75 per day, with insurance an extra US$17.50, and a second driver charged at US$15.

The speed limit right across the island is 25mph (40km/h). Permits (CI$7) are required as on Grand Cayman (see page 75) for scooters as well as jeeps, and the same regulations apply. And do take note of the signs stating that iguanas have right of way. Fuel is available both near McLaughlin's and on the north of the island at McCoy's Lodge. Prices are approximately CI$3.00 per imperial gallon, but may vary.

Tours of the island may be organised with Gladys Howard at Pirates Point (tel: 948 1010) in return for a US$25 donation to the National Trust. Alternatively, contact Little Cayman Beach Resort (tel: 948 1033) or Sam McCoy's Dive Lodge (tel: 948 0026).

WHERE TO STAY

Accommodation on Little Cayman is for the most part limited to the western end of the island, with a few private houses dotted here and there to the east. The majority of the accommodation is on an all-inclusive basis, in many cases with drinks as part of the package. Remember that all rates are subject to 10% government tax, unless otherwise stated.

Resort hotels

Little Cayman Beach Resort Guy Banks Rd, PO Box 51, Blossom Village; tel: 948 1033, US reservations: 1 800 327 3835; fax: 948 1040; email: lcbr@candw.ky; web: littlecayman.com (40 rooms)

A sense of light and air pervades this upmarket resort just a mile or so from the airport. All the rooms are in two-storey wooden buildings in a stunning beachside location, and each has one king or two double beds; AC, fan, TV; patio or balcony and pool view. Luxury oceanfront rooms also available. Air-conditioned Bird of Paradise restaurant (see page 185), beach bar, private beach with wide range of watersports. Facilities include floodlit tennis court, fitness centre, games room, library, gift shop, health and beauty spa. Dive centre run by Reef Divers (see page 188). Evening entertainment includes rum punch party on Mondays, and a Friday karaoke night. The resort operates a no-smoking policy except outside and at the bar.

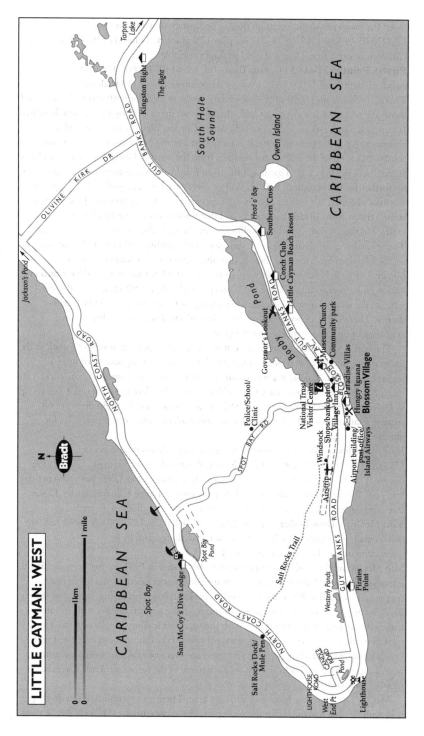

Rates: Per room per night, based on double occupancy (low/high season):
US$133.05–205.89/US$169.34–242.66, plus 12% gratuity. Transfers US$10 per person.
Children under 5 free. Dive and meal packages available.

Pirates Point PO Box 43 LC, Guy Banks Rd; tel: 948 1010; fax: 948 1011;
email: piratept@candw.ky; web: www.piratespointresort.com (10 chalets)
This all-inclusive and somewhat idiosyncratic resort is ideal for both certified divers and
those just seeking a few days' rest and relaxation. Set up in 1986 by the inimitable Gladys
B Howard, a larger-than-life Texan lady with a Cordon Bleu qualification and a
reputation for getting things done, it is located in a prime beachfront setting on the
southwestern tip of the island, just minutes from the airstrip. Gladys's passion for plants
is much in evidence, with a garden at the front filled with native trees and flowers – look
no further for the broadleaf, buttonwood or silver thatch that played such a big part in
Cayman's history. Set further back is a decent-sized swimming pool and Jacuzzi, just a
stone's throw from shaded hammocks and that turquoise sea. The beach here isn't
sandy, but there's some good snorkelling inside the reef, albeit in very shallow water.
The resort has a family atmosphere, and appeals to a slightly older clientele than others
on the island; indeed, most of them return time after time. Accommodation is in
homely individual chalets, six with ocean views (just ask for room 5!) and four further
back with air conditioning. The food is exceptionally good, with meals served buffet-
style on the terrace or in the comfortable dining room, and wine is included with
dinner. There's also a cosy, wood-panelled bar, adorned with the highly creative
craftwork of numerous guests over the years.

The staff at Pirates Point are all part of the dive team, taking it in turns to work in the
resort dining room etc as well as on the dive boat. The morning dive starts after a
leisurely breakfast, making it a relaxed affair with no pressure of time, and instructors are
on hand at all stages; if buoyancy is a problem, this is the place to sort it out. Courses up
to Divemaster include PADI, NAUI, SSI and universal referrals; night dives are on
request. Nature trail and fishing guides are also available, and there are bicycles for
guests to use.

Rates All-inclusive rates per person (low/high season): divers (two dives per day)
US$320/340 single, US$240/260 double; non-divers US$260/285 single, US$150/195
double, US$135/175 triple. All rates subject to 15% gratuity and US$8 per room per day
hotel tax. Rates include drinks, but not dive equipment rental. Children under 12 stay
free when sharing with parents; meals US$80 per day. No children under 5.

Sam McCoy's Dive Lodge PO Box 12 LC; tel: 948 0026, US: 800 626 0496; fax: 948
0057; email: mccoy@candw.ky; web: www.mccoyslodge.com.ky or
www.cayman.com.ky/com/sam (8 rooms)
Sam McCoy and his wife Mary opened McCoy's Lodge in 1984, having been the first to
introduce diving to Little Cayman. An all-inclusive resort based on the north coast
(opposite Bloody Bay Wall), the lodge offers packages based on diving, fishing or simply
R&R, including all meals, and transfer to and from the airport. Rooms with AC and
bathroom are large and comfortable, with sliding doors leading directly outside. Home-
cooked meals are served at a large communal table in the dining room decorated with
family photographs and mementos. The patio bar overlooks the sea, with a swimming
pool, Jacuzzi and hammocks nearby. As with many of the resorts on Little Cayman,
most of their clientele come back year after year.

McCoy's has two dive boats and a fishing boat. There's a maximum of ten divers per
trip, with flexible schedules; for the most part, dives concentrate on Bloody Bay Wall or

Above Smith's Cove, to the south of George Town (TH)

Below right Frangipani trees were planted in the past to mark Cayman graves. (TH)

Bottom right Colourful palm nuts at Bodden Town (TH)

Below Silver thatch tree, the national tree of the islands (TH)

Top Peter's Cave on Cayman Brac (KS)

Above Brown boobies nest high up in the bluff on Cayman Brac. (K)

Left First Cay walk, Cayman Brac (TH)

Below Juvenile brown booby (KS)

the nearby Jackson Reef. Dive courses can be arranged on request, as can snorkel trips around the island. Fishing is all based on light tackle, so bonefishing or fly fishing.

Rates per person per night, based on double occupancy and inclusive of all meals (low/high season): divers US$160/180 (includes two-tank morning dive, unlimited shore diving and optional night dive). Dive equipment is charged extra at US$12.50 each for BCD and regulator per day (a full set of equipment including mask and fins is US$25 a day). Non-divers US$105/115. Note that McCoy's defines the low season as June 1 – Oct 15, and winter as Oct 16 – May 31.

Southern Cross Guy Banks Rd, PO Box 44; tel: 948 1099; US reservations: 800 899 2582; international: 619 563 0017; fax: 948 1098; email: scc@candw.ky; web: www.southerncrossclub.com (11 chalets)

The first resort on Little Cayman, and indeed on the Cayman Islands as a whole, Southern Cross was opened in 1958, then taken over in 1995 by the current owner, Peter Hillenbrand, who has ensured that it retains every bit of its natural appeal. The resort's popularity is self-evident. Over two-thirds of its visitors have been before, and most of the rest have come through personal recommendation, with around 15% hailing from the UK.

Named after the constellation, which can be seen here in the winter at its most northerly point, the resort has an 800ft (243m) sea frontage on the southern side of the island, with uninterrupted views across to Owen Island and the reef just beyond. Each freshly painted chalet is individually designed, with en-suite facilities (two honeymoon suites have outdoor showers), separated from its neighbours by yards of sand, and looking out to sea. Visitors at Southern Cross stay on an inclusive basis, with separate packages available for diving, fishing and holiday visitors. Breakfast and lunch are served as a buffet in the spacious restaurant, with plate service at dinner. The bar is open all day, with service available from 4.00pm to non-residents. Friday night is barbecue night out on the deck, at US$18.75 inclusive, with outside bar. Plenty of locals gather here then; if you meet up with Obie (Edward Obadiah Scott, that is), tell him you read about him – he'll be chuffed!

Diving, fishing and other watersports are available, including guided fishing trips (see pages 190–1). In fact, the resort is one of only two on the island that offers fishing, and has two fishing boats, one deep-sea and one flat, moored at their own fishing dock. There is also a separate dive dock with two boats, each taking a maximum of 12 divers. Guests on a diving package who would prefer a day's fishing or sailing to diving can on occasion interchange the options subject to availability. Kayaks and bikes are provided free to guests, while sailboats are available for rent at US$25 per hour.

Rates Inclusive rates per person for seven nights, based on double occupancy (low/high season): divers (two dives per day) US$1,715/2,120; non-divers US$1,430/1,840. Rates include transfer from airport, three meals per day, service charge and government tax, but not dive equipment rental (see pages 190–1), nor drinks. No under 5s as a rule. Other packages available on request.

Villas and apartments

Conch Club Condominiums PO Box 51 LC, Guy Banks Rd; tel: 948 1033; fax: 948 1045; US tel: 800 327 3835; fax: 813 323 8827; email: refz79a@prodigy.com; web: www.conchclub.com (20 townhouses)

In joint ownership with Little Cayman Beach Resort, and very close by, the Conch Club features luxury self-catering two- and three-bedroom townhouses, each with patio, balcony and sea view. Ideal for families or small groups. Swimming pool. Other facilities shared with the resort (see page 180).

Rates per night low/high season: two bedroom (4 adults) US$300/375; three bedroom (6 adults) US$400/475; each additional adult US$25 per night. Cleaning and transfers (US$10 per person) extra. Meal plans available through Little Cayman Beach Resort.

The Club PO Box 51 LC, Guy Banks Rd; tel: 948 1033; email: theclub@reefseas.com; web: www.theclubatlittlecayman.com (8 villas)
Affiliated to Little Cayman Beach Resort, The Club boasts exclusive villas that have been elegantly furnished and equipped to a very high standard, each with three bathrooms. In addition to the swimming pool, dock and putting green, guests may use the facilities at the nearby resort.
Rates per night low/high season: one bedroom US$210/250; two bedroom US$325/375; three bedroom US$450/500 (oceanfront US$500/550). Meal plans available.

Kingston Bight Lodge PO Box 17 LC, Guy Banks Rd; tel: 948 1015; fax: 948 0006 (4 apartments, 8 rooms)
Despite a beachfront location overlooking the bay and Owen Island, Kingston Bight Lodge has had a chequered recent history. While it is scheduled to re-open in 2004, the signs aren't great. Until then, the bar is open from around midday, and in the evening from 6.00pm.

Paradise Villas PO Box 48 LC; tel: 948 0001, US: 877 3CAYMAN; fax: 948 0002; email: iggy@candw.ky; web: www.paradisevillas.com (12 villas)
Marc and Sabine have run these idyllic beachside villas and their affiliated dive school for a couple of years, with a laid-back approach that is disarming in its efficiency. Located just a short walk across the grass from Little Cayman's airstrip, but there's no need to worry about aircraft noise – the few planes that fly in each day are completely unobtrusive. Each one-bedroom villa has AC/fans, bathroom, kitchenette and lounge area, together with its own veranda back and front, a sea view and shady hammock and – if you're lucky – semi-resident iguana. Bike hire US$15 for the duration of your stay. Swimming pool; restaurant (Hungry Iguana). Dive school (Paradise Divers), with small gift shop. Fishing with the Iguana Fleet.
Rates per night (two people): winter US$185, summer US$165, plus 12% service

Village Inn Blossom Av; reservations through James Little at the Village Stores, tel: 948 1069; fax: 948 0069; email: villageinn11@hotmail.com (8 efficiencies, 3 apartments)
Opposite the clinic just a hundred yards or so from the sea, and almost as close to the airport, the blue-and-white painted Village Inn offers good-value monthly rentals for two people in a quiet location close to the shops. All units have AC and kitchenette.
Rates per month: efficiencies US$550; one-bedroom apartments US$875

A small number of individual houses and cottages on the island are available for rent, but most of these are organised by the owners. At present, just three privately owned properties can be rented through agencies. Tranquil Realty (PO Box 9, Blossom Village; tel: 948 1077; fax: 948 1078; email: bettyboo@candw.ky), has a two-bedroom condominium close to the lighthouse on the southwestern point of the island, and Cayman Villas on Grand Cayman (see page 53) have a couple of similar places on their books.

RESTAURANTS AND BARS

In order to have a liquor licence, establishments on Little Cayman must have at least ten rooms, so all bars and restaurants are linked to hotels or villa complexes. If transport is a problem, do give your chosen restaurant a ring – some of them, including McCoys, will collect you from your accommodation and take you back after your meal.

Bird of Paradise Little Cayman Beach Resort; tel: 948 1033. Good-value meals are served in the elegant, air-conditioned dining room, on a screened porch or on the patio. Buffet service. The menu changes nightly, and the resort will cater for individual requirements on request. Open 7.00–8.30am, 12.30–1.30pm, 6.30–8.00pm. Bar open Mon–Sat 11.30am–11.00pm; Sun midday–11.00pm. Karaoke night Fri.

Kingston Bight Tel: 948 1015. The bar at Kingston Bight Lodge is open in the evening from 6.00pm, and the restaurant is set to reopen in 2004, serving Cayman specialities. Beer at CI$3.25 a bottle is pretty good value.

Hungry Iguana Restaurant and Sports Bar Tel: 948 0007. Set in the grounds of Paradise Villas, the interior of this wood-panelled restaurant with its long bar makes no concessions to the bright Caribbean sunshine. By contrast, the shady veranda, with its view of the sea framed by sea-grape trees, is a relaxing place for lunch in the company of a couple of cheeky bananaquits. The only à la carte menu on Little Cayman ranges from burgers, sandwiches and pasta to fresh seafood and Caribbean/American dishes, with a daily lunchtime special at CI$6.95 and themed nights that include oriental, Indian, etc. Takeaway food is available to eat in your own villa. For entertainment, Friday night is disco night from 9.00pm, with a DJ and varied styles of music. Open daily midday–2.30pm, 5.30–9.00pm; Sunday brunch 11.00am–2.30pm. Bar closes Mon–Fri 1.00pm, and midnight on Sat/Sun. Happy hour 5.30–7.00pm daily.

McCoys Tel: 948 0026. Saturday night is barbecue night under the stars at 7.00pm, with plenty of traditional Cayman fare. Non-residents are welcome at US$15 per head (though do book 24 hours in advance) – the McCoys will pick you up if you don't have transport. On Wednesdays, there is jerk chicken and steak, also available to non-residents.

Pirates Point Tel: 948 1010. For non-residents, dinner at this resort should be booked no later than 10.00am on the day of reservation. Food is served buffet style in the small but comfortable and well-appointed restaurant, and is without doubt the best on the island. The fixed two-course menu at US$39.95 includes wine. Transport to and from your place of accommodation is also available.

Southern Cross Tel: 948 1099. The Friday barbecue out on the dock is open to all-comers, and is good value at US$18.75, with beer at US$3 and rum punch US$5. See page 183.

SHOPPING AND AMENITIES

Almost all Little Cayman's shops are to be found in the grandly named Little Cayman Mall, a handful of shops on the right just a few hundred yards from the airport as you head east on Guy Banks Road.

Food, drink and general supplies

Village Square Tel: 948 1069. The ultimate one-stop shop, the Village Square may not have a huge variety, but it does seem to have something of everything, including groceries, beer, hardware, fishing stuff, household goods, chandlery, camera films, newspapers and video rentals. Remember that everything on the island is brought in on the weekly boat, so prices are correspondingly high – you can expect to pay around US$4 for a loaf of decent bread. Open Mon–Sat 8.30am–6.00pm; Sun 9.00am–1.00pm.

Gifts and clothes
Gifts from Paradise The gift shop at Paradise Villas next to the airstrip has some classy T-shirts and a few gift items. Usually open Mon–Fri 9.00am–5.00pm.

Iguana Crossing Next to the car-hire place in Blossom Village. Come here for T-shirts, beachwear, sandals, jewellery, souvenirs, as well as wine and liquor, Cuban cigars, coffee and rum cake. Open Mon–Sat 8.30am–midday; 2.30–6.00pm; Sun 8.30–11.00am (but no alcohol may be served on Sunday).

Mermaids Tel: 948 0097. Little Cayman Beach Resort's gift shop sells souvenirs, clothes, postcards and treasure coins. Open Mon–Sat 10.00am–6.00pm; Sun 1.00–6.00pm. The dive shop at the resort also sells T-shirts etc.

Health and beauty
Next to Paradise Villas is the **Holistic Health Clinic** (tel: 948 1007). For some serious pampering, Southern Cross is planning to open a spa during 2004, with massage at US$80 per hour. A wider range of facilities is to be had down the road at Little Cayman Beach Resort:

Nature Spa Health & Beauty Tel: 948 0058. Opposite Little Cayman Beach Resort. A full range of services includes hairdressing, manicure and pedicure, facials and massage. Open Mon–Sat, 10.00am–6.00pm; Sun 1.00–6.00pm. Appointments necessary.

Photographic supplies
Reef Photo & Video Centre at Little Cayman Beach Resort; tel: 948 1063; email: edbeaty@candw.ky. Daily processing, custom underwater videos and equipment sales. Half-day rental with basic photo tips from US$39. Photography tuition from US$50 per hour. Open Mon–Fri 7.30am–5.00pm, Sat 7.30am–12.30pm.

OTHER PRACTICALITIES
Banks
Cayman National Bank, next to the shops at Little Cayman Mall, is open on Monday and Thursday from 9.00am to 2.30pm.

Church services
See page 192.

Communications
Post office
The only post office is by the airstrip and is open Mon–Fri 9.00–11.30am and 1.00–3.00pm (3.30pm on Friday).

Telephones
There is a public phone at the airport, one by the park on Blossom Avenue, and one at the Hungry Iguana. Both Little Cayman Beach Resort and Southern Cross also have public phones. Phonecards can be bought at the Island Airways office by the airstrip. There are no public internet facilities on the island.

Emergency telephone number
Police/doctor 911

Health and medical facilities

There is a nurse based at the **clinic** (tel: 948 1073) on Spot Bay Road, behind the school. The clinic is open Mon, Wed and Fri 9.00am–1.00pm; Tue and Thu 1.00–5.00pm. A doctor visits the clinic from Cayman Brac every Wednesday.

In an emergency, the nurse can be contacted out of hours on 948 1073. The nearest **hospital** is Faith Hospital on Cayman Brac, tel: 948 2225. Should there be a need for urgent hospital treatment, patients are put on the first flight off the island, but do note that the patient still has to pay for the ticket, so make sure that you are properly insured. In the unlikely event of a diving accident with a need for decompression, the plane flies to Grand Cayman at a maximum height of 500ft (150m).

There is no natural source of fresh **water** on the island. Drinking water is produced by desalination, with each of the resorts having its own reverse osmosis plant. This means that tap water is safe to drink, but it also means that water is very expensive, so conservation is the watchword here. Rain water is also collected in cisterns. Water for showers etc comes from wells and is mostly brackish.

Police

The police station on Spot Bay Road was opened in autumn 2000 as a base for the island's lone police officer; there are now two officers regularly seen on the beat. Before this, the role was handled by immigration and marine officers. To contact the police, dial 948 0100.

ACTIVITIES
Diving, snorkelling and fishing

Diving and Little Cayman are pretty well synonymous in the minds of most visitors. Renowned worldwide for the attractions of Bloody Bay Wall, the island has a total of 57 designated dive sites, and countless places that are good for snorkelling.

The Bloody Bay Marine Park, incorporating the area between Bloody Bay and Jackson's Point, is a regulated diving zone, in which only licensed vessels are permitted. Most of the dive sites around the island are either in the marine park or in replenishment zones (see map page 28). Under the rules that govern marine park status, boats are limited to a maximum of 20 divers on board at any one time. Even the resorts themselves are limited to the number of boats they may operate. It is therefore important to book diving in advance if you don't want to be disappointed.

On Bloody Bay Wall, each operator is limited by the Cayman Island Watersports Association to one visit per day, and may dive no deeper than 130ft (40m).

Fishing was the original basis of tourism on Little Cayman (diving came later), and remains a strong lure, with fishing packages run by several of the resorts. The biggest draw – aside, of course, from the relaxed pace of the island and the lack of pressure from boat captains – is that of bonefish, which are to be found in sheltered shallow waters such as surround Owen Island (also known as South Hole Sound Lagoon). Tarpon, too, are much sought after, particularly in Tarpon Lake just east of Kingston Bight. Offshore, deep-sea fishing focuses on blue marlin, dolphin, wahoo, tuna and barracuda. Bring your own tackle if you plan to go fly fishing.

Dive/snorkel/fishing operators

All of the island's resorts offer various diving, fishing and snorkelling opportunities to their guests. The following also welcome other visitors, space permitting:

Captain Castro's Fishing Excursions c/o the Village Square; tel: 927 7848.
If you want to go fishing, have a word with the guy at the airport with the pink sunglasses. Castro – his full name is Fidel Castro Christian – was born on the Brac, but has run fishing charters on Little Cayman for several years. Charters in his 17ft (5.2m) boat can be organised to go bonefishing, deep-sea fishing, or night fishing for shark or grouper – basically, whatever your interest, Castro will organise it – with advance reservation.
Rates US$150 per half day for one person for any type of fishing in the South Sound (including bonefishing). For two people, most trips cost US$250, but for deep-sea fishing the price is US$400 for two or three people. Night fishing for shark or grouper, on a catch-and-release basis, is US$150 per person,
Conch Club Divers PO Box 42; tel: 948 1026; fax: 948 1028; email: ccdivers@candw.ky; web: www.conchclub.com
Located at Conch Club Condominiums, this operator limits the number of divers to 15 per trip. PADI and SSI courses up to advanced standard. While many of their visitors stay at the condominiums here, all divers are welcome.
Rates Two-tank dive US$80; Resort course US$100; Open Water US$450; snorkel trip US$25. BCD/regulator US$12 each.
Paradise Divers PO Box 48LC; tel: 948 0001, US: 877 3CAYMAN; fax: 948 0002; email: pvillas@candw.ky; web: www.paradise-divers.com
A relaxed and friendly outfit where group dives are kept small and confidence is the watchword – it's not surprising that Paradise Divers regularly rates highly in surveys of dive operators. In the winter months *Banana Wind*, the fastest dive boat on Little Cayman, speeds out to the dive sites, while in summer, a pontoon boat comes right up on the sand not far from Bloody Bay Wall to collect its passengers. PADI and NAUI affiliated, with several PADI courses available, usually requiring advance reservation.
Rates Two-tank dive US$75; Resort course US$58; Open Water US$460; snorkel trip US$25. BCD/regulator US$10 each, but note that gear rental is a maximum of US$30 per day. Dive packages available on request for booking of five days or more.
Reef Divers Little Cayman Beach Resort; PO Box 51, Blossom Village; tel: 948 1033; US reservations: 800 327 3835; fax: 948 1040; email: lcbr@candw.ky; web: www.littlecayman.com
Established in 1993, Reef Divers has three 42ft custom-built boats and up-to-date equipment. Range of PADI courses, including nitrox. Night dives Tue and Thu, provided that there are at least six divers. Dive shop with sailboat and kayak rentals, plus T-shirts etc, but very little equipment.
Rates Two-tank dive US$75; Resort course US$100; Open Water US$450. BCD/regulator US$12 each. For dive packages, see Little Cayman Beach Resort (page 180).
Southern Cross (see page 183) Diving, fishing and other watersports are open to non-guests subject to availability.

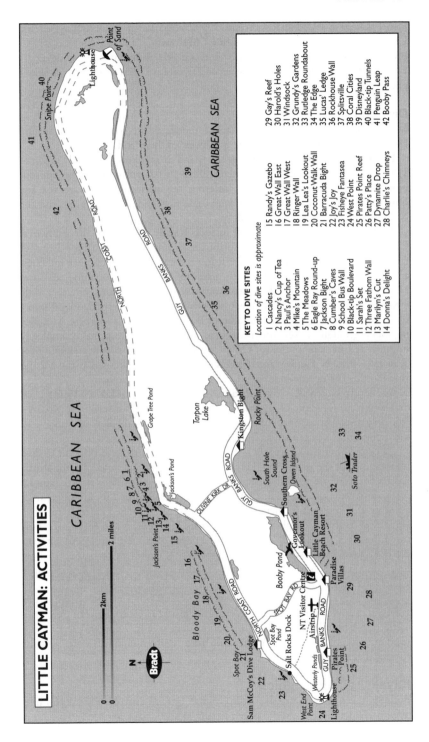

LITTLE CAYMAN: ACTIVITIES

CARIBBEAN SEA

CARIBBEAN SEA

KEY TO DIVE SITES

Location of dive sites is approximate

1 Cascades	15 Randy's Gazebo	29 Gay's Reef
2 Nancy's Cup of Tea	16 Great Wall East	30 Harold's Holes
3 Paul's Anchor	17 Great Wall West	31 Windsock
4 Mike's Mountain	18 Ringer Wall	32 Grundy's Gardens
5 The Meadows	19 Lea Lea's Lookout	33 Rutledge Roundabout
6 Eagle Ray Round-up	20 Coconut Walk Wall	34 The Edge
7 Jackson Bight	21 Barracuda Bight	35 Lucas' Ledge
8 Cumber's Caves	22 Joy's Joy	36 Rockhouse Wall
9 School Bus Wall	23 Fisheye Fantasea	37 Splitsville
10 Black-tip Boulevard	24 West Point	38 Coral Cities
11 Sarah's Set	25 Pirates Point Reef	39 Disneyland
12 Three Fathom Wall	26 Patty's Place	40 Black-tip Tunnels
13 Marilyn's Cut	27 Dynamite Drop	41 Penguin Leap
14 Donna's Delight	28 Charlie's Chimneys	42 Booby Pass

Rates Two-tank dive US$80; Resort course US$125 (includes gear); Open Water referral US$300; snorkel trip US$15. BCD/regulator US$12 each.

Fishing: Guided flats fishing trips, ideally for two anglers, with a maximum of three, US$150–180 for 3–4 hours; guided fishing on Tarpon Lake US$110. Deep-sea fishing prices on request.

Dive sites

Most of Little Cayman's 57 permanent moorings are located in or around Bloody Bay and Jackson Bay, to the northwest of the island.

Bloody Bay Wall to the north of the island drops almost vertically down to 1,200ft (365m) from a depth of a mere 18ft (5.4m). Giant sponges rise up from beautifully formed coral gardens, offering the perfect camouflage for any number of reef fish, while off the wall eagle rays glide gracefully by, and the occasional shark moves in the shadows.

Anchored dive sites on the wall include **Randy's Gazebo**, also known as Chimneys, which had us trying to formulate an underwater signal for 'wow'! A favourite with photographers, the site features corals of all shapes, sizes and hues, and so many marine creatures it's hard to focus on everything at once. Hawkshead turtles make their lazy way across the reef, and stingrays slide effortlessly by. At **Great Wall West**, the shallow reef drops suddenly off into a seemingly endless abyss; the sensation of floating in space is amazing. You may be lucky enough to see the occasional nurse shark on patrol, completely uninterested in your presence. Other popular sites on the wall include Great Wall East, Fisheye Fantasy and Three Fathom Wall (also known as the Mixing Bowl) – this last being the home of Freddie, the Nassau grouper.

As Bloody Bay Wall is renowned for boat diving, so **Jackson's Point** is an excellent place for shore diving and snorkelling. If you're not staying at McCoy's (the only resort on the north of the island), you'll need to take all your equipment, including tanks, as there are no independent dive operators based here.

Of course there are days when the prevailing winds make it difficult to dive on the north of the island, but there's no need to be disappointed, for the **south** has its fair share of good dive sites as well. Here, coral gardens beckon among reefs, mini walls and drop offs that would keep you absorbed for far longer than your air will allow. And there's also the wreck of the *Soto Trader*, which was sunk in 1976 after it caught fire en route from Grand Cayman. A 120ft (36.6m) cargo freighter, it lies today in the sand at a depth of around 50ft (15m), close to the dock used by most of the dive companies. It makes an intriguing shallow dive, though watch out for the fire coral on the hull, and close by you may spot a lone Goliath grouper lurking in the lee of a small reef.

In addition to Jackson's Point, there are several other places on the island where the **snorkelling** is superb, so it's really just a case of taking your pick. One of the most popular is reputed to be about half way to Point of Sand on the southern side of the island. At Point of Sand itself, though, do watch out for strong currents.

Kayaks/sailing dinghies

Both Southern Cross Club and Little Cayman Beach Resort have kayaks for hire by non-resident guests. At the Beach Resort, single kayaks cost US$10 per hour and two-person kayaks US$15 per hour, or US$40–90 per day. Southern Cross charges US$15 and $20 respectively, or US$30/40 for half a day. You can also hire Hobie Cats at the Beach Resort for US$25 an hour, or pedalboats at US$15.

Tennis/gym

The gym at Little Cayman Beach Resort is open to non-residents; contact the resort on 948 1033 for the current fees. Visitors may also use the resort's tennis court, at no charge. The best times to play are early morning or after 4.00pm, when it is cooler.

Hiking and heritage trails

There are plenty of places to explore Little Cayman on foot, though sadly two of the three trails established across the island some 200 years ago – the Spot Bay Trail and the Lighthouse Trail – have recently been paved for vehicles. Of course, you can still walk these, and with considerably greater ease than before. The Spot Bay Trail (now Spot Bay Road) across the western side of the island will take up to half an hour one way. The Lighthouse Trail (now called Candle Road) is a paved road with a dead end, and a loop that returns you to Guy Banks Road near Pirates Point. If you go up here, you may be rewarded with the sight of a rather larger iguana than you've seen elsewhere. The mile-long **Salt Rocks Trail** that links the North Coast Road with Guy Banks Road near the airstrip is the only one left in its natural state. It starts opposite the mule pen to the north, and is clearly marked by a signboard. Although the path is easy to follow, you'll need strong shoes and plenty of water. You should also be able to recognise (and thus avoid) the highly poisonous manchineel tree, which grows along the trail; with its apple-like fruit, small oval leaves and horizontal stripes on the bark, it's reasonably distinctive. The path is lined with a variety of native trees and plants, with bromeliads in evidence after about half way; visit in June to see these at their best. The orange sandy material to be seen in patches here and there is actually ground phosphate, which used to be exported from the island. The latter part of the trail once passed various homesteads, though little is left now except plants such as the tamarind, which were often grown in gardens as their seeds were used to flavour water. The trail finally emerges roughly in the middle of the airstrip, near the windsock.

A recently designated **Maritime Heritage Trail** is marked by a series of eight signboards. Backed by a leaflet produced by the tourist board, it tells the stories behind some of the many ships wrecked off these shores, and makes an interesting basis for a tour of the island.

For guided nature walks on the island, contact Gladys Howard at Pirates Point (see page 182).

ROUND-THE-ISLAND TOUR

The best way to see the island is undoubtedly by bike or, if you want to go right to the eastern tip, by hired jeep. Allow a couple of hours to do the shorter circuit by bike, which gives you time to complete it at leisure; you'll need longer if you're going to combine this with a visit to the museum or National Trust. The full tour of the island by jeep could be completed in not much more than an hour, but anything less than half a day wouldn't do it justice. Take a hat and plenty to drink.

The circular tour here is based on starting at the airport and heading east, but it could of course be started anywhere.

Blossom Village to Kingston Bight

The paved road heading east from the airstrip is lined by dense vegetation, occasionally broken by ponds and mangrove swamps. Flowering trees enliven the wayside, bringing splashes of red and yellow at the end of the year, while in spring the fluffy white of the cotton plant is to be seen all across the island. Part of Blossom Village lies behind the shops, and is accessed by the sandy Blossom Avenue just to the side of Paradise Villas. The newly designated Blossom Village Park, with its swings and picnic tables, has a memorial commemorating the 500th anniversary in 2003 of the discovery of the island by Christopher Columbus. There's also a small sandy beach here, ideal for families. A little further up the road is the island's cemetery, then it's just a few yards before you rejoin Guy Banks Road

Just a short walk east from the shops, set back from Guy Banks Road, is **Little Cayman Museum** (tel: 948 1033). The immaculately painted green-and-white building with its wooden veranda is surrounded by lawns, and flanked by artefacts from the collection. The museum houses personal and public memorabilia dating back 150 years or so. Originally the collection of Linton Tibbetts, a Bracker who went to the US with just $45 and returned a multi-millionaire, it tells the history of Little Cayman, as well as something of Cayman Brac. Tibbetts' collection is augmented by individual donations from the islanders, from a grandmother's sewing machine and plates to one of the turtle nets that were once effectively the lifeblood of the island. Open Thursday and Friday 3.00–5.00pm.

The tiny **Baptist church** next to the museum has now been closed, replaced by its grander new neighbour. All are welcome to attend the services at 11.00am and 7.30pm on Sunday, or the Wednesday Bible study at 7.30pm.

On the other side of the road is the recently built **National Trust Visitors' Centre** (open Mon–Sat 3.00–5.00pm). Overlooking Booby Pond, the centre was built as a result of the almost single-handed effort of Gladys Howard, the Texan-born owner of Pirates Point (see page 182) who fundraised tirelessly until the building was finally completed. The centre is staffed entirely by volunteers. Gladys now leads nature walks for visitors to the island in return for a US$25 donation to the National Trust (free to residents at Pirates Point); she also has a considerable fund of knowledge about Cayman history – contact her on 948 1010.

Inside the centre are panels featuring the natural history of the island, with a particular focus on the birds. Outside, telescopes on the porch and upstairs veranda enable visitors to watch the boobies across the pond. A number of local books and prints by local artists are for sale.

The centre is also home to Little Cayman's **library**. Housed in a small room off the main centre, the library mostly comprises paperback fiction, although there are some reference books as well. Visitors and residents alike may swap a book for a fee of just CI$1, or buy one for CI$3, with all proceeds going towards the National Trust.

The peaceful setting of **Booby Pond** is a haven for wildlife and has been designated an animal sanctuary and wetland of international importance under the UN Ramsar Convention. Like the other ponds on the Cayman Islands, Booby Pond is Crown land, while the land to the north is now owned by the National Trust. The natural beauty of the place can be somewhat deceptive, however. At the beginning of winter, the pond may look deep but has in fact just a few inches of water. By May, before the summer rain, much of the water has evaporated leaving a pretty smelly brackish residue.

The ancient breeding colony of well over 5,000 pairs of red-footed boobies and the attendant magnificent frigatebirds is the largest in the Caribbean. In the past, booby eggs formed part of the local diet, effectively checking the growth of the colony since boobies raise just one chick per year. Now, however, the colony is fully protected and numbers are rising fast.

At dawn, the sky is alive with boobies heading out to sea for their fishing grounds, attaining speeds of up to 40mph (64km/h). Frigatebirds glide effortlessly overhead, easily distinguished in flight by their forked tails. In the mating season (late November to January), the males display their distinctive red pouch. Known to locals as the 'man o' war', the frigatebird may co-exist with the booby, but it is also its arch enemy, hovering menacingly above the coastline as dusk approaches to terrorise the boobies as they return into releasing their day's catch.

Opposite the pond, not far from Little Cayman Beach Resort, is the Governor's Lookout, a small hide built for birdwatching, and the best place to see frigatebirds during the mating season.

Owen Island

Probably the nearest most of us will ever get to a desert island, Owen Island is located in the bay just a short kayak trip (or even a swim) from Southern Cross or – a little further – from Kingston Bight. The water here is very shallow and mostly thick with turtle grass; except at high tide it is actually quite possible to walk across. The small beach on the island is, quite simply, idyllic, with soft white sand backed by trees, and the odd piece of driftwood. Beyond is the edge of the reef. If you're planning to walk rather than wade out towards the reef, though, do take good shoes as this end of the island is rocky and it's tough going. The stretch of water between the island and the reef beyond is not deep, but watch out for currents around the tip of the island. There's plenty of underwater life here for snorkellers to observe, including young coral formations (take care not to knock them with your fins) and spiny lobster; you may even catch a glimpse of the occasional nurse shark as it slips through the narrow channel.

Further east

The road east from Kingston Bight is paved to within a mile or so of Point of Sand, before it turns into a sandy track, rough in parts, as far as Point of Sand and back along the north coast. The road is pretty flat, but drifting sand makes cycling over the last stretch particularly hazardous. That, coupled with the likelihood of punctures on the sharp stones and the lack of manoeuvrability of the island's rental bikes, makes it important to cycle only with extreme care beyond this point. A more sensible circuit for cyclists is to turn on to the paved crossover road, Olivine Kirk Drive, about 500 yards (450m) before Kingston

Bight, and head for the north side of the island, then west to complete a circuit of some eight miles (13km).

Continuing east along the southern road, you'll be following the coast. Inland, ponds line the roadside, many offering habitats to a wide variety of birds, including the West Indian whistling-duck. The largest of these ponds is the 15-acre **Tarpon Lake**, which lies on the left just past Kingston Bight. Popular with fishermen in search of the beautiful silver fish that make this their home in significant numbers, and a real delight for birdwatchers and photographers, it is accessed via a wooden boardwalk from the road. Evidence of earlier hurricanes can be seen in the dead trees whose skeletal limbs poke out of the water, though regeneration of the habitat is well under way.

As the road becomes rougher, the vegetation becomes less dense, coconut palms rise high above and rough tracks to the right offer tantalising glimpses of the Caribbean. Some six miles (10km) from Kingston Bight, the road veers to the left, with a track off to the right leading through to Point of Sand.

Point of Sand, marked as Sandy Point on some maps, is almost at the extreme east of the island, looking over towards Cayman Brac, five miles (8km) away across the channel. The water here is as clear as anywhere on the island, and sheltered by the reef. Snorkelling is excellent, but watch out for strong currents. The white sandy beach shifts with the changing tides and seasons, meaning that no map is ever quite accurate. It is backed by low bushes that offer little or no protection against the midday sun. Although there is a purpose-built wooden shelter back off the beach, the place is stacked with broken benches, so take an umbrella and/or sunhat, plus water and suncream, if you're heading out this way. The nearest place to get a drink is at Kingston Bight.

To complete the circuit of the island, return down the track to the point at which you forked off, then turn right and follow the road right round the coast, past the lighthouse. There is little along this road apart from trees, beaches and the occasional private house, so the choice of picnic spot is all yours. One significant development, though, is the imminent construction of **Little Cayman Marine Research Centre**. Dedicated on May 10 2003, the centre will occupy a 1,400ft stretch of the north shore, to the east of Bloody Bay Marine Park, and will be used to further the work of the Central Caribbean Marine Institute (see pages 29–30). At present there is a small beach shelter to mark the site, but when sufficient funds have been raised, and the Cayman-style building is finally complete, it will incorporate living accommodation for students alongside classrooms, laboratories and a library.

Approximately eight miles (13km) from Point of Sand, the road is again paved, but shortly before this you'll pass **Grape Tree Pond** and then **Jackson's Pond**, both offering good opportunities for birdwatching from viewing areas. Opposite the second of these is **Jackson's Point**, a good place for an afternoon's snorkel (and superb shore diving as well). From here, the road is again paved as it passes the northern side of the road across the island, Olivine Kirk Drive.

More or less opposite Sam McCoy's on your left is **Spot Bay Pond**; if you've missed the endangered West Indian whistling-duck at Grape Tree Pond, you may get to see it here, and to read about it on the information board that sits on the viewing platform.

Continue past Sam McCoy's to **Salt Rocks Dock**, where ships tie up each week to bring provisions to the island. This is also the site of the old **mule pen**, built in 1885 and the oldest surviving structure on the island. There is no diving from the docks, and no beach, but in summer some of the resort boats moor here, giving them easy access out to Bloody Bay Wall. Opposite the mule pen is the start of the Salt Rocks Trail (see page 191).

Almost at the western tip of the island is the **lighthouse**, not accessible to the public. Continue past here and Pirates Point and you'll find yourself back at the airstrip, with luck in time to enjoy a cool drink in a tree-shaded hammock.

Tarpon

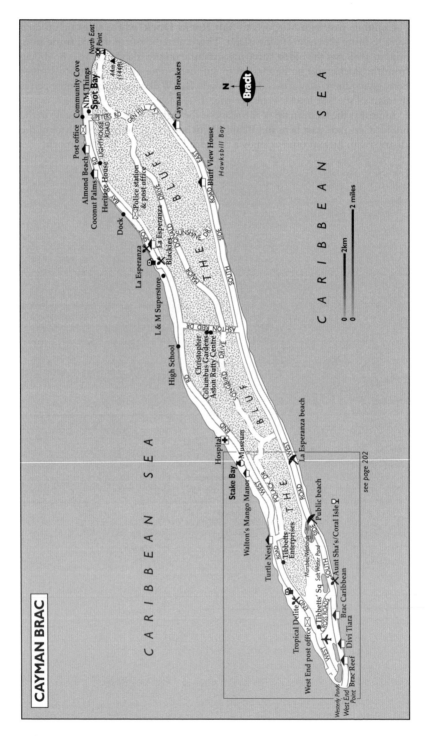

CAYMAN BRAC

Cayman Brac

On first acquaintance, Cayman Brac seems the poor relation of the Cayman Islands – more stepsister than true family. Short on white sandy beaches and with an apparently impenetrable interior, this Caribbean island lacks the clichéd Caribbean attractions. But appearances can be deceptive. Whereas Grand Cayman and, to a far lesser extent, Little Cayman are effectively ensnared by tourism, Cayman Brac very much retains its own personality. Here, you will meet the local people, or Brackers, in hotels, in restaurants, in the shops. Cayman food is the norm, not something to be sought out like a rare commodity. In fact, the whole ethos is that of Cayman – a gentler pace of life, a deeper sense of reality.

The Brac, so called after the Gaelic word for 'bluff', is 12 miles (19.3km) long from west to east, and nearly two miles (3km) across at its widest point, to the east. Located at 79° west, 19° 41' north, the island covers an area of just 14 square miles (36km²). It may be similar in size to Little Cayman, but there the similarity ends. Like some great fossilised whale, the bluff dominates almost the entire length of the island, seemingly impenetrable, and with only the western tip untouched by its presence. To the east, looming straight up from the sea, the highest point of this stark rock, at 144ft (43.9m), must have been a forbidding sight for sailors in days gone by. Cruel ironshore lies underfoot at the top, but beneath is a veritable labyrinth of limestone caves that have not only offered full rein to the imaginations of countless children over the years, but rather more soberly have served as shelters to generations of Brackers from the fierce storms that are occasionally meted out to the island.

There are four main settlements, all on the west or north of the island: West End, Stake Bay, Creek and Spot Bay, housing the island's 1,800 or so population. A considerable number of expatriate workers also live on the island, mostly from Jamaica and Honduras, swelling the population by almost double. Unlike on Grand Cayman, however, few foreigners here are employed in the tourism industry. Aside from the construction industry, some work in one of the island's three primary schools or the high school, and others in the local hospital. The few tourist venues are concentrated at the westernmost point of the island, where the land is flat, and wide sandy beaches are lapped by the blue waters of the Caribbean.

A little-known venue for discerning divers, and gaining popularity with keen climbers, the Brac is also ideally situated for the nature lover, with a number of designated hikes of varying degrees of difficulty. Safe and stress free, it is a welcoming place with no frills.

Locals will tell you that Cayman Brac is getting more crowded, with a lot of building. It's hard to take this on board by comparison with Grand Cayman, but clearly the Brackers like their island the way it is, and have no intention of letting the rest of the world spoil its natural beauty.

HISTORY

The first permanent settlers on the Brac, in 1833, were boatbuilders, sailors and turtle fishermen who came over from Grand Cayman to people this previously uninhabited island. Trade links were soon established with Jamaica, Cuba and Central America. Sixty years later, the population had risen to 528, and by 1934 it stood at 1,317.

Until 1968, one of the major exports from Cayman Brac was turtleshell, together with coconut, cattle and rope. Alongside these, from the early part of the 20th century until 1939, Cayman Brac traded in relatively low-quality phosphate, which was blasted out of the rock on Cotton Tree Land in the interior and transported by rail to waiting ships.

Time in Cayman Brac is effectively measured from the 1932 hurricane, which brought death and destruction to the Brac in devastating fashion. At the time of

THE '32 HURRICANE

On that fateful morning, it came with no warning,
Crashing waves sweeping o'er the land

From '1932 Hurricane' in *Traditional Songs from the Cayman Islands*

The lives of the islanders have been shaped across the years by the various hurricanes that have hit the Brac and the other two islands in the group. In 1980, the tidal surge caused by Hurricane Allen brought the sea some 300ft (100m) inland, throwing great stones against the bluff. Then, as so many other times, the islanders took refuge in the labyrinth of caves that lie within the bluff – a tough climb up to 80ft (24m) or so took them to a place of relative safety.

Undoubtedly the hurricane that caused the most damage in living memory was that of November 8 1932, which changed the lives of Brackers for ever. The Brac took the hurricane head on, with winds of 200mph (320km/h) and water crashing inland up to 800ft (244m). Indeed, the seas were so rough that some waves went right over the bluff. Later, as the storm died away and the waters subsided, a shark was found inland in the grounds of Spellman McLaughlin House on the northern side of the island, a rare light moment at a time of real tragedy.

One hundred and nine Brackers lost their lives that night, 40 of them in three separate ships at sea. Whole families were wiped out, from babies to grandparents. A mass gravesite for many of the victims of the hurricane lies near the sea on White Bay Road (see page 218).

the hurricane, life on Cayman Brac was pretty primitive by Western standards. Without electricity or telephones, and with very few cars, the islanders were effectively cut off from the outside world except by sea. The few products that were imported were brought in by boat, traded in exchange for turtleshell and rope.

Electricity came late to Cayman Brac. Until the 1960s, nobody had a stove either. Instead, every house had a hearth in a separate caboose – a shed off the main house with a walkway between the two. Each day, one of the islanders would carry a live coal by hand to his neighbours until every fire was lit.

NATURAL HISTORY

Vegetation on the bluff is dense, in spite of the precarious existence that is the lot of trees whose roots penetrate deep into the limestone in search of water. Tall, pale-green cacti stand alongside large succulents, overshadowed by dense trees, from mastic and wild sapodilla to red birch, silver thatch and coconut palms. Fruit trees grow wild, including vine pears, wild figs and some 20 varieties of mango, which may be picked in season. Where sunlight penetrates, bougainvillaea tumbles down the rockface, and from November to January, the roads are lined with 'Christmas flowers' – yellow elders or shamrock that decorate the trees right across the island.

Almost 200 species of birds have been identified on the Brac, making it a wonderful place for birdwatching. High up on the southern side of the island, a small colony of brown boobies nest in the bluff. Like their cousins, the red-footed boobies, these are pelagic birds, to some extent at the mercy of the magnificent frigatebirds that swoop down and steal their catch. All around, on both sides of the bluff, white-tailed tropicbirds may be seen, distinctive for their long white tails, like streamers.

Inland is the only place in the world where the Cayman Brac parrot nests. With a population of just 350, it is seriously endangered. Among other birds endemic to the Brac are the red-legged thrush, the loggerhead kingbird and the vitelline warbler.

While the exterior of the bluff hosts several bird species, the network of caves that meander through the bluff is home to a multitude of different creatures. Barn owls nest in dark corners, and five species of bat, of which the most populous is the Jamaican fruit bat, have colonised the caves. That unexpected squeaking isn't a bat, though, it's probably a hermit crab. Watch out for them on the floor of the caves – it's easy to tread on them by mistake. The caves themselves are a seemingly endless series of interconnecting tunnels. Stalactites and stalagmites reach out to touch each other, formed from calcium carbonate as a result of the slow and incessant drip, drip of water over countless centuries. Leggy tree roots dangle into nothingness, seeking out sufficient water to eke out their precarious existence.

If the bluff dominates most of the island, to the west is a very different landscape. Here, herons, egrets and numerous other waterfowl are attracted by the flat wetland terrain, as are countless migrant birds on their passage south.

The National Trust (see page 29) is engaged in long-term projects to preserve the unique wildlife and flora indigenous to Cayman Brac.

GETTING THERE
By air
The flight with Cayman Airways from Grand Cayman to Gerrard Smith International airport, at the westernmost tip of the island, takes between 40 minutes and an hour, depending on whether it's a direct flight or via Little Cayman. There are also Cayman Airways flights from Miami to Cayman Brac, with a short stopover in Grand Cayman. For details of schedules and prices, see pages 81–2. Note that passengers are not allowed to get off the plane in Grand Cayman when booked on a direct flight from Miami to Cayman Brac. A couple of small shops and a bar are the only facilities at the airport.

By sea
Surprisingly, there is no ferry service between Little Cayman and Cayman Brac, although the distance between the two islands is just five miles (8km). That said, most of the boat operators here run snorkel and dive trips to Little Cayman, so day trips by boat are straightforward to organise (see page 214).

GETTING AROUND
In a nutshell, getting around Cayman Brac can be a problem. Although the island is small, there is no road that runs right round so those at the easternmost point of the island have to cover a significant distance to get just a mile or so around to the south. There is no public transport (don't be deluded by the 'bus stop' signs – they're for school buses only) and though walking is fine in daylight, it's not ideal on unlit roads at night. The options are therefore taxis, some sort of hire vehicle – car, scooter or bike – or to hitchhike. On the positive side, some of the restaurants and dive operators will collect you from your accommodation and take you home afterwards – it's always worth asking.

Taxis
Taxis are few and far between, and not always available when you want them, even at the airport, so do book in advance. Contact numbers are as follows:

David Hurlston & Osmond Knight Tel: 948 2307/0435/0523. Airport US$7 per person one way; island tour US$15 per person.
Elo's Taxi Tel: 948 0220
Maple Edwards Tel: 948 0395

Vehicle hire
As on the other islands, drivers need an international driving licence or their local licence plus a Cayman Islands driving permit. If you buy your permit on Cayman Brac, it is slightly cheaper than on the other islands, at CI$4/US$5. The speed limit is 25mph in the vicinity of schools and the hospital, 30mph on Ashton Reid Drive and at the Cross Roads junction close to the hotels in the southwest, and 40mph elsewhere.

Fuel prices are a little higher than on Grand Cayman. Petrol is CI$2.45 (US$3.06) per gallon. There are just two fuel stations on the Brac – one opposite Salt Water Pond Walk on the north side of the island (open Mon–Sat 7.30am to around 8.30pm, and later at weekends; Sun 3.00–5.00pm); and the second at Watering Place, just west of Blackie's (open Mon–Sat 8.00am–8.00pm approx).

Cars

All car-hire companies will meet incoming flights by arrangement, and most offer a free pick-up service.

B&S Motorventures 126 Channel Rd, South Side; tel: 948 1646/2517; fax: 948 1676; email: the_rock@candw.ky; web: www.bandsmv.com. Steve and Nola Bodden run this place on the southwest side of the island as if they were your friends, and offer a wealth of useful information along the way. Vehicles range from cars at US$35 per day to jeeps at US$38 and 7- or 9-seater people carriers at US$48–55, including third party insurance; CDW is from US$7.50 per day. Weekly rates are based on six days' hire for six or seven days. For bicycles and scooters, see below.

Brac Rent-a-Car Tibbetts' Square; tel: 948 1515/0277; fax: 948 1380; email: scottaud@candw.ky; web: www.bracrentals.com. Range of cars including Jeeps. Rates low/high season from US$35/42 to US$50/55. Fully comprehensive insurance is extra. Open Mon–Fri 8.30am–5.00pm; Sat 8.30am–midday.

CB Rent-a-Car Tel: 948 2847/2424, US 800 228 0668; fax: 948 2329. Based at the airport, they have four-, five- and six-seater vehicles, with child safety seats available. Open daily 8.00am–6.00pm. Rates from US$35 per day all year round. Discount of 20% to members of AAA and AARP, travel agents and airline employees.

Four D's Car Rental Kidco Bldg, South Side; tel: 948 1599; fax: 948 0459/2513; email: 4_d@candw.ky. At US$35–40 per day in high season, including fully comprehensive insurance, these are the cheapest cars on the island, if not the best maintained, and the owners are certainly helpful. Every seventh day free. Open Mon–Fri 8.00am–5.00pm; Sun 9.00am–1.00pm.

Scooters and bicycles

For many visitors, scooters offer the ideal compromise between the high cost of car hire and the freedom of a bike, giving the opportunity to explore almost everywhere on the island except the unpaved roads on the bluff.

Bikes are an ideal form of transport in the daytime, with quiet flat roads all along the coast, and the main road across the island an easy cycle road. If you're planning to cycle up on the bluff, though, be prepared for very steep access roads, and check that the areas where you'll be cycling are paved: hotel bikes aren't geared for off-road cycling, and could prove very dangerous.

Both bikes and scooters may be hired from **B&S Motorventures** (see above). Scooters cost US$30 per day (US$180 for six–seven days); bicycles US$10 per 24 hours. Unlike the hotel bikes, though, these ones have gears and proper brakes. If you phone from your accommodation, someone from B&S will usually drive out to collect you.

Hitchhiking

One of the bonuses of having no transport is the opportunity to meet local people. Giving and taking of lifts is not uncommon: during a walk along Stake Bay Road, two separate vehicles stopped to offer us a lift in as many minutes. As anywhere, women on their own should obviously avoid any potentially threatening situation.

WHERE TO STAY

Cayman Brac has less choice of hotel accommodation than the other two islands in the group, although there are plenty of secluded villas and condominiums for

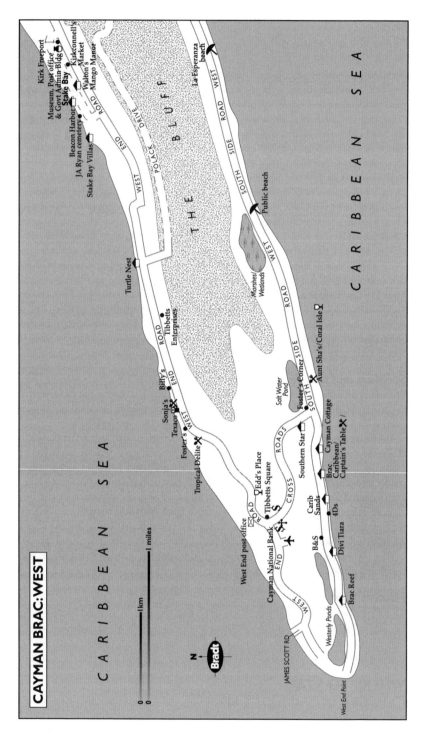

CAYMAN BRAC: WEST

CARIBBEAN SEA

CARIBBEAN SEA

CARIBBEAN SEA

THE BLUFF

N

Bradt

0   1km
0   1 miles

JAMES SCOTT RD

West End Point

Westerly Ponds

Brac Reef

Cayman National Bank

West End post office

WEST END ROAD

B&S

Divi Tiara

4Ds

Carib Sands

Southern Star

Edd's Place

Tibbetts Square

CROSS ROADS

Brac Caribbean/
Captain's Table

Cayman Cottage

Aunt Sha's/Coral Isle

SOUTH SIDE ROAD

Foster's Corner

Salt Water Pond

Marshes/
Wetlands

WEST ROAD

SOUTH SIDE ROAD

Public beach

La Esperanza beach

ROAD WEST

Mango Manor

Walton's Market

Kirkconnell's

Stake Bay

Museum, Post office
& Govt Admin Bldg

Kirk Freeport

Beacon Harbour

JA Ryan cemetery

Stake Bay Villas

WEST END ROAD

POLACK DRIVE

Turtle Nest

Tibbetts Enterprises

ROAD END

Billy's

Sonja's

Texaco

Foster's WEST

Tropical Delite

the more independent minded. The two resort hotels are located on the southwest point, close to the airport. Don't worry about noise, though; there are very few planes and those that there are are small and relatively quiet.

Resort hotels

Brac Reef Beach Resort PO Box 56 WE, South Side; tel: 948 1323; fax: 948 1207; US reservations: tel: 800 594 0843 or 345 323 8727; fax: 727 323 8827; email: bracreef@candw.ky; web: www.bracreef.com (40 rooms)
A relaxed resort situated at the southwest of the island, Brac Reef is the most upmarket of the island's hotels. All rooms overlook the pool, most with either a patio or private balcony, plus en-suite bathroom, AC/ceiling fan, TV, telephone and radio/alarm; a fridge or microwave may be rented. Luxury oceanfront rooms are also available. Meals are taken either in the air-conditioned restaurant (The Palms), or at the terrace bar (Tipsy Turtle). There are also a conference/banquet centre, swimming pool, games rooms, fitness centre, floodlit tennis court and health and beauty spa (tel: 948 1323), plus Polly's Landing boutique and gift shop; dive and photo shops. Evening entertainment.
    A beautiful private beach with hammocks and high shady 'lookout' – a perfect spot to relax in the cool breeze with a book – is also the place for a wide range of watersports. There is excellent snorkelling from the jetty. Diving is through Reef Divers, who are based on site. Bicycles are available free of charge for guests, while kayaks cost CI$5 per hour.
Rates per room per night for 2 people, low/high season: US$95/133. All rates subject to 12% service charge. Packages available for divers and non-divers alike.
Divi Tiara PO Box 238 STB, South Side; tel: 948 1553, US toll free: 800 367 3484; fax: 948 1316; email: tiarares@candw.ky; web: www.diviresorts.com (71 rooms)
The majority of guests at this multi-coloured Canadian-owned resort are from the US, although a few come from the UK, and most are either divers or honeymooners (or both!). It's also a good bet for families, with a relaxed atmosphere and friendly, mostly Caymanian, staff. Standard, deluxe (with sea view and cable TV) and luxury (with Jacuzzi) rooms, plus 12 one-bedroom timeshare apartments. Buffet-style restaurant. The bar is open 10.00am–midnight, with snacks available all day. In addition, a rustic beach bar overlooks a sandy beach where egrets and herons abound. Other facilities include a conference centre, swimming pool and tennis court. Shops with jewellery, coins and cigars, clothes, drinks and snacks are open 8.30am–5.30pm. Diving with Dive Tiara, and on-site dive and photo shop. Bikes available for guests.
Rates per room per night: standard US$101–182; deluxe US$134–241; luxury US$158–285. Children 16 and under free if sharing with adults (maximum 4 people per room). Apartments US$199–358 per night. Rates vary across four seasons, with the highest at Christmas, and the lowest from May to December. All rates subject to 10% service charge. Various packages available.

Guesthouses

Walton's Mango Manor PO Box 56, Stake Bay; tel/fax: 948 0518; email: waltons@candw.ky; web: www.waltonsmangomanor.com (5 rooms, house)
George and Lynne Walton's home away from home is conveniently located on the north of the island, just opposite the bluff, close to the museum, and with an ironshore beach at the bottom of the extensive garden. Near to the sea is a private, self-contained guesthouse, Sea Dreams (see page 206), and there's a beach shelter for those lazy days of sun and snorkelling. There's also, quite unexpectedly, a private synagogue (see box, *Beth*

BETH SHALOM

Many are the gifts that exchange hands in celebration of a special anniversary, but when George Walton set out to surprise his wife, Lynne, his present was altogether in a different league. The synagogue in the grounds of their guesthouse at Stake Bay was built to mark the occasion of their 35th wedding anniversary. Called Beth Shalom, or 'House of Peace' it is named after the New York synagogue in which the couple were married, and was dedicated in 2002 by the rabbi who conducted their wedding.

The simple curves of the white circular building, designed by an architect friend on the Brac, sweep up above the Star of David to deep-blue roof gables. Step through the heavy mahogany door and your eye is drawn upwards to the 12 star-like lights in the ceiling that symbolise the 12 tribes of Israel. The Torah – the first to be brought to the Brac – sits in the hand-carved wooden ark alongside the traditional ram's horn.

This is a temple of calm and tranquillity, and the Walton's are keen for it to be used by people of all faiths – whether as a place for quiet reflection or to celebrate that special occasion. They are happy, too, to show visitors around – do make the effort to visit.

Shalom, above). The model boats that adorn the traditional porched house were built by George's brother, Albert, a further example of whose work is on display in the museum in George Town.

Rates per room, per night low/high season: US$80–90/$90–100, including an excellent home-cooked breakfast.

Self-catering apartments and villas

There are several small cottages and villas both to the north and south of the Brac, and the following is just a selection. For other properties, contact **Tranquil Realty**, PO Box 90, South Side; tel: 948 1577; fax: 948 1578; email: tranquil@candw.ky; web: www.tranquilrealty.com, or the Department of Tourism (see page 210).

Almond Beach Hideaways Spot Bay; US tel: 866 222 8528; fax: 503 472 6394; email: kbryan@onlinemac.com; web: www.almondbeachhideaways.com (2 villas)
These two-bedroom individual villas on the beach each have a seafront patio, two bathrooms, kitchen, AC, laundry, phone, TV/VCR and barbecue.
Rates per villa per night: US$185 (two adults); US$210 (three adults); U$240 (four adults); children under eight free; children aged 9–16 US$20 per night (deduct 10% Jul–Sep). Minimum three-night stay. Maid service available US$10 per hour.
Beacon Harbor Foster's Rd, Stake Bay; US tel/fax: 956 544 4396; email: info@beaconharbor.com; web: www.beaconharbor.com (2 condominiums)
These large two-bedroom condominiums look out over the north side of the island near Stake Bay. Custom-built for divers, the units lie opposite three good dive sites and have downstairs toilets, outside showers and washdown facilities for scuba gear. Upstairs, each unit sleeps up to six people, with living room, kitchen, bathroom, AC/fans, TV/VCR, telephone and laundry.

Rates for two people: US$190 per night; US$1,150 per week. Each additional guest US$35 per night, US$205 per week.

Bluff View Contact John Byrnes, 46246 Weld CR #13, Ft Collins, CO 80524, USA; tel: 970 493 5801; fax: 970 493 2283; email: jbyrnes@frii.com (2 apartments)

Owned by the climbing fraternity on the Brac, Bluff View is on the south road towards the east end of the island. Backed up against the bluff, it's just 60yds (50m) from the sea. The traditional-style house has two independent one-bedroom apartments, one on each floor, each with large living room complete with double sofa bed, bathroom, fully equipped kitchen and AC. Separate laundry and outside shower.

Rates per week: US$570, including taxes

Brac Caribbean Beach Village PO Box 4, Stake Bay; tel: 948 2265, US: 866 THE BRAC; fax; 948 1111; email: bracarib@candw.ky; web: www.866thebrac.com (16 condominiums)

These luxury one- and two-bedroom beachside apartments in the southwest are built in a traditional style; each has a private balcony, living room, cable TV, phone, kitchen and three bathrooms. There is a sparkling swimming pool and restaurant (Captain's Table) on site. Diving is through Reef Divers. Laundry facilities.

Rates (two-bedroom apartment) per night: US$185 (two adults); US$215 (three adults); U$245 (four adults); children under 11 free; children aged 12–17 US$35 per night. Maid service US$35 per day.

Carib Sands PO Box 4 SPO; tel: 948 1121; fax: 948 1111; email: caribsan@candw.ky; web: www.866thebrac.com (37 condominiums)

Sister to the adjacent Brac Caribbean, this complex has its own swimming pool. Of the various condominiums, with between one and four bedrooms, some have a sea view, and all have kitchen, AC/ceiling fans and cable TV.

Rates per night: US$185 (one bedroom); U$245 (two bedroom); US$305 (three bedroom); U$465 (four bedroom). Children under 11 free; children aged 12–17 US$25 per night. Dive packages available through Reef Divers.

Cayman Breakers PO Box 202 SPO; tel/fax: 948 1463; email: caymanbreakers@yahoo.com; web: www.caymancondosonline.com (9 units)

These individual pink-washed houses with two storeys sit right on the beach on the south of the island. Each air-conditioned unit has two bedrooms and two bathrooms, a fully equipped kitchen and utility room, living room with sofa bed, satellite TV and VCR. Picnic tables and hammocks are set around the pool, barbecue grills and hammocks are set in a courtyard by the pool, and there's a rinse tank for divers. Courtesy bikes for guests.

Rates low/high season, four adults, eight days: US$880/990 (oceanview); US$990/1,100 (oceanfront balcony/patio view). Additional night US$126–141. Rates include 10% government tax.

Cayman Cottage PO Box 100 WPO, South Side; tel: 948 1617, US 505 898 6854; email: caymancottage@yahoo.com; web: www.caymancottage.com

This private house in the grounds of the owner's home is just 25yds (24m) from the beach in the southwest of the island. Bedroom, bathroom, living room, kitchen, with AC/ceiling fans and TV/VCR.

Rates per night: US$120 (two adults); US$130 (three/four adults). Children under 12 free.

La Esperanza PO Box 28, Stake Bay; tel: 948 0591; fax: 948 0525; email: lodging@candw.ky (4 apartments, 2 houses)

Located opposite the restaurant of the same name, La Esperanza is Caymanian owned and run and is arguably the most friendly place on the island to stay. Four comfortable two-bedroomed apartments (sleep 4–6) and two three-bedroomed/two-bathroom houses (sleep 6–8) are set in shady grounds; each has a kitchen, living room, TV, radio/cassette and AC/ceiling fans. Next to the restaurant is a small shop with basic groceries, T-shirts etc, and on the south side of the island is a private beach. Car rental for guests only is US$26 per day.

Rates per night for two people: US$71; three people US$85. Each additional person US$12 per night.

Sea Dreams Reservations through Walton's Mango Manor (see above)
The self-contained two-storey house in the garden of Walton's Mango Manor sleeps up to four people. Fully air conditioned, it has two bedrooms, two bathrooms, a living room with TV/VCR, a kitchen and laundry. If you don't fancy cooking, an excellent breakfast is available for US$6 per person.

Rates US1,000 per week for two people, US$1,200 for four people, all year round.

Stake Bay Villas PO Box 48 SB, Stake Bay; tel: 948 1646/2517; fax: 948 1676; email: the_rock@candw.ky; web: www.stakebayvillas.com (2 villas)
Down a lane to the left, just before the Stake Bay sign when coming from the airport, these new one-bedroom villas with screened balconies are right on the beach. Each villa sleeps up to four people (with sofa bed) and has AC, satellite TV, kitchen and laundry facilities.

Rates US$120 per night, two people. Additional guests US$25 per day. Minimum stay three nights.

Turtle Nest PO Box 50 Stake Bay, tel/fax: 948 2697; email: thetnest@candw.ky; web: www.thetnest.com
This privately owned house lies on the north coast, on the boundary between Cotton Tree Bay and Rock, next door to the owner's accommodation. Just 100yds (90m) from the sea, it sleeps up to four people. Modern bedroom, lounge, bathroom, kitchen with AC/fans, telephone and TV/VCR. Small pool in lovely private sand garden, with shady beach shelter.

Rates for two people: US$99 per night; additional adult US$20 per night.

Timeshare

Divi Tiara (see page 203) has 12 one-bedroom timeshare apartments in its resort complex, sharing the same facilities.

RESTAURANTS AND BARS

The Brac is not endowed with an enormous range of restaurants, but what it lacks in variety and style it makes up for in good traditional cooking. Both Captain's Table and La Esperanza will sometimes collect diners by arrangement.

Aunt Sha's Kitchen (at the Coral Isle) Tel: 948 1581. It's difficult to miss the bright pink building that is Aunt Sha's, situated all on its own on the southern side of the island. A good selection of Cayman-style food, including turtle stew and the excellent Cayman-style fish, as well as some Chinese dishes, is on offer at moderate prices. If asked, they will also prepare sandwiches to take away – chicken CI$4. Even on windy days, the open-air area overlooking the sea is sheltered, making it a better bet at lunchtime than the rather dark restaurant, and a great place to watch the frigatebirds wheeling overhead. At night, look out to sea – you may be lucky enough to spot the odd cruising shark in the shallows. Lively bar, pool room. Dancing on the outside terrace Wed, Fri and Sat from 8.00pm. Open Mon–Fri 9.00am–1.00am, Sat 9.00am–midnight,

Sun midday to midnight. Happy hour Fri/Sat 6.00–7.00pm (with special cocktails and snacks, plus 50 cents off beer).

Brac Reef Resort South Side; tel: 948 1323. The Palms restaurant features a fixed-price meal, although an à la carte menu is also available. Open for breakfast 7.00–9.00am (CI$12), lunch 12.30–1.30pm (CI$15), and dinner 6.30–8.00pm (CI$25). The shady terrace bar has snacks from CI$4.50, and fruit punch at CI$2. Open Mon–Thu 11.00am–11.00pm; Fri–Sat 11.00am–midnight; Sun midday–11.00pm. Happy hour Fri 5.00–7.00pm.

Captain's Table South Side; tel: 948 1418; fax: 948 1419; email: captable@candw.ky. Captain's Table is located in the southwest of the island, in front of Brac Caribbean Beach Village and near the resort hotels. The most cosmopolitan restaurant and bar on the Brac, it offers a wide-ranging menu including seafood, steaks and American-style dishes. The pleasant, airy restaurant has friendly service, or diners may opt for one of the tables by the pool. If you're short on transport, ring and they'll pick you up. Open Mon–Sat 11.30am–10.00pm; Sun midday–10.00pm. Happy hour Fri 7.00–9.00pm (but check times – they do change).

Divi Tiara (details above). Simple food, including a choice of main course, is served buffet-style. Menus are changed daily. Open for breakfast, lunch and dinner, 7.00am–10.00pm.

La Esperanza Stake Bay; tel: 948 0531. The dock at Bussy's, as this popular restaurant is widely known, has to be the best place on the island for a drink or meal as the sun goes down. Turn up on a Wednesday or at the weekend and you'll see Bussy or his wife slaving over a huge barbecue with mountains of jerk chicken prepared to their own recipe. Join the queue of locals for this unmissable treat, either to eat in or take away. At other times, try one of the fish dishes, including *akee* (salt fish) and dolphin, or mahi mahi. On Friday and Saturday nights, there is often live music; the rest of the week the juke box is as loud as the bar staff will allow! If transport is a problem, give them a ring – Bussy will usually collect you and take you home at the end of the evening. Restaurant open daily 9.00am–2.00pm, 6.00pm–10.00pm. Bar open Mon–Sat 9.00am–1.00pm; Sat 9.00am–midnight; Sun 11.00am–midnight.

The Palms See *Brac Reef*, above.

Sonia's White Bay Plaza; tel: 948 1214. Local food is served at lunchtime only, with dishes around CI$9 each. Open Mon–Sat 11.45am–2.30pm.

Tropical Delite West End; tel: 948 1272. This cool restaurant, formerly called G&M Diner, serves local dishes with daily specials. Turtle stew is a Sunday treat. Open Sun–Thu 6.30am–3.00pm; daily 6.30–10.00pm.

Fast food/snacks

Blackies Drive Thru Open 4.00–11.00pm daily for fast food and unmissable homemade ice-cream; do try the coconut or the rum toffee if they're available.

Golden Touch The jerk chicken stand just outside Edd's Place is owned by Barry Morgan and is open at weekends only.

Market Place Tibbetts' Sq The deli at this supermarket serves mostly takeaway meals for breakfast and lunch, plus pizzas from 3.00pm.

Martin's Pizzeria and Grill Tel: 917 5596. Based close to the airport, with a menu that features pizzas, burgers and other US-style fast food. Islandwide delivery service on Fri and Sat. Open Sun–Thu 9.00am–10.00pm; Fri to 1.00am; Sat to midnight.

Bars

Both the resort hotels have good bars, but those at La Esperanza and Aunt Sha's (the bar is called Coral Isle) are far more lively, and there's music at the Coral Isle on Wednesday, Friday and Saturday evenings. In addition, there is **Edd's Place** on Tibbetts' Square, a rather dingy but very noisy bar playing loud music. Outside, jerk chicken is available at weekends. Open Mon–Fri 9.00am–1.00am; Sat 9.00am–midnight, Sun midday–midnight.

SHOPPING AND AMENITIES
Dive/marine equipment

Both **Reef Divers** and **Divi Tiara** have shops selling dive equipment. See *Dive operators*, page 211, for details. For more general marine stores, including fishing equipment, and masks and snorkels, go to **Brac Marine** in West End, tel: 948 1518.

Food/general stores

Billy's Supermarket and Appliance Centre Cotton Tree Bay; tel: 948 1321. Just west of West End Primary School. Open Mon–Thu 8.00am–9.00pm, Fri/Sat 8.00am–10.00pm.

The Shoppe Next to Billy's. Open Mon–Sat 8.30am–midday, 1.00pm–8.30pm.

Kirkconnell's Market Stake Bay; tel: 948 2256. Just after Walton's Mango Manor on the left, a newly opened supermarket with plenty of variety and reasonable prices. Open Mon–Thu 8.00am–7.30pm; Fri 8.00am–8.00pm; Sat 8.00am–9.00pm.

L&M Bight Rd. Open Mon–Sat 9.00am–7.30pm.

Market Place Tibbetts' Sq; tel: 948 1296. Groceries, hardware, electrics and fishing tackle. Open Mon–Fri 8.00am–9.00pm; Sat 8.00am–10.00pm.

Tibbetts' Enterprises Cotton Tree Bay; tel: 948 1322. A general store on the bluff side of the road selling everything from hardware to snacks. Open Mon–Sat 7.30am–9.00pm.

Liquor stores

Brac Freeport Tibbetts' Sq; tel: 948 1332. Open Mon–Sat 9.00am–6.00pm.

Brac Distributors Foster's Corner, South Side; tel: 948 1537. Open Mon–Sat 8.00am–6.00pm.

Island Man Rumshop Spot Bay Rd (opposite Blackies); tel: 948 2548. Open Mon–Fri 9.00am–6.00pm; Sat to 6.30pm.

Photographic supplies and courses

Photographic supplies and processing are available at Fast Foto in Tibbetts' Enterprises (see above). Both dive operators on the Brac also have shops supplying photographic equipment and offering daily on-site film processing.

Photo Tiara Tel: 948 1553. Aside from camera rental, Divi Tiara's photo shop specialises in underwater photography courses. The basic course has two hours in the classroom followed by a dive with an instructor. For the truly hooked, there's the six-day Nikon School of Underwater Photography course, the only one in the Caribbean, for which an all-inclusive package is also available. For details, call US tel: 800 661 3483. Open daily 8.00am–5.00pm

Reef Photo & Video Centre Tel: 948 1340. Based at Brac Reef, the centre offers equipment sales and rentals, underwater videos and half-day camera rental including basic tuition for US$39. Open 7.30am–12.30pm; 1.30–5.00pm.

Souvenirs/gifts

It has to be said that Cayman Brac is not a mecca for shopping, but gifts and souvenirs are still to be found. Most of the general stores and even 4-D's car hire sell T-shirts and small nick-nacks, and there's also some beachwear at Market Place.

Kirk Freeport PO Box 893 GT, Stake Bay; tel: 948 2612; email: kirkfree@candw.ky. This small shop next to the museum has a surprisingly wide range of glass, silver, gold, black coral, china, jewellery etc, as well as T-shirts and casual clothing. A good place for gifts of all prices. Open Mon–Fri 10.00am–6.00pm, Sat 10.00am–1.00pm.

NIM Things Spot Bay; tel: 948 0461. Tenson Scott's local craft shop is an acronym for 'Native Island Made': everything here is handmade on the Brac, or painted by his daughter, Simone, whose gallery is next door. Don't go looking for sophistication – items on sale include shell crafts, straw bags and polished caymanite. And if you've time for a chat, Tenson can certainly fill the gap. Open Mon–Sat 9.00am–6.00pm.

Treasure Chest Tibbetts' Square; tel: 948 1333. Probably the best shop on the island for gifts and souvenirs, Treasure Chest is also within easy walking distance of the airport. So check in your bags, then wander back here for a last browse – it's much more convivial than sitting in an airport lounge. Open Mon–Sat 9.00am–5.00pm.

OTHER PRACTICALITIES
Communications
Post office and internet

The main post office is near Tibbetts' Square at West End, open Mon–Fri 8.30am–5.00pm. The computer here represents the only public internet access on the island, and costs CI$2.50 for quarter of an hour, CIS$3.50 for half an hour, or CI$6 for an hour (valid for up to a month). Sub post offices are located in the government administration building at Stake Bay (open Mon–Fri 8.30am–4.30pm), and at Watering Place, Creek and Spot Bay (open Mon–Fri 9.00–11.30am, 1.00–3.00pm; Fri to 3.30pm). First-day covers can be bought at West End and occasionally also at Stake Bay.

Telephones

There are public telephones in several places on the island, including Reef Divers, Salt Water Pond Walk, Stake Bay (government administration building), Spot Bay and the Aston Rutty Centre on the bluff, though they're by no means all in working order.

Health and medical facilities

Cayman Brac Clinic on Tibbetts' Square, tel: 948 1777, is open Mon–Sat 8.00am–midday; and Mon, Wed, Thu and Fri 3.00–6.00pm. The small government **Faith Hospital** is at Stake Bay, tel: 948 2243–5. For dental services, tel: 948 2618.

Water is produced by desalination from the island's reverse osmosis system, and is safe to drink from the tap.

Laundry

The new laundry and dry cleaner at Foster's Corner on South Shore Road is called Brac Suds, tel: 948 0689. If you leave your laundry at your place of accommodation before 9.00am, they will pick it up and return it to the front desk that evening.

Library

The modern public library (tel: 948 0472) is opposite the government administration building in Stake Bay. Open Mon, Wed–Fri 1.00–6.00pm, Tue 10.00am–3.00pm, Sat 10.00am–1.00pm.

Money and banking

The local branch of **Cayman National Bank** is opposite Tibbetts' Square in West End, and has an ATM. Open Mon–Thu 9.00am–2.30pm; Fri 9.00am–4.30pm. If the bank is closed, swipe your card outside the door to gain access to the ATM.

Brac Rent-a-Car (see page 201) are agents for Moneygrams. Open Mon–Fri 9.00am–4.30pm, Sat 9.00–11.30am. C.B. Motors offers Quik Cash. Open Mon–Thu 7.30am–8.30pm; Fri–Sat 7.30am–9.00pm; Sun 3.00–5.00pm

Tourist information

Cayman Brac Tourist Office (PO Box 194; tel: 948 1649/1849; fax: 948 1629) is tucked away on the north coast, to the west of the airport and next to the park. Open Mon–Fri 8.30am–5.00pm.

ACTIVITIES
Beaches and snorkelling

The only white sandy beaches on the island are on the southwest tip, where the two resort hotels and most of the villas are situated, and the public beach on the southern side of the island. The public beach is a lovely swimming beach with gentle rollers in front of the reef. Unfortunately, the place is spoiled by the wire enclosure that surrounds the picnic area. The showers don't work, the water smells and the toilets are filthy. Keep to the beach itself and you'll be fine.

Of course, you don't need expanses of white sand to go snorkelling. In many areas there are small stretches of sand and even if not, with a pair of old shoes to clamber across the rocks, you can set off pretty well anywhere. The reef on the Brac is far less extensive than on the other two islands. In the southwest, there is a long stretch running almost continuously through to the area beyond Salt Water Pond, with another stretch further east at Hawksbill Bay, making this side of the island the most attractive for snorkellers. To the south, there is also the wreck of the *Prince Frederick* (see page 212) which offers a different focus for an hour or so. To the north, the only place with a reef is just to the west of Spot Bay, but other good locations for snorkellers include Buccaneer's Barcadere, accessed along Robert Foster Lane near the airport, and Radar Reef, to the centre of the island near Stake Bay, where concrete steps lead down into the water. Note that strong currents at each end of the island make snorkelling at these points potentially hazardous, with the rocks to the east adding to the risks.

Diving

Diving off Cayman Brac is consistently rated among the best in the Caribbean, with calm conditions almost all year round, and most dive sites within five to 15 minutes' boat ride. All the dive operators on the island also visit Little Cayman, just five miles (8km) away, a boat trip of some 50 minutes.

Dive operators

There are just two dive operators on the island, both based in the southwest at the two resort hotels. Both offer diving off Little Cayman as well as Cayman Brac. Alternatively, you can contact Dee McKenzie for private tuition on tel: 948 1418; email: weedee@candw.ky.

Dive Tiara Tel: 948 1553. The dive school at Divi Tiara is in theory exclusively for their own guests, although in practice outsiders are occasionally accepted. A PADI five-star centre, it has five dive boats and offers all courses including nitrox.
Rates Two-tank dive US$66; Open Water US$425. BCD/regulator US$11 each.
Reef Divers PO Box 56, West End; tel: 948 1642 or 800 327 3835; fax: 948 1279; email: reefdive@candw.ky; web: www.bracreef.com
A highly efficient outfit, geared to guests at the affiliated Brac Reef Resort, Reef Divers also takes walk-in divers, space permitting. Be aware, though, that you will be fitting in to the requirements of their own guests. Dive shop, with films, T-shirts etc, is open 7.30am–12.30pm; 1.30–5.00pm.
Rates Two-tank dive US$75; Resort course US$125; Open Water US$450. BCD/regulator US$12 each.

Dive sites

There are plenty of sites to choose from among the Brac's 41 permanent dive moorings, which are for the most part concentrated in the western half of the island. Sites to the **north** are considered to be the most dramatic, with sudden drop offs as the wall plunges almost straight down from around 55–60ft (16.8–18.3m). It is the north, too, that has the best shore diving – in fact, there is no real shore diving to the southwest where the dive operations are based. Tunnels, crevices and narrow chasms characterise dives to the **south**, where you may come across any number of creatures as you turn a corner. Nurse sharks are often seen here under the overhanging rocks. At the other end of the spectrum, keep an eye out for the occasional exquisite air crab, or perhaps the extraordinary iron-shaped trunkfish. The swim-throughs at Tarpon Reef make it seem like fish city, with a central sandy clearing where you may spot a glittering silver tarpon just hanging in the water. Swim alongside or below it and you won't frighten it off. Less obvious, though, is the encrusted anchor that is suspended above a short tunnel at Anchor Wall.

Wrecks and other attractions

One of the most visited wrecks in the islands was in fact deliberately scuppered as a dive attraction. The 315ft (95m) Russian frigate, originally known simply as #356, was bought from Cuba by the Cayman Islands for US$275,000 and renamed the MV *Capt Keith Tibbetts* as a tribute to the local man who played a vital role in the development of the islands. The hull was cleaned out so that divers can swim through the cabins on the top three decks,

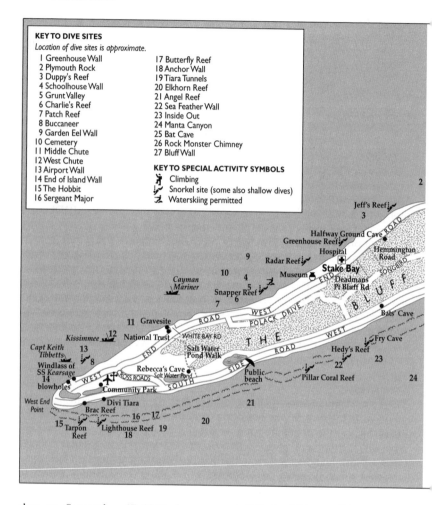

KEY TO DIVE SITES

Location of dive sites is approximate.

1 Greenhouse Wall
2 Plymouth Rock
3 Duppy's Reef
4 Schoolhouse Wall
5 Grunt Valley
6 Charlie's Reef
7 Patch Reef
8 Buccaneer
9 Garden Eel Wall
10 Cemetery
11 Middle Chute
12 West Chute
13 Airport Wall
14 End of Island Wall
15 The Hobbit
16 Sergeant Major

17 Butterfly Reef
18 Anchor Wall
19 Tiara Tunnels
20 Elkhorn Reef
21 Angel Reef
22 Sea Feather Wall
23 Inside Out
24 Manta Canyon
25 Bat Cave
26 Rock Monster Chimney
27 Bluff Wall

KEY TO SPECIAL ACTIVITY SYMBOLS

Climbing
Snorkel site (some also shallow dives)
Waterskiing permitted

then on September 17 1996 she was sunk 900yds (822m) offshore to the northwest of the island. Her bow rests in 80ft (24m) of water, with the stern at just 50ft (15m). As yet marine life is confined to angelfish, the occasional lobster and a lone moray. The wreck is usually dived from a boat, but can also be visited as a shore dive. Tanks may be hired from either of the dive operators (see page 211), but you'll obviously need transport to get them to the northern shore.

Just east of the frigate is the wreck of the 55ft (17m) *Cayman Mariner*, lying at a depth of 60ft (18m), while slightly inshore of that is the upturned hull of the 50ft (15m) steel tugboat, the *Kissimmee*.

On the southern side of the island, close to the bubble house, the iron-hulled *Prince Frederick* lies scattered 100ft (30m) offshore in about 50ft (15m) of water The Norwegian-registered ship went down in 1897, and is now a great place for snorkelling. A signboard at the side of the road marks the nearest point on the beach.

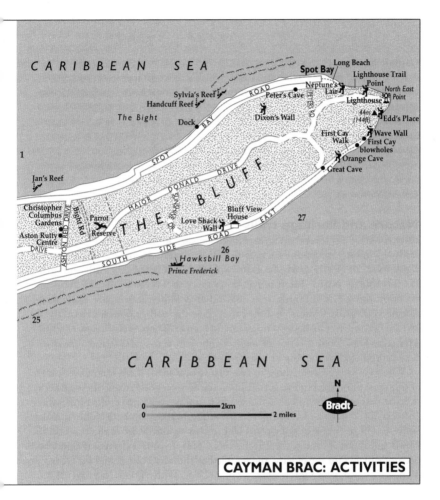

CAYMAN BRAC: ACTIVITIES

You'd have thought that there was sufficient natural life in these waters, but a recent addition to the underwater world is a bronze sculpture of dolphins. Created by marine sculptor Dale Evers, it was sunk on Radar Reef, near Stake Bay, in 2003.

Other watersports

Aside from diving and snorkelling, there are few organised watersports on the island. Those with access to a boat can waterski 100ft (30m) offshore west of the junction of Kirkconnell St, Bay Font and Foster's Road as far as Sarah's Rock. Swimming and diving here are permitted within 100ft (30m) of the shore.

The two resort hotels have kayaks available to guests. Brac Reef rents their kayaks out to non-residents at US$15 per person per hour.

Fishing

Fishing is extremely popular on the Brac, with bonefishing inside the reef, particularly along the coast to the southwest, and a variety of fish including snapper, grouper, tuna, marlin, wahoo and sailfish in the waters beyond. Fishing (and snorkelling) trips can be arranged through the following:

Captain Shelby's Tel: 948 0535; cell: 927 5413/917 7074
A courteous and helpful Caymanian, Captain Shelby runs boat trips for all purposes around the island and over to Little Cayman. Bring your own lunch (except for picnic trips, of course!).
Edmund Bodden GPO West End; tel: 948 1228
Specialists in bonefishing.
Gemini III Tel: 948 2517/2396; email: the_rock@candw.ky
Steve Bodden of B&S Motorventures (see page 201) organises deep-sea fishing charters aboard this 30ft (9.1m) cruiser. US$400 half day; US$600 full day.
Robin Walton Tel: 925 2382; email: robie@candw.ky

Nature and heritage trails

Cayman Brac has several designated heritage sites linked by walking and hiking trails, including attractions such as the Westerly Ponds, the bat caves and the lighthouse, all clearly marked on the ground and detailed in a leaflet produced by the tourist board. Interpretive signs give an overview of each trail and mention the species of birds, trees and other wildlife that you are likely to see during your walk. Visitors are asked to respect the trails, not to touch cacti, and to take nothing but mangoes – in season, of course! There is also a new Maritime Heritage Trail, with a series of eight signboards across the island linked to a leaflet produced by the tourist board.

Wherever you go, remember to take plenty of water – there is nowhere on the south coast or on the bluff to get a drink – and to wear good strong shoes or boots. A basic first-aid kit would be sensible too if you're going up on the bluff, where the terrain is rocky and very uneven. If you're heading up here alone, it makes sense to tell someone of your plans before you set off. Most of the trails on the bluff, and the caves too (except Rebecca's Cave), require a degree of agility and are not suitable for the elderly, the disabled or the very young. And for all except Rebecca's Cave, take a torch, even if you're going with a guide (see page 217).

If you have time for only one of the trails, consider the three-hour Lighthouse Trail, which starts from Spot Bay and combines Peter's Cave with some magnificent views to the north and east and some good hiking on the top of the bluff. See page 220.

Tennis

The tennis court at Divi Tiara (tel: 948 1553) may be used by non-residents for US$2 per person per day.

Climbing

Many thanks to John Byrnes. For further information, including details of equipment, technical descriptions of routes, and a copy of 'Bluff View Guide to Cayman Brac Climbing', email John Byrnes on jbyrnes@frii.com, or check out www.tradgirl.com/caymans.

Cayman Brac's newest sport is something of a well-kept secret. The 144ft (44m) bluff rising almost vertically from sea level is an open invitation to climbers, with a variety of walls with steep overhangs and sheer drops that will challenge even the most experienced, and with views to match. The best time of year to visit for climbing is from mid-November to early May. With seven different climbing areas around the island, facing south around to northwest, shady climbing can be had at any time of day or season.

Since 1995, a small group of climbers has been working to establish various routes on the eastern end of the bluff for the enjoyment of themselves and other visiting enthusiasts. Their house, Bluff View – otherwise known as the Climber House – is also used by climbers visiting the Brac. For details of renting the house, see page 205.

For the most part, routes on the bluff are suitable only for advanced climbers, with difficulty ratings ranging from 5.8 to 5.12c (UK 4c–7a). Many, particularly those around the lighthouse, involve a rappel (abseil) from the top of the bluff down to a stance just above the sea, before climbing back up the sheer rock face.

Safety

If something should go wrong when climbing on the bluff, remember that, unless there are other climbers around, no-one else on the island can rescue you. It is therefore important that climbers understand and take the responsibility for self-rescue. The emergency telephone number for fire department rescue is 911, but do be aware that this should be used only as an absolutely final resort since the local fire department has little capability for steep-rock rescue.

Bolts

The stainless-steel bolts originally used on the Brac corroded as a result of the constant exposure to salt water, and are no longer safe. In November 2000, a team of climbers began rebolting the various routes on the island with titanium glue-in Tortuga bolts (see www.ushba.com for details). The new bolts are easily recognisable as grey rings about 1½in (3.5cm) in diameter. They were developed specifically for marine environments and should provide safe climbing for many years to come. Climbers should not trust any of the old bolts they may encounter on the island, since they can fail without warning under body weight. By early 2004, 46 routes of every grade had been rebolted. For the latest information, see www.tradgirl.com/caymans.

Equipment

For the approach routes to climbs at the Point (around the lighthouse) and Edd's Place, strong shoes or hiking boots that cover your ankles and a pair of leather gloves to protect your hands are strongly recommended – the terrain is pretty rugged. A foam pad to sit on when changing shoes or having a bite to eat is an essential 'luxury'. Don't be put off by the sharp ironshore rock on the top of the bluff: once over the edge you'll find it much smoother.

There is nowhere on the island to rent climbing gear, so take everything you need with you, including ropes, quick draws, ascenders or prussiks, chalk, tape, etc. Climbers at the Point and Edd's Place will need two 165ft (50m) ropes, one for rappeling (abseiling) and one for leading.

Areas below are listed anti-clockwise around the island, starting at the westernmost area on the south side (see map pages 212–13).

Love Shack Wall is 2.7 miles (4.3km) east of Ashton Reid Road (also known as the Bluff road) on the south side of island, and a five-minute walk from the Bluff View house. The steep, overhanging wall, identifiable by its left angling crack, has powerful routes on pocketed rock.

Three routes: 5.11d to 5.12b/c (UK 6b–7a)

Orange Cave lies just past the Great Cave. Park at the end of South Road, then it's a pleasant ten-minute stroll further east. If you can tear your eyes from the ocean you'll spy the cave; a short scramble takes you to the base.

Five routes, 5.8 to 5.11b (UK 4c–6a), including Chum Buckets, which was the first climbing route to be established on the Brac.

Wave Wall is some 20 minutes' walk east of the Orange Cave. As you pass two huge boulders, keep an eye out for pieces of caymanite, but leave them where you find them – it's illegal to possess raw caymanite if you're not an islander. Go on through the rocks and traverse carefully along the seaside – big waves can make the approach dangerous or impossible if the surf is up. The route is shaded in the afternoon from about 2.00pm. Boots and gloves are recommended for the approach.

Ten routes, 5.8 to 5.12a (UK 4c–6c)

East Bluff or **Edd's Place**. Park at the lighthouse on top of the bluff and follow a faint path heading south. Continue southeast to the cliff edge, then to the right. The terrain ranges from tough ironshore rock to an easier concrete-like surface; in general walking is easier along the cliff edge. The total approach is only 0.7 miles (1.1km) but can take anything from 25 to 40 minutes. Routes require rappel (abseil) access.

Two routes, 5.10a and 5.11a (UK 5b–6b)

Northeast Point Usually just called **The Point**, this offers a unique experience even for very experienced climbers. The rock drops straight down for over 100ft (30m) directly into the water. From the top of the cliff and belay ledges, turtles, Atlantic bottlenose dolphins and large fish can be seen in the crystal blue water. As for the East Bluff, park at the lighthouse, then follow the trail left approximately 100yds (275m) to the main wall. All routes require rappel access.

Fifteen routes, 5.9–5.12 (UK 5a–6c)

Neptune's Lair Park in the Spot Bay turnaround at the east end of the island's northern road. Follow the trail east, then walk along the beach towards the huge Foreskin Rock in the sea. It's best to stay along the shore when entering the boulder area. Continue to the steep white limestone face, about 20–25 minutes from the car. Bring your snorkelling gear for a lunchtime break – there are some unusual corals in the sea here, and lots of other marine life too. Though the recently established routes may seem short compared to others on the island, the setting of Neptune's Lair is something of a 'must visit'.

Three routes, 5.11a to 5.12a approximately (UK 6a–6c)

Dixon's Wall is located 2.1 miles (3.4km) east of La Esperanza on the north of the island, with access across private land. The wall is steeper than it looks and is of the finest quality. North facing, it's shady most of the year.

Four rebolted routes, 5.11b–5.11d (UK 6b–6c)

New routes

Climbers putting up new routes must use the Tortuga bolts. If you are considering a new route, please let John Byrnes know in advance. Some specialised tools such as a glue gun may be available at Bluff View, and he has detailed written instructions and pointers on installation. Be forewarned that glue-in anchors are in general more tricky, time consuming and expensive to place properly than mechanical bolts.

TOURING THE ISLAND

There is no obvious tour of the island, since the road doesn't run right round. As many visitors stay in the area to the southwest, however, it makes sense to start from here and to treat it as two separate trips taking anything from an hour or two each to a full day, depending on your interests and the time you plan to spend walking. Obviously the two suggested itineraries could be combined. The bluff can be accessed from either the north or the south, so has been treated separately (see page 222).

Island tours are available from Maple Edwards, tel: 948 0395, mobile: 916 3714 (Miss Singer): a two-hour tour costs US$15 per person. Larger groups can be handled by B&S Tours (tel: 948 1646), who have a 29-seater, air-conditioned coach. Alternatively, round-the-island tours may be organised through one of the taxi companies (see page 200).

For guided **nature tours**, contact the District Administration Office, tel: 948 2222, ext 4420; web: www.naturecayman.com. T J Sevik (known to everyone simply as TJ) is the government's tour guide and leads nature tours around the island, for which there is no charge (although transportation is not included). His knowledge of the island is born of years of exploring both the bluff and the surrounding sea as a boy. He is passionate about his island, and his ability to spot the Brac's birds is excellent.

North side

Starting from the resorts to the southwest, head east along South Side Road, then turn left on to the Cross Road, with the end of the runway to your left. At the T-junction by Tibbetts' Square, turn left again and follow West End Road all the way to the end. Here, the road appears at first to peter out, but if you continue on through what looks like a car park you can turn right into James Scott Road, then cross Georgiana Drive to the sea. On the beach to the right lies the windlass (ship's winch) from the **SS Kearsage** of 1860. When the sea is up you can see blowholes here as well. You can continue along the beach and return to the main road via Robert Foster Lane, possibly stopping for a swim at Buccaneer Barcadere. The snorkelling is recommended here, too, but watch out for the sharp drop off.

Return the way you came, and on the right you will see the **tourist office**, a pretty cottage-like building in the Cayman style, painted in pink and blue pastels (tel: 948 1649; open Mon–Fri 8.30am–5.00pm). Behind the tourist office is **Cayman Brac Community Park**, where a short nature trail leads the visitor through a succession of labelled trees that are native to the island. The park is in good order, and the public toilets are clean, yet at most times the playground with its climbing frames and wendy houses, and the woodland area with barbecue grills, is almost eerily quiet.

Continuing east, pass the airport and Tibbetts' Square. Shortly after this on your left is Pioneer Lane, a good place to stop for a short **walk**, or perhaps some time on the beach watching the birds. Follow the lane to the sea where there is a sandy beach to the west – a rare commodity on this northern side of the island, where the beach is for the most part ironshore. If you turn right along the hurricane boulder path, you can return on a track to the main road. A little further along the main road, again to the left, is White Bay Road, the site of a **mass gravesite** from the 1932 hurricane. Nineteen people died here when the house that stood on this spot was destroyed in the storm. The site is set back from the road on the left near the sea, and is now marked by a simple panel, while just up the road is the National Trust building, open on Wednesday and Friday afternoons, or by appointment. For further information, contact Wallace Platts on 948 2390 or Claudette Upton on 948 0319.

Opposite White Bay Road is the start of the **Salt Water Pond Walk**, which leads south across the island, coming out beside Rebecca's Cave (see page 221). Although the trail is only at the beginning of the bluff, don't be fooled into thinking that the terrain will be easy – it's pretty tough going, even here, so allow at least an hour and possibly more to get to the cave. With luck you'll be rewarded with the sight of several native birds, such as the vitelline warbler or the Caribbean elaenia, as well as a wide variety of tropical plants along the trail.

As you head further east along West End Road, the road veers inland until the bluff towers over it to the right. A little way after this, you enter Stake Bay, where a short loop with the rather grandiose title of **Stake Bay Walk** will take you along Ryan's Drive to Stake Bay Road on the coast. On the corner here is the J A Ryan cemetery, burial site of the descendants of W S Ryan, one of the Brac's most illustrious citizens, who died in 1910 having reputedly been the first Bracker to marry, the first to go to sea as a master mariner, and the first to become a justice of the peace. Here, too, is the site of the original harbour where the schooners came in. Pass the older houses overlooking the sea and return along Kirkconnell Street, which brings you out near the museum on the main road.

Cayman Brac Museum was opened in 1983, housed in the old government building in Stake Bay. Of typical Cayman construction, it is an attractive wooden house with a shaded veranda. The new government administration building, a faceless modern block housing the post office, immigration office and much else besides, lies behind the museum.

The museum collection, somewhat dusty but nevertheless of genuine interest, effectively tells the story of Cayman Brac before the '32 hurricane, when life on the Brac was changed forever. The scale model of a schooner with its cargo of catboats on board, ready to go out to the fishing grounds, is a graphic reminder of the importance of the sea for the Brac. Personal and work-based artefacts and documents include some post 1932. Books are on sale. Open Mon–Fri 9.00–midday, 1.00–4.00pm; Sat 9.00–midday.

Just past the hospital on your right is the first of two trails that lie quite close together. **Deadman's Point Bluff Road** involves a climb up the steps on to the bluff, leading to a hike through endemic forest to Songbird Drive, which is effectively the backbone of the bluff. The path alternates between jagged karstic cliff rock, with its sinkholes and caves, and flat areas where grass overlies the rock. It passes through forest where several birds breed, including the loggerhead kingbird, the red-legged thrush, the white-crowned pigeon and the Zenaida dove. From August to May, you may also see migrant vireos, warblers and tanagers. Allow around an hour-and-a-half for the return hike, or turn left along Songbird Drive and return to West End Road via the parallel **Hemmington Road**.

A little further east on the main road is one of the few signposted caves on this northern stretch of the island. **Half Way Ground Cave**, so called because it's halfway up the bluff, is home to a small colony of bats, but little else. About a mile further on, past the high school and Ashton Reid Drive, is the **Bight Road**, a trail of about a mile that was traditionally used to get from the settlements in the north of the island to the provision grounds on the bluff and thence to the south shore. Today, the trail follows the western boundary of the 197-acre **parrot reserve** through ancient forest across to the southern edge of the bluff. Note that no dogs are allowed into the reserve, no fires are permitted, and visitors should refrain from contact with any animals.

The best time to see parrots is during the summer in early morning, from 6.00am to 8.00am, although you are more likely to hear than see them. Even if you're unlucky – and the Cayman Brac parrot is a shy creature, not easily spotted – you'll have the opportunity to spot many other endemic birds and plants in an environment that could be miles from civilisation, rather than just a few hundred yards. Allow about three hours for the full return trip, or stop at the mid point on Major Donald Drive and come back from there. There is also a one-mile (1.6km) circular National Trust **nature trail** off the southern end of Bight Road, leading into the parrot reserve, where 15 species of orchid have been identified on the route. In addition to the Cayman Brac parrot, you may also see the red-legged thrush or the vitelline warbler, while in the winter there are numerous migratory birds.

Back on Stake Bay Road, continue east past La Esperanza (do stop for a drink or a meal on their pontoon) into Spot Bay Road. On the right is **Heritage House** (tel: 948 0563), which is currently used for various functions, but where it is hoped to have a full-time information officer in the future. The house was bought by the government in 1998 from the Lazzari family, who arrived from Cuba in 1870 and later settled in Northeast Bay. John Antonio Lazzari opened a tannery in the grounds, using freshwater from the six wells to cure the skins. The family also kept livestock on the bluff as well as tending their plantations. A series of ladder steps built up the face of the bluff to allow them access to their animals are still in use. Today, visitors to the elegant house will also see panels about the local fauna set here and there among the original thatched outbuildings and wells, and tropical fruit trees – naseberry, soursop, tamarind, mango and custard apple – grow alongside other native species including coconut, sea grape and red birch. For information, contact Chevala Burke on tel: 948 2222, ext 4420.

Just before you come into Spot Bay, a path from the main road brings you to a set of historic steps up the north face of the bluff, leading up to the panoramic viewpoint known as Big Channel Road Outlook.

Spot Bay, in the northeast corner of the Brac, is a good starting point for some excellent walks. The picnic tables and natural shade at **Spot Bay Community Cove** would seem to make it a good spot for swimming (though there's a sharp drop off), but large notices indicate the contrary. There is a ramp here for small boats. Shortly beyond the cove, the road ends. From here, follow the path through sea-grape trees to the shore and **Long Beach**. The walk beneath the bluff can be pretty dramatic; rough seas mean that only climbers should proceed further east beyond the end of the beach. Allow up to an hour-and-a-half for the return walk back to the road.

Back in Spot Bay, follow Lighthouse Road on the bluff side to the Lighthouse Steps, which are the beginning of the **Lighthouse Trail** (allow up to three hours for the return walk from the bottom of the steps; strong shoes and water essential). Follow the steps up the northeast face of the bluff, and halfway up is the entrance to **Peter's Cave**, which has long been used as a hurricane shelter by the residents of Spot Bay. The cave is huge, with tunnels leading off in several directions, and it can get quite cold away from the entrance.

Continuing on up, you come out at the top to **Peter's Outlook**, with sweeping views across Spot Bay. There is a small car park nearby, at the end of Peters Road, so drivers up on the bluff can leave their vehicles and approach the caves from above. The trail takes you across uneven terrain through coarse shrubland. Halfway along the path, above the small outcrop of rock far below known as Little Cayman Brac, brown boobies breed in caves and ledges in the bluff. Eventually the path opens out into a stark area where the intermittent vegetation, dominated by the occasional solitary century plant, is regularly battered by the prevailing easterly winds. Seabirds wheel in the currents overhead, while underfoot the going remains tough. Here, at the easternmost tip of the island, stands the lighthouse, warning sailors heading west in the Caribbean of the imminent danger as they head for the bluff. In fact, there were until recently two lighthouses, the first dating from 1930s, but these old beacons have just been replaced.

South side

The westernmost point of the island affords views across the strait to Little Cayman some five miles (8km) away. Here, you are on the edge of the **Westerly Ponds** which, despite their location close to the airport at the western tip of the island, remain peaceful and unspoilt, a haven for wildlife. Formerly a mangrove swamp that became cut off from the sea, the ponds that you see today are still affected by the tides via an underground connection with the sea. The result is that the water is at best brackish, becoming hypersaline by the end of the dry winter season.

Boardwalks and viewing areas enable observation of over 100 species of birds on the wetlands, the majority on migration routes to Central and South America. West Indian whistling-ducks and the black-necked stilt are both in residence, as are several herons and egrets, their numbers augmented in winter by migratory species of heron. Of the other migrants, a small colony of least terns breeds on the edge of the lagoon in the summer, while up to 30 shorebirds have been spotted during the winter migration. Perhaps surprisingly, osprey, merlin and peregrine falcons nest in the surrounding red mangroves.

Following the road east from the ponds, pass the two resort hotels and the Cross Road, and you'll come to **Salt Water Pond** on your left. This small bird sanctuary attracts several species, and here, too, least terns breed in the summer months. There is talk of putting a boardwalk through this area for visitors.

Aunt Sha's, the florid pink building on the beach, is a pretty good place to stop for a snack at lunch time – the bar area overlooks the sea, and is much pleasanter than the restaurant in the daytime. It is also the last place on this stretch where you can get anything to drink, so stock up if you're planning a day out.

Not far from Aunt Sha's on the left is **Rebecca's Cave**, named in memory of 17-month old Rebecca Bodden who died nearby as her parents sought the shelter of the cave with her during an apparent lull in the 1932 hurricane. Tragically, the family was caught by the full force of the storm, and the little girl perished. Her tomb is in the cave, a sombre reminder of the island's past. A wild fig grows at the entrance to the cave, and to the side is the southern end of the Salt Water Pond Walk across the bluff (see page 218).

Near the public beach (see page 210), on the other side of the road, the **Marshes Wetlands** spread out at the foot of the bluff. Up to 35 species of birds have been spotted here, in and around the mangroves, while high above, several pairs of brown boobies have their nests, part of a small colony that inhabits this southern stretch of the bluff.

From the name, you could be forgiven for thinking that **Bats' Cave**, a couple of miles further on, is the only one inhabited by bats. It isn't, but it certainly has a lot of them. Five species of bat live here, including the most populous, the Jamaican fruit bat. Shine your torch up to the roof of the cave and you'll uncover whole colonies huddled together in each of the high narrow recesses; come in the evening at around 9.00pm and you'll see the bats in flight.

The extraordinary spaceship-style building on the right as you continue east is known as the Bubble House, said to be designed to withstand hurricane-force winds. Be that as it may, its construction bankrupted the original owner, and the half-completed building was for years empty and desolate. Today, it's finally complete and in private ownership. Ashton Reid Drive, the only paved road across the bluff, leads off to the left, then shortly after is the southern end of Bight Road and the parrot reserve (see page 219). From here, the distance between the sea and the bluff narrows. Sea-grape trees line the road, and just a few small houses are dotted along the coast; otherwise, there is little to detract from the natural beauty of this southern shoreline.

The road ends abruptly at the **Great Cave**, a mile or so from the lighthouse that marks the eastern end of the island at the top of the bluff. The name is somewhat misleading, as there are in fact several caves up in the bluff, linked one to another by narrow and winding passages that are almost impassable in places. To climb up to the caves, you'll need to be reasonably agile as the steps are not completely even, and to have good shoes and a torch. It doesn't take much to imagine the terror of being holed up here in a storm, in total darkness, with bats darting about overhead, no water and very little air.

Continuing on foot from the Great Cave, **First Cay Walk** leads east along the beach. The going is initially over rough shingle, which gradually gives way to ironshore where the sea rushes through blowholes and outcrops of caymanite decorate the otherwise uniform grey. Brown boobies and frigatebirds vie for the evening meal in the skies overhead, while from January to August migrant white-tailed tropicbirds may be seen. Beyond First Cay (the first large independent boulder on the beach) the seas can be pretty rough, and the area is not suitable for any but skilled climbers. Allow 1–2 hours for the return walk from the Great Cave, or bring a picnic and stay longer.

The Bluff

Although there are several access points up on to the bluff, there is only one paved road, Ashton Reid Drive, which crosses the island more or less in the centre. Once at the top, the main roads are now paved, but others are just gravel. If you're planning to take scooters or bikes up there, do ask for advice first. In some cases, hire companies ask customers not to use them on the bluff. It's a great place for a picnic, particularly near the lighthouse (see page 220), but wherever you go, remember to take plenty to drink. The nearest telephone in case of emergency is at the Aston Rutty Centre on Ashton Reid Drive.

By car, you can take Ashton Reid Drive straight up to Songbird Drive from either side of the island. If you're driving along here, take a few moments to pause at the new **Christopher Columbus Gardens** on the western side of the road. One of the projects of the year-long quincentennial celebrations in 2003, the gardens commemorate the explorer's discovery of the islands, and feature a relief of Columbus himself. A Wall of Distinction honours 500 people, past and present, who have made an outstanding contribution to the development of the island, while around the area boardwalks and paths allow access to the woodland area with its extraordinary limestone formations and attendant flora and fauna.

A second route from West End runs parallel to the edge of the bluff until Stake Bay, then winds on and up until it eventually meets Songbird Drive off to the left (if you miss this junction, you'll find yourself on the southern side of the bluff heading for Ashton Reid Drive). Whichever route you take, continue along Major Donald Drive towards the lighthouse, past Bight Drive hiking trail and the parrot reserve (see page 219). In fact, a good place to see (or hear) the Cayman Brac parrot early in the morning is the southeast corner of the intersection of Ashton Reid Drive and Major Donald Road. Much of this area is forested, interspersed with small areas of open pasture where cattle graze. The road is for the most part fenced off with colourful posts of red birch, which in time will regenerate to create a living hedge. In the forests, all sorts of fruit grow wild, including the vine pear, with its sweet yellow fruit, and the red, equally sweet, prickly pear.

Towards the end of Major Donald Drive, take a brief detour to the right down Green Hill Lane. At the end of the road, the view over the southern side of the bluff is spectacular, though definitely not for those without a head for heights – it's a sheer drop to the sea far below. Backtrack, then continue east a little while – the turning to the left is Peter's Road, which brings you to a small parking area and the steps above Peter's Cave (see page 220). Straight on, Major Donald Drive brings you out on to the eastern point of the bluff, which is also the end of the Lighthouse Trail (see page 220). Even if time is not on your side, savour just for a few moments this wild and windswept spot, watched over year round by the lighthouse beacon that stands like a sentinel at its eastern tip.

Appendix

ACCOMMODATION

The following is an at-a-glance summary of the various places to stay detailed in this guide, put together as an aid to planning your holiday. The type of accommodation indicated here is of necessity simplistic; for details of each venue, see the page number given.

Grand Cayman

Name	Location	Type	No rooms/ units	Page
Adam's Guest House	George Town	guesthouse	6	122
Anchorage Condominiums	Seven Mile Beach	condominiums	15	122
Annie's Place	George Town	guesthouse	2	122
Avalon Condominiums	Seven Mile Beach	condominiums	14	122
Beach Club Hotel & Dive Resort	Seven Mile Beach	resort hotel	41	120
Cayman Diving Lodge	East End	dive lodge	10	172
Cobalt Coast	West Bay	medium hotel	24	151
Comfort Suites	Seven Mile Beach	medium hotel	108	119
Compass Point	East End	dive resort	18	172
Courtyard Marriott	West Bay Rd	medium hotel	233	119
Driftwood Village	North Side	cottages	4	167
Eldemire's Guest House	George Town	guesthouse	13	122
Grand Caymanian	Safehaven	timeshare/ condominiums	132	123
Grand Morritt's	East End	timeshare	40	172
Harbour View	Seven Mile Beach	apartments	9	123
Hyatt Regency	West Bay Rd/SMB	luxury hotel	289	118
Indies Suites	West Bay Rd	medium hotel/ timeshare	40	119
Jeff's Guest Homes	West Bay	houses	2	152
Marriott Beach Resort	Seven Mile Beach	luxury	309	118
Morritt's Tortuga	East End	timeshare	177	172
Nautilus Apartments	West Bay	townhouses etc	4	152
Plantation Village	Seven Mile Beach	timeshare/ apartments	71	123
The Reef	East End	resort hotel/ condominiums	88	173

Name	Location	Type	No rooms/ units	Page
Retreat at Rum Point	Rum Point	condominiums	23	169
Ritz Carlton	Seven Mile Beach	luxury hotel	366	118
Sammy's Airport Inn	Airport	medium hotel	60	120
Seaview Hotel and Dive Centre	George Town	dive lodge	15	121
Seven Mile Beach Resort	Seven Mile Beach	condominiums	38	123
Spanish Bay Reef Resort	West Bay	resort hotel	66	153
Sunset House	George Town	dive lodge	59	121
Sunshine Suites	West Bay Rd	medium hotel	132	120
Treasure Island Resort	Seven Mile Beach	medium hotel	281	120
Turtle Nest Inn	Bodden Town	apartments	9	163
Villas of the Galleon	Seven Mile Beach	condominiums	59	123
Westin Casuarina	Seven Mile Beach	luxury hotel	343	118

Little Cayman

Name	Location	Type	No rooms/ units	Page
The Club		villas	8	184
Conch Club Condominiums		condominiums	20	183
Kingston Bight Lodge		apartments/rooms	12	184
Little Cayman Beach Resort		hotel	40	180
Paradise Villas		villas	12	184
Pirates Point		resort hotel	10	182
Sam McCoy's Dive Lodge		dive lodge	8	182
Southern Cross		resort hotel	11	183
Village Inn		apartments	11	184

Cayman Brac

Name	Location	Type	No rooms/ units	Page
Almond Beach Hideaways	Spot Bay	houses	3	204
Beacon Harbor	Stake Bay	condominiums	2	204
Bluff View House	South Side	self-catering apartments	2	205
Brac Caribbean Beach Village	Stake Bay	apartments	16	205
Brac Reef Beach Resort	South Side	resort hotel	40	203
Carib Sands	South Side	condominiums	37	205
Cayman Breakers	South Side	condominiums	9	205
Cayman Cottage	South Side	house	1	205
Divi Tiara	South Side	resort hotel	71	203
La Esperanza	Stake Bay	apartments/houses	6	205
Sea Dreams	Stake Bay	house	1	206
Stake Bay Villas	Stake Bay	villas	2	206
Turtle Nest	Stake Bay	house	1	206
Walton's Mango Manor	Stake Bay	guesthouse	5	203

Appendix 2

FURTHER READING
History

Bingner, Alice Grant *A Brief History of the Cayman Islands*, 1982

Craton, Michael *Founded upon the Seas, A History of the Cayman Islands and their People* Ian Randle Publishers, Jamaica, 2003

Hirst, George S S *A Handbook of the Cayman Islands* Kingston, Jamaica, 1907

Hirst, George S S *Notes on the History of the Cayman Islands*, 1910. The most detailed of Hirst's books includes a fascinating account of life on the islands at the turn of the century.

Kohlman, Aarona *Under Tin Roofs* Cayman Islands National Museum, 1993

Mitchell, David *Pirates* Thames & Hudson, 1976

Our Islands' Past Introductions by Philip Pedley. Cayman Islands National Archive and Cayman Free Press. A series of three books, bringing into the public domain some of the material currently held by the National Archive in George Town:
Volume I: *Edward Corbet's Report and Census of 1802 on the Cayman Islands*, 1992
Volume II: *The Wreck of the Ten Sails* Guest ed Dr Margaret E Leshikar-Denton, 1994
Volume III: *Traditional Songs from the Cayman Islands*, 1996

McLaughlin, Heather R *Cayman Yesterdays* Cayman Islands National Archive, 1991. A compilation of transcripts.

McLaughlin, Heather R *The '32 Storm* Cayman Islands National Archive, 1994

Ross, H E *Love's Dance – The Catboat of the Caymanes*, 1999. An illustrated account of Cayman's seafaring tradition, with plenty of reminiscences from former catboat sailors themselves.

Williams, Neville *A History of the Cayman Islands* Government of the Cayman Islands, 1970. Published to coincide with the tercentenary of the 1670 Treaty of Madrid, this is a readable account of Cayman history.

Whittington, Tricia *Back Then*, 2000. Reminiscences of North Side.

Biography

Dixon, H C *Cayman Brac, Land of My Birth*. A brief but affectionate account of the Brac written in the 1950s by a man who left the island to become a preacher.

Jackson, Will *Smoke-Pot Days* Cayman National Cultural Foundation, 1997. This biographical account of Cayman since the 1920s gives a pretty good insight into life both on land and at sea in the years when the islands were almost completely cut off from the outside world. It also tells of the effects, good and bad, of rapid developments wrought by tourism and development since the 1960s. *Up from the Deep* is by the same author.

Morse, Gay *So you want to live on an Island*, 2004. A light-hearted look at the trials and tribulations of life as a dive instructor on Little Cayman – and much more.

Tibbetts, Elsa M *The sea of bitter beauty*, 1984. An autobiographical tale of life on Cayman Brac.

Culture

Barnett, Dr Curtis L E *Toes in the Sand: Caymanian Tales and Thoughts*, published by the author, 1995. A rather worthy but nevertheless interesting collection of stories and essays investigating traditional Cayman values and culture and their effects on the population today. More recent is his *Mid-Millennial Isles*, 2004.

Fuller, Robert S *Duppies Is* Cayman Artventures, 1981. Real ghost stories of the occasionally spine-chilling variety, based on first-hand accounts of this peculiarly Cayman phenomenon, and with an impassioned introductory diatribe against the modern world and its effect on Cayman's duppies.

Muttoo, Henry with 'Jerry Craig', Karl *My Markings: The Art of Gladwyn K Bush* Cayman National Cultural Foundation, 1994

Nowak, H G (the Barefoot Man) *The People Time Forgot* Cayman Islands National Museum, 1987. Photographic record of Cayman people.

Poupeye, Veerle *Caribbean Art* Thames & Hudson, London, 1998. Although Cayman art is only touched on, almost in passing, Poupeye's book offers an interesting overview of art in the Caribbean as a whole.

Our Islands' Treasure volume 1, Pirates Week Commitee, 1980

Natural history

Bradley, Patricia *The Birds of the Cayman Islands* British Ornithologists' Union, 2000. The definitive record of all the birds on the Cayman Islands.

Bradley, Patricia, and Rey-Millet, Y-J *Birds of the Cayman Islands* Caerulean Press, 1995. An excellent field guide to Cayman birds, with useful information on habitats as well as detailed descriptions of endemic birds, and good colour photographs.

Brunt, M A, and Davies, J E (editors) *The Cayman Islands: Natural History and Biogeography* Kluwer Academic Publishers, 1994. A series of academic essays on a range of natural history subjects, including climate and tides, by individual writers who are each experts in their field.

Burton, F J, and Clifford, P *Wild Trees in the Cayman Islands* National Trust for the Cayman Islands

Greenberg, Idaz and Jerry *Corals & Fishes: Florida, Bahamas & Caribbean* Seahawk Press, 1999. A handy four-colour pocket guide to 260 species of fish, coral and other marine wildlife that inhabits the waters around Cayman.

Ground, Richard *Creator's Glory: Wildlife of the Cayman Islands* National Trust for the Cayman Islands, 1989

Humann, Paul *Reef Fish Identification* New World Publications, Florida, 2002. Probably the best (but at around US$40 also the most expensive) of the fish identification books available. In the same series are guides to coral and creature identification and fish behaviour.

O'Keefe *Sea Turtles: The Watchers' Guide* Larsen's, Florida, 1995

Proctor, George R *Flora of the Cayman Islands* HMSO, London, 1984

Sauer, Jonathan D *Cayman Islands Seashore Vegetation: A Study in Comparative Biogeography*, University of California Press, Los Angeles, 1982

Queen Elizabeth II Botanic Park, One with Nature Donning, USA, 2002

Diving guides
Frink, Stephen and Harrigan, William J *The Cayman Islands Diving Guide* Swan Hill Press, 1999
Humann, Paul *Cayman Underwater Paradise* Florida, 1979
Humann, Paul *Cayman Seascapes* Florida, 1986
Pierce, Jean *Diving and Snorkelling: Cayman Islands* Lonely Planet Pisces, 1999
Wood, Lawson *Dive Sites of the Cayman Islands* New Holland, London, 2001
Wood, Lawson *Shipwrecks of the Cayman Islands* Aquapress, Southend-on-Sea, 2004

General guides and photographic books
Boultbee, Paul G *Cayman Islands* Clio Press (World Bibliographic Series, vol 187), 1996
Humann, Paul *Beautiful Isles Cayman*, 1986
Driver, Jenny and Dilbert, Leonard (introduction) *Cayman Islands* Caribbean Publishing, 2002
Oliver, Ed and associates *The Postcards of the Cayman Islands* EDO Ltd, 1993. The combination of old and new postcards and attractive line drawings makes this an appealing souvenir.

Business
Doing Business in the Cayman Islands Price Waterhouse, World Firm, 1993

Fiction
Matthiessen, Peter *Far Tortuga* Vintage Books, 1988. Peter Matthiessen's achievement in bringing to life the seafaring tradition of these islands is not be underestimated. The *New York Review of Books* compared it to 'the best of Conrad or Stevenson'.
Meekings, Brian *The Storyman* Storyman Publishing, 1997. A collection of short stories based in Cayman and introducing several aspects of the islands' culture and natural history. Ideal for children of around primary school age.

WEBSITES
www.caymanislands.ky The Department of Tourism's main website.
www.divecayman.ky Dedicated to diving and divers, this is also run by the Department of Tourism.
www.caymanislands.co.uk Department of Tourism website angled towards the visitor from the UK.
www.gov.ky Cayman Islands' government website, particularly useful for up-to-date information on visas etc and a full listing of government departments. Also has some useful links, including news stories.
www.naturecayman.com Focused on the natural history of Cayman Brac, but also includes general information and a section on Little Cayman.
www.caymannetnews.com Daily news and stories from Cayman, though articles published within 72 hours are available on a subscription-only basis.

Index

Page numbers in bold indicate major entries; those in italic
indicate maps

accommodation 52–5,
  223–4
  Bodden Town 163
  Cayman Brac 201–6
  East End 172–3
  George Town and
    Seven Mile Beach
    115–24, *116–17*
  Little Cayman 180–4
  North Side 167
  Rum Point 169
  West Bay 151–4
activities 60–1
  Grand Cayman
    85–114, *110–11*
  Little Cayman 187–91,
    189
agriculture 11, 15
aircraft, private 45
airports 42
  Cayman Brac 200
  Grand Cayman 71
  Little Cayman 179
animals 17–21
architecture 33
arrival, Grand Cayman 71
art 32–3

banana boats 109
banks 50
  Cayman Brac 210
  Grand Cayman 82
  Little Cayman 186
Barkers 157
Barkers National Park
  25–6, 157
bars
  Cayman Brac 208
  Seven Mile Beach
    133–4
  West Bay 155
bats 17
Bats' Cave 221
beach erosion 26–7
beaches
  Cayman Brac 210
  Grand Cayman 140–2,
    160, 161, 174
  Little Cayman 193,
    194
Beth Shalom 204
bicycles
  Cayman Brac 201

bicycles *continued*
  Grand Cayman 76–7
  Little Cayman 179–80
birds 17–19
  Cayman Brac 199
  Little Cayman 199
birdwatching
  Cayman Brac 219,
    220, 221
  Grand Cayman 114
  Little Cayman 192–3
Blackbeard 4
Bloody Bay Wall 190
Blossom Village 192
blowholes, Grand
  Cayman 174
Blue Dragon project 20
blue iguana 19, 20, 166
bluff, Cayman Brac 197,
  218–19, 222
  hiking 215–16
boat charters, Grand
  Cayman 104–7
boat dives, Grand
  Cayman 97–102
boat operators
  Cayman Brac 214
  Grand Cayman 104–7
  Little Cayman 188–90
boat trips 104–7, 148–9
Bodden Town 163–4
Boggy Sand Road 155
booby, brown 19, 199
booby, red-footed 18,
  192–3
Booby Pond 192–3
books 225–27
bowling 140
Breakers 164
budgeting 50–1
buses 78
business 65–6
butterflies 20
Butterfly Farm 147

cameras 48
Capt Keith Tibbetts, MV
  208–9
car hire 51
  Cayman Brac 200–1
  Grand Cayman 75–6
  Little Cayman 180
catboat 6

caves, Cayman Brac 199,
  219, 220, 221
  Bats' 221
  Great 221
  Half Way Ground
    219
  Peter's 220
  Rebecca's 21
Cayfest 58
Cayman Brac 81–2, *196*,
  196–222, *202*
  accommodation
    201–6
  activities 210–17,
    212–13
  bank 210
  beaches 210
  caves 199
  climbing *212–13*,
    214–17
  communications 209
  day trips 81–2
  diving 211–13, *212–13*
  fishing 213–14
  flights 200
  history 198
  island tour 217–22
  medical facilities 209
  natural history 199
  nature trails 214, 217,
    219
  restaurants and bars
    206–8
  shopping 208–9
  tourist office 217
  transport 200–1
Cayman Brac
  Community Park 217
Cayman Brac Museum
  218
Cayman Carnival 59
Cayman Islands Bird
  Club 114
Cayman Islands National
  Museum 146–7
Cayman Islands Sailing
  Club 108
Cayman Islands Yacht
  Club 74
Cayman Kai 170
caymanite 13
Cemetery Beach 141
cemetery, Watler 160

Central Caribbean
  Marine Institute
  29–30, 194
Central Mangrove
  Wetland Area 26
charities **29–30**, 67
charts 45
Christopher Columbus
  Gardens 222
churches
  Grand Cayman 84
  Little Cayman 186, 192
Cimboco, MV 6–7
cinema 140
climate 13–14
climbing *212–13*, 214–17
clocktower, George Town
  146
clothes 48–9, 67
cocktails 56
Columbus, Christopher 3
conch shell house 147
conservation 25–30
conservation, marine
  27–9, 85–6
consulates 42
coral 22, 25
  black 23
Coral Gardens 103
crabs, land 20–1
credit cards 49
cruise ships 45, 73
culture 32–4, 67
customs 42, 74

decompression chamber
  83
dentist 83–4
disabled visitors 37
dive courses 87–8
  children 88
  less confident 88
dive equipment 86–7, 135
dive operators
  Cayman Brac 211
  Grand Cayman 90–6
  Little Cayman 188–90
dive organisations 87
dive sites
  Cayman Brac 211–13
  Grand Cayman
    96–102, *98–9*
  Little Cayman *189*, 190

dive supplies 135
diver down flag 86
diving
    Cayman Brac 211–13
    costs 91
    courses 87–8
    equipment 86–7, 135
    free 90
    Grand Cayman
        85–102, 98–9
    guides 227
    Little Cayman 187–90,
        189
    operators 211–13,
        85–102, 187–90
    night 89
    nitrox 89–90
    speciality 89–90
    technical 89–90
Dr Carey's 148
Drake, Sir Francis 3
drinks 56–7
driving 51
    permit 75, 180, 200
duppies 32
duty free 42
duty-free shops
    Cayman Brac 209
    Grand Cayman 135

East End 170–4
East End Lighthouse Park
    174
economy 8–11
education 30–1
eels, moray 24
electricity 66
Elmslie Memorial United
    Church 143
emergency telephone
    numbers 62–3
entertainment 140

families 37
fast food 132–3
fax, Grand Cayman 82–3
ferries 78–9
festivals 58–9
field guides 226–7
financial services 11
First Cay Walk 221
fish 23–4
fishing 11, 103–4
    Cayman Brac 213–14
    Grand Cayman 104
    Little Cayman 187–90
fishing supplies
    Grand Cayman 135
    Cayman Brac 208
flights 42–5
    Cayman Brac 200
    inter-island 81–2
    Little Cayman 179
    long-haul 46–7
food 54, 55–6

football 112
Fort George 143
frigatebird, magnificent
    18–19, 193
fuel 52
further reading 225–7

geography 12–14
George Town 124–7,
    142–9, 144–5
    accommodation
        115–24
    cafés and snack bars
        127
    east of 159–74, 160–1
    restaurants 124–7
    shopping 134–9
    south of 148
    trips from
    walking tour 143–6
Gimistory 59
glass-bottomed boats
    148–9
Goldfield 7
golf 110–12
gorgonians 22
government 7–8
Governor Michael Gore
    Bird Sanctuary 161–2
Grand Cayman, location
    71
Grand Harbour shopping
    mall 159
gravesites 31
Great Cave 221
green flash 35
Guard House Park 164
Gun Square 164
gyms
    Grand Cayman 112
    Little Cayman 191

hair braiding 138–9
health 46–7, 83–4
health and beauty
    Grand Cayman 138–9
    Little Cayman 186
Hell 156–7
Heritage House 219
Heritage Museum 155
Heritage One passport
    79
hickatee 20
highlights 36–7
hiking
    Cayman Brac 214,
        217–22
    Grand Cayman 114
    Little Cayman 191
history 3–7
    Cayman Brac 198–9
    Little Cayman 177–8
hitchhiking 51
    Cayman Brac 201
horseriding 113–14

hospitals
    Cayman Brac 209
    Grand Cayman 83
hurricane, 1932 178, 198
    mass gravesite 218
hurricanes 14–15

iguana, rock 19, 178
    blue 19, 20, 166
immigration 41–2
insects 20
insurance 47
    vehicle 75
International Fishing
    Tournament 104
internet 62
    Cayman Brac 209
    Grand Cayman 82–3
island tours
    Cayman Brac 217
    Grand Cayman 79–81
    Little Cayman 180

Jackson's Point 194
Jamaica 4–5, 7
jetbikes 108–9
jet skis 108–9
Jolly Roger 106

Kaibo Yacht Club 74–5
kayaks
    Cayman Brac 213
    Grand Cayman 108
    Little Cayman 190–1
Kearsage, SS 217

language 31
law 8
Legislative Assembly 143
library
    Cayman Brac 210
    George Town 146
    Little Cayman 192
licensing laws 57
Lighthouse Trail 220
liquor stores, Grand
    Cayman 136–7
Little Cayman 176,
    177–95, 181
    accommodation 180–4
    activities 187–91, 189
    bank 186
    boat operators 188–90
    day trips 81–2
    dive sites 189, 190
    diving 187–90
    fishing 187–90
    flights 179
    history 177–8
    island tour 191–5
    medical facilities 187
    natural history 178–9
    post office 186
    restaurants and bars
        184–5

Little Cayman continued
    shopping 185–6
    snorkelling 187–90,
        189
    telephones 186
    tours 180
    transport 179–80
Little Cayman Baptist
    Church 192
Little Cayman Museum
    192
live-aboard dive boats 96
location 11
    Cayman Brac 197
    Grand Cayman 71
    Little Cayman 177
Long Beach 219

magazines 63
Malportas Pond 168
mammals 17
mangroves 14–15
maps 52
marinas 74
marine parks 27–8, 28
Maritime Heritage Trail
    Cayman Brac 214
    Grand Cayman 79
    Little Cayman 191
Marshes Wetlands 221
Mastic Trail 164–6
mastic tree 165
Meagre Bay Pond wildlife
    sanctuary 164
medical facilities 47
    Cayman Brac 209
    Grand Cayman 83–4
    Little Cayman 187
medicinal plants 167
Milestones in our History
    146
money 49
money wiring
    Grand Cayman 50
    Cayman Brac 210
moorings 72, 81
Morgan's Harbour 75,
    157
mosquitoes 21
museums
    Cayman Brac 218
    Grand Cayman 146–7,
        155
    Little Cayman 192
music 33
music shops 139

National Gallery 147
National Trust for the
    Cayman Islands 29
National Trust Heritage
    Beach 174
National Trust Visitors'
    Centre, Little Cayman
    192

natural history 14–30
  Cayman Brac 199
  field guides 226–7
  Little Cayman 178–9
newspapers 63–4
nightlife 133–4
North Side 167–8

off licences, Grand
  Cayman 136–7
orchids 16
overseas workers 37
Owen Island 193

paddleboats 109
parasailing 108
parrot reserve, Cayman
  Brac 219
parrots 17–18, 199
Pedro Bluff 163
Pedro St James 5, **162**
people 30
Peter's Cave 220
Peter's Outlook 220
pharmacies 84
philatelic bureau 83
philately 64–5
phosphate mines 142,
  177–8, 198
photographic courses
  Cayman Brac 208
  Grand Cayman 139
photographic supplies
  Cayman Brac 208–9
  Grand Cayman 139
  Little Cayman 186
photography 60–1
  underwater **88–9**, 90
pirates 3–4
Pirates Week 59
plants 16–17, 169
  medicinal 167
Point of Sand 194
poisonous plants 17
police 8
  Little Cayman 187
politics 7–8
Port Authority 74
port fees 74
post 63
post office
  Cayman Brac 209
  George Town 83, 146
  Little Cayman 186
privilege-card programme
  79
Prospect 159–60
public holidays 57

Queen Elizabeth II
  Botanic Park 166

radio 64–5
rainfall 13
Rebecca's Cave 221

recipes 54
reef protection 81
reef, coral 22
religion 31–2
religious services, Grand
  Cayman 84
reptiles 19–20
restaurants
  Bodden Town 163
  Breakers 164
  Cayman Brac 206–7
  Cayman Kai 170
  East End 173
  George Town 124–7,
    144–5
  Little Cayman 184–5
  North Side 167–8
  Rum Point 169–70
  Seven Mile Beach
    127–32
  West Bay 154–5
roads 51
  Grand Cayman 75
rugby 112
rum cake factory 147,
  155
Rum Point 168–70
Rum Pointer 78–9

safety 48
sailing 108
  Little Cayman 190–1
Salina Reserve 26
Salt Rocks Trail 191
Salt Water Pond 220
Salt Water Pond Walk
  218
sand garden 166
Savannah 162
scooters
  Cayman Brac 201
  Grand Cayman 76–7
  Little Cayman 179
self-catering, Grand
  Cayman 133
settlement 4–5
Seven Mile Beach
  115–24, *116–17*,
  127–39, 141
  accommodation
    115–24
  cafés and snack bars
    132–3
  restaurants 127–32
  shopping and
    amenities 134–9
sharks 22
shopping 58
  Bodden Town 163–4
  Cayman Brac 208–9
  East End 173–4
  George Town and
    Seven Mile Beach
    134–9, 148
  Little Cayman 185–6

shopping *continued*
  North Side 168
  Rum Point 165
  West Bay 155
shore dives, Grand
  Cayman 96–7
silver thatch palm **9**, 15
slavery 5
Smith's Cove 142
snakes 20
snorkelling
  Cayman Brac 210
  Grand Cayman 102–3
  Little Cayman 187–90
South Sound 148
spas
  Grand Cayman 138–9
  Little Cayman 186
speed limits
  Cayman Brac 200
  Grand Cayman 75
  Little Cayman 180
sponges 22
sport 34
Spot Bay Community
  Cove 219
squash 112
Stake Bay Walk 218
Stingray Brewery 159
Stingray City 97–100
  sandbar 103
stingray, southern 23,
  97–100
submarines 148–9
submersibles 148–9
Sunset Reef, Siren 101

Tarpon Lake 194
taxes 10
taxis
  Cayman Brac 200
  Grand Cayman 72–3,
    77–8
telephones 61–3
  Cayman Brac 209
  Grand Cayman 82
  Little Cayman 186
television 64
temperature 13
tennis
  Cayman Brac 214
  Grand Cayman
    112–13
  Little Cayman 191
theatre 140
timeshare
  Cayman Brac 206
  Grand Cayman 53
tipping 50
tour operators 38–41, 45,
  80–1
tourism 9–10
tourist information 35–6,
  79
  Cayman Brac 210

tours
  Cayman Brac 217
  Grand Cayman 79–81
  Little Cayman 180
Town Hall, George
  Town 146
Tradition 143
travel agency 84
travellers' cheques 49
Treaty of Madrid 4
trees 16–17
tubing 109
Turtle Farm 155, **156–7**
turtle, pond 20
turtles, sea 25
  green 26, 157
turtling 6

UK Overseas Territories
  Conservation Forum
  29
urchins, sea 24

visas 41

walls, Grand Cayman
  100–1
water 47
waterskiing
  Cayman Brac 213
  Grand Cayman 109
watersports operators
  109–10
waverunners 108–9
weather 13–14
weather forecasts 45–6
websites 227
weddings 38–9
West Bay **151–8**, *150–1*
  accommodation 151–4
  bars 151
  National Trust
    walking tour 155
  restaurants 154–5
  shopping 155
  tour 155–7
West Indian whistling-
  duck 18, 168, 194
Westerly Ponds 220
windsurfing 108
work permits 66
Wreck of the Ten Sail
  Park 174
Wreck of the Ten Sail 171
wrecks
  Cayman Brac 211–13
  Grand Cayman 101–2
  Little Cayman 190

yacht clubs 74–5
yachts, private 45, 74